Clinical Dilemmas in

Inflammatory Bowel Disease

Clinical Dilemmas in

Inflammatory Bowel Disease

EDITED BY

Peter Irving

Centre for Gastroenterology
Institute of Cell and Molecular Science
Barts & the London, Queen Mary School of Medicine and Dentistry
London
UK

David Rampton

Centre for Gastroenterology
Institute of Cell and Molecular Science
Barts & the London, Queen Mary School of Medicine and Dentistry
London
UK

Fergus Shanahan

Department of Medicine
National University of Ireland Cork
Clinical Sciences Building
Cork University Hospital
Cork
Eire

Blackwell
Publishing

© 2006 by Blackwell Publishing Ltd

Blackwell Publishing, Inc., 350 Main Street, Malden, Massachusetts 02148-5020, USA
Blackwell Publishing Ltd, 9600 Garsington Road, Oxford OX4 2DQ, UK
Blackwell Publishing Asia Pty Ltd, 550 Swanston Street, Carlton, Victoria 3053, Australia

First published 2006

Catalogue records for this title are available from the British Library and
Library of Congress

ISBNs: 978-1-4051-3377-7 (Pbk trade version)
978-1-4443-3864-5 (Customised version 2010, not for trade sale)

Set in 8.75/12 pt Minion by Graphicraft Limited, Hong Kong
Printed and bound in the United Kingdom by TJ International, Padstow, Cornwall

Commissioning Editor: Alison Brown
Editorial Assistant: Saskia van der Linden
Development Editor: Fiona Pattison
Production Controller: Kate Charman

For further information on Blackwell Publishing, visit our website:
http://www.blackwellpublishing.com

The publisher's policy is to use permanent paper from mills that operate a sustainable
forestry policy, and which has been manufactured from pulp processed using acid-free and
elementary chlorine-free practices. Furthermore, the publisher ensures that the text paper
and cover board used have met acceptable environmental accreditation standards.

Contents

List of Contributors

Elspeth Alstead
Consultant Gastroenterologist
Whipps Cross University Hospital
Leytonstone
London
UK

Azhar Ansari
Locum Consultant Gastroenterologist
Guy's & St Thomas' NHS Foundation Trust
London
UK

Mark Appleyard
Director of Endsocopic Services
Royal Brisbane and Women's Hospital
Department of Gastrointestinal Services
Brisbane
Australia

Anne Ballinger
Consultant Gastroenterologist
Homerton University Hospital NHS
    Foundation Trust
London
UK

Sasha Beresford
IBD Specialist Pharmacist & Principal
    Pharmacist, High-Risk Medicines
    Monitoring
Barts and The London NHS Trust
Royal London Hospital
Whitechapel
London
UK

Charles N Bernstein
Professor of Medicine
University of Manitoba Inflammatory
    Bowel Disease Clinical and Research
    Center
Winnipeg, Manitoba
Canada

Henry J Binder
Professor of Medicine
Yale University School of Medicine
New Haven, CT
USA

Ingvar Bjarnason
Professor of Digestive Diseases
Guy's, King's, St Thomas' Medical School
London
UK

Stuart Bloom
Clinical Director
Middlesex Hospital
London
UK

Brian Bressler
Gastroenterologist Fellow
Mount Sinai Hospital/University Health
    Network
University of Toronto
Toronto, Ontario
Canada

Elizabeth Carty
Consultant Gastroenterologist
Department of Gastroenterology
Whipps Cross University Hospital
Leytonstone
London
UK

Roger Chapman
Department of Gastroenterology
John Radcliffe Hospital
Oxford
UK

Rakesh Chaudhary
Clinical Research Fellow
Department of Gastroenterology
Hammersmith Hospital
Imperial College
London
UK

Paul Collins
Clinical Lecturer
Department of Medicine
University of Liverpool
Liverpool
UK

Jean-Frédéric Colombel
Professor of Hepatogastroenterology
Service d'Hépato-Gastroentérologie
Hôpital Huriez
France

Juliet Compston
Professor of Bone Metabolism
University of Cambridge
Department of Medicine
Addenbrooke's Hospital
Cambridge
UK

William Connell
Director IBD Clinic
St Vincent's Hospital
Victoria
Australia

Nick Croft
Consultant Paediatric Gastroenterologist
Institute of Cell and Molecular Science
Barts & the London, Queen Mary School
    of Medicine and Dentistry
London
UK

Garret Cullen
Gastroenterology Specialist Registrar
Department of Gastroenterology
St. Vincent's University Hospital
Dublin 4
Ireland

Sue Cullen
Consultant Gastroenterologist
Wycombe General Hospital
High Wycombe
UK

Ana Paula Cunha
Department of Dermatovenereology
Hospital S.João
Porto
Portugal

Alexandra Daley
Specialist Registrar in Gastroenterology
King's College Hospital
London
UK

Helena Deeney
Specialist Registrar in Gastroenterology
Oldchurch Hospital
Romford
Essex
UK

Alex J Di Mambro
Clinical Science at South Bristol
Bristol Royal Infirmary
Bristol
UK

Raymond D'Souza
Gastroenterology Registrar
Royal London Hospital
Whitechapel
London
UK

Donald R Duerksen
Associate Professor of Medicine
University of Manitoba
St. Boniface Hospital
Winnipeg, Manitoba
Canada

Jayne Eaden
Consultant Gastroenterologist
Walsgrave Hospital
Coventry
UK

Michael Escudier
Consultant in Oral Medicine
Guy's, Kings & St Thomas' Hospital
London
UK

Brian Feagan
Professor of Medicine
University of Western Ontario
Ontario, Canada

Alastair Forbes
Professor of Gastroenterology and Clinical
    Nutrition
University College London
London
UK

Paul Fortun
Clinical Lecturer in Gastroenterology
The Wolfson Digestive Diseases Centre
University Hospital
Nottingham
UK

Graham R Foster
Professor of Hepatology
Hepatobiliary Group
Institute of Cell and Molecular Science
Barts & the London, Queen Mary School of
    Medicine and Dentistry
London
UK

Christoph Gasche
Associate Professor of Medicine
Department of Medicine
Medical University and General
    Hospital Vienna
Department of Medicine
Vienna
Austria

Subrata Ghosh
Professor of Gastroenterology
Imperial College London
Hammersmith Hospital
London
UK

Peter Gibson
Professor of Gastroenterology
Department of Medicine
Monash University
Box Hill Hospital
Victoria
Australia

Stephen L Grainger
Consultant Physician and
    Gastroenterologist
King George's Hospital
Barking
Essex
UK

Emma Greig
Consultant Gastroenterologist
Taunton and Somerset NHS Trust
Taunton
UK

David Grunkemeier
Division of Gastroenterology and
    Hepatology
Multidisciplinary IBD Center
University of North Carolina
USA

Laura Hancock
Research Fellow
Department of Colorectal Surgery
John Radcliffe Hospital
Oxford
UK

Ailsa Hart
Gastroenterology Specialist Registrar
University College Hospital
London
UK

Christopher Hawkey
Professor of Gastroenterology
The Wolfson Digestive Diseases Centre
University Hospital
Nottingham
UK

Barney Hawthorne
Consultant Gastroenterologist
University Hospital of Wales
Cardiff
UK

Daan Hommes
Department of Gastroenterology and
    Hepatology
Academic Medical Center
Amsterdam
Holland

Peter Irving
Centre for Gastroenterology
Institute of Cell and Molecular Science
Barts & the London, Queen Mary School of
    Medicine and Dentistry
London
UK

Mark Kelly
Specialist Registrar in Gastroenterology
Hope Hospital
Salford
UK

Alex Kent
Specialist Registrar in Gastroenterology
St. Mary's Hospital
London
UK

John Keohane
Department of Medicine and Alimentary
    Pharmabiotic Centre
University College Cork
National University of Ireland
Ireland

Jutta Köglmeier
Specialist Registrar in Paediatric
    Gastroenterology
Royal London Hospital
Whitechapel
London
UK

Stefanie Kulnigg
Division of Gastroenterology and
    Hepatology
Medical University
Vienna
Austria

Louise Langmead
Consultant Gastroenterologist
Department of Gastroenterology
University College London Hospitals
London
UK

Marc Lémann
Professor of Medicine
Department of Gastroenterology
Hôpital Saint-Louis
Paris
France

James Lindsay
Consultant Gastroenterologist
Barts and The London NHS Trust
Royal London Hospital
Whitechapel
London
UK

Linmarie Ludeman
Consltant Histopathologist
Gloucester Royal Hospital
Gloucester
UK

Mark Lust
Gastroenterology Fellow
St. Vincent's Hospital
Victoria
Australia

Yashwant Mahida
Professor in Medicine
Institute of Infection Immunity &
    Inflammation
University of Nottingham
Nottingham
UK

Richard Makins
Consultant Gastroenterologist
Department of Gastroenterology
Whipps Cross University Hospital
London
UK

Richard Marley
Consultant Hepatologist
Barts and The London NHS Trust
Royal London Hospital
Whitechapel
London
UK

Joel E D Mawdsley
Clinical Research Fellow
Centre for Gastroenterology
Institute of Cell and Molecular Science
Barts & the London, Queen Mary School of
    Medicine and Dentistry
London
UK

John Mayberry
Consultant Physician
University Hospitals of Leicester NHS Trust
Leicester
UK

Dermot McGovern
Research Fellow
Wellcome Trust Centre for Human Genetics
University of Oxford
Oxford
UK

Alison McLean
Consultant Radiologist
Barts and The London NHS Trust
Royal London Hospital
Whitechapel
London
UK

Neil Mortensen
Professor of Colorectal Surgery
Department of Colorectal Surgery
John Radcliffe Hospital
Oxford
UK

Debbie Nathan
Inflammatory Bowel Disease Fellow
Box Hill Hospital
Victoria
Australia

Jeremy Nightingale
Consultant Gastroenterologist
Digestive Disease Centre
Leicester Royal Infirmary
Leicester
UK

Alick N S Nkhoma
Beit Clinical Research Fellow
Hepatobiliary Group
Centre for Gastroenterology
Institute of Cell and Molecular Science
Barts & the London, Queen Mary School of
    Medicine and Dentistry
London
UK

Carlo Nunes
Clinical Research Fellow
Gastroenterology
Guy's & St Thomas' NHS Foundation
    Trust
London
UK

Diarmuid O'Donoghue
Consultant Gastroenterologist
Centre for Colorectal Disease
St. Vincent's University Hospital
Dublin 4
Ireland

Tim Orchard
Consultant Gastroenterologist
Imperial College London
St Mary's Hospital
London
UK

Miles Parkes
Consultant Gastroenterologist
Department of Gastroenterology
Addenbrooke's Hospital
Cambridge
UK

Chris Probert
Consultant and Reader in
    Gastroenterology
Clinical Science at South Bristol
Bristol Royal Infirmary
Bristol
UK

Eamonn Quigley
Professor of Medicine and Human
    Physiology
Head of the Medical School
National University of Ireland
Cork
Ireland

Graham Radford-Smith
Consultant Gastroenterologist
Department of Gastroenterology and
    Hepatology
Royal Brisbane and Women's Hospital
Brisbane
Australia

Reshma C Rakshit
Department of Gastroenterology
Leicester General Hospital
Leicester
UK

David Rampton
Professor of Clinical Gastroenterology
Centre for Gastroenterology
Institute of Cell and Molecular Science
Barts & the London, Queen Mary School
    of Medicine and Dentistry
London
UK

Jonathan Rhodes
Professor of Medicine
University of Liverpool
Liverpool
UK

Andrew Robinson
Consultant Gastroenterologist
Hope Hospital
Salford
UK

Paul Rutgeerts
Head of the IBD Research Unit
Division of Gastroenterology
University Hospital Gasthuisberg
Division of Gastroenterology
Leuven
Belgium

Matt Rutter
Consultant Gastroenterologist
University Hospital of North Tees
Teesside
UK

Vikram A Sahni
Radiology Specialist Registrar
Barts and The London NHS Trust
Royal London Hospital
Whitechapel
London
UK

Sunil Samuel
Institute of Infection, Immunity &
    Inflammation
University of Nottingham and University
    Hospital
Nottingham
UK

Jeremy D Sanderson
Consultant Gastroenterologist
Guy's & St Thomas' NHS Foundation Trust
London
UK

R Balfour Sartor
Distinguished Professor of Medicine,
    Microbiology & Immunology
Department of Medicine, Division of
    Gastroenterology & Hepatology
University of North Carolina
Chapel Hill
USA

David Scott
Departments of Medicine and
    Rheumatology
Guy's, King's, St Thomas' Medical School
London
UK

Vikrant Sibartie
Specialist Registrar in Gastroenterology
Alimentary Pharmabiotic Centre
Department of Medicine
Cork University Hospital
Cork
Eire

Rakesh Shah
Specialist Registrar in Gastroenterology
St Mark's Hospital and Academic Institute
Harrow
UK

Fergus Shanahan
Professor of Medicine and Director
Alimentary Pharmabiotic Centre
University College Cork
National University of Ireland
Cork
Eire

Neil A Shepherd
Consultant Histopathologist
Gloucestershire Royal Hospital
Gloucester
UK

Geoff Smith
Consultant Gastroenterologist
Department of Gastroenterology
Charing Cross Hospital
London
UK

A Hillary Steinhart
Head, Combined Division of
    Gastroenterology
Mount Sinai Hospital/University Health
    Network
University of Toronto
Toronto, Ontario
Canada

Sreedhar Subramanian
Clinical Research Fellow
School of Clinical Sciences
University of Liverpool
Liverpool
UK

Abid Suddle
Specialist Registrar in Hepatology
Department of Gastroenterology
Barts and The London NHS Trust
London
UK

Fernando Tavarela Veloso
Professor of Medicine
Head of Department of Gastroenterology
Hospital S. João
Porto
Portugal

Ana Terlevich
Clinical Science at South Bristol
Bristol Royal Infirmary
Bristol
UK

Thea Thomas
Specialist Registrar in Gastroenterology
Whipps Cross University Hospital
Leytonstone
London
UK

Simon Travis
Consultant Gastroenterologist
John Radcliffe Hospital
Oxford
UK

Mark Tremelling
Gastroenterology Specialist Registrar
Addenbrooke's Hospital
Cambridge
UK

Gert Van Assche
Division of Gastroenterology
University of Leuven Hospitals
Leuven
Belgium

Séverine Vermeire
Division of Gastroenterology
University of Leuven Hospitals
Leuven
Belgium

Wilfred Weinstein
Professor of Medicine, Digestive Diseases
Department of Medicine
David Geffen School of Medicine a UCLA
UCLA
Los Angeles
USA

Horace Williams
Clinical Research Fellow
Department of Gastroenterology
St Mary's Hospital
Imperial College
London
UK

Preface

In early 2004, we instigated at Barts and The London a weekly lunchtime clinical and academic IBD meeting. This is a multidisciplinary meeting, open not only to adult medical consultants and trainee gastroenterologists, but also to others including colorectal surgeons, pediatric gastroenterologists, nurses, the nutrition team, specialist pharmacists, visitors to the Unit, laboratory researchers and medical students: the average attendance is about twenty. During the meetings, we discuss patients we have encountered during the previous week who have presented difficult management problems, as well as practical day-to-day administrative issues. In addition, we decided at the outset of these meetings to ask, in rotation, attending staff each to give a 15-minute presentation on a discrete, current, controversial, important, practical, and often as yet unresolved topic relating to the care of patients with IBD. The subjects are selected by discussion between the group, and one talk is presented each week. The talks have proved extremely popular, both for the audience and the presenter, and it is out of them that the idea for this book arose.

Accordingly, this book contains a series of pithy, we hope enjoyable, sometimes provocative, but generally evidence-based articles on IBD topics which have been selected with a view to covering many of the areas that cause clinicians difficulties in decision making. As we have deliberately chosen some controversial topics, we should perhaps point out that as editors we do not necessarily agree with all that is written here; if we did the book might prove dull. In line with its origins, some of the chapters of the book have been written in the first instance by younger gastroenterologists, prior to final touches being added by established experts.

We hope that this approach will appeal both to consultant and trainee gastroenterologists, as well as other members of the IBD team. Inevitably, the book will soon become out of date, but we hope that in the interim readers will find that it provides a useful distillation and analysis of a wide range of current management dilemmas. Indeed, we hope that you might read the odd chapter on the bus or in the train, if not in the lavatory or on the beach.

We are very grateful to all our co-authors, almost all of whom delivered their chapters on time and with minimal hassling. We are particularly grateful too to the team at Blackwell's: Alison Brown for her enthusiasm about the project when we first discussed it with her, Fiona Pattison, Mirjana Misina and Linda Bolton for all their editorial work.

PMI, DSR, FS
March 2006

Part 1 Investigating IBD in the 21st Century

1 Capsule endoscopy: do we need it?

JOEL E D MAWDSLEY & MARK APPLEYARD

LEARNING POINTS

Capsule endoscopy

- Capsule endoscopy (CE) has a diagnostic yield of 40–70% in patients with suspected small bowel Crohn's disease where other investigations have been normal

- It is not yet clear whether CE provides additional information about the small bowel in patients with known Crohn's disease

- There is an emerging role for CE in differentiating Crohn's disease from indeterminate colitis

- Small bowel follow through (SBFT) is not reliable in predicting capsule retention and the role of the patency capsule is evolving

- SBFT before CE may in due course prove unnecessary in suspected small bowel Crohn's disease

---

Introduction

In addition to being the section of the gastrointestinal (GI) tract most commonly affected by Crohn's disease, the small bowel (SB) is also the most difficult region to visualize endoscopically. Wireless video capsule endoscopy (CE) is a new technology which, at least in part, overcomes this problem, by allowing complete non-invasive endoscopic imaging of the small bowel.

However, for CE to have a role in the diagnosis and management of small bowel Crohn's disease, it should fulfill several criteria: it should be safe, provide additional diagnostic information and its use should lead to clinically meaningful changes in patient management. In this chapter we discuss the limitations of other small bowel imaging techniques, the potential uses of CE in relation to Crohn's disease and the evidence to support its use in each scenario.

Limitations of other techniques for imaging small bowel

Imaging of the SB has been previously limited to the radiologic techniques of small bowel follow through (SBFT), enteroclysis (double contrast small bowel examination) and computed tomography (CT) enteroclysis, and the endoscopic techniques of push enteroscopy, double balloon enteroscopy and colonoscopy with ileal intubation.

SBFT is the most common technique used to assess small bowel Crohn's but it is relatively insensitive for subtle mucosal lesions. Enteroclysis and CT enteroclysis are more invasive than SBFT, requiring the passage of a catheter into the duodenum under sedation, and several investigators have found these techniques to be no more sensitive [1]. All three techniques result in significant radiation exposure, limiting the frequency with which they should be performed.

Push enteroscopy can only view the proximal small bowel 15–160 cm beyond the ligament of Treitz and is more invasive and technically difficult than CE. Double balloon enteroscopy is an exciting new technology which has the potential to biopsy and perform therapeutic endoscopy throughout the small bowel. However, the examination is invasive, time consuming and may not examine the entire small bowel even when the procedures are performed per orally and per anally. Visualization of the terminal ileum at colonoscopy is limited both to the distal 10–15 cm of SB and to those patients in whom the terminal ileum can be successfully intubated.

TABLE 1.1 Trials assessing the role of capsule endoscopy in the diagnosis and assessment of Crohn's disease.

Reference	N	Preceding investigation	Yield (%)	Comparator	Yield (%)
Diagnosis of small bowel Crohn's					
Fireman [5]	17	SBFT, EGD, colonoscopy (ileoscopy 6/17)	71	N/A	N/A
Ge [6]	20	SBFT, EGD, colonoscopy	65	N/A	N/A
Herrerias [7]	21	SBFT, EGD, colonoscopy (ileoscopy 17/21)	43	N/A	N/A
Arguelles-Arias [8]	12	SBFT, EGD, colonoscopy	75	N/A	N/A
Liangpunsakul [9]	40	SBFT, EGD, colonoscopy	7.5	CT enteroclysis	0
Eliakim [10]	35	N/A	73	SBFT	23
				CT enteroclysis	20
Voderholzer [11]	5	SBFT, EGD, colonoscopy	40	CT enteroclysis	40
Assessing disease activity/recurrence					
Buchman [12]	30	N/A	70	SBFT	67
Voderholzer [11]	8	N/A	75	CT enteroclysis	75
De Palma [15]	8	SBFT, OGD, colonoscopy, push enteroscopy	75	N/A	
Debinski [14]	10	N/A	N/A	CDAI, IBDQ, CRP	N/A
Differentiating SB Crohn's from indeterminate colitis					
Mow [13]	22	N/A	59	Ileoscopy	23
Whitaker [16]	7	Colonoscopy and ileoscopy	29	N/A	

CDAI, Crohn's Disease Activity Index; CRP, C-reactive protein; CT, computed tomography; IBDQ, Inflammatory Bowel Disease Questionnaire; N/A, not available; EGD, esophagogastroduodenoscopy; SBFT, small bowel follow through.

Capsule endoscopy

The Pillcam® capsule endoscope from Given Imaging© was first used in clinical trials in 2000 and was granted Food and Drug Administration (FDA) approval in 2001 (Table 1.1). Since then it has been used in over 200 000 individuals.

Capsule endoscopy images are different from standard endoscopic images. The images are seen through intestinal content without air insufflation. Minimum standard terminology is being developed to allow consistent image description, but more validation with histology is required [2]. In a recent large randomized placebo-controlled trial looking at intestinal inflammation in patients on non-steroidal anti-inflammatory drugs, 7% of those on placebo had small bowel abnormalities [3]; these data raises the question of what constitutes a normal small bowel appearance.

The appearance of Crohn's disease at CE ranges from gross mucosal ulceration and stricturing to subtle mucosal breaks and denuded villi. A CE scoring index has been proposed along the lines of the endoscopic ones, but has not been fully validated [4].

Diagnosis of suspected small bowel Crohn's disease

The majority of trials examining the role of CE in the management of Crohn's disease have studied the diagnostic yield of CE in patients with symptoms and features suggestive of Crohn's who have undergone normal SBFT, esophagogastroduodenoscopy (EGD) and colonoscopy (with attempted ileal intubation in some).

In prospective analyses of this nature, CE appears to provide significant additional information, with a diagnostic yield ranging between 43% and 71% [5–8]. Furthermore, in all of these studies the positive findings at CE led to a change in management with a resulting improvement in most patients (83–100%), although treatment outcomes are not well reported.

In a retrospective analysis, the diagnostic yield was lower at 7.5% [9]. However, CE compared favorably to enteroclysis and CT enteroclysis, which were reported as normal in all the patients with positive findings at CE. In addition, all the patients responded to instigation of medical therapy.

Other studies have compared the sensitivities of CE with other techniques for diagnosing SB Crohn's disease, by performing the tests in a sequential, blinded manner. In a study comparing sequential SBFT, CT enteroclysis and CE, Eliakim *et al.* [10] found the sensitivities for Crohn's to be 23%, 20%, and 73%, respectively. Volderholzer *et al.* [11] found CE made a new diagnosis of SB Crohn's in two of five patients with unexplained diarrhea, both of whom had normal prior CT enteroclysis.

In summary, current evidence suggests that CE has a diagnostic yield of 40–70% in patients with symptoms suggestive of Crohn's disease where SBFT, OGD and colonoscopy with attempted ileal intubation have been normal. Direct comparison of diagnostic yield with enteroclysis and CT enteroclysis favors CE. The new diagnosis of Crohn's by CE has led to the institution of a beneficial new treatment regimen in most patients.

Assessment of disease activity and recurrence

Few trials have examined whether CE is useful in assessing the SB in patients with known Crohn's. Buchman *et al.* [12] found SBFT and CE to have similar diagnostic yields at 66% and 70% in patients with suspected disease recurrence while Voderholzer *et al.* [11] found CE and CT enteroclysis each to have a diagnostic yield of 75%. Mow *et al.* [13] suggested three or more ulcers were diagnostic of Crohn's; they found CE was diagnostic in 40% and suspicious for Crohn's in 30% of patients, but did not make additional diagnoses compared with ileoscopy.

In a study to assess its potential for detection of early postoperative recurrence of Crohn's, the diagnostic yield of CE was 75% in patients with previous SB resection and suspected recurrence who had had normal SBFT, OGD, colonoscopy, and push enteroscopy [14].

Only one study has examined the role of CE in assessing response to therapy. In this, improvements in mucosal appearance at CE were seen in 8/10 patients given infliximab [15]; these correlated with changes in Crohn's Disease Activity Index (CDAI), Inflammatory Bowel Disease Questionnaire (IBDQ) scores and C-reactive protein (CRP).

In summary, CE appears to detect recurrent small bowel Crohn's disease with a diagnostic yield of approximately 70%. However, it is not clear whether CE adds usefully to the information provided by conventional imaging techniques in this setting, nor do we yet know whether findings at CE lead to beneficial changes in management. It is therefore too early to define the role for CE in the assessment of response to therapy and of postoperative disease recurrence.

Differentiating Crohn's disease from indeterminate colitis

In a retrospective study, CE detected SB lesions suspicious of Crohn's in 13/22 patients with a previous diagnosis of indeterminate colitis and in five led to a change in management [13]. There was, however, no comparison made to other conventional imaging techniques or to the use of antibodies to *Saccharomyces cerevisiae*/antineutrophil cytoplasmic antibody (ASCA/ANCA) serology. In a second study, CE identified lesions characteristic of CD in 2/7 patients with a diagnosis of indeterminate colitis and ongoing pain and/or diarrhea, all of whom had already undergone non-diagnostic ileoscopy [16].

Is capsule endoscopy safe in Crohn's disease?

In all of the studies discussed above, SBFT was performed prior to CE and patients with significant stricturing were excluded from CE. CE retention occurred in 1/71 (1.4%) patients with suspected Crohn's, and in 4/80 (5%) patients with known Crohn's disease. In the trials of suspected SB Crohn's, very few patients were excluded because of abnormal radiology and radiology did not reliably prevent retention; SBFT may not therefore be required prior to CE in this setting.

Concerns regarding capsule endoscope retention have lead to the development of the Patency capsule. This has the same dimensions as the Pillcam® capsule but contains only a simple tracer and is designed to disintegrate in the GI tract 40–100 hours after ingestion. In a multicenter study, the Patency capsule was passed intact in 41/80 patients with known small bowel strictures of whom 33 then underwent conventional CE. There were no cases of capsule retention although some patients did report abdominal pain [17].

Tolerability and capsule failure

In all the studies discussed, with the exception of patients in whom it was retained, the capsule was easily swallowed and well tolerated. Although there are no comparative preference data in these studies, in a different analysis 49/50 patients preferred CE to push enteroscopy [18].

In those studies where the data were given, the capsule failed to reach the colon before the end of its 8 hour battery life in 25/132 cases (failure rate 19%). However, in most cases, an incomplete examination did not affect diagnostic efficacy.

Conclusions

Although the number of studies is small, current evidence suggests that there is a role for CE in the diagnosis of suspected SB Crohn's disease. However, more work is required to determine the clinical significance of the more subtle mucosal lesions and whether CE can safely be performed without prior radiology. A role for CE in assessing patients with indeterminate colitis is slowly emerging but its role in assessing disease recurrence is less clear. The Patency capsule is likely to prove useful in patients with known or suspected small bowel strictures.

References

1 Ott DJ, Chen YM, Gelfand DW, Van SF, Munitz HA. Detailed per-oral small bowel examination vs. enteroclysis. Part II: Radiographic accuracy. *Radiology* 1985; **155**: 31–4 .

2 Korman LY. Standard terminology for capsule endoscopy. *Gastrointest Endosc Clin N Am* 2004; **14**: 33–41.

3 Goldstein JL, Eisen GM, Gralnek IM, Zlotnick S, Fort JG. Video capsule endoscopy to prospectively assess small bowel injury with celecoxib, naproxen plus omeprazole and placebo. *Clin Gastroenterol Hepatol* 2005; **3**: 133–41.

4 Kornbluth A, Legani P, Lewis BS. Video Capsule Endoscopy in Inflammatory Bowel Disease: past, present, and future. *Inflam Bowel Dis* 2004; **10**: 278–85.

5 Fireman Z, Mahajna E, Broide E, *et al.* Diagnosing small bowel Crohn's disease with wireless capsule endoscopy. *Gut* 2003; **52**: 390–2 .

6 Ge ZZ, Hu YB, Xiao SD. Capsule endoscopy in diagnosis of small bowel Crohn's disease. *World J Gastroenterol* 2004; **10**: 1349–52.

7 Herrerias JM, Caunedo A, Rodriguez-Tellez M, Pellicer F, Herrerias JM Jr. Capsule endoscopy in patients with suspected Crohn's disease and negative endoscopy. *Endoscopy* 2003; **35**: 564–8 .

8 Arguelles-Arias F, Caunedo A, Romero J, *et al.* The value of capsule endoscopy in pediatric patients with a suspicion of Crohn's disease. *Endoscopy* 2004; **36**: 869–73.

9 Liangpunsakul S, Chadalawada V, Rex DK, Maglinte D, Lappas J. Wireless capsule endoscopy detects small bowel ulcers in patients with normal results from state of the art enteroclysis. *Am J Gastroenterol* 2003; **98**: 1295–8.

10 Eliakim R, Suissa A, Yassin K, Katz D, Fischer D. Wireless capsule video endoscopy compared to barium follow-through and computerised tomography in patients with suspected Crohn's disease: final report. *Dig Liver Dis* 2004; **36**: 519–22.

11 Voderholzer WA, Ortner M, Rogalla P, Beinholzl J, Lochs H. Diagnostic yield of wireless capsule enteroscopy in comparison with computed tomography enteroclysis. *Endoscopy* 2003; **35**: 1009–14.

12 Buchman AL, Miller FH, Wallin A, Chowdhry AA, Ahn C. Videocapsule endoscopy versus barium contrast studies for the diagnosis of Crohn's disease recurrence involving the small intestine. *Am J Gastroenterol* 2004; **99**: 2171–7.

13 Mow WS, Lo SK, Targan SR, *et al.* Initial experience with wireless capsule enteroscopy in the diagnosis and management of inflammatory bowel disease. *Clin Gastroenterol Hepatol* 2004; **2**: 31–40.

14 Debinski HS, Hooper J, Farmer C. Mucosal healing in small bowel Crohn's disease following endoscopic therapy with infliximab using the Crohn's disease capsule endoscopic index. *Proceedings of the 4th International Conference on Capsule Endoscopy, Florida, USA.* 33.

15 De Palma GD, Rega M, Puzziello A, *et al.* Capsule endoscopy is safe and effective after small-bowel resection. *Gastrointest Endosc* 2004; **60**: 135–8.

16 Whitaker DA, Hume G, Radford-Smith GL, Appleyard MN. Can capsule endoscopy help differentiate the aetiology of indeterminate colitis? *Gastrointest Endosc* 2004; **59**: AB177.

17 Spada C, Spera G, Riccioni ME, *et al.* Given patency system is a new diagnostic tool for verifying functional patency of the small bowel. *Proceedings of the 4th International Conference on Capsule Endoscopy, Florida, USA.* 205.

18 Mylonaki M, Fritscher-Ravens A, Swain P. Wireless capsule endoscopy: a comparison with push enteroscopy in patients with gastroscopy and colonoscopy negative gastrointestinal bleeding. *Gut* 2003; **52**: 1122–6

Part 1 Investigating IBD in the 21st Century

2 Pathology reports – pitfalls for the unwary*

WILFRED WEINSTEIN

> ### LEARNING POINTS
>
> **Pathology reports**
>
> - Communication between pathologist and endoscopist is crucial and must be two-way
>
>   - Do not force the pathologist to make unrealistic diagnoses or rush to judgment
>
>   - Encourage the pathologist to avoid using hackneyed, vague, misleading, or non-actionable diagnoses
>
>   - The endoscopist's ego strength should be sufficient to allow the pathologist to complain about poor quality biopsies, lack of clinical information, or unrealistic expectations
>
>   - Educate each other! Send references of clinicopathologic importance in IBD to the pathologist
>
> - Ask questions that reflect *what is possible* to determine from biopsy pathology
>
> - Include clinical information relevant to the differential diagnosis

Introduction

Pitfalls in pathology reports are a product of misunderstanding or miscommunication in regards to the role of biopsy in the differential diagnosis of UC and Crohn's disease. Colonic biopsy has a limited role *by itself* in the initial

evaluation, differential diagnosis, and subsequent management of inflammatory bowel disorders. However, when taken together with the history, endoscopic findings, and clinical course it may significantly help to make the case for one type of IBD rather than another [1,2].

Pitfalls occur with the too-oft practice of not providing the pathologist with an adequate history and endoscopic description, or with unrealistic expectations of what biopsy can do in management. The pathologist may not have sufficient information about the clinical manifestations and therapy of the disorders. This results in failure to be descriptive alone, when the endoscopist pressures naively or prematurely for a single diagnosis. Compounding the pitfalls is the "silence of the pathologists" who put up with no historical or endoscopic information, inadequate biopsies, and unrealistic expectations. They rarely communicate these deficiencies to the clinician [3].

Special problems and how to minimize the risk of errors

Ulcerative proctitis

A biopsy is taken within a 10-cm segment of apparent diffuse inflammation in the rectum and the endoscopist asks the pathologist to "rule out ulcerative proctitis." The pathologist should never make this diagnosis unless a biopsy taken approximately 10 cm upstream is normal; that

---

*UNWARY: adj: not alert to danger or deception; "seduce the unwary reader into easy acquiescence" [*The American Heritage® Dictionary of the English Language*, 4th edn, Copyright © 2000 by Houghton Mifflin Company]. Not alert: easily fooled or surprised. Heedless, gullible [from dictionary.com].

rules out proctosigmoiditis. If the proximal biopsy is normal then one can have the "ulcerative proctitis talk" with the patient, indicating that 90% of the time the disorder does not migrate proximally [4]. If the endoscopist does not consider other possible relevant causes of ulcerative proctitis when biopsies are taken, an erroneous report is inevitable; as in mucosal prolapse due to solitary rectal ulcer syndrome (SRUS), mucosal trauma from digital removal of stool, anal intercourse, sexually transmitted disease [5], and ischemic proctitis, especially after aortoiliac bypass surgery.

Questions for the pathologist and avoiding unrealistic expectations

(Table 2.1)

"Rule out Crohn's disease"

This guarantees that the pathologic diagnosis will be *compatible with Crohn's disease* because almost any histologic findings are compatible with Crohn's disease. The solution is for the clinician to ask the pathologist if there are findings of focal inflammation in diffusely abnormal mucosa

TABLE 2.1 Lesion descriptions, relevant medications, history, and questions for the pathologist. (After Weinstein [3])

Lesion description
Simple language for mucosal abnormalities: thick folds rather than hypertrophic; define friability if used, i.e. single pass petechiae or bleeding; or spontaneous petechiae or oozing
Describe what was seen rather than an interpretive term such as colitis

Key drugs
Type of preparation (enemas or oral)
Current IBD treatment
Any other immunosuppressives (e.g. after transplantation)
Chemotherapy or radiotherapy (and when last treatment with same)
Current or recent NSAIDs, cocaine, methamphetamine
Current or recent antibiotics

History
Brief usually suffices
Duration of diarrhea, bloody or non-bloody
Risk factors for other disorders (see section on ulcerative proctitis)
Underlying cardiac or vascular disease if present

Question for the pathologist
Be as specific as possible (see text)

NSAIDs, non-steroidal anti-inflammatory drugs.

endoscopically and if there are non-crypt cell granulomas (because granulomas next to partially degraded crypts are a feature of UC). Neither finding clinches the diagnosis of Crohn's but the question alerts the pathologist that you are looking for more solid evidence than any small collection of inflammatory cells.

"Rule out UC in a patient with diffusely abnormal mucosa"

My favorite question in apparent UC endoscopically is in two parts:
1 *"It looks like UC but are there features to suggest something else?"* This alerts the pathologist to look for disorders that can mimic UC, such as infectious colitis (acute self-limited) or multifocal non-crypt associated granulomas that would suggest Crohn's disease or ischemic bowel. In endoscopically classic UC, biopsies help most when the findings do not fit.
2 *"Are there classic signs of underlying UC?"* This refers to crypt branching and subcryptal inflammatory infiltrates.

"Is it UC or Crohn's disease?"

Settings where that distinction is difficult to impossible in a single series of biopsies at any point in time include [2]: fulminant colitis, treated IBD, mild IBD, and new onset UC in children. A meeting of the two solitudes (clinician and pathologist) will: (i) inform the clinician about these special situations; and (ii) empower the pathologist to avoid being a collaborator in providing a definitive diagnosis when that is not possible. Fulminant or highly severe UC can be transmural and resemble Crohn's disease. In treated UC, mild UC, and in childhood UC at presentation (even with moderate to severe symptoms), the rectum may be spared and the inflammation more severe in proximal than distal parts of the colon [2,6]. Thus, Crohn's might be the erroneous diagnosis based upon patchiness and rectal sparing. Overall, the best time to make the distinction between UC and Crohn's disease in adults is in the untreated state when there are active but not fulminant symptoms.

The rush to judgment

The endoscopist should not rush to judgment, and furthermore not press the pathologist to collaborate in a rush to judgment. In patients with shorter term histories of diarrhea it may be most prudent to simply call it colitis, leave open the possibility of a self-limited disease, and treat with the usual drugs. The most common error we make is the knee jerk label of Crohn's for any focal endoscopic involvement. Drug-induced colitis (non-steroidal anti-inflammatory drugs [NSAIDs], cocaine, methamphetamines) might be responsible for a Crohn-like or an ischemic picture [7]. Aphthous lesions from PhosphoSoda preparations occur commonly in the left colon. Ischemic colitis appearances on biopsy may be produced by infections, not just the classic *Escherichia coli* OH:157, but also others such as *Salmonella*, *Shigella*, *Clostridium difficile*, and *Campylobacter jejuni*.

Biopsies taken near diverticula to look for IBD

But the endoscopist does not tell the pathologist about the diverticulosis. A bona fide segmental colitis, only in an area of diverticula, may represent diverticular colitis and not some other focal disease such as Crohn's disease [8] (see Chapter 61).

Colitis in the immunocompromised patient

In patients with common variable immunodeficiency, undergoing chemotherapy or radiotherapy, or with human immunodeficiency virus (HIV) with low CD4 counts, and after transplantation, the main role of the endoscopist is to rule out infectious causes or endogenous changes such as chemotherapy or radiation change. UC or Crohn's disease are difficult if not impossible diagnoses to make with assurance in these settings.

The pathologist's vague, meaningless, or non-actionable terminology1

Mild chronic inflammation is the greatest pandemic affecting the gastrointestinal tract. Usually these are cases with normal mucosa. Mild inflammation is present in the right colon in health, accompanied by scattered eosinophils and crypt mucus depletion, but not cryptitis. If the pathologist is not aware of this regional difference or if the endoscopist mixes right and left sided colonic biopsies into one fixative bottle, then irrelevant diagnoses may result for the unwary clinician.

Non-actionable terms unfortunately still abound. **Moderate dysplasia** in the colon is not a standard dysplasia grade, and there is no published action plan for it. **Unqualified atypia** may lead to panic and the term should not be used

unless accompanied by the adjective of **regenerative-type atypia**.

Clinical correlation recommended. What does this mean? Many pathologists use this as a covert term for "I'm concerned" or "I don't know what's going on histologically" to fit the clinical and/or endoscopic picture. Either sentiment is permissible. The solution is to remove the phrase and phone the clinician, or transmit any special concern in the pathology report.

Indeterminate colitis. This term should not be used in biopsy reports, ever. An elegant review is available for those of us who are perplexed by the diagnosis of indeterminate colitis [2].

Conclusion

Histology taken at ileocolonoscopy plays a central part in the diagnosis and management of IBD. Frequent and specific communication between clinician and pathologist is the best way to minimize the risk of erroneous conclusions being reached.

References

1 Fefferman DS, Farrell RJ. Endoscopy in inflammatory bowel disease: indications, surveillance, and use in clinical practice. *Clin Gastroenterol Hepatol* 2005; **3**: 11–24.

2 Guindi M, Riddell RH. Indeterminate colitis. *J Clin Pathol* 2004; **57**: 1233–44.

3 Weinstein WM. Mucosal biopsy techniques and interaction with the pathologist. *Gastrointest Endosc Clin N Am* 2000; **10**: 555–72.

4 Ghirardi M, Nascimbeni R, Mariani PP, Di Fabio F, Salerni B. [Course and natural history of idiopathic ulcerative proctitis in adults.] *Ann Ital Chir* 2002; **73**: 155–8.

5 Fried R, Surawicz C. Proctitis and sexually transmissible diseases of the colon. *Curr Treat Options Gastroenterol* 2003; **6**: 263–70.

6 Bernstein CN, Shanahan F, Anton PA, Weinstein WM. Patchiness of mucosal inflammation in treated ulcerative colitis: a prospective study. *Gastrointest Endosc* 1995; **42**: 232–7.

7 Cappell MS. Colonic toxicity of administered drugs and chemicals. *Am J Gastroenterol* 2004; **99**: 1175–90.

8 Jani N, Finkelstein S, Blumberg D, Regueiro M. Segmental colitis associated with diverticulosis. *Dig Dis Sci* 2002; **47**: 1175–81.

3 Non-invasive diagnosis and assessment

ALEX J DI MAMBRO, ANA TERLEVICH & CHRIS PROBERT

LEARNING POINTS

Non-invasive diagnosis and assessment

- C-reactive protein remains an important diagnostic and monitoring tool

- Raised fecal calprotectin correlates strongly with disease activity, has been used as a screening test for IBD and may predict relapse

- The combination of perinuclear antineutrophil cytoplasmic antibody (pANCA) and antibodies to *Saccharomyces cerevisiae* (ASCA) may help differentiate ulcerative colitis from Crohn's disease, especially in children

- In the right hands, abdominal ultrasound identifies active IBD in the terminal ileum and colon

- Analysis of fecal volatiles and genetic mutations may in the future alter the way we diagnose, monitor and treat IBD.

Introduction

Non-invasive assessment of IBD is desirable from the patient's point of view, as it is relatively painless and has few complications. However, it is also desirable from the clinical perspective: patients with chronic disease should not be exposed repeatedly to ionizing radiation, nor to endoscopic investigations, because of the potential risks from such procedures. In addition, in some parts of the world, endoscopy services are becoming over-stretched due, for example, to demands for colorectal cancer screening. In this synopsis, we discuss non-invasive methods for diagnosing and assessing IBD.

C-reactive protein

C-reactive protein (CRP), principally produced by hepatocytes, is part of the acute phase response. It has a short half-life and is therefore a useful marker to detect and monitor disease activity in Crohn's disease [1]. A raised CRP is, of course, non-specific, but, like a raised platelet count, can point to the possibility of IBD in patients presenting to the clinic with diarrhea and/or abdominal pain. In UC the acute phase response of CRP is, for unknown reasons, only modest, and CRP is not as good a marker of disease activity except in severe relapses, when a CRP >45 mg/L during treatment indicates a high risk of colectomy (see Chapter 42) [2]. Interestingly, recent trials of biologic agents in patients with Crohn's disease have found that those patients with raised CRP tend to respond better than those without (see Chapters 23, 31).

Plasma viscosity

Plasma viscosity is sometimes used alone, or in conjunction with CRP, to assess disease activity in IBD but is also non-specific. It has been shown to correlate well with CRP in both UC and Crohn's disease; however, it has a low sensitivity for detecting active Crohn's disease, being within the normal laboratory range in 48% of those with active disease [3].

Calprotectin

Calprotectin is a calcium-binding protein secreted predominantly by neutrophils. Elevated fecal calprotectin levels are found in many inflammatory diseases of the intestine [4] and have been proposed as a way of deciding which patients with diarrhea and abdominal pain need further investigation for IBD. Fecal calprotectin levels correlate strongly with IBD activity and may be used to predict relapse [5].

Serology – pANCA and ASCA

Recent papers have shown a strong association between certain antibodies and IBD.

Perinuclear antineutrophil cytoplasmic antibody (pANCA) is found in patients with rheumatoid arthritis, systemic lupus erythematosus, microscopic polyangitis, and also in IBD. The prevalence of pANCA is increased in patients with UC (30–80%) compared with healthy controls. In comparison, pANCA is found less commonly in patients with Crohn's disease (0–20%). In UC, pANCA appears independent of disease extent and activity; however, in Crohn's disease its presence has been associated with UC-like features [6]. pANCA can be subdivided according to which perinuclear antigen antibodies are directed against. In patients with UC, the antigen may be histone 1, but antibodies are not directed against proteinase 3, myeloperoxidase, elastase, lysozyme, or cathepsin G [7].

The prevalences of IgG and IgA antibodies to *Saccharomyces cerevisiae (ASCAs)* are increased in patients with Crohn's disease compared with controls and range from 35–76% [8]. Patients who are ASCA-positive are more likely to have disease of the ileum, or ileum and colon, than patients who are ASCA-negative. Furthermore, ASCA-positive patients have also been shown to be more likely to require ileocecal resection [9].

Combining pANCA with ASCA increases specificity. For example, in UC, pANCA alone has a sensitivity and specificity of 65% and 85%, respectively; however, when combined with a negative ASCA, the sensitivity is 57% and the specificity 97% [10]. The positive predictive value (PPV) is therefore increased from 74% to 92% when the antibodies are combined.

Combined pANCA and ASCA has also been used to increase diagnostic accuracy in categorizing indeterminate colitis. One recent study showed that pANCA-positive and ASCA-negative patients with indeterminate colitis often progressed to a diagnosis of UC (PPV 64%), whereas those who were pANCA-negative and ASCA-positive were more likely to have CD (PPV 80%) [11].

Although pANCA alone is unlikely to provide the basis for a non-invasive screening test for IBD, it appears that in combination with ASCA it may have some adjuvant uses in differentiating Crohn's disease from UC, in categorizing indeterminate colitis, and possibly in determining disease pattern in Crohn's disease.

Recently, two new potential marker antibodies have been described: OmpC and I2. The low sensitivity of the antibodies to detect either Crohn's disease or ulcerative colitis means they are unlikely to have a diagnostic role [12], but they may be useful in screening for a fistulizing/stenotic phenotype with Crohn's disease as they are strongly associated with this pattern in children (p < 0.006 and < 0.003 for OmpC and I2, respectively [13].

Abdominal ultrasound

Abdominal ultrasound offers a simple, accessible, and non-invasive method of detecting and monitoring IBD (in particular Crohn's disease) and yet, at least in the UK, it is under-utilized. It has an overall accuracy of 89% in identifying active terminal ileal and colonic Crohn's disease (see Chapter 4) [14]. Doppler sonography, with or without contrast, is a newer, non-invasive method of assessing the hyperdynamic splanchnic and mesenteric blood flow that occurs in active inflammation. It can detect early mucosal and transmural inflammatory lesions. Furthermore, repeated quantification of mesenteric blood flow is claimed to enable the prediction of relapse at 6 months after steroid-induced remission [15]. (The role of magnetic resonance imaging [MRI] is discussed in Chapter 4.)

Analysis of fecal volatiles

Some patients with IBD have observed that the gas they emit per rectum during periods of disease activity smells different to that emitted when their disease is quiescent. Recently, we have investigated the composition of gas emitted from stool samples to explore this observation further and have found that the volatile compounds of such gas are different from those found in healthy volunteers. Furthermore, the gas produced by such stool samples can be used to distinguish between UC and Crohn's disease. This observation may lead to a novel diagnostic test.

However, the technique is still under evaluation and these results need to be reproduced in larger series before its usefulness for non-invasive diagnosis or monitoring of IBD can be determined.

Genetic mutations and IBD

The first gene to be identified as a risk factor for Crohn's disease is the *NOD2/CARD15* gene on chromosome 16 (see Chapter 24). Mutations of the gene are significantly more common in patients with Crohn's disease than in healthy controls. However, although the odds ratio is impressive, the genetic mutations are present in fewer than half of the patients studied [16,17]. At present, screening for these genes or other mutations plays no part in the diagnosis or monitoring of IBD [18].

Conclusions

At present, CRP and plasma viscosity remain the only widely available means of non-invasive monitoring of IBD. Fecal calprotectin looks promising as a diagnostic pointer towards IBD; it has the advantage of being a test of luminal disease and is therefore unlikely to be influenced by extra-intestinal disease processes. pANCA and ASCA may have a role in distinguishing Crohn's disease from UC and, potentially, IBD from other gastrointestinal disorders. Ultrasound warrants further investigation as a non-invasive technique for both diagnosing and monitoring Crohn's disease. Analysis of fecal volatiles is still at an early stage of development but also appears promising. Genetic screening is unlikely, in the foreseeable future, to be used to make a diagnosis of IBD.

References

1 Vermeire S, Van Assche G, Rutgeerts P, *et al.* C-reactive protein as a marker for inflammatory bowel disease. *Inflamm Bowel Dis* 2004; **10**: 661–5.

2 Travis SP, Farrant JM, Ricketts C, *et al.* Predicting outcome in severe ulcerative colitis. *Gut* 1996; **38**: 905–10.

3 Lobo AJ, Jones SC, Juby LD, *et al.* Plasma viscosity in inflammatory bowel disease. *J Clin Pathol* 1992; **45**: 54–7.

4 Johne B, Fagerhol MK, Lyberg T, *et al.* Functional and clinical aspects of the myelomonocyte protein calprotectin. *Mol Pathol* 1997; **50**: 113–23.

5 Tibble JA, Sigthorsson G, Bridger S, *et al.* Surrogate markers of intestinal inflammation are predictive of relapse in patients with inflammatory bowel disease.*Gastroenterology* 2000; **119**: 15–22.

6 Vasiliauskas EA, Plevy SE, Landers CJ, *et al.* Perinuclear antineutrophil cytoplasmic antibodies in patients with Crohn's disease define a clinical subgroup. *Gastroenterology* 1996; **110**: 1810–9.

7 Cohavy O, Bruckner D, Gordon LK, *et al.* Colonic bacteria express an ulcerative colitis pANCA-related protein epitope. *Infect Immun* 2000; **68**: 1542–8.

8 Sandborn WJ. Serological markers in inflammatory bowel disease: state of the art. *Rev Gastroenterol Disord* 2004; **4**: 167–74.

9 Zholudev A, Zurakowski D, Young W, *et al.* Serologic testing with ANCA, ASCA and anto-Omp C in children and young adults with Crohn's disease and ulcerative colitis. *Am J Gastroenterol* 2004; **99**: 2235–41.

10 Quinton J-F, Sendid B, Reumaux D, *et al.* Anti-*Saccharomyces cerevisiae* mannan antibodies combined with antineutrophil cytoplasmic autoantibodies in inflammatory bowel disease: prevelance and diagnostic role. *Gut* 1998; **42**: 788–91.

11 Joossens S, Reinisch W, Vermeire S, *et al.* The value of serological markers in indeterminate colitis: a prospective follow-up study. *Gastroenterology* 2002; **122**: 1242–7.

12 Elitsur Y, Lawrence Z, Tolaymat N. The diagnostic accuracy of serologic markers in children with IBD – The West Virgina experience. *Journal of Clinical Gastroenterology* 2005; **39**: 670–73.

13 Dubinsky MC, Lin YC, Dutridge D, *et al.* Serum immune responses predict rapid disease progression among children with Crohn's disease: Immune responses predict disease progression. *American Journal of Gastroenterology* 2006; **101**: 360–67.

14 Pascu M, Roznowski AB, Muller HP, *et al.* Clinical relevance of transabdominal ultrasonography and MRI in patients with inflammatory bowel disease of the terminal ileum and large bowel. *Inflamm Bowel Dis* 2004; **10**: 373–82.

15 Ludwig D. Doppler sonography in inflammatory bowel disease. *Z Gastroenterol* 2004; **42**: 1059–65.

16 Russell RK, Nimmo ER, Satsangi J. Molecular genetics of Crohn's disease. *Curr Opin Genet Dev* 2004; **14**: 264–70.

17 Shaoul R, Karban A, Weiss B, *et al.* NOD2/CARD15 mutations and presence of granulomas in paediatric and adult Crohn's disease. *Inflamm Bowel Dis* 2004; **10**: 709–14.

18 Torok HP, Glas J, Lohse P, Folwaczny C. Alterations of the CARD15/NOD2 gene and the impact on management and treatment of Crohn's disease patients. *Dig Dis* 2003; **21**: 339–45.

Part 1 Investigating IBD in the 21st Century

4 What is the best way to image perianal Crohn's disease?

VIKRAM A SAHNI & ALISON MCLEAN

LEARNING POINTS

Imaging pelvic Crohn's disease

- Perianal fistulae associated with Crohn's disease are often complex and tend to recur if the full extent is under-diagnosed at presentation

- Magnetic resonance imaging (MRI) and endoanal ultrasound (with or without hydrogen peroxide) are the investigations of choice

- MRI has superior contrast resolution and can identify deep extensions of complex perianal disease

Introduction

Pelvic Crohn's disease encompasses a spectrum of conditions including perianal skin tags, fissures, ulcers, and perianal abscesses and fistulae. Six to 34% of patients develop anal fistulae [1] and the diagnosis and treatment of these fistulae can be particularly challenging.

Although simple perianal fistulae can be identified at examination under anesthesia (EUA) and then treated successfully without the need for diagnostic imaging [2], fistulae associated with Crohn's disease are frequently complex with secondary extensions and ramifications. Failure to appreciate the complexity of such fistulae at EUA could result in incomplete treatment and may be responsible for the high rate of recurrence [3].

Several imaging modalities have been employed to delineate fistulous tracks, each with advantages and limitations. Fistulae should be classified as described by Parks *et al.* [4] to provide the surgeon with a roadmap which should minimize both operative trauma to the anal sphincters and subsequent recurrence.

Imaging

Contrast fistulography has historically been used to delineate fistula anatomy. This involves cannulating the external opening and injecting water-soluble contrast material under X-ray control. However, the technique has been shown to be unreliable, with an accuracy of only 16% [5]. It gives little information about the immediate anatomic relations especially to the sphincter mechanism and levator plate. The complete extent of complex fistulae and deep abscesses may not be identified if they fail to fill with contrast.

Although valuable in the overall assessment of complex transmural Crohn's disease, **computed tomography (CT)** has major limitations in the evaluation of perianal disease. The density of the anal sphincter, levator muscle, active fistulae, and fibrotic tracks on CT images are very similar, so that it is difficult to differentiate between them unless the fistula has been outlined by air or contrast [6].

CT has a role in the guidance of drainage of deep pelvic abscesses. It is widely available and allows a safe approach for drainage in an area where multiple intervening structures must be avoided. A transabdominal or transgluteal approach may be used [7].

Anal endosonography uses a high-frequency endoanal probe (typically 10 MHz) to evaluate sphincter anatomy

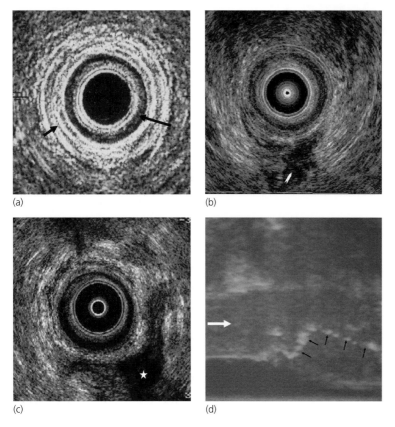

(a)

(b)

(c)

(d)

FIG 4.1 (a) Patient 1. Endoanal ultrasound demonstrating normal sphincter anatomy at the level of the mid anal canal (internal anal sphincter, long black arrow; external anal sphincter, short black arrow). (b) Patient 2. Endoanal ultrasound demonstrating posterior perianal fistula at the level of the mid anal canal (white arrowhead). (c) Patient 3. Endoanal ultrasound demonstrating posterior perianal collection at the level of the upper anal canal (white star). (d) Patient 4. Transrectal longitudinal ultrasound demonstrating thickened rectal wall (white arrow) with fistulous track (black arrows) extending above anal sphincter in rectal wall. The track is hyperreflective due to the presence of air within it. Fig. 4.1(a–c) courtesy of Dr. Mark Scott, Centre for Academic Surgery, Barts and The London, Queen Mary's School of Medicine and Dentistry, London, UK.

and provide high-resolution images of the internal and external sphincter. The internal sphincter appears as a hyporeflective ring while the external sphincter is of mixed reflectivity. Fistulous tracks appear as areas of low reflectivity unless they contain air, in which case they are hyperreflective (Fig. 4.1).

The advantage of anal endosonography is that it allows rapid evaluation in real time with no use of ionizing radiation. However, its primary limitation is the limited field of view it provides, which results in suboptimal visualization of the ischiorectal fossa and the supralevator area. This can lead to abscesses and fistulae being missed and, as a consequence, a high recurrence rate [8]. To compound this problem, endosonography cannot differentiate fistulae from scar tissue. Finally, in a proportion of patients with perianal inflammation, an endoanal probe cannot be tolerated because of anal stenosis or pain.

The advent of contrast-enhanced endosonography using hydrogen peroxide has improved the accuracy of the technique [9]. Hydrogen peroxide is introduced into the fistula track by cannulating the external orifice with an intravenous cannula. Within the fistula it generates small air bubbles which have a bright hyperreflective appearance.

The recent development of three-dimensional endoanal ultrasonography allows the axial images obtained from routine endoanal ultrasound to be reconstructed in the coronal and sagittal planes. West *et al.* [10] have shown that this technique, when combined with hydrogen peroxide, is comparable to endoanal MRI in detecting non-Crohn's perianal fistulae. Its capabilities in Crohn's disease are yet to be evaluated.

Some of the limitations of endoanal ultrasound can be overcome by using transcutaneous perianal ultrasound (PAUS) or transvaginal ultrasound. These two techniques, used in conjunction, allow for a larger field of view. In addition, they may be used when an endoanal probe cannot be tolerated. Wedemeyer *et al.* [11] have shown that transcutaneous PAUS has comparable sensitivity to MRI in detecting perianal fistulae and/or abscesses, yet is well tolerated and requires no special equipment.

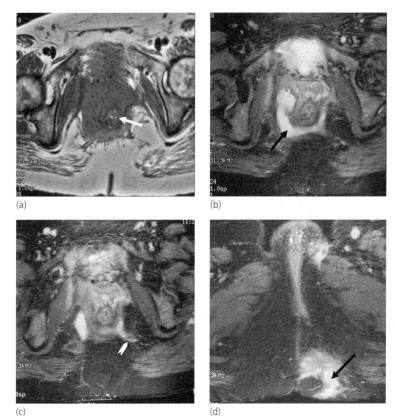

(a) (b)

(c) (d)

FIG 4.2 Patient 5. (a,b) T1 and Short Tau Inversion Recovery magnetic resonance imaging (STIR MRI) at the same level demonstrating anal sphincter mechanism (white arrow) and associated posterior horseshoe abscess (black arrow). The abscess involves both ischiorectal fossae. (c) STIR MRI demonstrating fistulous track extending to the left buttock (white arrowhead). (d) STIR MRI demonstrating left buttock abscess (black arrow).

Magnetic resonance imaging is a well-established technique for imaging perianal involvement in Crohn's disease. The value of the technique was first appreciated by Koelbel *et al.* [12], who imaged a small series of Crohn's patients with abdominopelvic fistulae. No absolute consensus of technique exists. However, most centers use a combination of T1, T2 (with or without fat suppression) and Short Tau Inversion Recovery (STIR) sequences in the axial and coronal plane. The T1 sequences provide anatomic information regarding the sphincter mechanism. The T2 and STIR sequences demonstrate the fistula track as high signal (Fig. 4.2).

Enhanced accuracy can be achieved by including imaging in the sagittal plane, instilling saline into the fistula track, or acquiring dynamic enhanced images with intravenous gadolinium.

The advantages of MRI are that it provides high soft tissue contrast resolution with true multiplanar capability. In addition, the wide field of view and lack of ionizing radiation make it attractive in young patients who may require multiple investigations [13].

The majority of MR examinations are acquired using a phased array torso receiver coil. However, endoanal receiver coils have been developed, and these provide excellent anatomic detail of the anal sphincters and the internal openings of fistulae [14]. The limitations are similar to those of endoanal ultrasound: a small field of view and poor patient tolerance in patients with extensive and painful perianal disease. In patients with extensive or complex pelvic disease, additional examination with a phased array torso coil is mandatory. Without this adjunct, the full extent of involvement would be missed, especially in the supralevator and ischiorectal compartments.

An extension of the role of MRI has been to assess the effects of antitumor necrosis factor, infliximab, on perianal Crohn's disease. Although external orifices stop draining after infliximab treatment, MRI has shown that fistula tracks often persist with residual inflammation. This has important implications for fistula recurrence and abscess formation and can guide further treatment [15].

Evidence and conclusions

In the assessment of pelvic Crohn's disease, MRI, and endoscopic ultrasound appear to be the investigations of choice.

Two prospective trials have compared these techniques with surgical EUA. Orsoni et al. [16] found rectal endoscopic ultrasound to be the most sensitive modality. The agreement of ultrasound and MRI with surgical evaluation of perianal fistulae was 82% and 50%, respectively. Schwartz et al. [17] found all three techniques had an accuracy of over 85%. By combining any two procedures the accuracy improved to 100%. The low agreement between MRI and EUA in the former study may be because a whole body coil was used rather than a phased array coil which provides thinner slices and better spatial resolution. Another major difference in the studies was that Orsoni et al. [16] used EUA as the gold standard. This may not have been appropriate given its known potential for underestimating the extent of disease. In contrast, Schwartz et al. [17] used a consensus opinion of all three techniques to establish the gold standard.

The preferred examination will depend on local expertise, the facilities available, and patient tolerance. Each case should be assessed individually and a combination of techniques may be required.

References

1 Williams DR, Coller JA, Corman ML, et al. Anal complications in Crohn's disease. Dis Colon Rectum 1981; 24: 22–4.

2 Shouler PJ, Grimley RP, Keighley MR, et al. Fistula-in-ano is usually simple to manage surgically. Int J Colorectal Dis 1986; 1: 113–5.

3 Seow-Choen, Phillips RK. Insights gained from the management of problematic anal fistulae at St Mark's Hospital, 1984–88. Br J Surg 1991; 78: 539–41.

4 Parks AG, Gordon PH, Hardcastle JD. A classification of fistula-in-ano. Br J Surg 1976; 63: 1–12.

5 Kuijpers HC, Schulpen T. Fistulography for fistula-in ano. Is it useful? Dis Colon Rectum 1985; 28: 103–4.

6 Halligan S. Imaging fistula-in-ano. Clin Radiol 1998; 53: 85–95.

7 Harisinghani MG, Gervais DA, Maher MM, et al. Transgluteal approach for percutaneous drainage of deep pelvic abscesses: 154 cases. Radiology 2003; 228: 701–5.

8 Makowiec F, Jehle EC, Starlinger M. Clinical course of perianal fistulas in Crohn's disease. Gut 1995; 37: 696–701.

9 Sudol-Szopinska I, Jakubowski W, Szczepkowski M. Contrast-enhanced endosonography for the diagnosis of anal and anovaginal fistulas. J Clin Ultrasound 2002; 30: 145–50.

10 West RL, Zimmerman DD, Dwarkasing S, et al. Prospective comparison of hydrogen peroxide-enhanced three-dimensional endoanal ultrasonography and endoanal magnetic resonance imaging of perianal fistulas. Dis Colon Rectum 2003; 46: 1407–15.

11 Wedemeyer J, Kirchhoff T, Sellge G, et al. Transcutaneous perianal sonography: a sensitive method for the detection of perianal inflammatory lesions in Crohn's disease. World J Gastroenterol 2004; 10: 2859–63.

12 Koelbel G, Schmiedl U, Majer MC, et al. Diagnosis of fistulae and sinus tracts in patients with Crohn disease: value of MR imaging. Am J Roentgenol 1989; 152: 999–1003.

13 Haggett PJ, Moore NR, Shearman JD, et al. Pelvic and perineal complications of Crohn's disease: assessment using magnetic resonance imaging. Gut 1995; 36: 407–10.

14 deSouza NM, Gilderdale DJ, Coutts GA, et al. MRI of fistula-in-ano: a comparison of endoanal coil with external phased array coil techniques. J Comput Assist Tomogr 1998; 22: 357–63.

15 Van Assche G, Vanbeckevoort D, Bielen D, et al. Magnetic resonance imaging of the effects of infliximab on perianal fistulizing Crohn's disease. Am J Gastroenterol 2003; 98: 332–9.

16 Orsoni P, Barthet M, Portier F, et al. Prospective comparison of endosonography, magnetic resonance imaging and surgical findings in anorectal fistula and abscess complicating Crohn's disease. Br J Surg 1999; 86: 360–4.

17 Schwartz DA, Wiersema MJ, Dudiak KM, et al. A Comparison of endoscopic ultrasound, magnetic resonance imaging, and exam under anaesthesia for evaluation of Crohn's perianal fistulas. Gastroenterology 2001; 121: 1064–72.

5 Surveillance colonoscopy in UC: alternatives and ways to improve outcome

MARK LUST & WILLIAM CONNELL

LEARNING POINTS

Surveillance colonoscopy in UC

- Colonoscopy with multiple random biopsies is currently the most widely used method of cancer surveillance in UC, but its overall efficacy and cost-effectiveness have not been substantiated

- Alternatives requiring further evaluation include:

  - prophylactic proctocolectomy

  - chemoprophylaxis with 5-aminosalicylic acid (5-ASA), folic acid and/or ursodeoxycholic acid

  - close clinical supervision

  - biomarkers such aneuploidy and p53

  - chromoendoscopy and magnifying endoscopy

Cancer risk in UC

Patients with UC face an increased risk of developing colorectal cancer (CRC), especially those with long-standing, extensive disease. The cumulative risk for cancer is estimated to be 2% at 10 years, 8% at 20 years, and 18% at 30 years [1]. Expressed in a different way, the lifetime prevalence of CRC in any patient with UC is 3.7%, increasing to 5.4% among individuals with pancolitis [1]. Individuals with extensive colitis are at greater risk of developing cancer than those with left-sided colitis, whereas the cancer risk in patients with proctitis is similar to that of the general population [2]. CRC is also increased among UC patients with coexisting primary sclerosing cholangitis [3], and possibly those with a family history of bowel cancer [4]. Recently, an important study from St. Mark's Hospital showed that active colonic inflammation represents a strong risk factor for the development of colorectal neoplasia in colitis [5]. The same group subsequently showed that macroscopic colonoscopic features helped predict the neoplasia risk in UC, and those with a normal-looking colon had a similar risk of developing colon cancer over 5 years of follow-up to the general population [6].

Endoscopic surveillance

Because most cancers complicating colitis are preceded by dysplasia, endoscopic surveillance has been recommended as a means to identify patients at imminent risk of carcinoma or to detect established cases of malignancy at an early and curable stage. Endoscopic surveillance involves regular (1–2 yearly) colonoscopic examinations of the entire bowel during which time multiple, random biopsies from flat mucosa or targeted biopsies from elevated or suspicious lesions are obtained. If dysplasia is detected, and confirmed by a separate pathologist, the predictive value of developing cancer is sufficiently high to justify prophylactic surgery [7]. Endoscopic surveillance is generally recommended in patients with extensive colitis or primary sclerosing cholangitis, usually commencing 8–10 years after disease onset, although patients with left-sided colitis may be included in similar programs starting 10–15 years after disease onset.

Although endoscopic surveillance is beneficial to many patients, its overall efficacy and cost effectiveness has never been substantiated. In particular, it does not always prevent the development of advanced cancer, and the exercise is costly, inconvenient, and requires considerable administrative effort. Accordingly, the overall value of endoscopic surveillance has been questioned, and alternative options proposed to manage the cancer risk in colitis [8].

Alternatives to endoscopic surveillance

Prophylactic proctocolectomy

Prophylactic proctocolectomy offers the best means to eliminate the risk of cancer, and this option should be seriously considered in those at highest risk of developing cancer. However, surgical resection of the large bowel is a major undertaking which may be associated with the development of various postoperative complications including pouchitis. Not surprisingly, many patients are unwilling to agree to this option, especially when their health is otherwise satisfactory.

Chemoprophylaxis

There is evidence that 5-aminosalicylic acid (5-ASA) therapy may confer protection against the development of CRC in IBD patients [9–11]. In contrast to most series, a population-based study from Denmark showed no increase in the cancer rate among patients with IBD, and a possible reason for this observation was the widespread use of maintenance 5-ASA therapy [9]. A retrospective case–control study showed that mesalazine in a dosage of 1.2 g/day or more reduced the risk of cancer by 81% in patients with UC [10], and a separate case–control analysis also suggested that sulfasalazine therapy may reduce the risk of CRC in UC [11]. However, these results differ from a Canadian population-based study which did not confirm any definite chemo-preventative effect of 5-ASA therapy [12]. It remains unclear if any anticancer effect from 5-ASA is purely due to a reduction in colonic inflammation or secondary to an induction of apoptosis and inhibition of cellular proliferation [8]. Other therapeutic agents with reported anticancer properties in IBD include folic acid, ursodeoxycholic acid (in those with coexisting primary sclerosing cholangitis), butyrate, and conjugated linoleic acid [8].

Clinical supervision

When UC patients present with symptoms of cancer, the tumor is usually diagnosed at an advanced stage when the prognosis is poor [13]. Therefore, a practice of clinical sup-

ervision and investigating new symptoms seems hazardous for UC patients, even if 5-ASA therapy is routinely used. Most patients who are informed of the association between colitis and cancer are not satisfied with this option.

Biomarkers

One of the limiting factors of dysplasia is that the diagnosis of dysplasia can be difficult to make in the presence of inflammation, and that considerable inter- and intra-observer variability applies [7]. An objective molecular marker that is reliably predictive of malignancy would be desirable to complement dysplasia in clinical practice. Like sporadic CRC, the major carcinogenic pathways leading to colitis-associated cancers involve chromosomal instability, microsatellite instability, and hypermethylation. However, the timing and frequency of key genetic changes are different, and abnormalities in these molecular pathways may be demonstrated in inflamed colonic mucosa even before any histologic evidence of dysplasia or cancer. Various markers that appear to indicate a subsequent risk of developing dysplasia or cancer include aneuploidy, p53, and mucin-associated sialyl Tn antigen [14]. There is insufficient evidence at present to support the use of these markers in clinical practice.

Chromoendoscopy and magnifying endoscopy

A major drawback of endoscopic surveillance is the limited ability to detect the presence of dysplasia from random colonic biopsies. If dysplasia was visible to the endoscopist, targeted biopsies could be obtained, thereby enhancing the diagnostic yield of endoscopic surveillance. Using a magnifying endoscope or chromoendoscopy (in which the colon is sprayed with indigo carmine or methylene blue) allows the endoscopist to recognize slight irregularities to the mucosal surface that cannot be appreciated by conventional endoscopy. Obtaining targeted biopsies from elevated or suspicious regions appears to be more accurate and time effective than a practise of taking large numbers of random, non-targeted biopsies [15,16].

Conclusions

In spite of its imperfections, endoscopic surveillance remains an effective means of reducing the cancer risk in most UC patients who do not wish to undergo prophylactic surgery. In future, however, patients may be stratified according to individual risk, and the conduct of surveillance streamlined to reflect the level of risk. In this way, the development of advanced cancer can hopefully be minimized, and cost reduced. If the pivotal association between disease activity and CRC can be substantiated, this observation promises to significantly influence the way in which endoscopic surveillance is practiced. For example, intensive surveillance (6–12 monthly) with endoscopic spraying and magnifying endoscopy may be appropriate among patients with chronically active extensive disease or those with coexisting primary sclerosing cholangitis. In contrast, patients with persistently inactive disease could undergo colonoscopic examinations less regularly, possibly 5 yearly. In those with active inflammation confined to the distal colon and in whom no other risk factor for bowel cancer applies, it may be reasonable to simply undertake annual flexible sigmoidoscopy (making sure that that the upper level of disease is reached), and colonoscopy every 5 years. Eventually, new biomarkers may supplant dysplasia as a means of predicting malignancy, but until this time the use of 5-ASA compounds should be encouraged to offer additional protection against the development of CRC.

References

1 Eaden JA, Abrams KR, Mayberry JF. The risk of colorectal cancer in ulcerative colitis: a meta-analysis. *Gut* 2001; **48**: 526–35.

2 Ekbom A, Helmick C, Zack M, Adami HO. Ulcerative colitis and colorectal cancer: a population-based study. *N Engl J Med* 1990; **323**: 1228–33.

3 Jayaram H, Satsangi J, Chapman RW. Increased colorectal neoplasia in chronic ulcerative colitis complicated by primary sclerosing cholangitis: fact or fiction? *Gut* 2001; **48**: 430–4.

4 Askling J, Dickman PW, Karlen P, *et al.* Family history as a risk factor for colorectal cancer in inflammatory bowel disease. *Gastroenterology* 2001; **120**: 1356–62.

5 Rutter M, Saunders B, Wilkinson K, *et al.* Severity of inflammation is a risk factor for colorectal neoplasia in ulcerative colitis. *Gastroenterology* 2004; **126**: 451–9.

6 Rutter MD, Saunders BP, Wilkinson KH, *et al.* Cancer surveillance in longstanding ulcerative colitis: endoscopic appearances help predict cancer risk. *Gut* 2004; **53**: 1813–6.

7 Connell WR, Lennard-Jones JE, Williams CB, *et al.* Factors affecting the outcome of endoscopic surveillance for cancer in ulcerative colitis. *Gastroenterology* 1994; **107**: 934–44.

8 Shanahan F, Quera R. Surveillance for ulcerative colitis-associated cancer: time to change the endoscopy and microscopy. *Am J Gastroenterol* 2004; **99**: 1633–6.

9 Langholz E, Munkholm P, Davidsen M, Binder V. Colorectal cancer risk and mortality in patients with ulcerative colitis. *Gastroenterology* 1992; **103**: 1444–51.

10 Eaden J, Abrams K, Ekbom A, *et al.* Colorectal cancer prevention in ulcerative colitis: a case–control study. *Aliment Pharmacol Ther* 2000; **14**: 145–53.

11 Pinczowski D, Ekbom A, Baron J, *et al.* Risk factors for colorectal cancer in patients with ulcerative colitis: a case–control study. *Gastroenterology* 1994; **107**: 117–20.

12 Bernstein CN, Blanchard JF, Metge C, Yogendran M. Does the use of 5-aminosalicylates in inflammatory bowel disease prevent the development of colorectal cancer? *Am J Gastroenterol* 2003; **98**: 2784–8.

13 Choi PM, Nugent FW, Schoetz DJ Jr, *et al.* Colonoscopic surveillance reduces mortality from colorectal cancer in ulcerative colitis. *Gastroenterology* 1993; **105**: 418–24.

14 Itzkowitz S. Colon carcinogenesis in inflammatory bowel disease: applying molecular genetics to clinical practice. *J Clin Gastroenterol* 2003; **36** (5 Suppl): S70–4.

15 Kiesslich R, Fritsch J, Holtmann M, *et al.* Methylene blue-aided chromoendoscopy for the detection of intraepithelial neoplasia and colon cancer in ulcerative colitis. *Gastroenterology* 2003; **124**: 880–8.

16 Rutter MD, Saunders BP, Schofield G, *et al.* Pancolonic indigo carmine dye spraying for the detection of dysplasia in ulcerative colitis. *Gut* 2004; **53**: 256–60.

6 Abnormal liver tests – what should we do about them?

RICHARD MARLEY & ABID SUDDLE

> ### LEARNING POINTS
>
> **Abnormal liver tests**
>
> In sick inpatients with IBD:
>
> - Abnormal liver function tests (LFTs) are common and often resolve spontaneously
>
> - Imaging of the liver with ultrasound or computed tomography (CT) is the investigation of choice
>
> In well outpatients with IBD:
>
> - A slowly progressive rise in LFTs, particularly the alkaline phosphatase, should prompt investigations for sclerosing cholangitis
>
> - Drug-induced hepatotoxicity may be mild and any change in treatment should be made after careful consideration of its effects on the patient's underlying IBD

Introduction

The interpretation and investigation of abnormal liver biochemistry is linked to the severity of the associated IBD (Table 6.1). Abnormal liver function tests (LFTs) are found in up to 50% of patients with IBD requiring surgery [1]. The causes of these are likely to be multifactorial and related to factors such as sepsis, malnutrition, and drug reactions. The prevalence of significant hepatobiliary disease in patients presenting in the outpatient setting is much lower, at approximately 5% in adult patients [2–4].

Investigation of liver function test abnormalities in sick inpatients with IBD

The focus of initial investigation for sick patients is imaging to look for reversible and treatable complications such as cholecystitis or ascending cholangitis, occurring on the background of cholelithiasis or primary sclerosing cholangitis. Other less common complications include hepatic abscesses and acute portal vein thromboses. The pattern of LFT abnormalities in all the above is unpredictable, so an ultrasound and/or Doppler examination of the liver and hepatic vessels is needed in all cases, with additional triphasic computed tomography (CT) of the liver and/or magnetic resonance cholangiopancreatography (MRCP) if the index of suspicion for any of the above is high.

It is important to monitor the vitamin K-corrected prothrombin time as a marker of hepatic synthetic function, because in patients with active IBD albumin levels may be difficult to interpret. Abnormal LFTs in this setting will usually resolve with effective treatment of the bowel disease. Only rarely is a liver biopsy indicated in such patients, usually to determine if drug hepatotoxicity is present.

Investigation of liver function test abnormalities in outpatients with IBD

The most important hepatobiliary disease associated with IBD is sclerosing cholangitis, both the large and small duct forms (see Chapter 56).

Liver abnormalities can arise due to diseases that have a

TABLE 6.1 Causes of abnormal liver biochemistry in IBD.

The "sick inpatient" with IBD
General
Sepsis
Drug-induced, e.g. antibiotics
Nutritional, e.g. steatohepatitis secondary to weight
loss/malnutrition, cholestasis secondary to TPN

Secondary to portal pyemia
Acute portal vein thrombosis
Hepatic abscess

Complications related to hepatobiliary disease
Ascending cholangitis
Cholecystitis

The "well outpatient" with IBD
Associated with IBD
Primary sclerosing cholangitis
Small duct cholangitis
Non-alcoholic fatty liver disease
Amyloidosis (Crohn's only)
(Autoimmune hepatitis/primary biliary cirrhosis)

Secondary to treatment of IBD
Drugs, e.g. azathioprine, methotrexate, 5-ASA compounds
Postoperative, e.g. steatohepatitis

Incidental to IBD
Alcoholic liver disease
Viral hepatitis
Metabolic/autoimmune conditions, e.g. hemochromatosis,
α_1-antitrypsin deficiency

5-ASA, 5-aminosalicylic acid; TPN, total parenteral nutrition.

recognized association with IBD, as a result of its treatment – both drug and surgical – and as a result of liver diseases that occur commonly in the absence of IBD (Table 6.1). A detailed history is therefore important, particularly alcohol history, drug history, and in regard to risk factors for viral hepatitis. All patients merit a full metabolic, autoimmune, and viral screen for causes of liver disease, and this should include lipid and glucose levels because of the rising incidence of non-alcoholic fatty liver disease in the general population.

The following three conditions are responsible for the majority of cases.

Sclerosing cholangitis

Patients should be fully investigated if they present with a progressive rise in hepatic alkaline phosphatase (see Chapter 56). This is particularly suggestive of sclerosing

cholangitis in the context of ulcerative colitis or large intestinal Crohn's disease. The presence or absence of a positive antineutrophil cytoplasmic antibody (ANCA) [5] should not influence more definitive investigations. MRCP is becoming increasingly sensitive in the diagnosis of large duct sclerosing cholangitis, although the decision to use this modality in place of endoscopic retrograde cholangiopancreatography (ERCP) should be based upon local experience and expertise. Normal biliary imaging together with worsening cholestatis should lead to liver biopsy, as small duct sclerosing cholangitis also requires treatment and monitoring for the development of cholangiocarcinoma.

Non-alcoholic fatty liver disease

This is the most common cause of abnormal liver biochemistry in IBD. The LFT abnormalities are often mild, showing a persistently elevated level of transaminases, gamma glutamyl transpeptidase and, less commonly, alkaline phosphatase. Diagnosis is often by exclusion of other diseases together with a suggestive ultrasound. Cofactors such as hyperlipidemia and insulin resistance should be looked for and treated, to slow down disease progression [6].

Reversal of the alanine aminotransferase : aspartate aminotransferase (ALT : AST) ratio, age >45 years, and a platelet count of <150 is predictive of advanced fibrosis, and such patients should be biopsied to confirm the diagnosis and stage the severity of their disease [7]. An aggressive steatohepatitis can occur in small bowel Crohn's disease, in particular following extensive resection.

Drug-induced hepatotoxicity

The three drugs most commonly used in IBD causing liver problems in patients with IBD are thiopurines (azathioprine and 6-mercaptopurine), methotrexate, and 5-aminosalicylic acid (5-ASA) compounds.

• Thiopurines can cause a variety of hepatic reactions including portal inflammation with cholestasis, peliosis hepatis, nodular regenerative hyperplasia, veno-occlusive disease and hepatoportal sclerosis [8].

• Although methotrexate can cause an idiosyncratic hepatotoxicity, the main concern is of progressive fibrosis and cirrhosis mediated by a toxic metabolite of microsomal origin. Surveillance liver biopsies have been advocated, based largely on experience from patients with dermatologic and rheumatologic conditions. However, a recent study in patients with IBD showed that cumulative doses of up to 5 g were associated with little hepatotoxicity [9]. It may be that serum markers of fibrosis become available that will accurately correlate with the degree of fibrosis [5].

• Both sulfasalazine and mesalazine can cause hepatic dysfunction, at a similar frequency. In 11 published clinical trials monitoring LFT abnormalities, the global incidence of mesalazine-induced liver dysfunction was 2.8% [10]. In a randomized trial comparing mesalazine with sulfasalazine, 3/115 patients treated with mesalazine developed hepatitis compared with 4/105 treated with sulfasalazine [11]. In most cases, an increase in the serum transaminases is seen; an acute hepatitis is confirmed on liver biopsy, if this is performed.

The diagnosis of drug-induced hepatotoxicity is usually made on the basis of a temporal relationship with starting and stopping the medications. Liver biopsy is often non-diagnostic but is useful in assessing the severity of liver disease when decisions need to be made about the risk–benefit ratio of continuing implicated medications in patients whose IBD is difficult to control.

Other conditions

The association between ileal Crohn's disease and gallstones is well documented [12]. Hepatic amyloidosis is seen infrequently in IBD, most commonly in chronically active Crohn's disease [13]. Hepatic granulomas are occasionally seen on liver biopsy in patients with Crohn's disease, although it is doubtful whether they are of clinical significance. It is unclear whether reported cases of primary biliary cirrhosis and autoimmune hepatitis occurring in patients with ulcerative colitis represent a true or chance association.

Conclusions

Biochemical liver abnormalities are common in patients with IBD. Interpretation of these abnormalities should be made in the context of the patient's clinical condition. In sick patients, the abnormalities require less investigation, although imaging of the liver is mandatory; these abnormalities frequently resolve with treatment of the underlying bowel disease. In outpatients, the main diagnoses that need to be considered are sclerosing cholangitis and drug-induced hepatotoxicity, as they may lead to significant morbidity and mortality if they go unrecognized.

References

1 Memon MI, Memon B, Memon MA. Hepatobiliary manifestations of inflammatory bowel disease. *HPB Surg* 2000; 11: 363–71.

2 Perret AD, Higgins G, Johnson HH, *et al*. The liver in ulcerative colitis. *Q J Med* 1971; 40: 211–38.

3 Olsson R, Danielson A, Jarnerot G, *et al*. Prevalence of primary sclerosing cholangitis in patients with ulcerative colitis. *Gastroenterology* 1991; 100: 1319.

4 Ahmad J, Slivka A. Hepatobiliary disease in inflammatory bowel disease. *Gastroenterol Clin North Am* 2002; 31: 329–45.

5 Terjung B, Worman HJ. Anti-neutrophil antibodies in primary sclerosing cholangitis. *Best Prac Res Clin Gastroenterol* 2001; 15: 629–42.

6 Kiyichi M, Gulten M, Gurel S, *et al*. Ursodeoxycholic acid and atorvastatin and the treatment of non-alcoholic steatohepatitis. *Can J Gastroenterol* 2003; 17: 713–8.

7 Shimada M, Hashimoto E, Kaneda H, *et al*. Nonalcoholic steatohepatitis: risk factors for liver fibrosis. *Hepatol Res* 2002; 24: 429–38.

8 Norris S. Drug and toxin-induced liver disease. In: *Comprehensive Clinical Hepatology*, 1st edn. 2000; 3.29: 1–20.

9 Te HS, Schiano TD, Kuan SF, *et al*. Hepatic effects of long-term methotrexate use in the treatment of inflammatory bowel disease. *Am J Gastroenterol* 2000; 95: 3150.

10 Deltenre P, Berson A, Marcellin P, *et al*. Mesalazine induced chronic hepatitis. *Gut* 1999; 44: 886–8.

11 Rachmilewitz D. Coated mesalazine versus sulphasalazine in the treatment of active ulcerative colitis: a randomised trial. *BMJ* 1989; 298: 82–6.

12 Lapidus A, Bangstad M, Astrom M, *et al*. The prevalence of gallstone disease in a defined cohort of patients with Crohn's disease. *Am J Gastroenterol* 1999; 94: 1261–6.

13 Cucion C, Sonnenberg A. The comorbid occurrence of other diagnoses in patients with ulcerative colitis and Crohn's disease. *Am J Gastroenterol* 2001; 96: 2107–12.

7 Is monitoring necessary?

RAKESH SHAH & ALASTAIR FORBES

LEARNING POINTS

Monitoring

- 5-Aminosalicylic acid (5-ASA) drugs are safe and well-tolerated

- Monitoring for hepatic and renal dysfunction is probably sensible

- We recommend:

  - Baseline full blood count, urea and creatinine and liver function tests

  - Full blood count, urea and creatinine and liver function tests 6-monthly for the first 2 years of therapy (full blood count 3-monthly for the first 6 months – sulfasalazine only)

  - Subsequent annual urea and creatinine

Introduction

Sulfasalazine and 5-aminosalicylic acid (5-ASA) are known to be effective in the management of patients with ulcerative colitis, and to a lesser extent, Crohn's disease [1]. Sulfasalazine has been used for many years, but both dose-dependent and idiosyncratic side-effects, attributed to the sulfapyridine constituent, are common. The 5-ASA moiety is the principal active constituent in therapy for inflammatory bowel disease, and the sulfapyridine component has come to be regarded as a rather toxic and dispensable transport molecule [2]. Other 5-ASA preparations (mesalazine, olsalazine, and balsalazide) lack the sulfapyridine constituent and are generally better tolerated than sulfasalazine [3].

Prescribers of potentially long-term drug therapy should be especially alert to possible side-effects and the need for appropriate monitoring. The 5-ASA drugs are no exception to this philosophy, and new symptoms or abnormal investigations should raise the possibility of side-effects and the question of dosage reduction or drug withdrawal. It is prudent to educate the patient on possible side-effects given that they may remain on the drug for many years.

Sulfasalazine is widely prescribed in rheumatoid arthritis and its toxicity profile is well rehearsed [4,5]; it should not be assumed that its side-effects will necessarily be as frequent in IBD. However, the reasonable supposition that sulfasalazine will exhibit a wider range of side-effects than other 5-ASAs has been borne out in IBD trials [6].

Side-effects

A wide range of adverse events may be seen with the 5-ASA drugs (Table 7.1). It should be noted that most of these are rare (less than 1/10 000 patients affected). Some side-effects common to both sulfasalazine and the alternative 5-ASAs are more frequent in one group than the other [5]. Risk quantification is difficult as generally only the more serious problems have been studied in depth.

Renal side-effects

Renal toxicity with sulfasalazine, although still cited as a side-effect, is very rare. Ten clinical trials involving 718 patients on sulfasalazine for more than 6 months yielded no

TABLE 7.1 Side-effects of sulfasalazine and 5-ASA drugs.

Side-effects common to sulfasalazine and the other 5-ASAs	Side-effects of sulfasalazine alone
Gastrointestinal	*Dermatologic*
Diarrhea*	Stevens–Johnson syndrome
Nausea/vomiting*†	Exfoliative dermatitis
Exacerbation of symptoms of colitis*	Epidermal necrolysis
	Pruritus
Abdominal pain*†	Periorbital edema
Acute pancreatitis	Stomatitis
Hepatitis	Parotitis
Neurologic	*Neurologic*
Headache*	Ataxia
Peripheral neuropathy	Aseptic meningitis
	Vertigo
	Tinnitus
Genitourinary	*Genitourinary*
Interstitial nephritis‡	Hematuria
Nephrotic syndrome	Crystalluria
	Oligospermia
Hematologic	*Respiratory*
Agranulocytosis†	Lung fibrosis
Anemia†	
Leukopenia†	
Thrombocytopenia†	
Pancytopenia†	
Others	
Hypersensitivity reactions†	
Lupus erythematosus-like syndrome	
Alopecia	

* Most common side-effects.
† More common with sulfasalazine.
‡ More common with mesalazine.

cases of deterioration in renal function [3]. There have been a very few case reports of sulfasalazine causing renal toxicity as part of a generalized hypersensitivity reaction [7]. It should be remembered also that IBD is itself complicated by renal disease independently of any therapeutic endeavors.

On the other hand, the association of 5-ASAs (and mesalazine in particular) with interstitial nephritis is now well established. This is a serious adverse effect, but one that is often reversible on drug withdrawal if detected early. In one report, complete recovery was seen in 85% of patients in whom the drug had been stopped within 10 months [8]. The pathogenesis of mesalazine-induced interstitial nephritis

is unclear, but may involve renal hypoxia resulting from local effects of mesalazine on renal blood flow, or perhaps a direct tubular toxic effect [9]. Interstitial nephritis as a result of mesalazine therapy is rare; from a review of 18 clinical trials lasting at least 6 months assessing the efficacy of mesalazine in IBD, only 1/1638 patients had a deterioration in renal function [3]. However, affected patients are at risk of end-stage renal failure requiring dialysis or transplantation. About half of all reported cases present within a year of drug initiation, but the range is wide (3 months–5 years) [8]. It is possible that the concurrent use of steroids can delay the presentation – steroids themselves having a modest role in the treatment of interstitial nephritis [9].

Hepatic side-effects

Liver disease is relatively common in inflammatory bowel disease, especially in patients with active and/or extensive disease. Most 5-ASA-induced hepatotoxicity is part of a more generalized hypersensitivity reaction and is rare [3].

Sulfasalazine is not normally associated with liver dysfunction other than in generalized hypersensitivity reactions characterized by systemic illness, rash, and fever [10]. Liver biopsies then show histologic features consistent with hypersensitivity. This is likely to be a result of the sulfapyridine constituent. Most cases present within 1 month of treatment initiation and are quickly reversible on drug withdrawal. However, rare cases of fulminant hepatic failure and death have been reported [11]. The degree of hepatic dysfunction tends to be worse in sulfasalazine-treated rheumatoid arthritis patients than in IBD patients.

Other forms of 5-ASA cause hepatic dysfunction still more rarely. In 17 clinical trials involving 1558 patients on mesalazine for more than 6 months there were two cases with raised transaminases that were thought to be mesalazine related [3]. There has also been a single case of histologically confirmed chronic hepatitis commencing more than 6 months after the initiation of mesalazine treatment [12]. Liver dysfunction improved on drug withdrawal.

Hematologic side-effects

The 5-ASAs have been associated with a wide range of hematologic side-effects in IBD. Agranulocytosis, red cell aplasia, leukopenia, thrombocytopenia and pancytopenia have all been reported. Antibody-mediated cell destruction and/or direct bone marrow suppression are thought possible mechanisms [13].

Arguably the best data on hematologic adverse reactions

to sulfasalazine come from a 1996 study involving over 10 000 patients [14]. These patients were identified from the UK General Practice Research Database, all having IBD or rheumatoid arthritis treated with sulfasalazine. Only 4/6286 IBD patients on sulfasalazine had an adverse hematologic reaction (one-tenth of the risk in the arthritis patients). These findings have been supported by more recent work [5]. The majority of sulfasalazine-associated hematologic side-effects occur within 3 months of starting treatment [3].

Over 4000 patients from the above UK study took other 5-ASAs for IBD, and in this group no hematologic side-effects were recorded [14]. However, case reports of leukopenia, thrombocytopenia, and pancytopenia have been made [15,16]. In contrast with sulfasalazine, most of these presented more than 3 months after initiation of treatment. In most cases the prognosis appears good if the drug is withdrawn.

Other side-effects

Pancreatitis occurs very occasionally and is apparently least rare with mesalazine [5]. The neurologic and dermatologic side-effects of sulfasalazine (Table 7.1) are all rare. A 5-ASA-related lupus-like syndrome incorporates an anti-nuclear antibody-positive migratory arthralgia and arthritis, which is unrelated to the underlying IBD [17]. Alopecia is probably a little more common with sulfasalazine, but case reports of reversible, dose-dependent hair loss also exist for other forms of 5-ASA [18].

Sulfasalazine predictably leads to reduced fertility in men through an almost inevitable oligospermia of uncertain pathogenicity [19]. It is highly likely to be secondary to the sulfapyridine constituent as most patients show a significantly improved sperm count after switching to other forms of 5-ASA. The drug should not be used in men planning a family.

Monitoring of patients on 5-ASA drugs

The recent British Society of Gastroenterology guidelines for IBD recognize that serious side-effects with 5-ASA drugs are rare. Monitoring of renal function during 5-ASA therapy is suggested in those with pre-existing renal impairment, comorbid disease, and in those on other potentially nephrotoxic drugs [20]. No other specific monitoring is advocated.

Decisions on monitoring need to take into account the severity of the side-effect in question, its frequency, and the cost and effectiveness of the monitoring strategy used. Clearly, it is important that the patient is counseled about the types and nature of possible side-effects when embarking upon potential long-term therapy. Given the observations above and recognizing the incomplete evidence base, we currently recommend:

• Baseline full blood count, urea and creatinine and liver function tests.

• Full blood count urea and creatinine and liver function tests 6-monthly for the first 2 years of therapy (full blood count 3-monthly for the first 6 months – sulfasalazine only).

• Subsequent annual urea and creatinine.

References

1 Sands BE. Therapy of inflammatory bowel disease. *Gastroenterology* 2000; **118**: S68–82.

2 Azad Khan AK, Piris J, Truelove SC. An experiment to determine the active therapeutic moiety of sulfasalazine. *Lancet* 1977; **2**: 892–5.

3 Cunliffe RN, Scott BB. Review article: monitoring for drug side effects in inflammatory bowel disease. *Aliment Pharmacol Ther* 2001; **16**: 647–62.

4 Capell HA, Maiden N, Madhok R, *et al.* Intention-to-treat analysis of 200 patients with rheumatoid arthritis 12 years after random allocation to either sulfasalazine or penicillamine. *J Rheumatol* 1998; **25**: 1880–6.

5 Ransford RAJ, Langman MJS. Sulfasalazine and mesalazine: serious adverse reactions re-evaluated on the basis of suspected adverse reaction reports to the Committee on Safety of Medicine. *Gut* 2002; **51**: 536–40.

6 Das KM, Eastwood MA, McManus JP, Sircus W. Adverse reactions during salicylazosulfapyridine therapy and the relation with drug metabolism and acetylator phenotype. *N Engl J Med* 1973; **289**: 491–5.

7 Chester AC, Diamond LH, Schreiner GE. Hypersensitivity to salicylazosulfapyridine: renal and hepatic toxic reactions. *Arch Intern Med* 1978; **138**: 1138–9.

8 World MJ, Stevens PE, Ashton MA, Rainford DJ. Mesalazine-associated interstitial nephritis. *Nephrol Dial Transplant* 1996; **11**: 614–21.

9 Corrigan G, Stevens PE. Review article: interstitial nephritis associated with the use of mesalazine in inflammatory bowel disease. *Aliment Pharmacol Ther* 2000; **14**: 1–6.

10 Fich A, Schwartz J, Braverman D, *et al.* Sulfasalazine toxicity. *Am J Gastroenterol* 1984; **79**: 401–2.

11 Marinos G, Riley J, Painter DM, McCaughan GW. Sulfasalazine-induced fulminant hepatic failure. *J Clin Gastroenterol* 1992; **14**: 132–5.

12 Deltenre P, Berson A, Marcellin P, *et al.* Mesalazine (5-aminosalicylic acid) induced chronic hepatitis. *Gut* 1999; **44**: 886–8.

13 Taffet SL, Das KM. Sulfasalazine: adverse effects and desensitization. *Dig Dis Sci* 1983; **28**: 833–42.

14 Jick H, Myers MW, Dean AD. The risk of sulfasalazine and mesalazine-associated blood disorders. *Pharmacotherapy* 1995; **15**: 176–81.

15 Kotanagi H, Ito M, Koyama K, Chiba M. Pancytopenia associated with 5-aminosalicylic acid in a patient with Crohn's disease. *J Gastroenterol* 1998; **33**: 571–4.

16 Farrell RJ, Peppercorn MA, Fine SN, Micjetti P. Mesalamine-induced thrombocytopenia. *Am J Gastroenterol* 1999; **94**: 2304–6.

17 Kirkpatrick AW, Bookman AA, Habal F. Lupus-like syndrome caused by 5-aminosalicylic acid in patients with inflammatory bowel disease. *Can J Gastroenterol* 1999; **13**: 159–62.

18 Netzer P. Diffuse alopecia as a side effect of mesalazine therapy in Crohn's disease. *Schweiz Med Wochenschr* 1995; **125**: 2438–42.

19 Di Paolo MC, Paoluzi OA, Pica R, *et al.* Sulfasalazine and 5-aminosalicylic acid in long term treatment of ulcerative colitis: report on tolerance and side-effects. *Dig Liver Dis* 2001; **33**: 563–9.

20 Carter MJ, Lobo AJ, Travis SPL. Guidelines for the management of inflammatory bowel disease in adults. *Gut* 2004; **53**(Suppl V): 1–16.

Medical Treatment: Making the Most of What We've Got – *5-ASA drugs*

8 Do they have a role in Crohn's disease?

VIKRANT SIBARTIE & BRIAN FEAGAN

LEARNING POINTS

Use of 5-ASA in Crohn's disease

- Unlike in UC, the role of 5-aminosalicylates (5-ASA) in treating active Crohn's or in maintaining remission in Crohn's disease is questionable

- 5-ASA may have a role in preventing relapse after surgery for small bowel Crohn's

- As in UC, 5-ASA may have a role in reducing the risk of colon cancer in extensive colonic Crohn's disease but this remains to be proven

- Particularly in view of its safety profile, it is reasonable to continue using 5-ASA in patients who are well-established on the drug if they believe it helps them

---

Introduction

While the efficacy of 5-aminosalicylates (5-ASA) in UC for induction of remission of mild to moderate disease and for maintenance of remission is well established, the role of these agents in Crohn's disease is now questionable. In contrast to the parent drug sulfasalazine, which seems to be effective in mild to moderately active Crohn's colitis, the 5-ASA compounds have a marginal or negligible effect, both in inducing and maintaining remission. Indeed, a case can be made for abandoning 5-ASA in the management of Crohn's disease.

Different formulations of 5-ASA

The prototype 5-ASA drug is sulfasalazine, which is composed of sulfapyridine linked by an azo-bond to 5-aminosalicylic acid (5-ASA), and reaches the colon intact, where it is split into its two component molecules by an azo reductase released by colonic bacteria. Sulfapyridine acts solely as a carrier molecule to the colon, where the active drug, 5-ASA, has its therapeutic effect.

As the sulfapyridine moiety is responsible for most of sulfasalazine's side-effects (see Chapter 7), other 5-ASA formulations have been devised. Because 5-ASA in its pure form is largely absorbed in the proximal small intestine, the different formulations ensure that it is delivered distally by either linking it to another carrier (e.g. olsalazine, balsalazide) or by the use of slow release (mesalazine ethycellulose-coated microgranules) and delayed release preparations (eudragit-coated mesalazine). 5-ASAs are available in oral, foam enemas, and suppository formulations. Although the latter two are helpful in UC limited to the rectum, only oral preparations of sulfasalazine and mesalazine have been adequately evaluated in Crohn's disease.

5-ASA in active Crohn's disease

Studies in the early 1980s by Malchow *et al.* [1] and Summers *et al.* [2] showed sulfasalazine to be effective in inducing remission in mildly active Crohn's disease, especially in Crohn's colitis, reflecting the site of action of the active portion of the drug after it is cleaved in the colon. However, the side-effects of sulfasalazine, which include nausea, headaches, rash, diarrhea, male infertility, and, more rarely, agranulocytosis and pancreatitis, are the main limitations of the drug. Doses of 2–4 g are effective, with higher doses of up to 6 g showing better efficacy at the expense of more side-effects.

Several trials have evaluated other 5-ASA, such as mesalazine, with a better side-effect profile than sulfasalazine. While some have shown slightly superior efficacy of mesalazine compared with placebo in mildly active Crohn's disease, others have demonstrated no benefit. The first convincing trial using mesalazine slow-release formulation in mild to moderate Crohn's disease was performed by Singleton *et al.* [3] in 1993 and showed a remission rate of 43% compared with 18% on placebo, the benefit being seen in both small and large bowel disease. A subsequent trial performed by the same investigator did not replicate these results, with no significant difference between mesalazine and placebo groups [4]. More recently, a meta-analysis by Hanauer and Stromberg [5] showed that 4 g/day mesalazine reduced the Crohn's Disease Activity Index (CDAI) by 18 points compared with placebo. However, such a small reduction does not translate into any significant improvement in clinical practice [6].

The overall data with mesalazine in active Crohn's disease remain, at best, dubious. Many clinicians have viewed 5-ASA as an attractive first option for Crohn's disease because of its favorable side-effect profile. It has therefore been used largely in mild to moderately active Crohn's disease involving the small bowel. However, this practice is not evidence-based and can no longer be recommended for the induction of remission of Crohn's disease.

5-ASA in maintaining remission of Crohn's disease

Results of studies involving the use of 5-ASA in the maintenance of remission of Crohn's disease have been conflicting. It is clear that sulfasalazine has no role when used for this indication [1,2].

The role of mesalazine is less clear: its effect, at a dosage of at least 2 g/day, may be dependent on disease location and whether remission was achieved with corticosteroids or with surgery. It is likely that mesalazine has no role when remission has been induced with steroids [7]. Indeed, a recent meta-analysis of seven trials of the use of mesalazine in maintaining remission of Crohn's disease showed no

benefit over placebo [8]. However, this review did not include patients who achieved remission with surgery. An earlier meta-analysis [9] suggested that benefit is found only in post-surgical patients predominantly with ileal involvement, and in patients with prolonged disease duration. In these patients, the risk of relapse after surgery was reduced by mesalazine by 13%. When this was put to the test prospectively with a randomized placebo-controlled trial of 318 post-surgical patients, mesalazine was no better than placebo at preventing relapse after 18 months of treatment in the entire group of patients [10]; however, retrospective analysis again showed benfit for mesalazine in patients with exclusively small bowel involvement.

Many physicians have abandoned the routine prescription of mesalazine for the maintenance of remission of Crohn's disease. The decision to continue this drug should only be made after careful consideration of the long-term cost balanced against a potentially small benefit in a select group of patients, possibly post-surgical patients with ileal disease. For those patients already on mesalazine, the decision to stop this medication can be difficult, especially in those who perceive it to be beneficial. One must bear in mind, in this setting, the strong placebo effect observed in most studies, and the relative safety of this drug.

5-ASA in chemoprevention of colon cancer

Colonic Crohn's disease increases the risk of colorectal cancer particularly in patients with extensive colitis [11]. The relative risk of developing colon cancer is 20 for those diagnosed before the age of 30 years. While several studies and epidemiologic data suggest that 5-ASA can reduce the risk of developing neoplasia in UC (see Chapter 51) [12], no studies have properly evaluated this in Crohn's colitis. It can be postulated that, if 5-ASA have little role in preventing relapses of Crohn's disease and thus have little anti-inflammatory effect in this setting, they may have no effect in preventing dysplasia and its progression to cancer. However, the mechanisms of chemoprevention of colon cancer by 5-ASA may rely on pathways not necessarily related to chronic inflammation, such as an increase in apoptosis of neoplastic polyps, antiproliferative effects on colon cancer cell lines, and stabilization of DNA [13]. Thus, there may be a role for 5-ASA in the chemoprophylaxis of colorectal cancer in Crohn's colitis, which may be a factor in the decision to use them in Crohn's colitis in remission. Further studies need to be performed to confirm if this role is more than just theoretical.

Conclusions

Although 5-ASA preparations have previously been widely used, the evidence base for their efficacy in active Crohn's disease or in the maintenance of remission has gradually crumbled in recent years. The main indications, themselves equivocal, are now only maintenance of post-surgical remission in patients with exclusively small bowel disease, and for the reduction of the risk of colonic neoplasia in patients with extensive Crohn's colitis.

References

1 Malchow H, Ewe K, Brandes JW, *et al.* European Cooperative Crohn's Disease Study (ECCDS): results of drug treatment. *Gastroenterology* 1984; **86**: 249–66.

2 Summers RW, Switz DM, Sessions JT Jr, *et al.* National Cooperative Crohn's Disease Study (NCCDS): results of drug treatment. *Gastroenerology* 1979; **77**: 847–69.

3 Singleton JW, Hanauer SB, Gitnick GL, *et al.* Mesalamine capsules for the treatment of active Crohn's disease: results of a 16-week trial. Pentasa Crohn's Disease Study Group. *Gastroenterology* 1993; **104**: 1293–301.

4 Singleton J. Second trial of mesalamine therapy in the treatment of active Crohn's disease. *Gastroenterology* 1994; **107**: 632–3.

5 Hanauer SB, Stromberg U. Oral Pentasa in the treatment of active Crohn's disease: a meta-analysis of double-blind, placebo-controlled trials. *Clin Gastroenterol Hepatol* 2004; **2**: 379–88.

6 Feagan BG. 5-ASA therapy for active Crohn's disease: old friends, old data, and a new conclusion. *Clin Gastroenterol Hepatol* 2004; **2**: 376–8.

7 Modigliani R, Colombel JF, Dupas JL, *et al.* Mesalamine in Crohn's disease with steroid-induced remission: effect on steroid withdrawal and remission maintenance. *Gastroenterology* 1996; **108**: 688–93.

8 Akobeng AK, Gardener E. Oral 5-aminosalicylic acid for maintenance of medically-induced remission in Crohn's Disease. The Cochrane Database of Systematic Reviews 2005, Issue 1. Art No.: CD003715.pub2. DOI: 10.1002/14651858.CD003715.pub2.

9 Camma C, Giunta M, Rosselli M, *et al.* Mesalamine in the maintenance treatment of Crohn's disease: a meta-analysis adjusted for confounding variables. *Gastroenterology* 1997; **113**: 1465–73.

10 Lochs H, Mayer M, Fleig WE, *et al.* Prophylaxis of postoperative relapse in Crohn's disease with mesalamine: European Cooperative Crohn's Disease Study VI. *Gastroenterology* 2000; **118**: 264–73.

11 Ekbom A, Helmick C, Zack M, Adami HO. Increased risk of large-bowel cancer in Crohn's disease with colonic involvement. *Lancet* 1990; **336**: 337–59.

12 Eaden J, Abrams K, Ekbom A, Jackson E, Mayberry J. Colorectal cancer prevention in ulcerative colitis: a case–control study. *Aliment Pharmacol Ther* 2000; **14**: 145–53.

13 Cheng Y, Desreumaux P. 5-Aminosalicylic acid is an attractive candidate agent for chemoprevention of colon cancer in patients with inflammatory bowel disease. *World J Gastroenterol* 2005; **11**: 309–14.

9 Steroids in Crohn's: are they obsolete?

DAVID RAMPTON

LEARNING POINTS

Steroids in Crohn's disease

- Steroids provide prompt symptom relief, at the expense of a high relapse rate and many side-effects

- Steroids should be avoided in patients with abscess, fistula, perianal disease or non-inflammatory complications

- When needed, steroids should be given for the shortest possible time, with concurrent calcium and vitamin D

- In ileocecal Crohn's, budesonide, which has fewer side-effects than prednisolone, should be prescribed

- Steroids have no role in maintenance of remission

- Patients on long-term steroids should be switched to steroid-sparing alternatives

---

TABLE 9.1 Problems associated with use of corticosteroids in Crohn's disease.

Problem	Reference
Inappropriate use	
Abscess, fistulous disease	3,4
Perianal disease	5
Uninflamed stricture	
Non-inflammatory diarrhea	Chapter 46
Remission maintenance	7,8
Inadequate response	
Failure to heal mucosa	10,11
Poorly sustained response	9,15,16
Steroid resistance	17,18
Side-effects	
Common to all settings	1
Specific to Crohn's: death, sepsis	3–6,21,22

Introduction

Since their introduction for treatment of active UC half a century ago, corticosteroids have become the mainstay of treatment of active IBD. In recent years, however, it has emerged that the use (and misuse) of steroids in IBD is associated with a range of limitations and complications which may in some patients outweigh their benefits (Table 9.1) [1,2]. These problems are specially pronounced in patients with Crohn's disease, in part because in this disease steroids tend to be prescribed for longer periods than in UC. This chapter outlines the adverse consequences of the use of steroids as they relate in particular to Crohn's disease, and indicates what measures can be taken to avoid them. Emerging evidence suggests that the use of steroids in Crohn's disease should be shrinking as recognition of their adverse effects increases and as the development of more effective and safer alternatives proceeds.

Inappropriate use

When steroids are to be used in the treatment of Crohn's disease, care has to be taken to avoid prescribing them for inappropriate indications (Table 9.1). In some of these, such as diarrhea resulting not from mucosal inflammation but from bile salt malabsorption, bacterial overgrowth, or short bowel syndrome (see Chapter 46), patients are unlikely to benefit. In others, steroids can even worsen the outcome.

For example, in patients with an abdominal mass resulting from an abscess with or without fistulation, use of steroids can cause severe sepsis and even death [3,4]. In patients with perianal disease, steroids may not only increase the risk of sepsis, but also compromise the response to concurrent thiopurine therapy [5]. When given to patients with intestinal obstruction resulting from uninflamed strictures, steroids do not relieve the symptoms and can increase the complications of subsequent surgery (see below) [6]. Lastly, steroids are not effective in maintaining remission in Crohn's disease whether given as prednisolone [7] or budesonide [8]; in this chronic setting, the use of prednisolone in particular puts patients at special risk of steroid-induced side-effects (see below).

Inadequate response

Poor mucosal healing

While approximately 50% of patients with active Crohn's disease given prednisolone under trial conditions enter remission on symptomatic and laboratory criteria, and a further third improve in 4 weeks [9], in only one-quarter is this accompanied by mucosal healing [10,11]. Thus, steroids contrast with azathioprine, liquid formula diet, and above all infliximab, treatment with each of which is often associated with complete mucosal healing [12–14].

Rapid relapse after steroid withdrawal

The failure of steroids to improve mucosal appearances may explain the high rate of steroid dependency which follows their initiation and of relapse which occurs after their discontinuation. Indeed, at 1 year after starting on steroids, approximately half of patients are still on them, or will have relapsed and needed surgery [9,15].

Factors predicting poor response to steroids

Factors predicting a poor response to steroids include previous bowel resection, perianal disease, and a high pretreatment Crohn's Disease Activity Index (CDAI) [16]. At a molecular level, a poor response to steroid therapy has also been associated with overexpression of glucocorticoid receptors [17], and of the multidrug resistance (*MDR*) gene [18]; it is likely that in the foreseeable future other genotypes will be identified that predict steroid resistance and dependence.

Side-effects

Side-effects common to all indications

Side-effects common to all clinical situations in which corticosteroids are used include glucose intolerance and diabetes, fluid retention, hypertension, weight gain, hyperlipidemia, osteoporosis, avascular necrosis of the hip, myopathy, mood changes, Cushingoid facies, acne, reduced wound healing, infection, dyspepsia, glaucoma, cataracts, growth retardation in children, and adrenal suppression. Most of these do not need rehearsal here and are reviewed by Rutgeerts [2]. However, it is only recently that a dose-related link between steroid usage and cardiovascular complications has been recognized [19]. Because in most instances the risks of side-effects are dose- and duration-related, every effort should be made to restrict the use of prednisolone to the minimum period needed to obtain remission.

Side-effects more specific to Crohn's disease

In routine practice, the most common side-effect of steroids prescribed long-term is probably osteoporosis, not least because it is compounded by the adverse effects on bone loss of Crohn's disease itself [20]. This side-effect has led to the recommendation that, whenever given steroids, patients with Crohn's should be given concurrent "bone protective" therapy (e.g. with calcium and vitamin D tablets); other measures to prevent or reverse bone loss are reviewed elsewhere (see Chapter 55). Recognition of the inhibitory effects of steroids on growth in children with Crohn's has led to the widespread adoption of a liquid formula diet as primary therapy for active disease in patients in this age group (see Chapter 41).

Some side-effects specific to Crohn's have been referred to above [3–5]. Others include an approximately fourfold increase in the risk of septic complications in patients having elective bowel surgery after treatment with steroids [6]. Additionally, steroids appear to increase substantially the risk of major intra-abdominal or pelvic abscess in patients with Crohn's disease [21]. Overall, steroids appear to increase the risk of sepsis nearly threefold and of death twofold in Crohn's disease [22].

Can side-effects be avoided by use of newer formulations?

Although use of budesonide reduces the risk of many of these adverse effects, this preparation is effective only in patients with active ileocecal Crohn's, and appears to be marginally less potent than prednisolone [8]. There is no good evidence that an enteric-coated preparation (prednisolone EC) reduces dyspeptic symptoms. However, oral formulations of prednisolone are being developed to release the steroid in the colon and thus reduce its systemic absorption and side-effects; their efficacy in either Crohn's or UC requires confirmation. An ingenious new technique for delivering dexamethasone involves incorporating it, as a metabolic precursor, in autologous erythrocytes [23]; it is claimed that this methodology will minimize steroid-induced side-effects.

Conclusions

Corticosteroids are clearly neither a panacea nor a poison, and are not yet obsolete. For most adult patients with active Crohn's, corticosteroids provide a quick reduction in symptoms and in laboratory evidence of inflammation, together with an improvement in general well-being. For these patients, a prompt withdrawal of steroids, with their replacement if necessary by an immunomodulator such as azathioprine, represents a reasonable compromise to balancing symptom relief against the risk of side-effects. What should be aimed for, and is now feasible in the vast majority of patients, is the avoidance of the prescription of conventional oral prednisolone for anything but active inflammatory disease, or for a period of longer than a few weeks. Recent developments in therapy such as the more widespread use of thiopurines in adults, and of liquid formula diets in children, together with the introduction of infliximab for very sick patients in both age groups, have made this goal realizable. The advent of further biologic and other therapies in the coming years (see Chapter 31) should eliminate, once and for all, steroid-related complications in patients with Crohn's disease.

References

1 Present DH. How to do without steroids in inflammatory bowel disease. *Inflamm Bowel Dis* 2000; **6**: 48–57.

2 Rutgeerts PJ. Review article: the limitations of corticosteroids therapy in Crohn's disease. *Aliment Pharmacol Ther* 2001; **15**: 1515–25.

3 Malchow H, Ewe K, Brandes JW, *et al*. European Cooperative Crohn's Disease Study (ECCDS): results of drug treatment. *Gastroenterology* 1984; **86**: 249–66.

4 Felder JB, Adler DJ, Korelitz BI. The safety of corticosteroid therapy in Crohn's disease with an abdominal mass. *Am J Gastroenterol* 1991; **86**: 1450–5.

5 Wheeler SC, Marion JF, Present DH. Medical therapy, not surgery, is the appropriate first line treatment for Crohn's enterovesical fistula. *Gastroenterology* 1998; **114**: A113.

6 Aberra FN, Lewis LJ, Hass D, *et al*. Corticosteroids and immunomodulators: post-operative infectious complication risk in inflammatory bowel disease patients. *Gastroenterology* 2003; **125**: 320–7.

7 Summers RW, Switz DM, Sessions JT, *et al*. National Cooperative Crohn's Disease Study: results of drug treatment. *Gastroenterology* 1979; **77**: 847–69.

8 Kane SV, Schoenfeld P, Sandborn WJ, *et al*. The effectiveness of budesonide therapy for Crohn's disease. *Aliment Pharmacol Ther* 2002; **16**: 1509–17.

9 Munkholm P, Langholz E, Davidsen N, Binder V. Frequency of glucocorticoid resistance and dependency in Crohn's disease. *Gut* 1994; **35**: 360–2.

10 Olaison G, Sjodahl R, Tagesson C. Glucocorticoid treatment in ileal Crohn's disease: relief of symptoms but not of endoscopically viewed inflammation. *Gut* 1990; **31**: 325–8.

11 Modigliani R, Mary JY, Simon JF, *et al*. Clinical, biological and endoscopic picture of attacks of Crohn's disease. Evolution on prednisolone. *Gastroenterology* 1990; **98**: 811–8.

12 D'Haens G, Geboes K, Ponette E, Penninckx F, Rutgeerts P. Healing of severe recurrent ileitis with azathioprine therapy in patients with Crohn's disease. *Gastroenterology* 1997; **112**: 1475–81.

13 Fell JM, Paintin M, Arnaud-Battandier F, *et al*. Mucosal healing and a fall in mucosal pro-inflammatory cytokine mRNA induced by a specific oral polymeric diet in paediatric Crohn's disease. *Aliment Pharmacol Ther* 2000; **14**: 281–9.

14 D'Haens G, van Deventer S, van Hogezand R, *et al*. Endoscopic and histological healing with infliximab anti-tumour necrosis factor antibodies in Crohn's disease: a European multicentre trial. *Gastroenterology* 1999; **166**: 1029–34.

15 Faubion WA, Loftus EV, Harmsen WS, Zinsmeister AR, Sandborn WJ. The natural history of corticosteroid therapy for inflammatory bowel disease: population-based study. *Gastroenterology* 2001; **121**: 255–60.

16 Gelbmann CM, Rogler G, Gross V, *et al*. Prior bowel resections, perianal disease, and a high initial Crohn's disease activity index are associated with corticosteroid resistance in active Crohn's disease. *Am J Gastroenterol* 2002; **97**: 1438–45.

17 Sandborn WJ, Faubion WA. Clinical pharmacology of inflammatory bowel disease therapies. *Curr Gastroenterol Rep* 2000; **2**: 440–5.

18 Farrell RJ, Murphy A, Long A, *et al*. High multidrug resistance (P-glycoprotein 170) expression in inflammatory bowel disease patients who fail medical therapy. *Gastroenterology* 2000; **118**: 279–88.

19 Wei L, MacDonald TM, Walker, BR. Taking glucocorticoids

by prescription is associated with subsequent cardiovascular disease. *Ann Intern Med* 2004; **141**: 764–70.

20 Bernstein CN, Leslie WD. Review article: Osteoporosis and inflammatory bowel disease. *Aliment Pharmacol Ther* 2004; **19**: 941–52.

21 Agrawal A, Durrani S, Leipor K, *et al.* Effect of systemic corticosteroid therapy on risk for intra-abdominal or pelvic abscess non-operated Crohn's disease. *Clin Gastroenterol Hepatol* 2005; **3**: 1215–20.

22 Lichtenstein GR, Cohen RD, Feagan BG, *et al.* Safety of infliximab and other Crohn's disease therapies: updated TREAT Registry data with over 10,000 patient-years of follow-up. *Gastroenterology* 2005; **128** (Suppl): W1034.

23 Annese V, Latino A, Rossi L, *et al.* Erythrocytes-mediated delivery of dexamethasone in steroid-dependent IBD patients – a pilot uncontrolled study. *Am J Gastroenterol* 2005; **100**: 1370–5.

Medical Treatment: Making the Most of What We've Got — *Antibiotics for Crohn's disease*

10 Antibiotics: which, when, and for how long?

ALEX KENT & JEAN-FRÉDÉRIC COLOMBEL

LEARNING POINTS

Antibiotics for Crohn's disease

- Intestinal inflammation in IBD is caused by an altered immune response to commensal enteric flora in a genetically susceptible host

- Metronidazole and ciprofloxacin:

  - seem to provide clinical benefit, although controlled trials are few

  - are best for patients with active colonic and perianal Crohn's

  - are less effective for uncomplicated ileal disease

  - can reduce recurrence rates after ileocolic resection

  - are beneficial in pouchitis

- Treatment needs to be long-term subject to toxicity and tolerance

- Non-absorbable antibacterial agents such as rifaximin need further investigation

- There is no evidence to support the use of antituberculous drugs in IBD

Introduction

The etiology of Crohn's disease remains uncertain, and to date no therapy is curative. Although genetic and environ-mental factors are involved, there is growing evidence that enteric flora are integral to this process. Currently, treatment is aimed at modifying the pathogenic mechanisms involved, mostly by using anti-inflammatory drugs (mesalazine, corticosteroids) or immunosuppressant agents. There is a paucity of data regarding treatment with antibiotics, yet their use has a long tradition. Antibiotics are used in penetrating disease with subsequent fistula or abscess formation, in severe disease motivated by fear of complications, and as an attempt to delay surgical interventions. The therapeutic effects are presumed to be mediated through the alteration of the bacterial flora, but some antibiotics also possess innate immunomodulatory activity [1].

Antibiotics in the treatment of IBD – "why and when": arguments from animal and human models of the disease

The gastrointestinal tract surface mucosa separates the inside of the body from the outside world. In adults, the number of living microbial cells inhabiting the gut amounts to about 10 times the number of cells constituting the human body. Within the terminal ileum, approximately 10^7 living bacteria may be found in 1 g of intestinal contents; in the colon, this value is up to 10^{12}. Most (>99%) are anaerobes. The inherent barrier function of the intestinal mucosa prevents bacterial translocation through, and invasion into, the bowel wall, and a subsequent pathologic tissue reaction. The enteric immune system regulates the interactions between microbial antigens and immuno-competent cells [2]. Recent research has focused on the pathogenetic role of the mucosal barrier, and disturbance of its function has emerged as a keystone in the chain of events leading to chronic IBD.

The role of intestinal flora in IBD has received much attention recently, being supported by a number of observations: the lack of intestinal inflammatory response in experimental models employing germ-free animals [3]; the concentration of intestinal bacteria in IBD is higher than in healthy controls and increases progressively with the severity of the disease, with the concentration higher in areas where IBD occurs more frequently [4]; diversion of the fecal stream is therapeutic, with subsequent flare-up of the inflammatory process when the fecal stream is restored [5], unless the small bowel effluent undergoes ultrafiltra-tion [6]; and in IBD there is loss of immunologic tolerance to enteric flora [7].

Animal models, combined with experimental and clinical data also suggest that:
• Only some commensal bacteria are pathogenic
• The response to bacteria is, at least in part, determined by the host, suggesting that only some patients are likely to respond to antibiotic treatment
• Disease site is important; colonic and postoperative ileal Crohn's disease respond better to antibiotic treatment than unoperated small bowel disease
• Antibiotics are better at preventing than treating intesti-nal inflammation

What antibiotics to use, when and for how long? – evidence from clinical trials

Metronidazole and ciprofloxacin

What are the antibiotics of choice for patients with IBD? Agents that provide a broad-spectrum reduction of both aerobic and anaerobic enteric flora would seem to have the highest probability of success. The two antibiotics most widely studied in Crohn's disease are metronidazole and ciprofloxacin, alone or in combination. Metronidazole is a nitroimidazole with antimicrobial activity against Gram-positive and Gram-negative anaerobes, whereas ciprofloxacin, a quinolone, is effective against enteric Gram-negative and anaerobic Gram-positive organisms but does not influence bacteroides. However, in two rodent models of colitis, Rath

et al. [8] found that for established intestinal inflammation, the combination of imipenem and vancomycin is more effective (than either ciprofloxacin or metronidazole). Thus, metronidazole and ciprofloxacin may not be the optimal antibiotic combination for all subsets of patients with Crohn's disease; broader spectrum antibiotics, such as imipenem or meropenem, may provide greater efficacy in certain clinical settings and require controlled evaluation.

Crohn's disease

Further support for the utility of antibiotics as primary therapy for mild to moderately active Crohn's disease comes from a prospective trial [9] of ciprofloxacin versus mesalazine showing equivalent rates of remission (56% vs 55%). Moreover, Sutherland *et al.* [10] found that 10 or 20 mg/kg metronidazole was more effective than placebo in patients with colonic involvement. Although this trial had insufficient statistical power to prove the efficacy of antibiotics for patients with colonic Crohn's disease, the observation that antibiotics work best when there is colonic involvement is consistent across clinical studies [11].

A study by Rutgeerts *et al.* [12] indicated that after patients had undergone ileal resection and ileocolic ana-stomosis, administration of metronidazole for 3 months tended to delay symptomatic recurrence and decrease the rate of severe endoscopic lesions when compared with placebo, although differences did not reach significance at 1-year follow-up. However, a subsequent study [13] of 12 months' treatment with ornidazole showed that the clinical and endoscopic recurrence was significantly reduced at 1 year when compared with placebo. Thus, experimental and clinical information point to important distinctions between antibiotic effects on the colon and on the intact and operated ileum.

It is generally accepted that antibiotics are effective in perianal Crohn's disease, albeit usually without complete healing. However, they may maintain comfort and improve quality of life for long periods of time [14]. The useful-ness of metronidazole in treating perianal fistulas in Crohn's disease has been suggested by various uncontrolled studies [15]. There are also uncontrolled observations that concomitant use of ciprofloxacin and metronidazole is particularly effective in perianal Crohn's disease [11,16].

Oral ciprofloxacin (500–750 mg/day for 6 months) has been reported to be significantly more effective than placebo in UC, but concomitant treatments such as steroids and/or mesalazine make it difficult to draw definitive conclusions

[17]. Alone, or when combined with corticosteroids, metronidazole does not offer benefit in UC [18]. On the other hand, it appears clinically to improve pouchitis when compared with placebo [19], while its effect on endoscopic and histologic features remain controversial [19,20]. Ciprofloxacin is also reportedly effective in metronidazole-resistant pouchitis [21].

Other antibiotics

Various studies have pursued the hypothesis of a causative role of atypical mycobacteria (see Chapter 11). A recent meta-analysis of antimycobacterial therapy for Crohn's disease identified eight randomized trials, six of which were included in the study [22]. The conclusion of the authors was that treatment of Crohn's disease with antimycobacterial antibiotics was ineffective without a course of corticosteroids to induce remission.

Both co-trimoxazole and vancomycin failed to show any clinical efficacy in IBD, whereas tobramycin seems to provide only marginal benefits.

More recently, rifaximin, a non-absorbable antibacterial agent, has been investigated in preliminary studies. At a dosage of 800 mg/day the drug was significantly superior to placebo in promoting clinical improvement in patients with steroid-resistant UC [23] and appeared to induce remission in most patients with clinical flare-up during mesalazine maintenance treatment, thus sparing steroid use [24]. In subjects with active Crohn's disease, 600 mg/day rifaximin for 16 weeks induced a substantial decrease in the Crohn's Disease Activity Index (CDAI) [25]. The combined use of rifaximin and ciprofloxacin was also found to promote both clinical and endoscopic improvement in cases of metronidazole-resistant pouchitis [26].

Duration of treatment

There is great variation between studies in treatment length. In clinical studies of ileocolonic Crohn's disease, sustained symptomatic improvement has been reported with up to 2 years of continuous ciprofloxacin plus metronidazole therapy [11]. In perineal Crohn's disease, metronidazole continues to be effective for up to 36 months, with exacerbation of disease with reduction or discontinuation of the antibiotic [15]. Treatment needs to be long-term with attention paid to side-effects. Metronidazole is known to be associated with various untoward effects (e.g. peripheral neuropathy, metallic taste, gastrointestinal disturb-

ances) with a reported incidence of 50% or more [12]. Ciprofloxacin is better tolerated, but more expensive, and can induce nausea, diarrhea, and skin rashes. The concomitant use of both antibiotics significantly increases the incidence of side-effects and the number of drug withdrawals. The use of a non-absorbable antibiotic such as rifaximin, virtually devoid of systemic side-effects [23,24], represents an attractive alternative which should be further investigated in controlled trials.

Conclusions

The pathogenesis of IBD would support the use of antibiotics in treatment. Studies have shown a response to antibiotics in the settings of ileocolonic and perianal Crohn's disease and after ileocolic resection. There is limited evidence for their use in UC, but they are useful in pouchitis. Ciprofloxacin and metronidazole are the most widely used antibiotics, but their use is limited by their side-effects. Newer antibiotics with excellent tolerability, such as rifamixin, need further evaluation.

References

1 Sands B. Therapy of inflammatory bowel disease. *Gastroenterology* 2000; **118**: 568–82.

2 Schulze J, Sonnenborn U. The role of the gut flora in inflammatory bowel diseases. In: Shimoyama T, Axon A, Lee A, Podolsky DK, O'Morain C, (eds.) *Helicobacter Meets Inflammatory Bowel Disease*. Medical Tribune, 2002: 393–417.

3 Dianda L, Hanby A, Wright N, *et al*. T-cell receptor-alpha-beta-deficient mice fail to develop colitis in the absence of a microbial environment. *Am J Pathol* 1997; **150**: 91–7.

4 Swidsinski A, Ladhoff A, Pernthaler A, *et al*. Mucosal flora in inflammatory bowel disease. *Gastroenterology* 2002; **122**: 44–54.

5 D'Haens G, Geboes K, Peeters M, *et al*. Early lesions of recurrent Crohn's disease caused by infusion of intestinal content in excluded ileum. *Gastroenterology* 1998; **114**: 262–7.

6 Harper P, Lee E, Kettlewell M, Bennett M, Jewell D. Role of the fecal stream in the maintenance of Crohn's colitis. *Gut* 1985; **26**: 279–84.

7 Duchmann R, Schmitt E, Knoll P. Tolerance exists towards resident intestinal flora in mice but is broken in active inflammatory bowel disease. *Clin Exp Immunol* 1995; **102**: 448–55.

8 Rath H, Schultz M, Freitag R, *et al*. Different subsets of enteric bacteria induce and perpetuate experimental colitis in rats and mice. *Infect Immun* 2001; **69**: 2227–85.

9 Colombel J, Lémann M, Cassagnou M, *et al.* A controlled trial comparing ciprofloxacin with mesalazine for the treatment of active Crohn's disease. *Am J Gastroenterol* 1999; **94**: 674–8.

10 Sutherland L, Singleton J, Sessions J, *et al.* Double blind, placebo controlled trial of metronidazole in Crohn's disease. *Gut* 1991; **32**: 1071–5.

11 Greenbloom S, Steinhart A, Greenberg G. Combination ciprofloxacin and metronidazole for active Crohn's disease. *Can J Gastroenterol* 1998; **12**: 53–6.

12 Rutgeerts P, Hiele M, Geboes K, *et al.* Controlled trial of metronidazole treatment for prevention of Crohn's recurrence after ileal resection. *Gastroenterology* 1995; **108**: 1617–21.

13 Rutgeerts P, Van Assche G, D'Haens G, *et al.* Ornidazole for prophylaxis of post-operative Crohn's disease: final results of a double blind placebo controlled trial. *Gastroenterology* 2002; **122**: A80 (Abstract).

14 Present D. Crohn's fistula: current concepts in management. *Gastroenterology* 2003; **124**: 1629–35.

15 Brandt L, Bernstein L, Boley S, Franks M. Metronidazole therapy for perineal Crohn's disease: a follow-up study. *Gastroenterology* 1982; **83**: 33–7.

16 Solomon M, McLeod R, O'Connor B. Combination ciprofloxacin and metronidazole in severe perianal Crohn's disease. *Can J Gastroenterol* 1993; **7**: 571–2.

17 Turunen U, Farkkila M, Hakala K, *et al.* Long-term treatment of ulcerative colitis with ciprofloxacin: a prospective double-blind, placebo-controlled study. *Gastroenterology* 1998; **115**: 1072–8.

18 Chapman R, Selby W, Jewel D. Controlled trial of intra-venous metronidazole as an adjunct to corticosteroids in severe ulcerative colitis. *Gut* 1986; **27**: 1210–2.

19 Madden M, McIntyre A, Nicholls R. Double-blind crossover trial of metronidazole versus placebo in chronic unremitting pouchitis. *Dig Dis Sci* 1994; **39**: 1193–6.

20 Shen B, Achkar J, Lashner B, *et al.* A randomized trial of ciprofloxacin and metronidazole to treat acute pouchitis. *Inflamm Bowel Dis* 2001; **7**: 301–5.

21 Hurst R, Molinari M, Chung T. Prospective study of the incidence, timing and treatment of pouchitis in 104 consecutive patients after restorative proctocolectomy. *Arch Surg* 1996; **131**: 497–500.

22 Borgaonkar M, MacIntosh D, Fardy J. A meta-analysis of antimycobacterial therapy for Crohn's disease. *Am J Gastroenterol* 2000; **95**: 725–9.

23 Gionchetti P, Rizzello F, Ferrieri A, *et al.* Rifaximin in patients with moderate or severe ulcerative colitis refractory to steroid treatment: a double-blind placebo-controlled trial. *Dig Dis Sci* 1999; **44**: 1220–1.

24 Guslandi M, Giollo P, Testoni P. Corticosteroid-sparing effect of rifaximin, a nonabsorbable oral antibiotic, in active ulcerative colitis: preliminary clinical experience. *Curr Ther Res Clin Exp* 2004; **65**: 292–6.

25 Shafran I, Johnson L, Hamm L, Murdocj R. Efficacy and tolerability of rifaximin, a nonabsorbed oral antibiotic, in the treatment of active Crohn's disease: results of an open-label study. *Am J Gastroenterol* 2003; **98**: S250.

26 Gionchetti P, Rizzello F, Venturi A, *et al.* Antibiotic combination therapy in patients with chronic treatment-resistant pouchitis. *Aliment Pharmacol Ther* 1999; **13**: 713–8.

Medical Treatment: Making the Most of What We've Got — *Antibiotics for Crohn's disease*

11 *Mycobacterium avium paratuberculosis* in Crohn's disease: player or spectator?

GEOFF SMITH & FERGUS SHANAHAN

LEARNING POINTS

Mycobacterium avium paratuberculosis in Crohn's disease

- *Mycobacterium avium paratuberculosis* (MAP) is widespread in the environment

- While humans may rarely become infected with MAP, the evidence for MAP as a direct cause of Crohn's disease is tenuous

- Even if MAP has no direct causative role in most patients with Crohn's disease, it might have a secondary disease-modifying influence

- Results of anti-mycobacterial therapy have been conflicting, with recent controlled trials failing to show benefit

Introduction

The concept that Crohn's disease might be related to an intestinal mycobacterial infection is not new. Dalziel, a Scottish clinician, proposed the link in 1913 [1]. Since then, successive generations of investigators using increasingly sophisticated technology have tried to resolve the controversy surrounding the role of mycobacteria in what is now known as Crohn's disease. *Mycobacterium avium* subspecies *paratuberculosis* (MAP) is an acid-fast bacillus comprising part of the *Mycobacterium avium* complex (MAC) that infects the enteric tract of many animals (Johne's disease), causing a granulomatous inflammation with pluribacillary and paucimicrobial forms paralleling leprosy in humans. Transmission to humans in milk or water has been suggested but analysis of retail milk stocks has produced conflicting results [2–4]. The potential public health significance of environmental exposure to MAP has been highlighted by several commissioned reports from expert groups in Europe and North America on the relationship between MAP and Crohn's disease [3,5–8]. None has concluded a direct causative link, but most called for more research.

Evidence for detection of MAP in Crohn's disease

Evidence implicating MAP as a cause of Crohn's disease includes detection of the organism in human tissues, immunoreactivity against the organism, and clinical responses to anti-mycobacterial therapy in patients.

Viable MAP was detected in tissue from patients with Crohn's disease almost 30 years ago and since then several research groups have used culture-dependent and molecular methods of detection of MAP. Many of these reports were summarized by Quirke in 2001 [9]. Overall, of 25 studies reported between 1980 and 2004, MAP was identified in 12% of 529 controls and 19% of 708 patients with Crohn's, a non-significant difference ($P = 0.06$). Positive results were also seen in 40/278 patients with UC (14.5%). More recently, studies using laser capture microdissection have shown that detection of bacterial DNA within granulomas in Crohn's disease is not specific to MAP because other forms of bacterial DNA including that from *Escherichia coli* are also detectable [10]. This may suggest that several commensals or pathogens are more numerous in Crohn's secondary to mucosal barrier dysfunction or to an innate immune abnormality, rather than a direct causative link.

Some investigators have used *in situ* hybridization to identify MAP within tissue from Crohn's patients. In one study, 35/48 samples from 33 patients were reported to be positive, with no positives in the control groups (patients with UC or no gastrointestinal disease) [11]. MAP has also been reported to be identifiable in the blood of patients with Crohn's disease using both culture- and molecular-dependent methods. Positive results were found in 46% of patients with Crohn's disease, 45% of those with UC, and 20% without IBD [12]. However, as with any detection technique, all of these studies should be controlled with a search for bacteria other than MAP, and need to be interpreted with caution.

If the presence of MAP causes the aggressive intestinal inflammation that characterizes Crohn's disease, one would expect to detect strong immunoreactivity against the stimulating organism. However, evidence for a brisk host response has not been found and surveys of anti-mycobacterial serologic activity have shown no difference between Crohn's and controls [13].

Responses to anti-mycobacterial treatment

Regardless of the evidence for the presence of *Mycobacterium paratuberculosis* in patients with Crohn's disease, the critical clinical issue is whether the disease responds to anti-mycobacterial therapy. When good responses have been reported, they have generally been with broad-spectrum macrolides, raising the possibility of a non-specific antibiotic effect. Table 11.1 summarizes the reported trials of anti-mycobacterial therapy in Crohn's disease. The results require cautious interpretation because the sensitivity of MAP to these antibiotic regimens was not determined

TABLE 11.1 Examples of controlled clinical trials of anti-MAP therapy in Crohn's disease.* Statistically significant results in **bold type.**

Reference	Number	Controls	Therapy	Outcome measure	Rx vs. placebo
Shaffer 1984 [14]	27	27	Rifampicin Ethambutol	CDAI Clinical	No difference No difference
Afdhal 1991 [15]	25	24	Clofazimine	Remission	64% vs 50%
Prantera 1994 [16]	20	20	Ethambutol Clofazamine Dapsone	Relapse on therapy	**16% vs. 65%** **$P = 0.03$**
Swift 1994 [17]	63	63	Rifampicin Isoniazid Ethambutol	Surgery CDAI	24% vs. 22% no difference
Thomas 1998 [18]	65	65	Rifamicin Isoniazid Ethambutol	Relapse on therapy at 5 years Surgery	**26 vs. 52%** **($P = 0.04$)** 8% vs. 18%
Goodgame 2001 [19]	15	16	Clarithromycin Ethambutol	HBAI	No difference

CDAI, Crohn's Disease Activity Index; HBAI, Harvey Bradshaw Activity Index.
* Selby *et al.* in Australia have recently completed a trial of combination anti-MAP therapy (clarithromycin, rifabutin, and clofazimine) over a 2-year period that showed no difference between the treatment and control groups for the primary efficacy criterion (unpublished).

in each case. More recently, a multicenter study in Australia of triple anti-MAP therapy over a 2-year period has been completed with negative results (WS Selby, verbal communication, British Society of Gastroenterology, Birmingham, March 2005). A meta-analysis of early studies prior to 2000 concluded that while anti-microbial therapy may be effective in maintaining steroid-induced remission of Crohn's, it is not effective in inducing remission [20]. Since then, controlled trials have failed to show convincing evidence for the use of these antibiotics.

Discussion

The story of *Helicobacter pylori* and peptic ulcer disease should serve as a lesson against the folly of dismissing an infectious basis to any chronic idiopathic disorder in humans. Furthermore, growing acceptance that Crohn's is a heterogeneous syndrome permits the possibility that a subset of patients might have an infectious basis to their disease. Reports of detection of MAP appear to reflect the widespread prevalence of the organism in the environment, and it seems likely that MAP may occasionally cause a chronic infection in humans [21,22]. However, evidence for the role of MAP in causing Crohn's disease is more tenuous and some features of the disease seem to be at variance with an infectious cause in most patients. These include the lower prevalence of Crohn's in rural areas, the lack of occupational risk in farmers where exposure to MAP would be maximal, and the reduced risk of Crohn's disease in conditions of overcrowding and poor sanitation which would favor transmission of an infectious agent. In addition, it is difficult to reconcile an infectious cause with therapeutic responses in patients with Crohn's disease to immunosuppression and immunomodulatory drugs such as anti-tumor necrosis factor (anti-TNF-α). Indeed, disseminated *Mycobacterium tuberculosis* is an established risk after therapeutic antagonism of TNF-α with infliximab [23]. If MAP causes Crohn's disease, disseminated MAP would be expected in some patients after infliximab, but this has not been described.

Although detection of increased bacteria in the tissues of patients with Crohn's disease is not specific to MAP [10], and even if MAP has no direct causative role, its presence in the intestinal mucosal microenvironment may still have pathophysiologic significance. MAP and other bacterial DNA have immunomodulatory properties and theoretically could have a secondary influence on the clinical course of the disease. However, until there is convincing controlled clinical evidence to show that an anti-MAP strategy can beneficially affect the long-term outcome, routine antimycobacterial agents cannot be recommended for patients with Crohn's disease.

References

1 Dalziel TK. Chronic interstitial enteritis. *BMJ* 1913; **ii**: 1068–70.

2 Chacon O, Bermudez LE, Barletta RG. Johne's disease, inflammatory bowel disease, and Mycobacterium paratuberculosis. *Annu Rev Microbiol* 2004; **58**: 329–63.

3 Gould G, Franken P, Hammer P, Mackey B, Shanahan F. International Life Sciences Institute (ILSI) Europe: report on *Mycobacterium avium subsp. Paratuberculosis* (MAP) and the food chain. ILSI Europe Report series, August 2004. www.ilsi.org/file/RPMyco.pdf

4 Gao A, Mutharia L, Chen S, *et al.* Effect of pasteurisation on survival of Mycobacterium paratuberculosis in milk. *J Dairy Sci* 2002; **85**: 3198–205.

5 National Institute for Allergy and Infectious Disease (NIAID). Crohn's disease: is there a microbial etiology? Recommendations for a research agenda. Report of a meeting held at National Institute for Health, Washington, DC 14 December 1998. www.niaid.nih.gov/dmid/meetings/crohns.htm

6 European Commission. Possible links between Crohn's disease and paratuberculosis: report of the scientific committee on animal health and animal welfare. www.europa.eu.int/comm/food/fs/sc/scah/out38–en.pdf

7 Rubery E. A review of the evidence for a link between exposure to Mycobacterium paratuberculosis (MAP) and Crohn's disease (CD) in humans. A report for the UK Food Standards Agency. June 2001. www.foodstandards.gov.uk/multimedia/pdfs/MAPcrohnreport.pdf

8 National Association for Colitis and Crohn's Disease. Report of the NACC expert group into the evidence linking Mycobacterium paratuberculosis (MAP) and Crohn's disease, December 2003. www.nacc.org.uk/MAPver9.pdf

9 Quirke P. Antagonist. Mycobacterium avium subspecies paratuberculosis is a cause of Crohn's disease. *Gut* 2001; **49**: 755–60.

10 Ryan P, Kelly RG, Lee G, *et al.* Bacterial DNA with granulomas of patients with Crohn's disease: detection by laser capture microdissection and PCR. *Am J Gastroenterol* 2004; **99**: 1539–43.

11 Sechi L, Manuela M, Francesco T, *et al.* Identification of Mycobacterium avium subsp. Paratuberculosis in biopsy specimens from patients with Crohn's disease identified by in situ hybridisation. *J Clin Microbiol* 2001; **39**: 4514–7.

12 Naser SA, Ghobrial G, Romero C, Valentine JF. Culture

of Mycobacterium avium subspecies paratuberculosis from the blood of patients with Crohn's disease. *Lancet* 2004; **364**: 1039–44.

13 Bernstein C, Blanchard JF, Rawsthorne P, Collins MT. Population-based case control study of seroprevalence of mycobacterium paratuberculosis in patients with Crohn's disease and ulcerative colitis. *J Clin Micro* 2004; **42**: 1129–35.

14 Shaffer JL, Hughes S, Linaker BD, *et al*. Controlled trial of rifampicin and ethambutol in Crohn's disease. *Gut* 1984; **25**: 203–5.

15 Afdhal NH, Long A, Lennon J, *et al*. Controlled trial of antimycobacterial therapy in Crohn's disease: clofazimine versus placebo. *Dig Dis Sci* 1991; **36**: 449–53.

16 Prantera C, Kohn A, Mangiarotti R, *et al*. Antimycobacterial therapy in Crohn's disease: results of a controlled, double-blind trial with a multiple antibiotic regimen. *Am J Gastroenterol* 1994; **89**: 513–8.

17 Swift GL, Srivastava ED, Stone R, *et al*. Controlled trial of anti-tuberculous chemotherapy for two years in Crohn's disease. *Gut* 1994; **35**: 363–8.

18 Thomas GA, Swift GL, Green JT, *et al*. Controlled trial of antituberculous chemotherapy in Crohn's disease: a five year follow up study. *Gut* 1998; **42**: 497–500.

19 Goodgame RW, Kimball K, Akram S, *et al*. Randomized controlled trial of clarithromycin and ethambutol in the treatment of Crohn's disease. *Aliment Pharmacol Ther* 2001; **15**: 1861–6.

20 Borgaonkar MR, MacIntosh DG, Fardy JM. A meta-analysis of antimycobacterial therapy for Crohn's disease. *Am J Gastroenterol* 2000; **95**: 725–9.

21 Hermon-Taylor J, Barnes N, Clarke C, Finlayson C. *Mycobacterium paratuberculosis* cervical lymphadenitis, followed five years later by terminal ileitis similar to Crohn's disease. *BMJ* 1998; **316**: 449–53.

22 Greenstein RJ. Is Crohn's disease caused by a mycobacterium? Comparisons with leprosy, tuberculosis, and Johne's disease. *Lancet Infect Dis* 2003; **3**: 507–14.

23 Keane J, Gershon F, Wise RP, *et al*. Tuberculosis associated with infliximab, a tumour necrosis factor α-neutralising agent. *N Engl J Med* 2001; **345**: 1098–104.

12 TPMT testing: is it essential?

AZHAR ANSARI & JEREMY D SANDERSON

LEARNING POINTS

Thiopurine methyl transferase testing

- Azathioprine and 6-mercaptopurine (6-MP) undergo three-way competitive metabolism via xanthine oxidase, thiopurine methyl transferase (TPMT) and the purine salvage pathway

- Allelic polymorphism influences TPMT activity: 1/10 people has 50% activity, and 1/300 no activity

- Individuals with no TPMT activity inevitably develop life-threatening myelotoxicity when given standard doses of a thiopurine

- Heterozygotes are at risk of nausea and myelotoxicity, usually avoidable by using 50% of the standard dose

- TPMT deficiency explains only a proportion of cases of thiopurine-induced myelotoxicity: blood count monitoring is mandatory in all patients

- Most thiopurine-induced side-effects are not TPMT-related

- TPMT testing before starting treatment with a thiopurine is optimal practice

---

Introduction

One of the classic applications of pharmacogenetics to clinical medicine is the influence of polymorphisms in the thiopurine methyl transferase (TPMT) gene on the risk of developing potentially severe adverse effects on treatment with the thiopurine drugs, azathioprine, and 6-mercaptopurine (6-MP) [1]. The ability to test an individual's risk of toxicity to a drug prior to starting treatment is an attractive concept, yet, despite obvious benefits, the uptake of pharmacogenetic testing is often low. One typical example of this is the infrequent testing for the cytochrome p450 mutation, CYP2C9, as a predictor of excessive anticoagulation on warfarin [2]. Add to this the fact that adverse effects to drugs are responsible for a staggering 6% of hospital admissions in the UK and you have a rather paradoxical situation [3]. Is TPMT testing before starting azathioprine or 6-MP an IBD dilemma or should it be an automatic decision?

Thiopurine metabolism

After ingestion, azathioprine is rapidly converted to 6-MP (Fig. 12.1). Three pathways then compete to metabolize 6-MP such that the drug is oxidized to thiouric acid by xanthine oxidase (XOD), methylated to 6-methyl-MP by TPMT, or entered along the purine salvage pathway leading to the formation of thioguanine nucleotides (TGN) [1]. TGN are considered responsible for the cytotoxic and immunosuppressive effects of the thiopurines.

Unlike XOD, TPMT activity varies according to a number of common allelic polymorphisms. One in 10 of the Caucasian population is heterozygous and has 50% TPMT activity. Moreover, 1 in 300 are homozygous (or

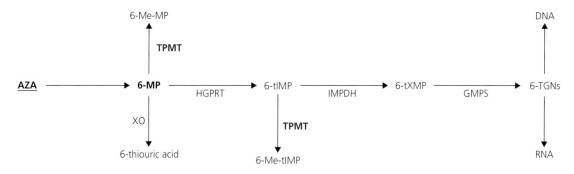

FIG 12.1 Simplified metabolism of azathioprine (AZA), 6-mercaptopurine (6-MP). On absorption, AZA is rapidly converted to 6-MP. 6-MP availability is reduced either by methylation to 6-methylmercaptopurine (6-Me-MP), catalyzed by thiopurine methyl transferase (TPMT), or by conversion to 6-thiouric acid by xanthine oxidase (XO). Cytotoxic and immunosuppressive thioguanine nucleotides (TGN) are formed via the salvage enzyme hypoxanthine guanine phosphoribosyltransferase (HGPRT). GMPS, guanine monophosphate synthase; IMPDH, inosine monophosphate dehydrogenase; 6-tIMP, 6-thioinosine monophosphate; 6-Me-tIMP, 6-methyl-thiomosine monophosphate; 6-tXMP, 6-thioxanthosine monophosphate.

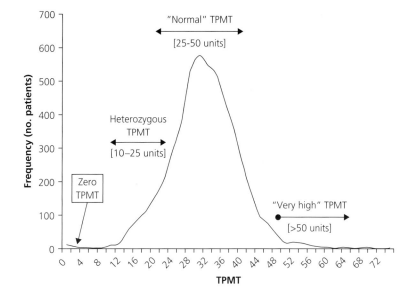

FIG 12.2 Distribution of TPMT activity (pmol 6-MMP/hour/mgHb) in 7000 individuals referred to the Purine Research Laboratory, Guy's Hospital, 1992–2002. (After Sanderson *et al.* [1])

compound heterozygotes) and have zero TPMT activity [4]. These individuals are completely unable to methylate 6-MP; much more of the drug is therefore metabolized to TGN, so that there is a risk of severe, potentially fatal myelosuppression during treatment with azathioprine or 6-MP [5]. Heterozygous individuals, treated with standard doses of azathioprine or 6-MP, are also at increased risk of bone marrow toxicity [6]. Interestingly, nausea often prompts withdrawal of thiopurines in this group before the

onset of myelosuppression, although the mechanism for this is unclear [7].

In patients with wild type TPMT genotype, the enzyme activity follows a near normal distribution (Fig. 12.2) although some individuals have very high activity. The genetic basis for this, if any, is not known. One could predict from the metabolism of thiopurines that those with higher TPMT activity should form fewer TGN as a result of higher methylation capacity. TGN levels have a broad correlation with clinical efficacy and one would therefore expect higher TPMT activity to be associated with reduced clinical response. In IBD this is the case, with response rates reduced to around 30% in patients with higher TPMT activity [7].

Should TPMT be tested before starting thiopurine therapy?

The most important advantage of TPMT testing before treatment is therefore the avoidance of potentially life-threatening myelotoxicity resulting from treatment of an individual with zero TPMT. At 1 in 300, this seems reassuringly unlikely to any individual IBD physician (who may come across one or two such patients in a career). However, this rarity is offset by the life-threatening nature of the toxicity and is considered by many sufficient to justify pretreatment testing in all patients. TPMT testing, either as enzyme activity or as genotype, however, has cost implications, although (in the UK) testing is relatively inexpensive at around £30 (US$50). Furthermore, health economic analyses have been performed for pretreatment TPMT testing using a variety of models and outcomes are favorable [8].

In addition to avoiding treatment of a "zero" patient, prior knowledge of TPMT status allows the prescriber to tailor the dose of azathioprine or 6-MP to an individual to minimize the risk of toxicity. This has not been addressed prospectively but a retrospective review of a 50% dosing strategy in patients heterozygous for TPMT receiving azathioprine confirms that toxicity is largely avoided and the efficacy matches that for those with normal TPMT activity receiving full dose treatment. It is theoretically possible to treat an individual with zero TPMT activity with extremely low doses of azathioprine (e.g. <5 mg) but, in general, the drug should be avoided in this group [9].

Relation of TPMT level to thiopurine-induced side-effects

Azathioprine and 6-MP are associated with a range of adverse effects with withdrawal rates as high as one-third of patients when they are used for treatment of Crohn's disease [7]. Meta-analyses of clinical trials produce lower rates with withdrawal reported in approximately 10% [10]. Infection (0.3–7.4%), a flu-like myalgic illness (2.3%), nausea and vomiting (1.4%), pancreatitis (1.4%), myelo-suppression (1.4–5%), and hepatitis (0.3–1.3%) are the most commonly reported adverse effects [1,11–13].

Importantly, variation in TPMT activity predicts only a small proportion of this toxicity. This fact is sometimes used as an argument against testing, albeit somewhat perversely, because it is akin to acquitting the proven perpetrator of one of a series of major crimes because they were not responsible for all of the others.

It is likely that other pharmacogenetic loci will explain some of the other adverse effects seen with thiopurines. For example, recent studies have implicated a role for polymorphism in the inosine triphosphatase (ITPa) gene in the flu-like myalgic illness seen with thiopurines [14].

Other side-effects are more likely to be hypersensitivity phenomena or idiosyncratic. Drug interactions are important, particularly with the xanthine oxidase inhibitor, allopurinol, which will divert 6-MP away from oxidation by XOD leading to an increase in TGN and myelotoxicity [15]. By the same mechanism, allopurinol could in theory be used to advantage to increase the effect of azathioprine in non-responders (similar to the use of ketoconazole to increase the bioavailability of cyclosporine) and a recent study in IBD has found this to be a safe and effective approach [16].

Could TPMT testing make blood count monitoring unnecessary?

Myelosuppression is the most important risk from treating individuals with TPMT deficiency. However, as with other side-effects, only a proportion of cases of myelosuppression overall occur in patients with TPMT deficiency [17]. Other cases may occur as a result of drug interactions, intercurrent infection (e.g. parvovirus), rare polymorphisms (e.g. 5′-nucleotidase deficiency), and, in most cases, an unknown cause. These cases, which can generally be managed with temporary withdrawal or reduction in dosage of the thiopurine, emphasize the need for blood monitoring during thiopurine treatment regardless of TPMT testing. Many physicians will argue that intensive blood monitoring and slow dose escalation (starting at 1 mg/kg azathioprine) is a safe substitute for TPMT testing before starting treatment. However, because case reports and anecdotal experience indicate that myelosuppression is inevitable in those with zero TPMT exposed to thiopurines, reliance on patients' regular and frequent attendance for a blood test is a risky strategy for avoiding this potentially lethal side-effect.

Can knowledge of TPMT levels be used to facilitate escalation of thiopurine dosage in non-responders?

The reasons for failure to respond to thiopurine treatment are undoubtedly multifactorial and include non-adherence and symptoms requiring a fundamentally different approach (e.g. surgery). For patients with very high TPMT activity, one would predict that escalating the dose of azathioprine or 6-MP to above that conventionally used in IBD would be associated with improved efficacy. This has not been addressed in any formal study. However, in practice, dose escalation in the presence of dominant methylation simply increases the potentially hepatotoxic methylated metabolite levels without a significant rise in TGN levels [18]. The ideal answer in this situation would be a TPMT inhibitor but, apart from the weak inhibitory effect of aminosalicylates [19], no such agent exists. Allopurinol coadministration is the alternative, but this should only be undertaken with cautious monitoring of blood counts.

Conclusions

Recent data show the increasing use of azathioprine and 6-MP for Crohn's disease such that 60% of patients with the disease receive a thiopurine [20]. Moreover, a greater emphasis on the need for adequate dosing and the possible benefits of therapeutic monitoring with TGN levels [11], suggest that higher doses are being used with a greater chance of toxicity. Crohn's disease patients also seem particularly prone to thiopurine-related toxicity [21]. The use of azathioprine and 6-MP in IBD needs to be undertaken in an effective but safe manner. Pretreatment testing of TPMT is an important part of this and the arguments in favor of this approach are compelling.

References

1 Sanderson J, Ansari A, Marinaki T, Duley J. Thiopurine methyltransferase: should it be measured before commencing thiopurine drug therapy? *Ann Clin Biochem* 2004; **41**: 294–302.

2 Sanderson S, Emery J, Higgins J. CYP2C9 gene variants, drug dose, and bleeding risk in warfarin-treated patients: a HuGEnet systematic review and meta-analysis. *Genet Med* 2005; **7**: 97–104.

3 Pirmohamed M, James S, Meakin S, Green C, *et al*. Adverse drug reactions as cause of admission to hospital: prospective analysis of 18 820 patients. *BMJ* 2004; **329**: 15–9.

4 Weinshilboum RM, Otterness DM, Szumlanski CL. Methylation pharmacogenetics: catechol O-methyltransferase, thiopurine methyltransferase, and histamine N-methyltransferase. *Annu Rev Pharmacol Toxicol* 1999; **39**: 19–52.

5 McBride KL, Gilchrist GS, Smithson WA, Weinshilboum RM, Szumlanski CL. Severe 6-thioguanine-induced marrow aplasia in a child with acute lymphoblastic leukemia and inhibited thiopurine methyltransferase deficiency. *J Pediatr Hematol Oncol* 2000; **22**: 441–5.

6 Relling MV, Hancock ML, Rivera GK, *et al*. Mercaptopurine therapy intolerance and heterozygosity at the thiopurine S-methyltransferase gene locus. *J Natl Cancer Inst* 1999; **91**: 2001–8.

7 Ansari A, Hassan C, Duley J, *et al*. Thiopurine methyltransferase activity and the use of azathioprine in inflammatory bowel disease. *Aliment Pharmacol Ther* 2002; **16**: 1743–50.

8 Oh KT, Anis AH, Bae SC. Pharmacoeconomic analysis of thiopurine methyltransferase polymorphism screening by polymerase chain reaction for treatment with azathioprine in Korea. *Rheumatology (Oxford)* 2004; **43**: 156–63.

9 Ansari A, Escudier M, Shobowale-Bakre M, *et al*. Responses to low dose azathioprine in patients with heterozygous thiopurine methyl transferase deficiency. *Gastroenterology* 2001; **120** (Suppl.1): A626.

10 Cosnes J, Nion-Larmurier I, Beaugerie L, *et al*. Impact of the increasing use of immunosuppressants in Crohn's disease on the need for intestinal surgery. *Gut* 2005; **54**: 237–41.

11 Dubinsky MC, Yang H, Hassard PV, *et al*. 6-MP metabolite profiles provide a biochemical explanation for 6-MP resistance in patients with inflammatory bowel disease. *Gastroenterology* 2002; **122**: 904–15.

12 Bajaj JS, Saeian K, Varma RR, *et al*. Increased rates of early adverse reaction to azathioprine in patients with Crohn's disease compared to autoimmune hepatitis: a tertiary referral center experience. *Am J Gastroenterol* 2005; **100**: 1121–5.

13 Pearson DC, May GR, Fick GH, Sutherland LR. Azathioprine and 6-mercaptopurine in Crohn's disease: a meta-analysis. *Ann Intern Med* 1995; **123**: 132–42.

14 Pearson DC, May GR, Fick G, Sutherland LR. Azathioprine for maintaining remission of Crohn's disease. *Cochrane Database Syst Rev* 2000: CD000067.

15 Present DH, Meltzer SJ, Krumholz MP, Wolke A, Korelitz BI. 6-Mercaptopurine in the management of inflammatory bowel disease: short- and long-term toxicity. *Ann Intern Med* 1989; **111**: 641–9.

16 Lowry PW, Szumlanski CL, Weinshilboum RM, Sandborn

WJ. Balsalazide and azathioprine or 6-mercaptopurine: evidence for a potentially serious drug reaction. *Gastroenterology* 1999; **116**: 1506.

17 Marinaki AM, Duley JA, Arenas M, *et al.* Mutation in the ITPA gene predicts intolerance to azathioprine. *Nucleosides Nucleotides Nucleic Acids* 2004; **23**: 1393–7.

18 Kennedy DT, Hayney MS, Lake KD. Azathioprine and allopurinol: the price of an avoidable drug interaction. *Ann Pharmacother* 1996; **30**: 951–4.

19 Sparrow MP, Hande SA, Friedman S, *et al.* Allopurinol safely optimizes thioguanine nucleotide metabolites in inflammatory bowel disease patients not responding to azathioprine. *Aliment Pharmacol Ther* 2005; **22**: 441–6.

20 Colombel JF, Ferrari N, Debuysere H, *et al.* Genotypic analysis of thiopurine S-methyltransferase in patients with Crohn's disease and severe myelosuppression during azathioprine therapy. *Gastroenterology* 2000; **118**: 1025–30.

21 Sandborn W, Sutherland L, Pearson D, *et al.* Azathioprine or 6-mercaptopurine for inducing remission of Crohn's disease. *Cochrane Database Syst Rev* 2000: CD000545.

Part 2 Medical Treatment: Making the Most of What We've Got – *Immunomodulators*

13 6-Mercaptopurine or azathioprine?

DERMOT MCGOVERN & SIMON TRAVIS

LEARNING POINTS

6-Mercaptopurine or azathioprine?

- 6-Mercaptopurine (6-MP) and its pro-drug, azathioprine, have subtle differences in their efficacy and tolerability
- Half of patients intolerant of azathioprine are able to take 6-MP but serious toxicity, such as leukopenia and pancreatitis, are common to both
- Azathioprine may be a more powerful immunosuppressant than 6-MP
- Data comparing the two drugs directly in IBD are lacking
- Either drug is a reasonable choice as the first-line thiopurine; azathioprine may be slightly more effective in patients who tolerate it.

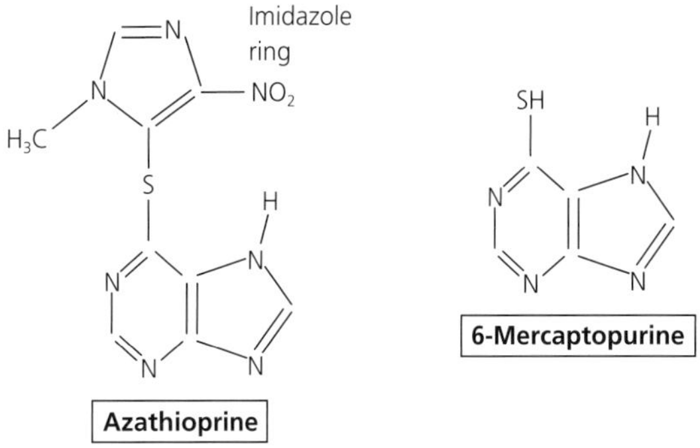

FIG 13.1 Chemical structures of azathioprine and 6-mercaptopurine.

Introduction

Azathioprine (AZA) and 6-mercaptopurine (6-MP) are effective cytotoxic therapies and immunosuppressants for organ transplantation, leukemia, and inflammatory conditions. 6-MP was first introduced in 1951 and AZA was synthesized from 6-MP to act as a pro-drug that protected the 6-MP moiety from catabolism (Fig. 13.1). AZA and 6-MP are, for the purposes of meta-analyses he and reviews, usually considered as the same drug. For historic reasons, AZA is the thiopurine of choice for the majority of gastroenterologists in the UK and Europe, whereas 6-MP is almost exclusively used in parts of North America. The efficacy of AZA or 6-MP in IBD is beyond doubt [1,2] but evidence from thiopurine therapy in IBD suggests these drugs to be heterogeneous. Important but subtle differences between AZA and 6-MP are revealed by an understanding of thiopurine metabolism and supported by analysis of clinical data.

Thiopurine metabolism

AZA is rapidly converted to 6-MP by a non-enzymatic glutathione-dependent reaction, releasing an imidazole derivative. 6-MP is then subject to metabolism by one of three competing enzymes (see Fig. 12.1) including thiopurine methyltransferase (TPMT) which catalyzes methylation of 6-MP to 6-methyl-mercaptopurine. *TPMT* mutations are common within the Caucasian population and there is significant interindividual variation in TPMT activity (see Chapter 12). Xanthine oxidase (XO), catalyzes 6-MP to thiourate, and hypoxanthine-guanine-phosphoribosyltransferase (HPRT) leads to the 6-thioguanine nucleotides (6-TGNs), thought to be the most active metabolite of thiopurine therapy. There is less interindividual variation in the activity of XO or HPRT.

Thiopurine intolerance

Three studies have now demonstrated that at least 50% of IBD patients "intolerant" of AZA can tolerate 6-MP [3–5]. 6-MP is 55% of the molecular weight of AZA and 88% of AZA is converted to 6-MP, giving a conversion factor of approximately 50% when converting the dose of AZA to 6-MP. Early AZA intolerance is independent of TPMT activity and much of this intolerance may be caused by the imidazole derivative cleaved when AZA is converted to 6-MP [3]. There are no data suggesting that patients intolerant of 6-MP can accept AZA. Large series examining the toxicity of AZA or 6-MP are rare. An audit of 624 IBD patients from Oxford (in which almost all received AZA) demonstrated that 28% experienced side-effects [6]. In contrast, a study from New York of 356 patients taking 6-MP demonstrated that 15% experienced toxicity [7]. These data might suggest that physicians should consider abandoning AZA in favor of 6-MP but there are other factors to consider.

Is azathioprine more effective than 6-MP?

In vitro evidence suggests that AZA is a more effective immunosuppressant than 6-MP. Examples include the following observations. AZA is more inhibitory than 6-MP in the human mixed lymphocyte reaction (a test of T lymphocyte function) [8] and 24 analogs of AZA lacking the 6-MP analog showed some activity in the human mixed lymphocyte reaction [9]. Furthermore, the cytostatic and cytocidal properties of 6-MP can be antagonized by exogenous purine administration, but AZA has an additional effect due to imidazole derivatives that is not antagonized by purines [10]. Also of interest is that AZA may have antibacterial properties *in vitro*, which lends a symmetry to the potential immunomodulation by imidazole antibiotics, but this has not been compared with 6-MP [11]. AZA suppresses pro-inflammatory cytokines [9] and suppresses

the human mixed lymphocyte reaction in the Lesch–Nyhan syndrome (HPRT deficiency) more potently than does 6-MP. This indicates that 6-TGNs are not responsible for all thiopurine immunosuppression [12]. Finally, inhibition of T lymphocyte proliferation by 6-MP is dependent on adenine ribonucleotide depletion, while AZA inhibits proliferation independently of this depletion [13]. These data demonstrate that AZA immunosuppression occurs through mechanisms other than those exerted by the mercaptopurine moiety alone and strongly implicate the imidazole derivative as the source of this additional immunosuppression.

Pharmocokinetic factors

Further important differences were highlighted when Cuffari *et al.* [14] compared 6-TGN levels in patients taking branded Imuran, or generic AZA and 6-MP. Patients receiving Imuran or 6-MP achieved significantly higher 6-TGN levels than generic AZA. The improved bioavailability of Imuran and 6-MP compared with generic AZA has implications for dosing and brand choice when considering thiopurine therapy or poor response. Significant differences in urinary thiopurine metabolites were also observed when the same individual was given AZA and then 6-MP, suggesting that AZA and 6-MP undergo metabolism via different pathways [15]. Approximately 12% of oral AZA was excreted in a form that could not have been converted to 6-MP. To add to the debate, the demonstration that a specific thioguanine nucleotide, thioguanosine triphosphate (TGTP) accounts for the mechanism of action through inhibition of Rac-1 signaling and promoting T-cell apoptosis [16], will see the evolution of new thiopurine compounds.

Comparative *in vivo* data

Remarkably, there is only a single *in vivo* comparison between AZA and 6-MP. This study investigated the effect of immunosuppressants on the survival of nephrectomized dogs receiving renal homotransplants. Nine out of 15 dogs treated with AZA survived beyond 20 days with good renal function compared with 6/15 treated with 6-MP. Dogs treated with AZA survived for longer (mean 35 days) than those on 6-MP (22 days), although no formal statistics were performed. Interestingly, this benefit of AZA over 6-MP occurred despite more frequent bone marrow suppression in the 6-MP (5 dogs) than AZA group (1 dog). This suggests that the additional benefit from AZA may be independent of 6-TGN production.

Nevertheless, in contrast to *in vitro* experiments and the animal data, some clinical evidence suggests that 6-MP may have an advantage over AZA. Herein lies the premise that all thiopurines are not created equal.

The Cochrane meta-analysis of thiopurine therapy for Crohn's disease demonstrated an odds ratio for induction of remission of 2.36 (95% confidence interval [CI] 1.57–3.53) for AZA/6-MP compared with placebo [1]. When trials using 6-MP were removed from the analysis, the odds ratio dropped to 2.04 (95% CI 1.24–3.35), but when AZA was removed the pooled odds ratio of 6-MP versus placebo increased to 3.10 (95% CI 1.55–6.21). These data suggest an increased efficacy of 6-MP over AZA but it is important to note that the odds ratios are still within the 95% confidence intervals.

Conclusions

Why should there be a difference between *in vitro* studies and the clinical evidence? The data illustrate the heterogeneity of AZA and 6-MP. *In vitro* and *in vivo* evidence indicate that the AZA imidazole derivative may contribute to increased immunosuppressive properties, but may also be responsible for increased toxicity. The Cochrane review, however, suggests that 6-MP may be the more effective of the two drugs in clinical practice. We believe that these data are not mutually exclusive. AZA may be the more potent immunosuppressive on a "per protocol" analysis of thiopurine therapy, but as a result of AZA's increased imidazole-related toxicity profile, 6-MP is better tolerated and more efficacious than AZA on an "intention to treat" analysis. At present, clinicians may choose either drug with justification, while recognizing that for those who can tolerate AZA, there may be added value.

References

1 Sandborn W, Sutherland L, Pearson D, *et al.* Azathioprine or 6-mercaptopurine for inducing remission of Crohn's disease. *Cochrane Database Syst Rev* 2000; **2**: CD000545.

2 Hawthorne AB, Logan RFA, Hawkey CJ, *et al.* Randomised controlled trial of azathioprine-withdrawal in ulcerative colitis. *BMJ* 1992; **305**: 20–22.

3 McGovern DP, Travis SP, Duley J, *et al.* Azathioprine intolerance in patients with IBD may be imidazole-related and is independent of TPMT activity. *Gastroenterology* 2002; **122**: 838–9.

4 Boulton-Jones JR, Pritchard K, Mahmoud AA. The use of 6-mercaptopurine in patients with inflammatory bowel disease after failure of azathioprine therapy. *Aliment Pharmacol Ther* 2000; **14**: 1561–5.

5 Bowen DG, Selby WS. Use of 6-mercaptopurine in patients with inflammatory bowel disease previously intolerant of azathioprine. *Dig Dis Sci* 2000; **45**: 1810–3.

6 Fraser AG, Orchard TR, Jewell DP. The efficacy of azathioprine for the treatment of inflammatory bowel disease: a 30 year review. *Gut* 2002; **50**: 485–9.

7 Present DH. 6-Mercaptopurine in the management of inflammatory bowel disease: short- and long-term toxicity. *Ann Intern Med* 1989; **111**: 641–9.

8 Al-Safi SA, Maddocks JL. Strength of the human mixed lymphocyte reaction (MLR) and its suppression by azathioprine or 6-mercaptopurine. *Br J Clin Pharmacol* 1985; **19**: 105–7.

9 Louis E, ANEYF, Belaiche J. High dose azathioprine but not 6-mercaptopurine inhibit the production of pro-inflammatory cytokines in inflammatory bowel diseases: an *in vitro* study. *Gastroenterology* 2000; **118**: A4202.

10 Sauer H, Hantke U, Wilmanns W. Azathioprine lymphocytotoxicity. Potentially lethal damage by its imidazole derivatives. *Arzneimittelforschung* 1988; **38**: 820–4.

11 Danielsson DE, Persson S. Antibacterial activity of azathioprine (Imuran) against anaerobic intestinal bacteria: implications in Crohn's disease. *Curr Chemother* 1978; **8**: 295–8.

12 Szawlowski PW, Maddocks JL. Azathioprine suppresses the mixed lymphocyte reaction of patients with Lesch–Nyhan syndrome. *Br J Clin Pharmacol* 1985; **20**: 489–91.

13 Dayton JS, Turka LA, Thompson CB, Mitchell BS. Comparison of the effects of mizoribine with those of azathioprine, 6-mercaptopurine, and mycophenolic acid on T lymphocyte proliferation and purine ribonucleotide metabolism. *Mol Pharmacol* 1992; **41**: 671–6.

14 Cuffari C, Hunt S, Bayless TM. Enhanced bioavailability of azathioprine compared to 6-mercaptopurine therapy in inflammatory bowel disease: correlation with treatment efficacy. *Aliment Pharmacol Ther* 2000; **14**: 1009–14.

15 Elion GB. The George Hitchings and Gertrude Elion Lecture. The pharmacology of azathioprine. *Ann N Y Acad Sci* 1993; **685**: 400–7.

16 Tiede I, Fritz G, Strand S, *et al.* CD28-dependent Rac 1 activation is the molecular target of azathioprine in primary human CD4+ T lymphocytes. *J Clin Invest* 2003; **111**: 1143–5.

14 Thiopurines: how long should we use them for?

ALEXANDRA DALEY & MARC LÉMANN

LEARNING POINTS

Thiopurines

- Most patients relapse after short courses of thiopurines

- Even after 4 years of thiopurine-induced remission, controlled data show that relapse is more common on drug withdrawal

- If there is an increased risk of lymphoma with prolonged thiopurine therapy it is small

- The decision to withdraw thiopurine treatment should be discussed with the patient and made on an individual basis

Introduction

Azathioprine has been routinely used to treat both Crohn's disease and UC since the 1960s. Azathioprine effectively maintains remission for up to 4 years in many patients [1]. However, there appears to be no clear consensus on the duration of treatment, and if, or when, it should be stopped after a period of stable remission. There remain concerns that long-term therapy may have unwanted side-effects, notably an increased risk of developing malignant disease.

A nationwide survey of consultant members of the British Society of Gastroenterology, conducted in 1999, indicated that British gastroenterologists use azathioprine frequently [2]. Forty-six percent use azathioprine for less than 2 years in any individual patient, but 17% continue treatment for more than 4 years. Interestingly, clinicians with greater experience of IBD tend to use higher maintenance doses for longer periods, and commence treatment in patients with less extensive disease.

Effects of withdrawal of thiopurines after short-term therapy

Several trials have shown that the withdrawal of azathioprine after short periods of treatment results in increased relapse rates compared with continuation of therapy. In 1978, O'Donoghue *et al.* [3] performed a double-blind trial involving 51 Crohn's patients. All had taken azathioprine for ≥6 months. Those who continued therapy had a relapse rate of 0% at 6 months and 5% at 1 year, whereas those who received placebo had rates of 25% and 41%, respectively. A recent open but randomized controlled trial in Crohn's patients also demonstrated an increased relapse rate following withdrawal of azathioprine after 2 years of treatment [4]. Although involving only a small number of patients, this study showed that 85% of subjects remained in remission if continued treatment was given, but only 47% did so if given placebo. In those previously treated with higher doses of the drug, the difference in relapse rates was even greater. In patients with UC, Hawthorne *et al.* [5] reported a randomized, withdrawal, placebo-controlled trial which has also shown that continuing treatment for at least 2 years is beneficial in those who have achieved remission on azathioprine.

Effects of withdrawal of thiopurines after longer term therapy

The usefulness of maintaining azathioprine beyond 4 years of full clinical remission was challenged in 1996 by Bouhnik et al. [1] They reviewed a series of 157 patients with Crohn's disease treated with azathioprine for at least 6 months. All patients had achieved remission for at least 6 months without steroid use. They compared the relapse rate of patients who continued on azathioprine treatment with those who stopped treatment. During the first 4 years of follow-up, patients who stopped treatment were at a higher risk of relapse than those who continued on azathioprine; however, after 4 years of sustained remission, the probability of relapsing was the same whether azathioprine was continued or not. This therefore suggested that, following a prolonged period of remission on azathioprine, there was no benefit in continuing treatment.

In contrast, another case note review of patients with IBD suggested that the length of time for which thiopurines were taken did not affect relapse rates [6]. In this study, 222 patients in remission stopped taking azathioprine; 115 had taken the drug for less than 2 years, 79 for between 2 and 4 years, and 36 for greater than 4 years. The proportion of patients who relapsed after stopping treatment was not significantly different between these groups.

Recently, a double-blind, placebo-controlled, non-inferiority, multicenter GETAID trial of azathioprine withdrawal in Crohn's disease found that stopping treatment did increase relapse rates when the drug had been taken for a long period [7]. Eighty-three patients were included after a long period of disease quiescence on azathioprine (minimum 42 months; median duration of therapy on entering the trial 55 months). Over the subsequent 18 months, 21% of those taking placebo relapsed, compared with only 8% of those who continued to take azathioprine, indicating that relapse is more likely if treatment is stopped after more than 3.5 years. Two biologic markers, a high CRP level and a low plasma hemoglobin concentration, were found in multivariate analysis to be associated with a higher relapse rate. In contrast, the presence of ileocolonic residual lesions or ulceration at colonoscopy, and the duration of azathioprine before inclusion, were not predictive of relapse. A long-term follow-up (median duration after azathioprine withdrawal 54 months) of these patients has also been reported recently [8], showing a cumulative probability of relapse after azathioprine withdrawal at 5 years of 63%.

These data strongly suggest that azathioprine maintenance therapy should be continued beyond 3.5 years.

Why consider withdrawing thiopurine therapy at all?

A major issue surrounding the prolonged use of azathioprine is the theoretical concern that long-term immunosuppression with such drugs may increase the risk of malignancy, particularly non-Hodgkin's lymphoma. Two studies have refuted this. Fraser et al. [9] conducted a retrospective case note review of 2204 patients with IBD, 626 of whom were given azathioprine for a mean duration of 27 months. Over a mean period of over 13 years, with mean follow-up from commencement of azathioprine of nearly 7 years, there was no significant difference in numbers of cancers observed between those who had or had not taken the drug. Connell et al. [10] also showed no increased risk of malignancy over that of the general population in 755 patients with IBD taking thiopurine therapy over a median follow-up of 9 years. However, a recent meta-analysis of six reported studies suggested a fourfold increase in the relative risk of lymphoma [11]. In addition, some Epstein–Barr virus (EBV) related lymphoma cases appear clearly linked to immunosuppressive therapy [12]. Although further clarification of this issue is required, the absolute risk remains small.

Conclusions

It is still not clear for how long patients should be treated with thiopurines in IBD. Relapse is common following withdrawal after short courses of treatment, and although there has previously been conflicting evidence regarding the need for continuation of treatment after longer durations of therapy, recent controlled data suggest the risk of relapse remains high after 4 years of treatment, which should therefore be continued. The risk of malignancy associated with long-term immunosuppression is low, but present, and should be discussed with the patient.

References

1 Bouhnik Y, Lémann M, Mary JY, et al. Long term follow-up of patients with Crohn's disease treated with azathioprine or 6-mercaptopurine. Lancet 1996; 347: 215–9.

2 Stack WA, Williams D, Stevenson M, Logan RFA. Immunosuppressive therapy for ulcerative colitis: results of a nationwide

survey among consultant physician members of the British Society of Gastroenterology. *Aliment Pharmacol Ther* 1999; **13**: 569–75.

3 O'Donoghue DP, Dawson AM, Powell-Tuck J, Bown RL, Lennard-Jones JE. Double-blind withdrawal trial of azathioprine as maintenance treatment for Crohn's disease. *Lancet* 1978; **2**: 955–7.

4 Vilien M, Dahlerup JF, Munck LK, *et al.* Randomized controlled azathioprine withdrawal after more than 2 years treatment in Crohn's disease: increased relapse rate the following year. *Aliment Pharmacol Ther* 2004; **19**: 1147–52.

5 Hawthorne AB, Logan RF, Hawkey CJ, *et al.* Randomized control trial of azathioprine withdrawal in ulcerative colitis. *BMJ* 1992; **305**: 20–2.

6 Fraser AG, Orchard TR, Jewell DP. The efficacy of azathioprine for the treatment of inflammatory bowel disease: a 30 year review. *Gut* 2002; **50**: 485–9.

7 Lémann M, Mary JY, Colombel JF, *et al.* Groupe d'Etude Thérapeutique des Affections Inflammatoires du tube Digestif (GETAID). A randomized double-blind controlled withdrawal trial in Crohn's disease patients in long term remission on azathioprine. *Gastroenterology* 2005; **128**: 1812–8.

8 Treton X, Bouhnik Y, Mary JY, *et al.* Azathioprine withdrawal in patients with Crohn's disease maintained on prolonged remission under treatment is associated with a high risk of relapse. *Gastroenterology* 2004; **126**: A167.

9 Fraser AG, Orchard TR, Robinson EM, Jewell DP. Long-term risk of malignancy after treatment of inflammatory bowel disease with azathioprine. *Aliment Pharmacol Ther* 2002; **16**: 1225–32.

10 Connell WR, Kamm MA, Dickson M, *et al.* Long term neoplasia risk after azathioprine treatment in inflammatory bowel disease. *Lancet* 1994; **343**: 1249–52.

11 Kandiel A, Fraser AG Korelitz BI, *et al.* Increased risk of lymphoma among inflammatory bowel disease patients treated with azathioprine and 6-mercaptopurine. 2005; **54**: 1121–5.

12 Dayharsh GA, Loftus EV Jr, Sandborn WJ, *et al.* Epstein–Barr virus-positive lymphoma in patients with inflammatory bowel disease treated with azathioprine or 6-mercaptopurine. *Gastroenterology* 2002; **122**: 72–7.

15 Making the most of methotrexate

EMMA GREIG, JOHN KEOHANE & BRIAN FEAGAN

LEARNING POINTS

Methotrexate

- Methotrexate is an alternative to thiopurines for steroid-resistant or steroid-dependent patients

- It is effective for both the induction (25 mg/week parenterally) and maintenance of remission (15 mg/week) in chronically active Crohn's disease

- The minimum effective dose is unknown, and there are not yet sufficient data to recommend the use of methotrexate orally

- While a controlled trial did not confirm its effectiveness in UC, the optimal dose and route of administration have not been conclusively studied

---

Introduction

Methotrexate has an established role in the management of several immuno-inflammatory disorders, most notably rheumatoid arthritis. In contrast to its widespread use by rheumatologists, methotrexate is used relatively sparingly by gastroenterologists for IBD. It was not until the late 1980s that Kozarek *et al.* [1] suggested that methotrexate had a possible role of refractory inflammatory bowel disease. Their initial report was an open label study of parenterally administered methotrexate. Since then, additional other open label studies and controlled trials have supported its use in the treatment in refractory Crohn's disease.

The mode of action of methotrexate is not completely understood; it has multiple effects including inhibition of dihydrofolate reductase, generation of adenosine, decreased expression of interleukin 1 (IL-1), and the induction of apoptosis [2]. At high doses, its primary action is antagonism of dihydrofolate reductase leading to inhibition of DNA, RNA, and protein synthesis. However, at the lower doses used in the management of IBD, inhibition of other folate-dependent enzymes may determine the immunomodulatory effects responsible for the action of methotrexate [3].

Evidence for the role of methotrexate in managing patients with either Crohn's disease or UC is discussed below. Route of administration (oral or parenteral) may be an important variable when considering efficacy, but conclusive studies are lacking. In addition, strategies for monitoring and reducing the risk of toxicity with methotrexate are summarized.

Induction of remission of Crohn's disease

The largest randomized, placebo-controlled trial of methotrexate included patients with chronic active Crohn's and showed that 25 mg/week intramuscularly for 16 weeks concurrently with tapering oral corticosteroids was signficantly more likely to achieve remission (39%) compared with placebo (19%) [4]. It was also noted that most patients responded to methotrexate by the eighth week, which contrasts with historic reports of a more delayed onset of action with purine analogs. However, 17% of patients receiving methotrexate withdrew from the study because of side-effects, compared with 2% in the placebo group. The adverse effects included asymptomatic elevation in serum aminotransferases, nausea, skin rash, pneumonia, and optic neuritis. Several smaller studies have used lower doses or oral administration and have yielded equivocal or negative results [5,6].

Specific studies have addressed time to remission comparing thiopurines with methotrexate. Two small comparative studies of methotrexate and either azathioprine or 6-mercaptopurine have shown no statistically significant difference in induction of remission between these therapies [7,8]. This is despite the latter study using high-dose methotrexate therapy with initiation at 25 mg/week intravenously, switching to 25 mg/week orally after 3 months [8]. In addition, a single-blind trial over 16 weeks using subcutaneous methotrexate showed no differences in obtaining remission at either 25 or 15 mg/week [9], with no differences in toxicity between the two groups. This was confirmed by a retrospective study where improvement and remission were highest with parenteral therapy but appeared dose-independent [10]. Both improvement and remission with methotrexate were more likely in patients under 40 years [10]. Blood levels of methotrexate do not appear to predict either efficacy or toxicity [9].

Maintenance of remission of Crohn's disease

The landmark study compared intramuscular methotrexate at 15 mg/week in the maintenance of remission in patients who had achieved remission using intramuscular methotrexate at 25 mg/week for 16 weeks [11]. Patients were followed for 40 weeks and remission was sustained in 65% of those receiving methotrexate compared with 39% of those taking placebo, a statistically significant difference. Of the patients who did relapse, fewer in the methotrexate group received steroids (28%) compared with the placebo group (58%, $P = 0.01$). No severe adverse events were noted in the methotrexate group and only one withdrew because of nausea.

Oral preparations used at lower doses showed a trend towards maintaining remission at 20 mg/week but not at 12.5 mg/week [5,6]. Unfortunately, there are no published data showing that methotrexate can maintain remission if this is achieved using surgery or another pharmacologic therapy than methotrexate itself.

In stable Crohn's disease, it appears that oral bioavailability is highly variable and averages 73% that of subcutaneously administered methotrexate [12]. Concomitant folic acid has no significant effect on bioavailability [12].

There appears to be a consensus from recent studies that immunosuppressive therapy, in general, does not increase early postoperative complications in elective surgery [13,14]. Whether methotrexate has any advantages over thiopurines is less clear in terms of efficacy at induction or maintenance of remission [15].

Ulcerative colitis

A randomized, multicenter, placebo-controlled trial showed that methotrexate at 12.5 mg/week given as an oral dose was no better than placebo in inducing remission, time to remission, or time to relapse after gaining remission [16]. A further randomized study comparing methotrexate (15 mg/week orally), 6-mercaptopurine (1.5 mg/kg/day), and aminosalicylates (3 g/day) added to oral prednisolone, showed no significant difference between methotrexate and aminosalicylates in obtaining or maintaining remission in UC [7]. This study showed a relapse rate of 86% over 6 months for those patients allocated to receive methotrexate compared with azathioprine (36%), with a similar rate of drug withdrawal for both azathioprine and methotrexate due to side-effects [7].

Methotrexate might be of greater benefit in UC if administered by the intramuscular route; a small, uncontrolled study in patients intolerant of or resistant to azathioprine showed promising results using a dosage of 12.5 mg/week [17]. However, randomized trial data are lacking and at present there is no evidence for using methotrexate to either gain or maintain remission in UC.

Toxicity of methotrexate

The most common side-effects of methotrexate are gastrointestinal toxicity, including nausea, anorexia, stomatitis, and diarrhea. These side-effects can be offset by either the parenteral administration of methotrexate or by the coadministration of folic acid 1–5 mg/day [18,19]. This stems from earlier research in rheumatoid arthritis, where there was 80% reduction in mucosal and gastrointestinal side-effects with low-dose folic acid. No difference in the efficacy of methotrexate with the coadministration of folic acid was found [19]. More serious side-effects such as bone marrow depression are seldom seen with the low doses used in IBD. Coadministration of other antifolate agents such as co-trimoxazole may increase the toxic effects of methotrexate on bone marrow. In addition, non-steroidal anti-inflammatory agents, penicillin, renal impairment, and old age are all particular factors that may worsen bone marrow toxicity with methotrexate. Full blood counts every 2 weeks for 1–2 months and then every 2–3 months for the duration of treatment are advisable to monitor for delayed bone marrow suppression [18,20]. Patients should seek medical help if they experience symptoms suggestive of infection, to rule out significant neutropenia as well as opportunistic infections.

Hepatic fibrosis is one of the most feared long-term side-effects associated with methotrexate. This concern arose principally from studies of patients with psoriasis and dermatologists have traditionally taken a vigilant approach to monitoring for liver fibrosis with routine biopsy at intervals after cumulative doses of 1–5 g. However, the incidence of liver disease appears to be significantly lower in patients with rheumatoid arthritis than in psoriasis [21]. Guidelines for monitoring by the American College of Rheumatology include liver blood tests every 4–8 weeks, and adjusting the dose accordingly but no routine liver biopsies of patients with normal results [22]. In a study of patients with IBD treated with methotrexate after receiving a cumulative dose of 1.5–5.4 g over 1–5 years, liver histology showed that only 1/20 patients had developed hepatic fibrosis in the absence of abnormal liver function tests [23]. Despite the poor correlation between transaminases and histology, it seems reasonable to recommend monitoring liver tests every 2–3 months [22], and liver biopsy is probably only necessary in those patients with persistently abnormal liver function tests, or for those with a cumulative dose of greater than 5 g [23]. Methotrexate should be used judiciously and sparingly in patients with a greater risk of hepatotoxicity; these include those who drink more than 7 units of alcohol per week, those weighing over 40% greater than average, and those with diabetes mellitus [22].

Hypersensitivity pneumonitis may occur in up to 10% of patients with rheumatoid arthritis treated with methotrexate [22], and represents the other serious long-term side-effect. Any unexplained shortness of breath or persistent cough requires a chest radiograph, blood gases, and lung function testing, particularly looking at carbon monoxide diffusing capacity [3].

Special considerations – pediatrics and reproductive age

Methotrexate appears to be an effective alternative to 6-mercaptopurine in the pediatric age range but only limited data for small numbers of patients are available in this population [24]. Conception and pregnancy should be avoided within 6 months of treatment of either partner, because methotrexate is teratogenic and abortifacient [25]. Breast feeding should be avoided also, because of the mutagenic effects of methotrexate [25].

Conclusions

The available evidence suggests that methotrexate at 25 mg/week parenterally (intramuscularly or subcutaneously) is effective in the induction of remission of Crohn's disease, and at 15 mg/day is effective in the maintenance of remission of such patients. The minimum effective dose is unknown, but there is insufficient evidence to base a recommendation of lower dose oral methotrexate in either setting [26]. There is no role for the use of methotrexate in UC using current evidence. The optimum duration of treatment is unknown; one reviewer has suggested 3–4 years [27]. Finally, more trials are needed to establish the synergistic effect of coadministration with infliximab for managing chronic active Crohn's disease or fistulating disease.

References

1 Kozarek RA, Patterson DJ, Gelfand MD, *et al*. Methotrexate induces clinical and histologic remission in patients with refractory inflammatory bowel disease. *Ann Intern Med* 1989; **110**: 353–6.

2 Seitz M. Molecular and cellular effects of methotrexate. *Curr Opin Rheumatol* 1999; **11**: 226–32.

3 Egan LJ, Sandborn WJ. Methotrexate for inflammatory bowel disease: pharmacology and preliminary results. *Mayo Clin Proc* 1996; **71**: 69–80.

4 Feagan BG, Rochon J, Fedorak RN, *et al*. Methotrexate for the treatment of Crohn's disease. The North American Crohn's Study Group Investigators. *N Engl J Med* 1995; **332**: 292–7.

5 Oren R, Moshkowitz M, Odes S, *et al*. Methotrexate in chronic active Crohn's disease: a double-blind, randomised, Israeli multicenter trial. *Am J Gastroenterol* 1997; **92**: 2203–9.

6 Arora S, Katkov W, Cooley J, *et al*. Methotrexate in Crohn's disease: results of a randomised, double-blind, placebo-controlled trial. *Hepatogastroenterology* 1999; **46**: 1724–9.

7 Mate-Jimenez J, Hermida C, Cantero-Perona J, Moreno-Otero R. 6-Mercaptopurine or methotrexate added to prednisone induces and maintains remission in steroid-dependent inflammatory bowel disease. *Eur J Gastroenterol Hepatol* 2000; **12**: 1227–33.

8 Ardizzoni S, Bollani S, Manzionna G, *et al*. Comparison between methotrexate and azathioprine in the treatment of

chronic active Crohn's disease: a randomised, investigator-blind study. *Dig Liver Dis* 2003; **35**: 619–27.

9 Egan LJ, Sandborn WJ, Tremaine WJ, *et al.* A randomised dose–response and pharmacokinetic study of methotrexate for refractory inflammatory Crohn's disease and ulcerative colitis. *Aliment Pharmacol Ther* 1999; **13**: 1597–604.

10 Chong RY, Hanauer SB, Cohen RD. Efficacy of parenteral methotrexate in refractory Crohn's disease. *Aliment Pharmacol Ther* 2001; **15**: 34–44.

11 Feagan BG, Fedorak RN, Irvine EJ, *et al.* A comparison of methotrexate with placebo for the maintenance of remission in Crohn's disease. North American Crohn's Study Group Investigators. *N Engl J Med* 2000; **342**: 1664–6.

12 Kurnik D, Loebstein R, Fishbein E, *et al.* Bioavailability of oral vs. subcutaneous low-dose methotrexate in patients with Crohn's disease. *Aliment Pharmacol Ther* 2003; **18**: 57–63.

13 Tay GS, Binion DG, Eastwood D, Otterson MF. Multivariate analysis suggests improved perioperative outcome in Crohn's disease patients receiving immunomodulator therapy after segmental resection and/or strictureplasty. *Surgery* 2003; **134**: 565–72.

14 Colombel JF, Loftus EV Jr, Tremaine WJ, *et al.* Early postoperative complications are not increased in patients with Crohn's disease treated perioperatively with infliximab or immunosuppressive therapy. *Am J Gastroenterol* 2004; **99**: 878–83.

15 Alves A, Panis Y, Joly F, *et al.* Could immunosuppressive drugs reduce recurrence rate after second resection for Crohn's disease. *Inflamm Bowel Dis* 2004; **10**: 491–5.

16 Oren R, Arber N, Odes S, *et al.* Methotrexate in chronic active ulcerative colitis: a double-blind, randomised, Israeli multicenter trial. *Gastroenterology* 1996; **110**: 1416–21.

17 Paoluzi OA, Pica R, Marcheggiano A, *et al.* Azathioprine or methotrexate in the treatment of patients with steroid-dependent or steroid-resistant ulcerative colitis: results of an open-label study on efficacy and tolerability in inducing and maintaining remission. *Aliment Pharmacol Ther* 2002; **16**: 1751–9.

18 Morgan SL, Baggott JE, Vaughn WH, *et al.* Supplementation with folic acid during methotrexate therapy for rheumatoid arthritis: a double-blind, placebo-controlled trial. *Ann Intern Med* 1994; **121**: 833–41.

19 Oritz Z, Shea B, Suarez-Almazor ME, *et al.* The efficacy of folic acid and folinic acid in reducing methotrexate induced gastrointestinal toxicity in rheumatoid arthritis: a meta-analysis of randomized controlled trials. *J Rheumatol* 1998; **25**: 36–43.

20 Cunliffe RN, Scott BB. Review article: monitoring for drug side-effects in inflammatory bowel disease. *Aliment Pharmacol Ther* 2002; **16**: 647–62.

21 Ruderman EM, Crawford JM, Maier A, *et al.* Histologic liver abnormalities in an autopsy series of patients with rheumatoid arthritis. *Br J Rheumatol* 1997; **36**: 210–3.

22 Kremer JM, Alarcon GS, Lightfoot RW, *et al.* Methotrexate for rheumatoid arthritis: suggested guidelines for monitoring liver toxicity: American College of Rheumatology. *Arthritis Rheum* 1994; **37**: 316–28.

23 Te HS, Schiano TD, Kuan SF, *et al.* Hepatic effects of long-term methotrexate use in the treatment of inflammatory bowel disease. *Am J Gastroenterol* 2000; **95**: 3150–6.

24 Mack DR, Young R, Kaufman SS, *et al.* Methotrexate in patients with Crohn's disease after 6-mercatopurine. *J Pediatr* 1998; **132**: 830–5.

25 Connell W, Miller A. Treating inflammatory bowel disease during pregnancy: risks and safety of drug therapy. *Drug Saf* 1999; **21**: 311–23.

26 Alfadhli AA, McDonald JWD, Feagan BG. Methotrexate for induction of remission in refractory Crohn's disease. *Cochrane Database Syst Rev* 2004; **4**: Art. No.: C DOI: 1002/14651858.CD003459.pub2

27 Modigliani R. Immunosuppressors for inflammatory bowel disease: how long is long enough? *Inflamm Bowel Dis* 2000; **6**: 251–7.

Part 2 Medical Treatment: Making the Most of What We've Got – *Immunomodulators*

16 Cyclosporine: balancing risk and benefit

HELENA DEENEY & BARNEY HAWTHORNE

LEARNING POINTS

To use cyclosporine safely in refractory acute severe colitis

- Counsel patient about risks, benefits, and alternatives; some may opt for infliximab or colectomy

- Check baseline renal function, BP, liver function tests, cholesterol, magnesium

- Do not use cyclosporine if cholesterol 115 mg/dL (<3 mmol/L), magnesium 1.4 mEq/L (<0.7 mg/dL), hypertension, renal impairment, epilepsy, sepsis, age >80 or poor general condition

- Give cyclosporine 2 mg/kg/day intravenously aiming for levels 200–300 ng/mL; alternatively consider oral microemulsion 5–6 mg/kg twice daily

- Monitor BP and renal function: reduce dose or stop if BP rises, or if creatinine rises by >25% or above 150 µmol/L

- Stop if no improvement over 7 days

- In responders, convert to oral cyclosporine 5–6 mg/kg/day twice daily, monitoring by trough levels (100–200 ng/mL); add thiopurine

- Taper corticosteroids over 2–3 weeks after response achieved

- Stop cyclosporine after 3 months

Introduction

Cyclosporine has a well-established use in the prevention of organ graft rejection. It is a fungal metabolite with potent immunosuppressive action brought about by its selective action against T-cell-mediated immune responses. The use of cyclosporine in the management of acute severe UC has long been a contentious issue. Concerns about its efficacy and side-effects (particularly opportunistic infection) have limited its widespread use. There is a perception that it delays, rather than prevents surgery. Until the recent controlled study of infliximab (see Chapter 20), cyclosporine was the only drug of proven benefit in salvaging patients who fail intravenous corticosteroids, and in whom surgery would otherwise be inevitable. The challenge remains to maximize the safety of cyclosporine without compromising its efficacy.

Short-term response in acute severe colitis

In UC, the landmark randomized controlled trial was reported by Lichtiger *et al.* [1], who used 4 mg/kg as a continuous infusion in 20 patients who had failed to respond to 7 days of intravenous corticosteroids. Nine of 11 in the cyclosporine group responded (82%), versus none in the placebo group. The trial was terminated prematurely because of the dramatic response rates. These high short-term response rates have been confirmed in a number of other uncontrolled studies [2–5]. The onset of action is rapid, and if patients have not responded after 7 days' treatment, cyclosporine should be stopped and surgery considered. Responders are converted to oral microemulsion cyclosporine in a dosage of 5–6 mg/kg/day in twice daily dosage.

Cyclosporine and surgery

Although there is a risk of drug toxicity, many patients will opt for cyclosporine rather than undergo colectomy. Cohen *et al.* [6] assessed 42 patients who received cyclosporine during an acute severe relapse and found that patients who retained their colon felt physically and psychologically healthier with a better quality of life than those who had undergone colectomy.

If rescue treatment with cyclosporine fails, patients who go on to have surgery do not appear to have an increased risk of perioperative complications, provided that the treatment is for a defined period and that the surgery is not delayed [7].

Long-term results

Although short-term response rates are generally 70–80%, long-term results are not as good, with most case series recording colectomy-free outcomes of 40–50% at 2 years [2–5]. Results are considerably better with the addition of thiopurines, the Chicago study [2] showing that while 40% of patients were colectomy-free at 5 years without their use, this figure rose to 66% in those receiving azathioprine or 6-mercaptopurine. Thiopurines are best started after discharge from hospital, cyclosporine being continued for 3 months, allowing time for their slow onset of action. Used in this way, cyclosporine is best considered as a bridging therapy, with rapid onset of action, to induce remission, and allow time for the slow onset maintenance therapy of the thiopurines.

Is cyclosporine safe?

The main concern over the use of cyclosporine is that of dose-related toxicity. The three most important issues are renal function, infections, and neurotoxicity. Other side-effects include anaphylaxis, hepatotoxicity, and, with long-term use, gingival hyperplasia and hypertrichosis.

In all patients there is a reversible decline in renal function, caused by afferent arteriolar vasoconstriction. Of more concern is the risk of irreversible renal damage. This is generally thought to be uncommon, but a study in 192 patients taking cyclosporine for non-renal autoimmune disease, in whom renal biopsy was performed, showed evidence of nephropathy in 21% [8]. Cyclosporine can also cause tubular dysfunction, causing hyperuricemia, metabolic acidosis, hypophosphatemia, and hypomagnesemia.

Widely reported opportunistic infections include *Pneumocystis carinii*, *Aspergillus*, *Nocardia*, *Staphylococcus*, cytomegalovirus, *Listeria* and herpes simplex. A Belgian report of 86 patients, all of whom had received intravenous cyclosporine between 1992 and 2000 [3], showed that side-effects were common and mostly reversible. However, one patient suffered a cardiac arrest following an anaphylactic reaction caused by the cyclosporine solvent. Although resuscitation was successful, the patient was left with cognitive impairment. Three patients (3.5%) died of opportunistic infections. One diabetic patient had failed to improve on cyclosporine and underwent surgery; postoperative recovery was complicated by fatal *Aspergillus fumigatus* pneumonia. The other two patients both responded to cyclosporine but died following discharge from hospital, one from *Aspergillus* pneumonia and the other from *Pneumocystis carinii* pneumonia (PCP). Both were taking triple immunosuppression on discharge (i.e. steroids, azathioprine, and cyclosporine). The risk of infection is significantly increased by the concurrent use of high-dose corticosteroids, and this report illustrates the hazards of an aggressive high-dose treatment regimen. If used in low-dose (2 mg/kg intravenously), PCP prophylaxis is probably not necessary, particularly if high-dose corticosteroids are tailed rapidly (over 2–3 weeks in responders).

In Lichtiger *et al.*'s study [1], a fit occurred in one patient. Low levels of either cholesterol or magnesium reduce the seizure threshold. These should therefore be checked before starting intravenous cyclosporine; it should not be started at all, or should be given orally, if the cholesterol is below 3 mmol, (as the effect of low cholesterol relates to the carrier in the intravenous preparation, and does not apply to the oral formulation). Magnesium should be corrected if low (noting that cyclosporine itself can cause renal losses of magnesium). Headaches are common and again dose-related, as are parasthesiae, but other rare neurologic effects include coma, spasticity, and ataxia. Neurotoxicity is also compounded by hypertension and high-dose corticosteroids.

There are a large number of potential drug interactions with cyclosporine (Table 16.1). There is growing evidence that the toxicity of cyclosporine can be reduced by careful patient selection, and by less aggressive treatment regimens, as discussed below. A treatment schema is shown in the Learning Points above.

Cyclosporine monotherapy

The risk of opportunistic infections would be reduced greatly if cyclosporine could be used without corticosteroids. In

TABLE 16.1 Drug interactions.

Agents increasing cyclosporine levels
Grapefruit juice
Erythromycin/clarithromycin
Itraconazole/ketoconazole
Fluconazole/miconazole
Ursodeoxycholic acid
Diltiazem/nicardipine/verapamil
High-dose methylprednisolone
Danazol
Progestogens
Cimetidine

Drugs increasing risk of nephrotoxicity
Aminoglycosides
Co-trimoxazole/trimethoprim
Quinolones
Amphotericin

Agents reducing cyclosporine levels
Rifampicin
St John's wort
Carbamazepine/phenytoin/phenobarbital
Ticlopidine

a small, randomized, double-blind controlled trial to look at the efficacy of intravenous cyclosporine monotherapy in comparison with glucocorticoids [9], 9/14 patients receiving cyclosporine (64%) responded, compared with 8/15 (53%) given methylprednisolone. These differences were not significant, but the likelihood of a type 2 error is high. Several patients failing monotherapy subsequently responded to combination therapy. A more important question therefore is whether cyclosporine plus corticosteroids is more effective than cyclosporine alone. This has only been addressed in one small study of 30 patients, reported in abstract form [10]. In this, 67% responded to cyclosporine monotherapy (4 mg/kg), whereas 93% responded to cyclosporine in combination with intravenous prednisolone (1 mg/kg). It seems likely that monotherapy is safer, although less efficacious.

Low-dose cyclosporine

The initial studies using 4 mg/kg/day cyclosporine by continuous infusion produced levels of 339–620 ng/mL [1]. A study from Leuven [11] has now compared 4 mg/kg with 2 mg/kg in a randomized trial in 73 patients. Response rates at 14 days were over 80% in both groups, with blood levels of 332 ng/mL (4 mg/kg) and 237 ng/mL (2 mg/kg). Side-

effects did not differ significantly, apart from a trend towards more hypertension in the high-dose group. Over 40% of the patients did not receive corticosteroids. Other case series have shown similar response rates with low-dose intravenous cyclosporine [12]. Similar blood levels can be achieved using oral microemulsion cyclosporine, with comparable results [13,14]. Although there is no definitive guidance about necessary cyclosporine blood levels, it seems that levels of 200–300 ng/mL are as effective as much higher concentrations.

Conclusions

The key to safe use of cyclosporine is careful selection of patients with refractory colitis: their general condition should be good, there should be no evidence of sepsis, and the drug should be avoided in very elderly patients. As cyclosporine is principally used as a bridge to long-term maintenance therapy with thiopurines, it should perhaps not be used in patients unlikely to tolerate these drugs, or in those with long-standing chronic active disease where colectomy may be more appropriate. It is clear that lower doses are effective, although the optimum drug levels are still unclear. Oral cyclosporine can achieve similar drug levels, but there are not yet any controlled trials of this preparation in acute severe colitis. Monotherapy is safer, but probably not as effective as combined therapy with corticosteroids. Many clinicians will recommend colectomy as the safest option in patients failing intravenous corticosteroids, but the consequences for patients are permanent and highly undesirable (permanent ileostomy or ileoanal pouch). Infliximab as an alternative medical approach is discussed in Chapter 20.

References

1 Lichtiger S, Present DH, Kornbluth A, *et al.* Cyclosporin in severe ulcerative colitis refractory to steroid therapy. *N Engl J Med* 1994; **330**: 1841–51.
2 Cohen RD, Stein R, Hanauer SB. Intravenous cyclosporine in ulcerative colitis: a five-year experience. *Am J Gastroenterol* 1999; **94**: 1587–92.
3 Arts J, D'Haens G, Zeegers M, *et al.* Long term outcome of treatment with intravenous cyclosporin in patients with severe ulcerative colitis. *Inflamm Bowel Dis* 2004; **10**: 73–8.
4 Stack WA, Long RG, Hawkey CJ. Short and long term outcome of patients treated with cyclosporine for severe acute ulcerative colitis. *Aliment Pharmacol Ther* 1998; **12**: 973–8.

5 Hyde GM, Thillainayagam AV, Jewell DP. Intravenous cyclosporin as rescue therapy in severe ulcerative colitis: time for a reappraisal? *Eur J Gastroenterol Hepatol* 1998; **10**: 411–3.

6 Cohen RD, Brodsky AL, Hanauer SB. A comparison of the quality of life in patients with severe ulcerative colitis after total colectomy versus medical treatment with intravenous cyclosporin. *Inflamm Bowel Dis* 1999; **5**: 1–10.

7 Hyde GM, Jewell DP, Kettlewell MG, *et al.* Cyclosporin for severe ulcerative colitis does not increase the risk of perioperative complications. *Dis Colon Rectum* 2001; **44**: 1436–40.

8 Feutren G, Mihatsh MJ. Risk factors for cyclosporine-induced nephropathy in patients with autoimmune diseases. International Kidney Biopsy Registry of Cyclosporine in Autoimmune Disease. *N Engl J Med* 1992; **326**: 1654–60.

9 D'Haens G, Lemmens L, Geboes K, *et al.* Intravenous cyclosporine versus intravenous corticosteroids as single therapy for severe attacks of ulcerative colitis. *Gastroenterol* 2001; **120**: 1323–9.

10 Svanoni F, Bonassi U, Caporuscio S. Effectiveness of cyclosporine A (cyclosporine) in the treatment of active refractory ulcerative colitis. *Gastroenterology* 1998; **114**: A1096.

11 Van Assche G, D'Haens G, Noman M, *et al.* Randomized, double-blind comparison of 4 mg/kg versus 2 mg/kg intravenous cyclosporine in severe ulcerative colitis. *Gastroenterol* 2003; **125**: 1025–31.

12 Rowe FA, Walker JH, Karp LC, *et al.* Factors predictive of response to cyclosporine treatment for severe, steroid-resistant ulcerative colitis. *Am J Gastroenterol* 2000; **95**: 2000–8.

13 Actis GC, Aimo G, Priolo G, *et al.* Efficacy and efficiency of oral microemulsion cyclosporine versus intravenous and soft gelatin capsule cyclosporine in the treatment of severe steroid-refractory ulcerative colitis: an open-label retrospective trial. *Inflamm Bowel Dis* 1998; **4**: 276–9.

14 Campbell S Travis S, Jewell D. Cyclosporine use in acute ulcerative colitis: a long-term experience. *Eur J Gastroenterol Hepatol* 2005; **17**: 79–84.

Medical Treatment: Making the Most of What We've Got – *Infliximab*

17 Contraindications – absolute or relative?

RAKESH CHAUDHARY & SUBRATA GHOSH

LEARNING POINTS

Contraindications

- Avoid infliximab in active sepsis or recent history of severe or opportunistic infection

- Screen for and treat latent tuberculosis (TB)

- Premedicate with steroids if considering reinfusion in patients with history of acute infusion reaction

- Stop treatment if drug-induced lupus develops (but *not* if positive for ANA antibody without lupus syndrome)

- Avoid use in pregnancy (although there is no current evidence of harm) unless benefit outweighs risk. Breast feeding is not recommended. Contraception is recommended

- Avoid in advanced heart failure

- Careful consideration is required if there is a history of malignancy, especially lymphoproliferative

- Use with caution in patients with obstructive lesions

- Avoid in patients with a history of demyelinating disease

Introduction

The increased importance and use of infliximab in IBD necessitates appreciation of its contraindications, whether absolute or relative. The absolute contraindications are denoted by the acronym STOIC (S, sepsis; T, tuberculosis; O, optic neuritis; I, infusion reaction (severe); C, cancer).

Relative contraindications include pregnancy, heart failure, and obstruction resulting from fibrostenotic disease without significant inflammation.

Infection

As infliximab neutralizes the activity of tumor necrosis factor α (TNF-α), there is the theoretic risk that it may alter normal immune responses to pathogens. This is reflected in studies that indicate that severe infection occurs in up to 8% of infliximab-treated patients (Table 17.1) [1–4]. Vigilance for evidence of sepsis is therefore required throughout the treatment course.

An increased susceptibility to opportunistic infections has also been described with anti-TNF therapy; this is exacerbated in patients on concomitant steroids and additional immunosuppressive agents. Tuberculosis, in particular, is now well recognized and screening of prospective patients as per the British Thoracic Society guidelines is recommended (see Chapter 18). This relies on tuberculosis (TB) history, chest X-ray, and ethnicity and duration of residence in UK. Regional differences in screening guidelines exist and European and US guidelines include tuberculin skin testing. Reactivation of latent TB usually occurs in the first 12 months following treatment initiation, most cases presenting within 2 months of initiation of therapy. Following the introduction of TB education programs and screening of latent TB by chest X-ray, skin test, and risk history, the rate of TB has declined to less than 1/1000 patients exposed. Treatment of latent TB should be initiated prior to infliximab therapy. Active TB should be considered a

TABLE 17.1 Summary of major adverse events (as percentages) in trials and large series (cohort size).

	ACCENT I (573) (%)	ACCENT II (306) (%)	Colombel et al. [3] (500) (%)	Ljung et al. [4] (217) (%)
Severe infection	4	4.6	4.0	8.3
Opportunistic infection	0.2	0.6	1	0.9
Serious infusion reaction	1.0	0.3	0.4	3.7*
Drug-induced lupus	0.3	0	0.6	0.5
Non-Hodgkin's lymphoma	0.2	0	0.2	1.4
Demyelination	0	0	0.2	0
Heart failure	0	0	0.2	0
Mortality rate	0.5	0†	1.4	1.4

* Severity not assessed.
† Two deaths during long-term follow-up.

contraindication to infliximab until anti-TB therapy leads to successful resolution.

Histoplasmosis, *Cryptococcus*, *Nocardia*, coccidioidomycosis, aspergillosis, listeriosis, cytomegalovirus infection, systemic candidiasis, toxoplasmosis, blastomycosis, and *Pneumocystis carinii* pneumonia after treatment with infliximab have been reported. In the TREAT registry, however, current use of cortocosteroids, but not infliximab or immunomodulator use, was associated with an increase in serious infections (odds ratio 2.3, 95% confidence interval [CI] 1.6–6.1) [5].

Administration of anti-TNF therapy is contraindicated in patients with abscess, active infection, with a recent severe life-threatening infection, or recent severe opportunistic infection. In fistulizing disease, caution is required, with appropriate surgical drainage performed and infection brought under control before considering infliximab.

Demyelination

The association of demyelination with anti-TNF therapy is highlighted in a paper by Mohan *et al.* [6] in which 20 rheumatology patients on anti-TNF treatment developed neurologic symptoms. Discontinuation of therapy largely resulted in partial or complete clinical resolution. Brain magnetic resonance imaging studies demonstrated bilateral changes consistent with demyelination. In view of this link with a demyelinating syndrome, the use of infliximab in patients with multiple sclerosis or a previous history of optic neuritis is contraindicated. In addition, patients on treatment with infliximab should be monitored for the development of neurologic signs and symptoms. Withdrawal of treat-

ment is advocated if demyelination occurs. Preliminary reports suggest that even in the absence of anti-TNF therapy there may be an association of demyelinating diseases and IBD [7].

Immunogenicity and autoimmunity

The development of antibodies against infliximab is now well described and associated with reduced duration of response to treatment. The incidence of antibodies to infliximab (ATI) is increased in the absence of concurrent immunosuppressive therapy and the use of an episodic therapy regimen. In a study of episodic infliximab therapy, the presence of ATI at concentrations of 8.0 µg/mL or greater prior to repeat infusion predicted a shorter duration of response (35 days compared with 71 days amongst patients with concentrations of less than 8.0 µg/mL; $P < 0.001$) and a higher risk of infusion reactions (relative risk, 2.40; $P < 0.001$) [8]. Immune consequences, in terms of adverse events, include the occurrence of the acute severe infusion reactions and delayed serum sickness-like reactions (see Chapter 19).

Prevention is clearly the best policy. Immunosuppressive therapy is best initiated before starting infliximab therapy and should be continued throughout treatment. Pretreatment with hydrocortisone intravenously and regular maintenance infusions every 8 weeks decrease immunogenicity. However, in the presence of an acute infusion reaction, reinfusion may be considered depending on the severity of the reaction. Patients with cardiopulmonary symptoms, hives, wheezing, stridor, or hypotension should not undergo repeat infliximab administration. Reinfusion may be attempted following premedication with steroids, antihistamines, or paracetamol. A reduction in infusion rate on reinfusion may also be beneficial. Serum-sickness episodes tend to occur following a significant interval between successive infusions, with most episodes occurring after the second infusion, and can be treated with a course of oral steroids.

During treatment with infliximab antinuclear antibody (ANA), anti-double-stranded antibodies, and antihistone antibodies may develop and be rarely associated with a lupus-type syndrome. The vast majority of patients who develop autoantibodies do not progress to drug-induced lupus [9]. The development of ANAs does not therefore require discontinuation of treatment per se. In the presence of a lupus-type syndrome, treatment should be terminated and specialist advice or treatment sought as appropriate.

Malignancy

There is currently no evidence linking anti-TNF therapy with an increased risk of solid tumors. A causal relationship between infliximab and the development of malignancy seems unlikely. For patients with a history of malignancy, caution is recommended, with adequate consideration of benefits against risk of recurrence. For those free of recurrence for 5 years, use of infliximab is currently considered safe.

There is some concern regarding the increased risk of lymphoproliferative malignancy, in particular non-Hodgkin's lymphoma, with anti-TNF therapy in rheumatoid arthritis and possibly Crohn's disease. The cumulative rate of lymphoma per 1000 patients exposed is 0.18. Immunosuppression, particularly when used for organ transplantation, is associated with an increased frequency of lymphomas, with Epstein–Barr virus (EBV) implicated in the pathogenisis. There are confounding factors: it is possible that Crohn's disease patients (in particular, the severe group selected for anti-TNF therapy) may be at an increased risk of lymphoma; and concurrent immunosuppressant use with azathioprine and methotrexate may also increase the incidence of lymphoma. Definitive conclusions are not yet possible, although vigilance and event reporting by clinicians is important.

Pregnancy

In murine models, anti-TNF agents do not appear to cause problems such as teratogenicity in pregnancy. A study examining the outcome of 96 women exposed to infliximab during pregnancy concluded that the outcome did not differ from that of the general population (see Chapter 40) [10]. Preliminary indications from the TREAT registry suggest that miscarriages, neonatal complications, and fetal malformation rates were not increased with exposure to infliximab. Intentional use of infliximab in 10 women did not result in any obvious fetal malformations [11]. Nevertheless, in view of the limited data, it is not recommended that pregnant patients receive infliximab – however, individual cases should be considered on their merits. The use of appropriate birth control is therefore advised during treatment with infliximab. A period off anti-TNF therapy (ideally 6 months) is recommended before conception. However, if a patient does conceive while on infliximab, current evidence would be in favor of continuation of pregnancy after discussion with the patient.

It is not known whether infliximab is secreted during lactation (although recent reports suggest that it is not), hence breast feeding is not recommended. Placental transfer of infliximab to the neonate has been reported. As active inflammation is detrimental to outcome of pregnancy, infliximab may have to be considered if other medical therapies are unsuccessful, and if a patient conceives on infliximab, a decision about whether or not to proceed with the pregnancy needs to be taken in conjunction with the patient and her partner.

Heart failure

TNF-α is known to be increased in cardiac failure in proportion with disease severity. An initial pilot study concluded that anti-TNF therapy improved cardiac and patient status. A total of 150 patients with New York Heart Association (NYHA) class III and IV heart failure were then treated with infliximab to see if anti-TNF therapy improved cardiac status [12]. The findings were not anticipated: infliximab did not improve cardiac function but, at doses >5 mg/kg, adversely affected patients with increased hospitalization and death resulting from worsening heart failure. Current advice is not to treat patients with moderate to severe heart failure with infliximab and for the cessation of its administration in patients with worsening cardiac failure. Careful consideration should be given to use in patients with mild to moderate heart disease, weighing up risks with expected benefits. Close monitoring is advocated, especially if increasing infliximab dosage to 10 mg/kg.

Obstructive lesions

Initial concern that patients with stenotic lesions might develop bowel obstruction following infliximab have not been borne out by recent experience (such as the TREAT registry). Infliximab can be used to treat patients with inflammatory strictures but caution is required in patients with symptoms resulting from fibrostenotic disease. It should not be used in patients with subacute obstructive symptoms in the absence of objective evidence of inflammation.

Conclusion

It is important to bear in mind the relative and absolute contraindications of infliximab use, especially because the use of anti-TNF therapy is rapidly becoming more widespread. The presence of active infection is the most important of the contraindications, especially relevant in the treatment of Crohn's disease. On the other hand, other contraindications are becoming more relative with increasing experience, such as use in pregnancy.

References

1 Hanauer SB, Feagan BG, Lichtenstein GR, *et al*. Maintenance infliximab for Crohn's disease: the ACCENT I randomised trial. ACCENT I Study Group. *Lancet* 2002; **359**: 1541–9.

2 Sands BE, Anderson FH, Bernstein CN, *et al*. Infliximab maintenance therapy for fistulizing Crohn's disease. *N Engl J Med* 2004; **350**: 876–85.

3 Colombel JF, Loftus EV Jr, Tremaine WJ, *et al*. The safety profile of infliximab in patients with Crohn's disease: the Mayo clinic experience in 500 patients. *Gastroenterology* 2004; **126**: 19–31.

4 Ljung T, Karlen P, Schmidt D, *et al*. Infliximab in inflammatory bowel disease: clinical outcome in a population based cohort from Stockholm County. *Gut* 2004; **53**: 849–53.

5 Lichtenstein GR, Cohen RD, Feagan BG, *et al*. Safety of infliximab and other Crohn's disease therapies: updated TREAT Registry data with over 10 000 patient-years of follow-up. *Gastroenterology* 2005; **128** (Suppl 2): W1034.

6 Mohan N, Edwards ET, Cupps TR, *et al*. Demyelination occurring during anti-tumor necrosis factor alpha therapy for inflammatory arthritides. *Arthritis Rheum* 2001; **44**: 2862–9.

7 Gupta G, Colleen M, Brensinger JM, Gelfand JDL. Are patients with inflammatory bowel disease (IBD) at increased risk for multiple sclerosis, demyelination or optic neuritis? *Gastroenterology* 2005; **128** (Suppl 2): M1149.

8 Baert F, Norman M, Vermiere S, *et al*. Influence of immunogenicity on the long-term efficacy of infliximab in Crohn's disease. *N Engl J Med* 2003; **348**: 601–8.

9 Vermeire S, Noman M, Van Assche G, *et al*. Autoimmunity associated with anti-tumor necrosis factor alpha treatment in Crohn's disease: a prospective cohort study. *Gastroenterology* 2003; **125**: 32–9.

10 Katz JA, Antoni C, Keenan GF, *et al*. Outcome of pregnancy in women receiving infliximab for the treatment of Crohn's disease and rheumatoid arthritis. *Am J Gastroenterol* 2004; **99**: 2385–92.

11 Mahadevan U, Kane S, Sandborn WJ, *et al*. Intentional infliximab use during pregnancy for induction or maintenance of remission in Crohn's disease. *Aliment Pharmacol Ther* 2005; **21**: 733–8.

12 Chung ES, Packer M, Lo KH, Fasanmade AA, Willerson JT. Randomized, double-blind, placebo-controlled, pilot trial of infliximab, a chimeric monoclonal antibody to tumor necrosis factor-alpha, in patients with moderate-to-severe heart failure: results of the anti-TNF Therapy Against Congestive Heart Failure (ATTACH) trial. Anti-TNF Therapy Against Congestive Heart Failure Investigators. *Circulation.* 2003; **107**: 3133–40.

Medical Treatment: Making the Most of What We've Got – *Infliximab*

18 How can we prevent tuberculosis?

SASHA BERESFORD & DAVID RAMPTON

LEARNING POINTS

Infliximab and TB

- Infliximab increases the background rate of tuberculosis (TB) approximately fivefold

- Infliximab-associated TB is often extrapulmonary

- Patients needing infliximab should have a careful history for previous TB and chest X-ray, but, in the UK at least, tuberculin testing is unnecessary

- Patients with active TB should have full anti-tuberculous chemotherapy, and those with inadequately treated previous TB should have chemoprophylaxis before infliximab

- In other patients, the risk of infliximab-induced TB in their ethnic group should be compared with that of chemoprophylaxis-related hepatitis

- Black African patients aged over 15 years, South Asian patients born outside the UK, and patients from other ethnic groups resident in the UK for less than 5 years with no past history of TB and a normal chest X-ray should usually be given isoniazid for 6 months when starting infliximab

- All patients on infliximab need careful clinical monitoring for TB

Introduction

Infliximab is of proven benefit in the treatment of refractory, chronic, active Crohn's disease [1] as well as in rheumatoid arthritis [2], psoriatic arthropathy, and anky-losing spondylitis [3]; it may have a role, too, in ulcerative colitis (see Chapter 20). When care has been taken to limit its use to patients without specific contraindications, the side-effects of infliximab to date have been few and largely restricted to infusion reactions. However, an increased risk of tuberculosis (TB) was noted soon after the introduction of infliximab in the USA and Europe in the late 1990s. This chapter outlines the extent of this risk and describes the current British approach to reducing it to a minimum [4].

How common is TB in patients with Crohn's disease?

In rheumatoid arthritis not treated with anti-TNF therapy, the incidence of TB is 6.2/100 000/year in the USA [5]. In Crohn's disease that has not been treated with infliximab, the incidence of TB is unknown; indeed, in some patients it may be difficult, initially at least, to distinguish the one diagnosis from the other.

In the general population in the UK, and probably in patients with Crohn's disease too, the incidence of TB depends on a range of factors which include age, ethnicity, and country of birth [6], as well as use of corticosteroids and immunomodulatory therapies such as azathioprine. Ethnicity is a particularly important risk factor. The annual risk of TB in the UK is increased at least 30-fold in black Africans aged over 15 years, while in South Asians born outside the UK, the risk of TB is increased by a similar extent; it is even greater in people from other ethnic groups resident in the UK for less than 5 years [4].

How common is TB in patients given infliximab?

In both Crohn's disease and rheumatoid arthritis, it is thought that infliximab increases the background risk of TB approximately fivefold [4].

Post-marketing surveillance in the USA and elsewhere showed 70 cases of TB associated with use of infliximab to mid-2001 [7] and 242 cases to 2003 [4]. Because the number of reported cases is relatively low, figures for incidence of TB in this setting carry wide confidence limits. Bearing in mind this caveat, the incidence of TB reported to the Federal Drug Administration in the USA during treatment with infliximab was recently 144/100 000 [8]; it appears to be even higher outside the USA [9,10].

Most cases of TB have occurred within the first 12 weeks of treatment with infliximab [8,11]. The frequency of TB has been much higher than of other opportunistic infections in patients on infliximab, and over 50% of cases are extra-pulmonary [7,8,12]. Although the incidence of infliximab-related TB may now be falling because of improved risk assessment, chemoprophylaxis (see below) and/or report-ing fatigue, complacency is clearly inappropriate; the mortality of TB in the early days of its recognition in asso-ciation with use of infliximab was 5–10% (Schering Plough, data on file).

Approaches to prevention of TB in patients to be given infliximab

Recommendations from several sources agree that patients in whom use of anti-tumor necrosis facor (TNF) therapy is being considered should have a careful history of any prior TB, and its treatment, checked, and a chest X-ray performed [4,12,13].

History of TB and/or abnormal chest X-ray

Patients with a history of TB or an abnormal chest X-ray should be referred for assessment by a specialist with expertise in TB. Those with active TB should receive standard anti-tuberculous chemotherapy for a minimum of 2 months before starting on infliximab. Patients with a chest X-ray consistent with previous TB, or with a history of previous extrapulmonary TB which has been fully treated, should be carefully monitored during infliximab therapy; those in whom treatment may have been inade-quate should have active TB excluded by appropriate investigation and should be given chemoprophylaxis before starting infliximab.

No history of TB and normal chest X-ray

Some guidelines have suggested that a tuberculin test should be used to direct the approach in this, which is much the largest, group of patients with Crohn's disease in whom infliximab is being considered [1,12,13]. Recent data, how-ever, have confirmed a very high incidence of anergy in patients with Crohn's [14]. Indeed, because under present NICE guidelines [15] all patients with Crohn's disease in the UK needing infliximab will be chronically ill and currently or recently taking corticosteroids and/or immunomodula-tory drugs, tuberculin testing will not assist in decision-making and is unnecessary [4].

What does need to be considered in the UK, as elsewhere, is the annual risk of TB in individual patients to be given infliximab; as indicated above, this is increased approx-imately fivefold by infliximab, and still further in some ethnic groups. This risk needs to be balanced against the risk of side-effects caused by TB chemoprophylaxis, itself dependent on the regimen to be used [4]. The most widely used of these is isoniazid for 6 months, which has a hepatitis risk rate of approximately 280/100 000 treated pati-ents [4]. Two shorter regimens, rifampicin with isoniazid for 3 months, and rifampicin with pyrazinamide for 2 months, cause serious hepatitis much more commonly (1800 and 6600/100 000 treated patients, respectively) [4].

These considerations mean that, in general, Caucasians in the UK with no history of TB, and a normal chest X-ray, need no TB chemoprophylaxis. In contrast, even if they have no TB history, and their chest X-ray is normal, black Africans aged over 15 years, South Asians born outside the UK, and other ethnic groups resident in the UK for less than 5 years have such a high risk of TB while on infliximab that they should usually be offered isoniazid for 6 months when starting it [4]. In other non-Caucasian ethnic groups, data on the risk of TB is too limited for it to be possible to make definitive recommendations.

Monitoring patients on infliximab

Regardless of their risk of developing TB, all patients on infliximab should be monitored carefully for symptoms such as fever, weight loss, or cough; gastroenterologists should be alert to the possibility of extrapulmonary as well as the more familiar lung disease. The slightest suspicion of TB should prompt immediate referral to a specialist TB physician.

Conclusions

TB is one of the most serious complications associated with the use of infliximab; indeed, fatalities have been reported. In every patient in whom therapy with infliximab is being considered, a strategy should be determined based on their history, chest X-ray, and ethnicity (Fig. 18.1). Although for ethical reasons a clinical trial to confirm it will be impossible, it is likely that implementation of these recommendations will dramatically reduce the risk of TB developing in

FIG 18.1 Algorithm to indicate the approach to prevention of tuberculosis (TB) in patients on immunosuppressants who need infliximab or other anti-tumor necrosis factor α (TNF-α) therapy. The high incidence of anergy in patients with Crohn's disease who take immunosuppressants [14] makes tuberculin skin testing unreliable and unnecessary. The decision about TB chemoprophylaxis in individual patients with no history of TB and a normal chest X-ray is dependent on a comparison of their ethnicity-related risk of acquiring TB during anti-TNF therapy, and the risk of drug-induced hepatitis during chemoprophylaxis (see text and reference [4]). (For recommendations about the prevention of TB in the small minority of patients in whom infliximab without concomitant immunosuppressive therapy is being considered, see reference [4]). CXR, chest X-ray.

patients given infliximab and other agents, biologic (see Chapter 31) or otherwise, which reduce the production or effects of TNF [10].

References

1 Rutgeerts P, van Assche G, Vermeire S. Optimizing anti-TNF treatment in inflammatory bowel disease. *Gastroenterology* 2004; **126**: 1593–610.

2 Maini SR. Infliximab treatment of rheumatoid arthritis. *Rheum Dis Clin North Am* 2004; **30**: 329–47.

3 Braun J, Sieper J. Biological therapies in the spondyloarthropathies: the current state. *Rheumatology* 2004; **43**: 1072–84.

4 British Thoracic Society Standards of Care Committee. BTS recommendations for assessing risk, and for managing *M. tuberculosis* infection and disease in patients due to start anti-TNF alpha treatment. *Thorax* 2005; in press.

5 Wolfe F, Michaud K, Anderson J, Urbansky K. Tuberculosis infection with rheumatoid arthritis and the effect of infliximab therapy. *Arthritis Rheum* 2004; **50**: 372–9.

6 Rose AMC, Watson JM, Graham C, *et al.* Tuberculosis at the end of the 20th century in England and Wales: results of a national survey in 1998. *Thorax* 2001; **56**: 173–9.

7 Keane J, Gershon S, Wise RP, *et al.* Tuberculosis associated with infliximab, a tumor necrosis factor-alpha neutralizing agent. *N Engl J Med* 2001; **345**: 1098–104.

8 Wallis RS, Broder MS, Wong JY, Hanson ME, Beenhouwer DO. Granulomatous infectious diseases associated with tumor necrosis factor antagonists. *Clin Infect Dis* 2004; **38**: 1261–5.

9 Keane J, Gershon SK, Braun MM. Tuberculosis and treatment with infliximab. *N Engl J Med* 2002; **346**; 625–6.

10 Gomez-Reino JJ, Carmona L, Valverde VR, Mola EM, Montero MD, BIOBADASER Group. Treatment of rheumatoid arthritis with tumour necrosis factor inhibitors may predispose to significant increase in tuberculosis risk: a multicenter active-surveillance report. *Arthritis Rheum* 2003; **48**: 2122–7.

11 Weinblatt ME, Keystone EC, Furst DE, *et al.* Adalimumab, a fully human anti-tumour necrosis factor alpha monoclonal antibody, for the treatment of rheumatoid arthritis in patients taking concomitant methotrexate: the ARMADA trial. *Arthritis Rheum* 2003; **48**: 855.

12 Gardam MA, Keystone EC, Menzies R, *et al.* Anti-tumour necrosis factor agents and tuberculosis risk: mechanisms of action and clinical management. *Lancet Infect Dis* 2003; **3**: 148–55.

13 Sandborn WJ, Hanauer SB. Infliximab in the treatment of Crohn's disease: a user's guide for clinicians. *Am J Gastroenterol* 2002; **97**: 2962–72.

14 Mow WS, Abreu-Martin MT, Papadakis KA, *et al.* High incidence of anergy in inflammatory bowel disease patients limits the usefulness of PPD screening before infliximab therapy. *Clin Gastroenterol Hepatol* 2004; **2**: 309–13.

15 National Institute for Clinical Excellence (NICE). Guidance on the use of infliximab for Crohn's disease. Technology Appraisal Guidance No. 40, 2002.

GERT VAN ASSCHE, SÉVERINE VERMEIRE & PAUL RUTGEERTS

LEARNING POINTS

Infusion reactions to infliximab

- Infusion reactions occur in 20–50% of patients treated with maintenance infliximab

- Acute infusion reactions to infliximab can be managed easily and most patients can be retreated safely

- Acute and delayed infusion reactions are linked to formation of antibodies to infliximab

- To reduce the incidence of infusion reactions, optimize infliximab maintenance by:

  ○ concomitant immunosuppression

  ○ systematic 8-weekly infliximab

  ○ steroid pretreatment in patients with a history of infusion reactions or a drug holiday >3 months

Introduction

The immunogenicity of the chimeric anti-tumor necrosis factor (TNF) antibody, infliximab, is a clinical reality and results in a decreased duration of response and/or drug intolerance resulting from infusion reactions. Infusion reactions can be managed with medical prophylaxis and slow infusion rates, but optimizing treatment strategies to avoid anti-infliximab antibody formation is paramount. Both concomitant immunosuppressants and corticosteroid pretreatment have been shown to decrease the immunogenicity and infusion reactions associated with infliximab treatment.

Type and incidence of infusion reactions associated with infliximab therapy

Acute infusion reactions in patients treated with infliximab typically occur during or within 2 hours of the infusion. Most of the acute infusion reactions are immunoglobulin G (IgG) related and are anaphylactoid-like rather than true anaphylactic reactions. Symptoms may vary from shortness of breath, chest pain, palpitations, flushing, fever, headache, and sometimes urticaria and hypotension. The possibility of the more rare, true anaphylactic reaction that is IgE-mediated should be considered in patients with urticaria and hypotension. An integrated safety report of 1140 patients with Crohn's disease treated with infliximab or placebo reported that 19.6% of patients treated with infliximab will eventually develop an infusion reaction, compared with 7.1% placebo-treated patients (Centocor, Malvern, PA, data on file). In a cohort of rheumatoid arthritis patients, infusion reactions occurred in 8.8% of infusions but 53% of 116 patients had at least one reaction [1]. Serious infusion reactions are rare (approximately 1%).

Delayed hypersensitivity typically occurs 5–9 days after an infusion and is unusual before 5 days. If occurring after 2 weeks, alternate diagnoses should be considered. The clinical presentation includes arthralgias (which may include unusual locations such as the temporomandibular joint or the jaw), back pain or spasm, myalgias, fever, skin rash, and leukocytosis. In a study by Hanauer *et al.* [2], delayed infusion reactions occurred in 25% of patients retreated after an interval of at least 2 years since previous administration of infliximab. Serum complement and urinalysis were both normal, indicating that delayed hypersensitivity-like reactions were not true type 3 hypersensitivity reactions. Typically, delayed hypersensitivity-type reactions are self-limited, resolving over 24–72 hours. The longer the "drug holiday" interval between infusions, the greater the risk, with delayed hypersensitivity rates ranging from 0.2% for infusions administered within 2 weeks of the last infusion, up to 3% for patients whose last infusion was 30–54 weeks previously.

Relation of infusion reactions to the immunogenicity of infliximab

The murine portion of the chimeric (25% murine, 75% human) antibody infliximab is most likely responsible for the immunogenicity observed with the drug and for the formation of antibodies to infliximab (ATIs) [3]. The formation of these ATIs is linked to the occurrence of infusion reactions. In a cohort study of 125 Crohn's disease patients treated with 5 mg/kg infliximab for moderate to severely active luminal Crohn's disease, or three doses of 5 mg/kg at weeks 0, 2, and 6 for fistulizing Crohn's disease in an episodic treatment schedule, up to 61% (38/125) of patients developed ATIs [4]. The presence of ATIs was clearly associated with an increased risk of infusion reactions and subsequently a loss of response. A total of 27% of patients developed infusion reactions. Farrell *et al.* [5] evaluated 53 consecutive patients with Crohn's disease treated with infliximab using a three-dose induction regimen followed by an on-demand schedule. From the initial 68% of patients who responded over time, approximately 50% lost their response and this was associated with positive ATIs in 73% of them. In the episodic retreatment arm of the ACCENT I study, the cumulative incidence of ATI amounted to 30% after 72 weeks, which was significantly higher than the 10% and 7% in the group of patients treated with 8-weekly systematic treatment with 5 or 10 mg/kg infliximab infusions [6]. In the ACCENT I trial, 4.5% of the infliximab (and 2.7% of the placebo) infusions were associated with an infusion reaction and 2.4% of the patients (14/573) met the definition of a delayed hypersensitivity reaction. Although the incidence of infusion reactions was similar in the episodic and systematic retreatment arms, ATIs were more likely to be present in patients with episodic treatment. Hence, the incidence of infusion reactions and of ATIs is highly variable and appears to depend on the maintenance treatment schedule [6–8].

Treatment of acute and delayed hypersensitivity reactions

Acute infusion reactions are treated by temporarily interrupting the infusion and administration of an antihistaminic (e.g. 50 mg diphenhydramine p.o. or 50 mg promethazine i.m.) and acetaminophen. This practice is based on expert opinion and experience in large cohorts. [9] In severe cases, or in patients with a previous history of infusion reactions, 100–250 mg hydrocortisone i.v. should be given. The infusion can be restarted after resolution of all symptoms at a slower rate. All infliximab infusions should be given by an easy to calibrate infusion pump in these patients and the initial rate after resolution of symptoms should be as low as 10 mL/hour with a stepwise increase every 15 minutes and constant monitoring of vital signs.

The treatment of delayed hypersensitivity reactions includes prednisone starting at 40–100 mg/day. Most of these patients have malaise and disabling arthralgias. Hence, short hospitalization is usually required and steroids should be tapered over 2 weeks to avoid symptom recurrence.

Management of patients with a history of infusion reactions (Fig. 19.1)

Patients with a known history of an immediate infusion reaction should be treated prophylactically with antihistamine therapy (see above) and 250 mg hydrocortisone 30 minutes prior to the start of the infusion. A reduced initial infusion rate is also advisable [9]. Using this strategy, most patients with previous reactions can be safely retreated. Patients with delayed hypersensitivity can be retreated if they are given systemic corticosteroids (e.g. 40 mg prednisolone p.o.) 3 days prior to, and 2 days after infusion [10], but controlled data are lacking and recurrence of a delayed reaction despite this strategy precludes further infliximab infusions.

Conclusions

Several strategies can be employed to minimize the risk of acute and delayed infusion reactions in patients treated with infliximab [11,12]. Based on the experience of randomized controlled trials and of prospective cohort studies it is clear that systematic maintenance treatment every 8 weeks, concomitant immunosuppression with azathioprine or methotrexate, and steroid pretreatment from the first infusion onward reduces the risk of ATIs and, most likely,

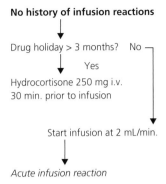

No history of infusion reactions

Drug holiday > 3 months? — No

Yes

Hydrocortisone 250 mg i.v.
30 min. prior to infusion

Start infusion at 2 mL/min.

Acute infusion reaction

- STOP infusion
- Administer antihistaminic and acetaminophen
- Administer hydrocortisone 250 mg in case of severe symptoms
- Restart infusion at reduced rate after symptom resolution (10 mL/hour,
  gradual increase every 15 min.)
- Survey patient and monitor vital signs every 15 min.
  Stop further infusion if symptoms redevelop

Previous infusion reaction

Administer
- Antihistaminic (acetaminophen)
- Hydrocortisone 250 mg 30 min. prior to infusion

Start infusion at reduced rate
(10 mL/hour, gradual increase every 15 min.)

FIG 19.1 Suggested algorithm to manage infliximab related acute infusion reactions.

the risk of infusion reactions. Which of these strategies will optimally protect the patient is unclear, although steroid pretreatment appears to be inferior to concomitant immunosuppressives [5]. Even so, there are no data showing that a combination of the strategies is useful. Whatever, patients intolerant of immunosuppressives should receive infliximab retreatment systematically to decrease the chance of developing ATIs. Novel, more "humanized" anti-TNF antibodies such as adalimumab (see Chapter 31) will probably become available in the near future as a treatment option for patients with intolerance to infliximab infusions.

References

1 Wasserman, M, Weber D, Guthrie J, *et al*. Infusion-related reactions to infliximab in patients with rheumatoid arthritis in a clinical practice setting: relationship to dose, antihistamine pretreatment and infusion number. *J Rheumatol* 2004; **31**: 1912–7.

2 Hanauer SB, Rutgeerts PJ, D'Haens G, *et al*. Delayed hypersensitivity to infliximab (Remicade®) re-infusion after 2–4 year interval without treatment. *Gastroenterology* 1999; **116**: G3174.

3 DeShazo R, Kemp S. Allergic reactions to drugs and biological agents. *JAMA* 1997; **278**: 1895–906.

4 Baert F, Noman M, Vermeire S, *et al*. Influence of immunogenicity on the long-term efficacy of infliximab in Crohn's disease. *N Engl J Med* 2003; **348**: 601–8.

5 Farrell RJ, Alsahli M, Jeen YT, *et al*. Intravenous hydrocortisone premedication reduces antibodies to infliximab in Crohn's disease: a randomized controlled trial. *Gastroenterology* 2003; **124**: 917–24.

6 Hanauer SB, Feagan BG, Lichtenstein GR, *et al*. ACCENT I Study Group. Maintenance infliximab for Crohn's disease: the ACCENT I randomised trial. *Lancet* 2002; **359**: 1541–9.

7 Rutgeerts P, D'Haens G, Targan S, *et al*. Safety of retreatment with anti-tumor necrosis factor antibody (infliximab) to maintain remission in Crohn's disease. *Gastroenterology* 1999; **117**: 761–9.

8 Hanauer S, Wagner C, Bala M, *et al*. Incidence and importance of antibody responses to infliximab after maintenance of episodic treatment in Crohn's disease. *Clin Gastroenterol Hepatol* 2004; **2**: 542–53.

9 Sandborn W, Hanauer S. Infliximab in the treatment of Crohn's disease: a user's guide for clinicians. *Am J Gastrenterol* 2002; **97**: 2963–72.

10 Panaccione R. Overcoming "delayed-type hypersensitivity reactions" in patients receiving repeated doses of infliximab: a report of 5 cases. *Gastroenterology* 2002; **122**: A613.

11 Rutgeerts P, Van Assche G, Vermeire S. Optimizing anti-TNF treatment in inflammatory bowel disease. *Gastroenterology* 2004; **126**: 1593–610.

12 Sandborn W. Optimizing anti-tumor necrosis factor strategies in inflammatory bowel disease. *Curr Gastroenterol Rep* 2003; **5**: 501–5.

20 Use in ulcerative colitis

SREEDHAR SUBRAMANIAN & JONATHAN RHODES

LEARNING POINTS

Use of infliximab for UC

Pros:

- Effective treatment for moderate to severe relapse of UC refractory to corticosteroids
- Generally well tolerated, safer than cyclosporine

Cons:

- Intravenous route
- Small but significant drug-associated mortality
- Cost

The need for better therapies for UC

The mainstays of therapy in UC comprise mesalazine, thiopurines, and corticosteroids. Limited alternative therapeutic options exist for patients in whom corticosteroids need to be avoided or in steroid-refractory patients who cannot tolerate azathioprine or 6-mercaptopurine; moreover, approximately 25% of patients with UC (and approximately one-third of patients admitted with severe colitis) still require colectomy. Thiopurines are ineffective in the acute setting because of the considerable delay in their onset of action. Cyclosporine is effective in severe colitis but up to one-third of patients fail to respond and many of those that

do respond need a colectomy eventually (see Chapter 16) [1]. Furthermore, its use is associated with a range of side-effects and a possible drug-associated mortality of 3.5% [2]; this exceeds the <1% mortality reported for management of severe colitis in specialist centers. There is therefore a clear need for more effective and safer therapy for patients with severe colitis, and with steroid-refractory or steroid-dependent disease. Infliximab has recently emerged as a therapeutic option for such patients.

The role of TNF-α in ulcerative colitis

In UC, a variety of inflammatory cells including polymorphonuclear leukocytes, lymphocytes, and macrophages are recruited to the site of inflammation; these in turn secrete a range of pro-inflammatory cytokines resulting in the recruitment of further inflammatory cells. Lymphocytes and macrophages produce tumor necrosis factor α (TNF-α). TNF-α up-regulates expression of E-selectin, intercellular adhesion molecule-1 (ICAM-1) and vascular cell adhesion molecule-1 (VCAM-1), leading to increased neutrophil adhesion, neutrophil recruitment, and synthesis of interleukin 8 (IL-8) and monocyte chemoattractant protein [3].

In cotton-top tamarins, the naturally occurring primate model of UC, therapy with CDP571, a humanized monoclonal antibody to TNF-α, produces weight gain and reduction in disease activity. This led to the initial trial of anti-TNF therapy in UC: CDP571 produced a significant reduction in the Powell–Tuck score and C-reactive protein by 1 week but the effect was not sustained beyond 2 weeks [4].

Infliximab has been proposed to act in several different ways including neutralization of TNF-α, lysis of activated TNF-α-producing immune cells, and apoptosis of activated T cells and macrophages [5]. Etanercept, the recombinant TNF-α receptor, is highly effective in rheumatoid arthritis but ineffective in Crohn's disease, suggesting that the action of infliximab in Crohn's disease is unlikely to be simply via neutralization of free TNF-α. Studies of etanercept have not yet been reported in UC.

Evidence for efficacy of infliximab in UC

Open-label trials. Several small, uncontrolled studies that showed promising results are outlined in Table 20.1.

Randomized trials. Sands *et al.* [7] reported the first randomized, double blind, placebo-controlled trial of infliximab in steroid-refractory UC. Only 11 patients were

TABLE 20.1 Studies reporting use of infliximab in ulcerative colitis.

Author	Year	Number of patients	Type of study	Infliximab dose (mg/kg)	Follow-up period	Response rate (%)	Remission rate (%)	Colectomy rate (%)
Chey [6]	2001	16	Retrospective	5	>4 months	88	88	6
Sands [7]	2001	11	Randomized, double-blind placebo-controlled	5, 10, or 20	10 weeks	50 vs. 0	12.5 vs. 0	12.5 vs. 100
Kaser [8]	2001	6	Retrospective	5	5$\frac{1}{2}$ months	100	66	0
Actis [9]	2002	8	Retrospective	5	9 months	50	25	50
Su [10]	2002	27	Retrospective	5	16 months	66	44	18.5
Probert [11]	2003	43	Randomized, double-blind placebo-controlled	5 or 10	6 weeks	39 vs. 30	27 vs. 11	0 vs. 5
Gornet [12]	2003	18	Retrospective	5	24 months	50	39	7
Kohn [13]	2004	13	Retrospective	5	12 months	77	62	15
Ochsenkuhn [14]	2004	13	Randomized, double-blind steroid-controlled	5	13 weeks	83 vs. 85	50 vs. 71	NA
Armuzzi [15]	2004	9	Randomized, double-blind steroid-controlled	5	10 months	50 vs. 50	45 vs. 40	NA
Järnerot [16]	2005	43	Randomized, double-blind placebo-controlled	5	3 months	71 vs. 33	40 vs. 33	29 vs. 67
ACT I [17]	2005	364	Randomized, double-blind placebo-controlled	5* or 10+	30 weeks	52.1,* 50.8† vs. 29.8	33.9,* 36.9† vs. 15.7	NA
ACT II [18]	2005	364	Randomized, double-blind placebo-controlled	5* or 10†	30 weeks	47.1,* 60† vs. 26	25.6,* 35.8† vs. 10.6	NA

enrolled, eight of them receiving infliximab at various doses (two received 20 mg/kg, three 10 mg/kg, and three 5 mg/kg) and the remaining three received placebo. Four (50%) patients responded in the treatment group in contrast to none of those in the placebo group, all of whom underwent colectomy by 2 weeks.

In a randomized, double blind, placebo-controlled trial from Bristol, 43 patients received two infusions of infliximab or placebo at weeks 0 and 2 [11]. Non-responders were offered open-label 10 mg/kg infliximab. After 6 weeks, there were no differences in remission rates or sigmoidoscopic scores between the treatment and placebo groups. Of the 20 patients given open-label infliximab, remission was achieved in 3/11 (37%) patients who had previously received infliximab and 1/9 (11%) patients who had not. This is the only negative study of infliximab in UC so far.

Armuzzi *et al.* [15] reported a randomized, open-label, methylprednisolone-controlled trial with 10 patients in each arm in which an infliximab induction regimen (0, 2, and 6 weeks) followed by 8-weekly maintenance was as effective as corticosteroids in maintaining remission as well as permitting withdrawal of steroids. In a similar study, a 50% remission rate occurred in the infliximab group compared with a 72% rate in the corticosteroid group at week 13 [14].

In a recent randomized, double-blind trial in steroid-refractory severe or moderately severe UC, patients were randomized to infliximab or placebo either on day 4 after initiation of corticosteroid treatment if they fulfilled the index criteria for fulminant UC on day 3, or on day 6–8 if by day 5–7 they fulfilled index criteria for severe or moderately severe UC. Forty-five patients were included (24 infliximab, 21 placebo). Seven (29%) patients in the infliximab group and 14 (66%) in the placebo group had a colectomy ($P = 0.017$) within 3 months of randomization. After 3 months, eight patients (6/15 infliximab, 2/6 placebo) were in complete clinical and endoscopic remission [16].

The ACT I and II [17,18,19] trials, are very similar randomized, placebo-controlled trials. ACT I recruited patients with active UC despite use of corticosteroids and thiopurines. Three hundred and sixty-four patients with moderate to severe UC on endoscopy and a Mayo score of 6–12 were randomized to receive placebo or infliximab, 5 mg/kg or 10 mg/kg, at weeks 0, 2, and 6, and at 8-weekly intervals through to week 46. Response was defined as a decrease in the Mayo score of ≥30% and ≥3 points, accompanied by a decrease in rectal bleeding score. Remission was defined as a Mayo score ≤2 and mucosal healing

by endoscopy score. At week 30, clinical response was achieved in 52.1% in the 5 mg/kg infliximab group, 50.8% in the 10 mg/kg group vs. 29.8% in placebo-treated patients ($P < 0.001$). There was a significant difference in the remission rates at week 30 (33.9% with 5 mg/kg infliximab, 36.9% with 10 mg/kg vs. 15.7% with placebo; $P = 0.001$). Infliximab-treated patients also achieved significantly better mucosal healing and corticosteroid withdrawal rates.

The ACT II trial also randomized 364 patients with UC refractory to at least one standard therapy (5-ASA, steroids, or thiopurines) to receive infliximab 5 mg/kg, 10 mg/kg, or placebo at weeks 0, 2, 6, 14, and 22. At week 30, clinical response was achieved in 47.1% in the 5 mg/kg group, 60% in the 10 mg/kg group vs. 26% with placebo ($P < 0.001$). Remission rates at week 30 were 25.6% with 5 mg/kg infliximab, 35.8% with 10 mg/kg, and 10.6% with placebo ($P = 0.003$ and $P < 0.001$). Infliximab-treated patients again achieved better mucosal healing and corticosteroid withdrawal rates.

Safety

Infliximab is well tolerated by most patients [20]. Approximately 4% develop an infusion reaction, which may be serious in 1%. Delayed hypersensitivity reactions (serum sickness-like illness) develop 5–9 days following infusion in approximately 2%, with features that include arthralgia, myalgia, fever, skin rash, and leukocytosis. Reactivation of latent tuberculosis may occur and all patients should be screened pretreatment at least by chest X-ray. In Crohn's disease, a study of 500 treated patients has suggested a drug-associated mortality of 1% in association with a mean of 4 infusions [20]. The principal cause of mortality is infection.

In the ACT I and II trials, one patient given infliximab died of histoplasmosis, four patients had pneumonia and one tuberculosis; in addition, one patient developed optic and another a peripheral neuropathy.

Cost

For a 70-kg individual, the cost of a single 5 mg/kg infusion is approximately £1800 (US $3100). Formal health economic evaluations are yet to be conducted for infliximab in UC, but if this strategy reduces hospital admission, surgery, and time off work in addition to improving quality of life, it may well prove to be cost-effective.

Conclusions

Until recently, data about the efficacy of infliximab in UC were conflicting, possibly as a result of the differing severity of patients being studied. However, Järnerot et al.'s [16] recent controlled study in moderate to severe disease and the ACT I and II trials have established the usefulness of infliximab in UC [19]. The ACT II trial included some patients who had been treated only with mesalazine and most clinicians will consider infliximab maintenance therapy to be inappropriate on current evidence for this group of patients. However, it is likely that infliximab will rapidly become a useful alternative to cyclosporine in the treatment of moderate to severe steroid-unresponsive colitis.

References

1 D'Haens G, Lemmens L, Geboes K, et al. Intravenous cyclosporine versus intravenous corticosteroids as single therapy for severe attacks of ulcerative colitis. Gastroenterology 2001; 120: 1323–9.

2 Arts J, D'Haens G, Zeegers M, et al. Long-term outcome of treatment with intravenous cyclosporin in patients with severe ulcerative colitis. Inflamm Bowel Dis 2004; 10: 73–8.

3 Sartor RB. Cytokines in intestinal inflammation: pathophysiological and clinical considerations. Gastroenterology 1994; 106: 533–9.

4 Evans RC, Clarke L, Heath P, et al. Treatment of ulcerative colitis with an engineered human anti-TNF alpha antibody CDP571. Aliment Pharmacol Ther 1997; 11: 1031–5.

5 ten Hove T, van Montfrans C, Peppelenbosch MP, van Deventer SJ. Infliximab treatment induces apoptosis of lamina propria T lymphocytes in Crohn's disease. Gut 2002; 50: 206–11.

6 Chey WY. Infliximab for patients with refractory ulcerative colitis. Inflamm Bowel Dis 2001; 7(Suppl 1): S30–3.

7 Sands BE, Tremaine WJ, Sandborn WJ, et al. Infliximab in the treatment of severe, steroid-refractory ulcerative colitis: a pilot study. Inflamm Bowel Dis 2001; 7: 83–8.

8 Kaser A, Mairinger T, Vogel W, Tilg H. Infliximab in severe steroid-refractory ulcerative colitis: a pilot study. Wien Klin Wochenschr 2001; 113: 930–3.

9 Actis GC, Bruno M, Pinna-Pintor M, Rossini FP, Rizzetto M. Infliximab for treatment of steroid-refractory ulcerative colitis. Dig Liver Dis 2002; 34: 631–4.

10 Su C, Salzberg BA, Lewis JD, et al. Efficacy of anti-tumor necrosis factor therapy in patients with ulcerative colitis. Am J Gastroenterol 2002; 97: 2577–84.

11 Probert CS, Hearing SD, Schreiber S, et al. Infliximab in moderately severe glucocorticoid resistant ulcerative colitis: a randomised controlled trial. Gut 2003; 52: 998–1002.

12 Gornet JM, Couve S, Hassani Z, et al. Infliximab for refractory ulcerative colitis or indeterminate colitis: an open-label multicentre study. Aliment Pharmacol Ther 2003; 18: 175–81.

13 Kohn A, Prantera C, Pera A, et al. Infliximab in the treatment of severe ulcerative colitis: a follow-up study. Eur Rev Med Pharmacol Sci 2004; 8: 235–7.

14 Ochsenkuhn T, Sackmann M, Goke B. Infliximab for acute, not steroid-refractory ulcerative colitis: a randomized pilot study. Eur J Gastroenterol Hepatol 2004; 16: 1167–71.

15 Armuzzi A, De Pascalis B, Lupascu A, et al. Infliximab in the treatment of steroid-dependent ulcerative colitis. Eur Rev Med Pharmacol Sci 2004; 8: 231–3.

16 Järnerot G, Hertervig E, Friis-Liby I, et al. Infliximab as rescue therapy in severe to moderately severe ulcerative colitis: a randomized, placebo-controlled study. Gastroenterology 2005; 128: 1805–12.

17 Rutgeerts P, Feagan BG, Olson A, et al. A randomized placebo-controlled trial of infliximab therapy for active ulcerative colitis: ACT I trial. Gastroenterology 2005; Suppl 2: A-105.

18 Sandborn WJ, Racmilewitz D, Hanauer SB, et al. Infliximab induction and maintenance therapy for ulcerative colitis: the ACTII trial. Gastroenterology 2005; Suppl 2: A-104.

19 Rutgeerts P, Sandborn WJ, Feagan BG et al. Infliximab for induction and maintenance therapy for ulcerative colitis. N. Eng J Med 2005; 353: 2462–76.

20 Colombel JF, Loftus EV Jr, Tremaine WJ, et al. The safety profile of infliximab in patients with Crohn's disease: the Mayo clinic experience in 500 patients. Gastroenterology 2004; 126: 19–31.

Part 2 Medical Treatment: Making the Most of What We've Got – *Infliximab*

21 Infliximab and surgery: health or hazard?

DAVID RAMPTON

Introduction

Many patients with chronic active refractory or fistulating Crohn's disease improve substantially on treatment with infliximab [1]. Indeed, so marked is the response in a minority of patients with Crohn's that the juxtaposition of the words infliximab and surgery is almost an oxymoron. It is now clear, however, that many patients with Crohn's disease will, despite treatment with infliximab, require surgery for complications of their disease.

The aim of this chapter is to review the effects of infliximab on the number of operations needed by treated patients, on the operative findings and necessary procedures, and on postoperative complications, and recovery and recurrence rates. It will be seen that few conclusions can be reached and that further prospective controlled data are needed. One reason for this relates to case selection in reported series; these inevitably exclude patients with abscess and obstruction, because, while being common indications for surgery in Crohn's disease, they are contraindications to the use of infliximab.

Effect of infliximab on the need for surgery

In an early retrospective case-note review of 26 patients given infliximab for internal and perianal fistulous Crohn's disease, 23% showed a complete and 46% a partial response. However, 19 (73%) eventually needed or declined surgery because of a failure to respond sufficiently well [2].

Whether positive or negative, uncontrolled data are of limited value. In the controlled ACCENT I trial in patients with chronic active Crohn's disease, the effects of regular 8-weekly "scheduled" infusions of infliximab, given as maintenance therapy for a period of a year, were compared with those of "episodic" infusions, given on recurrence of symptoms [3]. Surgery was needed in 14/188 (7%) patients on episodic infliximab, a significantly greater proportion than in those given regular infusions (11/385, 3%; $P = 0.01$) [4]. In a further analysis of these data, it was found, perhaps unsurprisingly, that the need for surgery fell in proportion to the percentage time that patients were in remission [5].

TABLE 21.1 Influence of infliximab on surgery in Crohn's disease.

Effects of infliximab	References
Need for surgery-reduced	2,4–6
Operative findings/procedures-none	8–10
Operative complications-unclear	8,11–13
Postoperative recurrence-no data	–

In patients participating in the ACCENT II maintenance trial of infliximab in fistulous (largely perianal) Crohn's disease [6], surgery was needed in 45/143 (30%) patients on placebo, compared with only 10/139 (7%) of those on infliximab [7].

While the evidence thus suggests that infliximab, particularly if given regularly, does indeed reduce the need for surgery, what is its effect on the operation itself in those patients who come to surgery despite its prior use (Table 21.1)?

Effect of infliximab on operative findings and procedures

It has been suggested that prior treatment with infliximab, by reducing disease activity and even inducing mucosal healing [8], might clean the operative field and result in less extensive surgery in patients with Crohn's disease. Unfortunately, the only currently available data addressing this question are again retrospective.

In one study, a case-note review of 100 operations showed that there was no difference in the length of resection or the number of strictureplasties performed between patients pretreated with infliximab in combination with an immunomodulatory drug ($n = 22$) and those given the immunomodulator alone ($n = 72$) [9]. In two other small preliminary retrospective studies, infliximab again did not reduce the length of resection [10,11]. Clearly, further controlled studies are needed to indicate whether pretreatment with infliximab could be used to make elective surgery in Crohn's disease less radical.

Effect of infliximab on the risks of surgery

By inducing mucosal healing [8], infliximab might reduce the complications of surgery. In contrast, as a result of its immunosuppressive effects, the drug might have the opposite effect, increasing, in particular, the risk of sepsis. What do existing data show?

In one case-note review, the outcome of surgery was compared in 40 infliximab-treated patients with that in 39 infliximab-naïve controls [12]. There were no differences between the two groups in early and late minor or major complications, or in length of stay. However, infliximab was associated with a trend to an increased risk of perioperative infection (15 vs. 2%), a difference possibly attributable to the more widespread use of steroids and immunosuppressive drugs in the infliximab-treated patients (75 vs. 40%). At the Mayo Clinic, a review of 270 patients' case-notes showed no association between septic (19% patients) and non-septic (7%) complications and perioperative treatment with infliximab ($n = 52$), steroids ($n = 107$), and/or immunosuppressive drugs ($n = 105$) [13]. Indeed, in the study from Wisconsin referred to above [9], there was a lower rate of postoperative abscess, leak, and fistula in patients on immunomodulators including infliximab (6%), than in those not on such therapy (25%).

In a series from Stockholm County, of 191 patients given infliximab for Crohn's over a 2-year period, 33 needed surgery, 18 having a colectomy, seven having perianal procedures, and the remainder miscellaneous procedures [14]. Eighteen percent of the patients had "severe" complications which included delayed wound healing, anastomotic leak and sepsis, pelvic abscess, and small bowel obstruction. More alarmingly, of 8/22 patients given infliximab for refractory acute severe UC coming to colectomy, all but one had a severe complication; two older patients died of pulmonary embolus and sepsis. This operative complication rate was not replicated in another small group of Scandinavian patients with UC coming to surgery after failing to respond adequately to infliximab [15]. Further and larger studies are needed to elucidate whether the extraordinary Stockholm County surgical complication rate is indeed a feature of use of infliximab in patients with UC, or rather a reflection of its use in that series as a last ditch measure in extremely sick and frail patients in whom every possible medical therapy was being tried in an effort to avoid surgery (see Chapter 20).

Effect of infliximab on postoperative recurrence rate

There are as yet no data on whether infliximab reduces postoperative recurrence of Crohn's disease.

Conclusions

Data are so scarce, and to such an extent retrospective and uncontrolled, that it is difficult to draw firm conclusions. Furthermore, a factor complicating interpretation of existing data is that two of the most common indications for surgery in Crohn's disease, sepsis and stricturing disease, are contraindications to the use of infliximab; case series are therefore inevitably not randomly selected. Nevertheless, infliximab given as regular maintenance therapy probably does reduce the need for surgery in both chronic active and perianal fistulous Crohn's disease. In patients coming to surgery despite use of infliximab, there is no clear effect on the operative procedure needed. Similarly, there is no consensus yet on whether infliximab alters surgical complication rates, and no evidence at all on whether it might reduce postoperative recurrence. In all these contexts, prospective controlled trials are needed to define further the effects of infliximab in patients coming to surgery.

References

1 Rutgeerts P, Van Assche G, Vermeire S. Optimizing anti-TNF treatment in inflammatory bowel disease. *Gastroenterology* 2004; **126**: 1593–610.

2 Poritz LS, Rowe WA, Koltun WA. Remicade does not abolish the need for surgery in fistulising Crohn's disease. *Dis Rectum* 2002; **45**: 771–5.

3 Hanauer SB, Feagan BG, Lichtenstein GR, *et al*. Maintenance infliximab for Crohn's disease: the ACCENT I randomised trial. *Lancet* 2002; **359**: 1541–9.

4 Rutgeerts P, Feagan BG, Lichtenstein GR, *et al*. Comparison of scheduled and episodic treatment strategies of infliximab in Crohn's disease. *Gastroenterology* 2004; **126**: 402–13.

5 Lichtenstein GR, Yan S, Bala M, Hanauer SB. Remission in patients with Crohn's disease is associated with improvement in employment and quality of life and a decrease in hospitalizations and surgeries. *Am J Gastroenterol* 2004; **99**: 91–6.

6 Sands BE, Anderson FH, Bernstein CN, *et al*. Infliximab maintenance therapy for fistulising Crohn's disease. *N Engl J Med* 2004; **350**: 876–85.

7 Lichtenstein GR, Yan S, Bala M, Blank M, Sands BE. Infliximab maintenance treatment reduces hospitalizations, surgeries, and procedures in fistulizing Crohn's disease. *Gastroenterology* 2005; **128**: 862–9.

8 D'Haens G, van Deventer S, van Hogzand R, *et al*. Endoscopic and histological healing with infliximab anti-tumour necrosis factor antibodies in Crohn's disease: European multi-centre trial. *Gastroenterology* 1999; **166**: 1029–34.

9 Tay GS, Binion DG, Eastwood D, Otterson MF. Multivariant analysis suggests improved peri-operative outcome in Crohn's disease patients receiving immunomodulatory therapy after segmental resection and/or stricturoplasty. *Surgery* 2003; **134**: 565–72.

10 Marchal L, D'Haens G, Van Assche G, *et al*. Pre-operative treatment with infliximab does not reduce the length of resected bowel in Crohn's disease. *Gastroenterology* 2003; **124** (Suppl 1): A216.

11 Colombel JF, Loftus EV, Tremaine WJ, *et al*. Pre-operative infliximab does not decrease the area of resected bowel at surgery in Crohn's disease. *Gastroenterology* 2003; **124** (Suppl 1): A523.

12 Marchal L, D'Haens G, van Assche G, *et al*. The risk of post-operative complications associated with infliximab therapy for Crohn's disease: a controlled cohort study. *Aliment Pharmacol Ther* 2004; **19**: 749–54.

13 Colombel JF, Loftus EV, Tremaine WJ, *et al*. The safety profile of infliximab in patients with Crohn's disease: the Mayo Clinic experience in 500 patients. *Gastroenterology* 2004; **126**: 19–31.

14 Ljung T, Karlen P, Schmidt D, *et al*. Infliximab in inflammatory bowel disease: clinical outcome in a population based cohort from Stockholm County. *Gut* 2004; **53**: 849–53.

15 Järnerot G, Hertevig E, Friis-Liby I-L, *et al*. Infliximab as rescue therapy in severe to moderately severe ulcerative colitis: a randomized placebo-controlled study. *Gastroenterology* 2005; **128**: 1805–11.

Medical Treatment: Making the Most of What We've Got – *Nutritional therapy for Crohn's disease*

22 Nutritional therapy for Crohn's disease: is it for adults?

DONALD R DUERKSEN & CHARLES N BERNSTEIN

LEARNING POINTS

Nutritional therapy

Enteral nutrition as primary therapy in adults with Crohn's disease:

- is clinically efficacious
- avoids side-effects of immunomodulators and corticosteroids

Disadvantages of enteral therapy include:

- patients' intolerance
- the necessity for enteral access
- its high cost
- its lesser effectiveness than corticosteroids
- early relapse after discontinuation

Introduction

In 1973 Voitk *et al.* [1] noted that patients receiving nutritional therapy prior to surgery frequently went into clinical remission. This led to the hypothesis that enteral feeding may have a primary role in the treatment of active Crohn's disease, and subsequently many small prospective studies examining the effect of enteral feeding on Crohn's disease have been performed.

Nutrition therapy as an alternative to corticosteroid therapy has been embraced in pediatric gastroenterology where issues of growth and the negative effects of corticosteroids are important (see Chapter 41). In adult patients, however, there appears to be less use of nutrition as primary therapy for Crohn's disease. In this chapter, we review: (i) the mechanism of benefit; (ii) the data supporting the use of nutrition therapy to induce and maintain remission in Crohn's disease; (iii) unanswered questions regarding nutrition therapy; and (iv) provide recommendations for its role in adult patients.

Mechanism of benefit

The mechanism by which enteral nutrition induces clinical remission is unclear. Theories regarding mechanism of benefit include reduction in fat content, modification of bacterial flora, exclusion of dietary components not found in enteral formula diets, reduction in microparticles such as titanium dioxide and aluminosilicates, decreasing colonic fecal bile salt load (due to low-fat diets decreasing enterohepatic circulation of bile acids), and provision of specialized nutrients such as glutamine in chemically defined diets [2]. Bowel rest does not appear to be of major importance in effecting a remission [3]. While no differences have been demonstrated when comparing remission rates with

TABLE 22.1 Meta-analyses comparing enteral nutrition with corticosteroid treatment.

	Fernandez [10]	Griffiths [9]	Messori [11]	Heuschkel [13]	Zachos [12]
Trials (*n*)	9	8	7	5	6
Patients (*n*)	419	413	353	147	292
EN resp (%)	58	57	58	84	51
Steroid resp (%)	79	81	79	88	75
OR (steroids vs. EN)	0.35	0.35	0.35	0.95	0.34
95% CI	0.23–0.53	0.23–0.53	0.23–0.53	0.67–1.34	0.20–0.56
Intolerance	37	21		8	

EN, enteral nutrition; resp, response; OR, pooled odds ratio.

polymeric vs. elemental formulas, formulas lower in long chain triglycerides may be most beneficial [4].

Evidence for effectiveness in the treatment of active disease (Table 22.1)

There have been no large randomized, placebo-controlled studies examining the role of enteral feeding in Crohn's disease. Studies have compared enteral feeding with corticosteroids, which have a remission rate of approximately 80% [5]. Early trials examining the role of enteral nutrition in active Crohn's disease demonstrated a 60–80% remission rate [6–8]. Three meta-analyses in the mid-1990s examined trials of enteral feeding in Crohn's disease and concluded that enteral feeding was not as effective as corticosteroid therapy, but that remission rates were approximately 60%, which is considerably greater than the placebo response of 20% in drug trials for Crohn's disease [9–11]. More recently, the Cochrane collaboration has conducted a systematic review of studies examining the role of enteral feeding in active Crohn's disease and has come to similar conclusions [12]. The response rates may be different in pediatric populations where a meta-analysis showed equivalent response to steroids and improved growth in enterally fed individuals [13]. Patients whose remission has been induced by enteral nutrition have a relatively high relapse rate after discontinuation of the feed. In order to improve remission rates, exclusion diets (avoidance of foods that appear to provoke symptoms on systematic reintroduction of solid food) have been advocated [14]. However, in a double-blind, controlled trial, Pearson *et al.* [15] concluded that while food sensitivities may occur, they are variable and poorly reproducible, and do not appear to influence remission rates in Crohn's disease.

Evidence for effectiveness in the maintenance of remission

There have been even fewer studies examining the role of enteral feeding in the maintenance of remission in Crohn's disease. Two different approaches utilizing enteral feeding have been used to prevent flares of Crohn's disease. One approach allows patients to eat normally and at regular intervals, and then institutes exclusive enteral feeding for a prolonged period. Study protocols have typically allowed 3 months of ad lib diet followed by 1 month of exclusive enteral feeding [16,17]. These small controlled studies (*n* = 6, *n* = 8) have demonstrated a decreased Crohn's Disease Activity Index (CDAI), decreased steroid use, and improved growth in patients receiving intermittent exclusive enteral feeding for 1 year as compared with the year prior to enteral feeding.

An alternative, perhaps more practical approach, is to administer daily nutrition supplements to individuals who have sustained a remission with enteral feeding. Harries *et al.* [18] performed a randomized cross-over study where enterally treated patients received an average of 550 calories of an oral polymeric formula and demonstrated improved anthropometrics, serum proteins, and creatinine height index compared with those taking no supplements. In a retrospective study of patients continuing to supplement with a semi-elemental formula via nasogastric tube 4–5 times/week after remission was achieved with enteral feeding, there was an improved 1-year remission rate (57%) compared with patients not taking the supplements (21%) [19]. Moreover, in a randomized controlled study of 39 patients, there was an improved 1-year remission rate (48 vs. 22%) in patients receiving 760 kcal/day of an oral semi-elemental supplement [20]. These same investigators also demonstrated similar

1-year remission rate when supplementation with a semi-elemental and polymeric formulas were compared [21].

In summary, studies examining the role of enteral feeding in maintaining remission in Crohn's disease are smaller and less well controlled than studies assessing their role in inducing remission. The available studies suggest a benefit with either intermittent exclusive supplementation or continuous partial supplementation. Further comparative studies with medication therapies are needed to define the role of enteral nutrition in maintaining remission in Crohn's disease.

Clinical use of nutrition as primary therapy in adults

There are no published data on the frequency that nutrition therapy is used in adult patients with active Crohn's disease. However, it appears that enteral nutrition is infrequently used as a primary treatment of Crohn's disease in adults. The potential reasons for this include: (i) growth issues are less relevant than in pediatrics; (ii) the logistics of feeding tube insertion is a deterrent; (iii) more aggressive use of immunomodulators and biologic therapies; and (iv) patients' intolerance of enteral nutrition.

Unanswered questions

While there appears to be a significant clinical benefit of enteral nutrition in inducing clinical remission, there are many unanswered questions regarding this therapy; for example, the optimal enteral formula is unknown. While initially elemental formulas were considered the most likely to induce remission, polymeric formulas also seem effective. Because of small trial numbers, it is not possible to conclude, based on randomized controlled studies, whether elemental formulas offer any advantage over polymeric formulas [12]. Other questions for which there are no prospective data available are summarized in Table 22.2. Enteral formulas with low long chain triglyceride content may be the most effective in inducing a remission [4], but large randomized studies are lacking.

Conclusions

Clinical trials have demonstrated a benefit of enteral nutrition in inducing remission in patients with active Crohn's disease. In the setting of increasing therapeutic options for

TABLE 22.2 Unanswered questions regarding enteral nutrition as primary therapy for Crohn's disease.

Elemental vs. polymeric formula
Optimal amount of fat in formula
Optimal fatty acid content of formula
Mechanism of action of enteral feeding
Optimal regimen for maintaining remission
Diet during enteral feeding
Response to nutrition therapy of colonic vs. ileal disease

Crohn's with immunomodulator therapies, enteral nutrition as a primary therapy in adult is limited by intolerance as well as the necessity of enteral access in many patients.

However, there does appear to be a role for enteral therapy in adult patients with Crohn's disease. We would recommend that it be strongly considered in the following circumstances:

1 Crohn's patients requiring hospitalization for treatment of active disease

2 Patients with active Crohn's disease refractory to corticosteroids and other biologic and immunosuppressive therapies

3 Patients with active Crohn's disease and significant side-effects to corticosteroid, immunosuppressive, and biologic therapies

4 To maintain remission in recurrent relapsing Crohn's disease when other agents such as azathioprine, methotrexate, and infliximab have failed

5 Patients interested in alternatives to immunosuppressive therapy

References

1 Voitk AJ, Echave V, Feller JH, Brown RA, Gurd FN. Experience with elemental diet in the treatment of inflammatory bowel disease. Is this primary therapy? *Arch Surg* 1973; **107**: 329–33.

2 Goh J, O'Morain CA. Review article: nutrition and adult inflammatory bowel disease. *Aliment Pharmacol Ther* 2003; **17**: 307–20.

3 Greenberg GR, Fleming CR, Jeejeebhoy KN, *et al.* Controlled trial of bowel rest and nutritional support in the management of Crohn's disease. *Gut* 1988; **29**: 1309–15.

4 Gorard DA. Enteral nutrition in Crohn's disease: fat in the formula. *Eur J Gastroenterol Hepatol* 2003; **15**: 115–8.

5 Summers RW, Switz DM, Sessions JT Jr, *et al.* National Cooperative Crohn's Disease Study: results of drug treatment. *Gastroenterology* 1979; **77**: 847–69.

6 Gonzalez-Huix F, de Leon R, Fernandez-Banares F, *et al.* Polymeric enteral diets as primary treatment of active Crohn's disease: a prospective steroid controlled trial. *Gut* 1993; **34**: 778–82.

7 Lochs H, Steinhardt HJ, Klaus-Wentz B, *et al.* Comparison of enteral nutrition and drug treatment in active Crohn's disease. Results of the European Cooperative Crohn's Disease Study. IV. *Gastroenterology* 1991; **101**: 881–8.

8 O'Morain C, Segal AW, Levi AJ. Elemental diet as primary treatment of acute Crohn's disease: a controlled trial. *BMJ (Clin Res Ed)* 1984; **288**: 1859–62.

9 Griffiths AM, Ohlsson A, Sherman PM, Sutherland LR. Meta-analysis of enteral nutrition as a primary treatment of active Crohn's disease. *Gastroenterology* 1995; **108**: 1056–67.

10 Fernandez-Banares F, Cabre E, Esteve-Comas M, Gassull MA. How effective is enteral nutrition in inducing clinical remission in active Crohn's disease? A meta-analysis of the randomized clinical trials. *JPEN J Parenter Enteral Nutr* 1995; **19**: 356–64.

11 Messori A, Trallori G, D'Albasio G, *et al.* Defined-formula diets versus steroids in the treatment of active Crohn's disease: a meta-analysis. *Scand J Gastroenterol* 1996; **31**: 267–72.

12 Zachos M, Tondeur M, Griffiths AM. Enteral nutritional therapy for inducing remission of Crohn's disease. *Cochrane Database Syst Rev* 2001; **3**: CD000542.

13 Heuschkel RB, Menache CC, Megerian JT, Baird AE. Enteral nutrition and corticosteroids in the treatment of acute Crohn's disease in children. *J Pediatr Gastroenterol Nutr* 2000; **31**: 8–15.

14 Riordan AM, Hunter JO, Cowan RE, *et al.* Treatment of active Crohn's disease by exclusion diet: East Anglian multi-centre controlled trial. *Lancet* 1993; **342**: 1131–4.

15 Pearson M, Teahon K, Levi AJ, Bjarnason I. Food intolerance and Crohn's disease. *Gut* 1993; **34**: 783–7.

16 Belli DC, Seidman E, Bouthillier L, *et al.* Chronic intermittent elemental diet improves growth failure in children with Crohn's disease. *Gastroenterology* 1988; **94**: 603–10.

17 Polk DB, Hattner JA, Kerner JA Jr. Improved growth and disease activity after intermittent administration of a defined formula diet in children with Crohn's disease. *JPEN J Parenter Enteral Nutr* 1992; **16**: 499–504.

18 Harries AD, Jones LA, Danis V, *et al.* Controlled trial of supplemented oral nutrition in Crohn's disease. *Lancet* 1983; **1**: 887–90.

19 Wilschanski M, Sherman P, Pencharz P, *et al.* Supplementary enteral nutrition maintains remission in paediatric Crohn's disease. *Gut* 1996; **38**: 543–8.

20 Verma S, Kirkwood B, Brown S, Giaffer MH. Oral nutritional supplementation is effective in the maintenance of remission in Crohn's disease. *Dig Liver Dis* 2000; **32**: 769–74.

21 Verma S, Holdsworth CD, Giaffer MH. Does adjuvant nutritional support diminish steroid dependency in Crohn disease? *Scand J Gastroenterol* 2001; **36**: 383–8.

23 Trials and tribulations – interpreting clinical trials in IBD

ELIZABETH CARTY & DAVID RAMPTON

LEARNING POINTS

Interpreting clinical trials

- The heterogeneity of IBD makes the design, execution, and interpretation of clinical trials particularly difficult

- Results may be misleading because of patient groups being poorly matched by phenotype (site, extent, activity, and behavior of disease), genotype, concurrent therapy, and smoking

- Statistical design and analysis of trials is often suboptimal

- Therapeutic goals are more meaningful endpoints than changes in clinical or other scores

---

Introduction

As in other areas of medicine, the key test of the therapeutic usefulness of a potential new agent for IBD is the randomized, double-blind, controlled clinical trial [1,2]; open-label pilot studies have frequently given misleadingly positive results. In this chapter, the difficulties associated with designing, executing, and particularly interpreting clinical trials in IBD are discussed. Confounding factors common to other diseases, such as mistaken diagnosis, comorbidity, poor compliance, and inadequate dosage or duration of the test therapy, will not be considered further here. Space constraints also prevent reiteration here of the CONSORT recommendations relating to the conduct and reporting of clinical trials [3].

The difficulties in interpreting clinical trials in IBD are primarily related to the heterogeneity of the disease and its effect on trial design.

Disease heterogeneity

Site and extent of disease

In UC, differences in disease extent have important implications for the response to particular drug delivery systems. For example, topically active agents administered as suppositories or enemas will not benefit patients with extensive colitis. Such considerations are even more relevant in Crohn's disease, in which any part of the bowel, from mouth to anus, can be affected. Furthermore, perianal fistulous disease cannot be equated to that occurring within the abdominal cavity, the former responding better than the latter to, for example, infliximab (see Chapter 48). In interpreting trial results, therefore, consideration of how the study was stratified for disease site and extent is essential (see below).

Disease behavior

The natural history of Crohn's disease depends on whether it is penetrating or non-penetrating [4], the former indicating a more aggressive form of disease. Furthermore, the symptoms of Crohn's disease may be brought about by several different pathologic processes, ranging from mucosal inflammation through stricturing to abscess and fistula formation. Patients with different pathologic explanations for their presentation may show different responses to a test therapy.

Other factors

Other factors influencing patients' response include smoking habit, concurrent therapy, and the time since discontinuation of previous treatments. The immunosuppressive effectiveness of thiopurines, for example, takes up to 4 months to be lost. Factors less easy to identify in interpreting trials are aspects of gut physiology that may influence a test drug's pharmacokinetics; these may differ between patients and include malabsorption due to small intestinal disease and abnormalities of intraluminal pH and gut transit [5].

Genotype

Genetic studies in IBD are revealing genotypes that not only identify susceptibility to the disease but also determine disease behavior and response to therapy (see Chapter 24). For example, thiopurine methyl transferase (TPMT) strongly influences metabolism of the thiopurines (see Chapter 12), while the multidrug resistance gene (*MDR*) affects response to corticosteroids, methotrexate, and cyclosporine [6]. Furthermore, failure of anti-tumor necrosis factor (TNF) therapy with infliximab has been linked to polymorphisms in the TNF/lymphotoxin-α region [7] and to the pANCA+/ASCA− antibody profile [8]. Unrecognized genotypic differences between patients are likely to contribute to variability of response in therapeutic trials.

Trial design

Stratification

The heterogeneity of IBD indicates that clinical trials should be stratified prospectively to minimize differences between patients treated with novel and comparator drugs (Table 23.1). Unfortunately, trials to date have usually been too small to match patient groups satisfactorily; retrospective subgroup analysis and type 2 statistical errors have occurred too often.

Remission induction vs. remission maintenance studies

Clinical trials in IBD must be aimed clearly either at induction of or maintenance of remission. In placebo-controlled induced trials in Crohn's disease, placebo response rates may be high in patients with low serum C-reactive protein [9]. Conversely, responses to biological therapies are often best in patients with a high C-reactive protein. Restricting recruitment in induction trials to patients with

TABLE 23.1 Points to consider when reviewing clinical trials in IBD.

Disease heterogeneity
Site and extent of disease
Disease behavior (e.g. penetrating vs. non-penetrating Crohn's)
Smoking
Concurrent and recent therapies
Gut physiology affecting pharmacokinetics
Genotype affecting disease behavior and response to drugs

Trial design
Stratification
Remission induction vs. remission maintenance
Choice of comparator
Endpoints (scores vs. goals)
Statistics

a raised C-reactive protein is therefore desirable. In trials of remission maintenance, factors increasing the likelihood of relapse should be matched in the control and test groups. In Crohn's disease, for example, these include site of disease and its behavior [4], time since previous relapse or surgery, smoking habit [10], and levels of inflammatory markers such as serum C-reactive protein [11] and fecal calprotectin [12].

Choice of comparator

Argument persists as to whether a novel agent should be compared with an existing therapy or placebo. In severe active IBD, use of a placebo is unethical. Indeed, it has been argued that placebos should never be used when conventional therapy is known to be effective [13]. However, many clinicians feel that use of a placebo group in patients with mild to moderate, rather than severely active IBD, allows clearer assessment of the therapeutic potential of a new agent. A further potential advantage of placebo-controlled studies is that the size of the trial can be smaller than when standard comparator therapy is used, because the difference sought in power calculations will be larger. This results in exposure of fewer subjects to a potentially ineffective and/or toxic novel agent. When placebos are used, clear withdrawal criteria must be established. In turn, analysis of results must be on an intention-to-treat rather than per protocol basis.

Endpoints

Objective measurement of disease activity and definition of outcome is contentious, particularly in Crohn's disease [2].

There is a lack of widely accepted hard endpoints, death fortunately being too rare in either form of IBD to be a useful measure of drug efficacy. A range of less clear-cut outcome measures has instead been employed.

Clinical activity indices

There are several clinical activity indices for both UC [14,15] and Crohn's disease [16,17]. Most combine subjective and objective measurements to produce a score; these range from symptoms recorded in patients' daily diaries to blood results and mucosal appearances at endoscopy. The multiplicity of such scores indicates their inadequacy. Difficulties include the unreliability of symptom recording by patients, inappropriate weighting of certain variables, the poor correlation between clinical scores and disease activity assessed biochemically and endoscopically [18], and problems in defining remission and in identifying clinical as opposed to statistically significant improvement.

Quality of life scores

Quality of life scores have been used to assess response in clinical trials in IBD [19]. To date, however, it is widely felt that these serve best as a secondary rather than primary outcome measure [2].

Therapeutic goals

Several well-defined and clinically relevant goals have been proposed as preferable to clinical scoring. In Crohn's disease, these include reduction of steroid dosage, avoidance of surgery, and closure of fistulae, although this may mask underlying abscess formation.

Laboratory measures of inflammation

Unfortunately, although serum C-reactive protein, orosomucoid, erythrocyte sedimentation rate (ESR), and platelet count correlate directly and hemoglobin and albumin indirectly with disease activity in IBD, no single or set of blood tests is reliable as a measure of response to novel therapies. Four day fecal excretion of indium-labeled leukocytes provides a better guide [20], but is cumbersome and involves radio-isotopes. Fecal calprotectin is a promising alternative [12].

Mucosal appearance and histology

The mucosal appearances at ileocolonoscopy can be assessed and scored at least semi-objectively in ulcerative and Crohn's colitis [18,21], and at the ileocolonic anastomosis after surgery [22]. However, colonoscopic assessment of the mucosal response has not been widely undertaken in clinical trials because the procedure is neither pleasant nor entirely safe, particularly in active colitis. Perhaps the wireless endoscopy capsule (see Chapter 1) may prove useful in trials in non-stricturing small bowel Crohn's in the future.

No score to assess mucosal inflammation microscopically has achieved widespread usage [20]. In Crohn's disease, the patchy distribution of inflammation leads to a risk of sampling error.

Statistical considerations

Detailed discussion of potential statistical defects in trial design and analysis is beyond the scope of this chapter. However, all too commonly, trials in IBD are compromised by, for example, inadequate (or even absent) power calculations, under-powering, failure to use odds ratios and confidence limits to compare treatments, post hoc subgroup analysis, and inappropriate use of multiple uncorrected retrospective comparisons, of one-tailed P values and of parametric rather than non-parametric statistics.

Conclusions

To address some of the problems outlined above, the International Organization of Inflammatory Bowel Disease has recently outlined the current position with respect to activity indices, definition of patient subpopulations, treatment indications, and efficacy endpoints in trials of patients with Crohn's disease [2]. If this consensus is adhered to in trials of patients with Crohn's, and if a similar one is developed for UC, inconsistencies between trials may be reduced and comparisons facilitated. Meanwhile, clinicians must remain alert to the many pitfalls associated with the interpretation of clinical trials in IBD.

References

1 Feagan BG, McDonald JW, Koval JJ. Therapeutics and inflammatory bowel disease: a guide to the interpretation of randomized controlled trials. *Gastroenterology* 1996; **110**: 275–83.

2 Sandborn WJ, Feagan BG, Hanauer SB, *et al.* A review of activity indices and efficacy endpoints for clinical trials of medical therapy in adults with Crohn's disease. *Gastroenterology* 2002; **122**: 512–30.

3 Moher D, Schulz KF, Altman DG. The CONSORT statement: revised recommendations for improving the quality of reports of parallel-group randomised trials. *Lancet* 2001; **357**: 1191–4.

4 Brzinski A, Lashner BA. Natural history of Crohn's disease. In: Allan RN, Rhodes JM, *et al.* (eds.) *Inflammatory Bowel Diseases*, 3rd edn. Churchill Livingstone, 1997: 475–86.

5 Nugent SG, Kumar D, Rampton DS, Evans DF. Intestinal luminal pH in inflammatory bowel disease: possible determinants and implications for therapy with aminosalicylates and other drugs. *Gut* 2001; **48**: 571–7.

6 Tremaine WJ. Failure to yield: drug resistance in inflammatory bowel disease. *Gastroenterology* 2002; **122**: 1165–7.

7 Taylor KD, Plevy SE, Yang H, *et al.* ANCA pattern and LTA haplotype relationship to clinical responses to anti-TNF antibody treatment in Crohn's disease. *Gastroenterology* 2001; **120**: 1347–55.

8 Esters N, Vermeire S, Joossens S, *et al.* Serological markers for prediction of response to anti-tumor necrosis factor treatment in Crohn's disease. *Am J Gastroenterol* 2002; **97**: 1458–62.

9 Schreiber S, Rutgeerts P, Fedorak RN, *et al.* A randomized, placebo-controlled trial of certolizmab pegol (CDP870) for treatment of Crohn's disease. *Gastroenterology* 2005; **129**: 807–18.

10 Sutherland LR, Ramcharan S, Bryant H, Fick G. Effect of cigarette smoking on recurrence of Crohn's disease. *Gastroenterology* 1990; **98**: 1123–8.

11 Belluzzi A, Brignola C, Campieri M, *et al.* Effect of an enteric-coated fish-oil preparation on relapses in Crohn's disease. *N Engl J Med* 1996; **334**: 1557–60.

12 Tibble JA, Sigthorsson G, Bridger S, Fagerhol MK, Bjarnason I. Surrogate markers of intestinal inflammation are predictive of relapse in patients with inflammatory bowel disease. *Gastroenterology* 2000; **119**: 15–22.

13 Rothman KJ, Michels KB. The continuing unethical use of placebo controls. *N Engl J Med* 1994; **331**: 394–8.

14 Powell-Tuck J, Bown RL, Lennard-Jones JE. A comparison of oral prednisolone given as single or multiple daily doses for active proctocolitis. *Scand J Gastroenterol* 1978; **13**: 833–7.

15 Walmsley RS, Ayres RC, Pounder RE, Allan RN. A simple clinical colitis activity index. *Gut* 1998; **43**: 29–32.

16 Best WR, Becktel JM, Singleton JW, Kern F Jr. Development of a Crohn's disease activity index. National Cooperative Crohn's Disease Study. *Gastroenterology* 1976; **70**: 439–44.

17 Harvey RF, Bradshaw JM. A simple index of Crohn's disease activity. *Lancet* 1980; **1**: 514.

18 Cellier C, Sahmoud T, Froguel E, *et al.* Correlations between clinical activity, endoscopic severity, and biological parameters in colonic or ileocolonic Crohn's disease. A prospective multicentre study of 121 cases. The Groupe d'Etudes Therapeutiques des Affections Inflammatoires Digestives. *Gut* 1994; **35**: 231–5.

19 Irvine EJ, Feagan B, Rochon J, *et al.* Quality of life: a valid and reliable measure of therapeutic efficacy in the treatment of inflammatory bowel disease. Canadian Crohn's Relapse Prevention Trial Study Group. *Gastroenterology* 1994; **106**: 287–96.

20 Saverymuttu SH, Camilleri M, Rees H, *et al.* Indium-111 granulocyte scanning in the assessment of disease extent and activity in inflammatory bowel disease: a comparison of colonoscopy, histology and fecal indium-111 excretion. *Gastroenterology* 1986; **90**: 1121–8.

21 Baron J, Connell A, Leonard-Jones A. Variation between observers in describing mucosal changes in proctocolitis. *BMJ* 1964; **1**: 89–92.

22 Rutgeerts P, Geboes K, Vantrappen G, *et al.* Predictability of the postoperative course of Crohn's disease. *Gastroenterology* 1990; **99**: 956–63.

24 Genetics – clinical and therapeutic applications

MARK TREMELLING & MILES PARKES

> ### LEARNING POINTS
>
> **Genetics**
>
> - Genetics is defining distinct disease subsets in IBD, particularly in Crohn's disease
>
> - To date, *NOD2/CARD15*, *IBD5/OCTN*, *MDR*, and genes in the HLA region have been confirmed as increasing the risk of IBD
>
> - It is possible that these and other genetic advances will alter disease management in the future
>
> - Advances in pharmacogenetics have already altered disease management and are likely to continue to do so

Introduction

Since the publication of the first IBD genome scans in 1996, the field of IBD genetics has made substantial progress – arguably more so than in any equivalent complex disease. Even with the current incomplete state of knowledge, genetic studies and their sequelae have provided some of the first truly penetrating insights into pathogenic mechanisms in IBD.

To what extent does this have practical implications? It may be too early to ask this question – both because the field has much more to yield and because the ramifications of the first major breakthrough, *NOD2*, have yet to be worked through fully. Furthermore, any clinical benefit will not be *fully* realized until years after its scientific implications have been completely elucidated. However, even now

it is clear that the genetic dissection of IBD will ultimately lead to a quantum leap forward in the way we understand and manage these diseases.

In this chapter, we briefly summarize genetic progress in IBD to date, and then describe the areas in which the practical and clinical impact is most likely to be felt

Broad linkage regions resolved to level of association and gene identification

1 *NOD2/CARD15* was reported in 2001 to be the Crohn's disease predisposing gene in the IBD1 linkage, having been identified using both a classic positional cloning strategy and a candidate gene approach [1,2]. The three common and many rare variants that predispose to Crohn's disease cluster around the leucine-rich region [3] subsequently shown to be important in the intracellular binding of muramyl dipeptide (MDP) ubiquitous in bacterial cell walls. Being heterozygous for one of these variants gives a 1–3 times increased risk of Crohn's disease, and carrying two copies confers an up to 40-fold risk.

2 *IBD5/OCTN:* Crohn's disease linkage on chromosome 5 has been fine-mapped to reveal a widely replicated 250 kb "IBD5 risk haplotype" [4], recently also implicated in UC. This association may be due to variants in the *OCTN* gene cluster which encode solute transporters [5].

3 *MDR* (multidrug resistance protein) is implicated as a positional candidate gene on chromosome 7 linkage, and by *mdr1* mouse knock-out developing IBD-like illness. MDR encodes p-glycoprotein 170, an ATP-dependent transmembrane transporter which pumps amphiphillic

and hydrophobic molecules, including bacterial antigens, out of cells. Its complex association with UC awaits full characterization [6].

4 *HLA* had been investigated as a candidate locus before linkage studies also firmly implicated this region. The most replicated associations are HLA DRB1*0103 with severe UC and extra-intestinal manifestations [7–9], and TNF –857 with IBD overall [10]: full linkage disequilibrium patterns around these alleles await characterization.

At least five more strong and replicated linkages await resolution, and imminent genome-wide association scans are likely to be more powerful still.

Assessing the impact

By what yardstick can one measure the impact of IBD genetics? It is perhaps helpful to consider the original and radical goals, and assess the extent to which the field has measured up – in particular by asking whether IBD genetics has:

1 redefined Crohn's disease and UC, and delineated the heterogeneity within these categories according to prognosis and treatment response

2 provided potential for diagnostic tests

3 produced insights into the pathogenesis of IBD, including environmental triggers

4 lead to the development of rational, individualized therapies

Heterogeneity within Crohn's disease and UC

Clinicians will recognize distinct patterns of distribution and behavior within Crohn's disease and UC, often breeding true in multiply affected families and indicating a genetic basis. With identification of *NOD2* and HLA risk alleles the genetic determinants of some of this heterogeneity are beginning to be characterized.

NOD2 mutations have been found in all forms of Crohn's disease, but a consistent pattern is of association with young age of onset and ileal disease [11,12]. Stricturing behavior and need for surgery may also be associated, although are probably secondary to ileal involvement – and disease behavior is known to be an unstable phenotype compared to extent. Within the HLA region, the rare DRB1*0103 allele is reproducibly associated with extensive UC and the need for colectomy as well as with IBD-associated large joint

arthropathy, erythema nodosum, and iritis [9]. At an individual level, DRB1*0103 is too rare to be clinically useful (present in 3% controls vs. 14% UC requiring surgery) [8]. However, it does illustrate that when more "severity" alleles have been identified and genotyping is readily available (see below) it might be possible to identify prospectively individuals with an adverse prognosis and manage their IBD differently, perhaps with earlier use of more aggressive medical therapy.

To date, no genetically stratified drug trials have been reported in IBD but, with knowledge of *NOD2* and its fundamental role in disease pathogenesis, these should not be long coming. Industry cannot afford to risk rejecting a useful but genotype-specific therapy because of failure to account for known heterogeneity within Crohn's disease, and as more genes are identified, such stratification will become more common.

Genetics has not yet redefined Crohn's disease (e.g. "*NOD2* positive Crohn's disease" vs. "*NOD2* negative Crohn's disease"), but if distinct prognoses or treatment response profiles are identified for genetically determined subgroups then it is likely that at least some reappraisal will occur. One of the first edifices to fall might be Crohn's colitis, which the emerging genetic evidence indicates is likely to be different pathogenetically to small bowel Crohn's disease.

Genetics to diagnose IBD?

The reality is that at a population level genetics has poor predictive value. Thus, while *NOD2* is likely to be the strongest IBD susceptibility gene, of all individuals carrying two mutant *NOD2* genes only 4% will develop Crohn's disease. Furthermore, the IBD5 risk haplotype, including OCTN risk alleles, are carried by 46% of healthy individuals (vs. 53% affecteds), and the TNF –857 "risk" allele is in fact the common allele, present in 90% of controls (vs. 92% affecteds). While the ability to risk stratify will increase as more genes are found and factored into the equation, genetics alone is unlikely to provide a pure diagnostic test given the major environmental influence and the high frequency of many "risk alleles" in the general population.

Individuals whose risk is magnified by virtue of a high "load" of genetic risk alleles may in the future be identified as suitable for risk modification by use of, for example, vaccines to as-yet unidentified environmental triggers. Clearly, this is highly speculative.

What has been the impact on understanding of IBD pathogenesis?

Discovery of *NOD2* was of immediate interest given its homology to toll-like receptors (TLR) and hence a putative role in bacterial recognition and innate immunity via activation of NFκB pathways. While this was consistent with prior understanding of the importance of gut flora in Crohn's disease pathogenesis, it has confounded expectations by the fact that mutations cause *loss* of function (i.e. less NFκB in response to MDP stimulation *in vitro*) and that the gene is only expressed intracellularly – in monocytes, Paneth cells, and epithelial cells [1,2].

Although conflicting functional evidence has emerged, progress is now being made towards resolving these apparent contradictions. Mouse models have shown interplay between *NOD2* and TLR, with the former modulating response through TLR pathways, possibly varying according to the stimulating antigen [13,14]. Although *NOD2* knock-out mice do not develop intestinal inflammation, defensin production is lower and they are much more susceptible to infection with the intracellular organism *Listeria*, given orally, than wild-type mice.

In human peripheral blood mononuclear cells, MDP induced little TNF-α/IL-1 but strong IL-8 chemokine secretion, and markedly up-regulated TNFα/IL-1 in response to TLR ligands. These effects were not seen in cells from *NOD2* double mutants and it is postulated that absence of this up-regulating "priming signal" may lead to failure of the innate immune system to clear pathogens and a subsequently abnormal adaptive immune response [15].

Although the genetic data are yet incomplete, functional studies in progress regarding OCTN are revealing interesting effects on transport of substrates, such as ergothioneine, with possible roles in oxidative stress.

One of the strengths of the genetic approach is that it asks difficult and often unexpected questions of cell biologists and immunologists. Finding the answers to these questions will reveal fundamental insights into the pathogenesis of IBD.

Is individualized therapy or gene therapy a realistic prospect?

This depends on a number of factors. Delineating heterogeneity within Crohn's disease and UC is one aspect of this but even genetically defined disease subgroups may not be homogenous in terms of treatment response or intolerance.

The latter may be determined by an entirely separate group of genes involved in, for example, drug metabolism (see Chapter 12). It is in the convergence of data regarding these different aspects that individualized therapy may emerge. Another assumption is that the relevant genotyping will be impossibly expensive – but with costs plummeting and chip technology advancing (a customized "IBD chip" to genotype all relevant loci in individuals presenting with IBD symptoms is entirely conceivable), this is unlikely to be a barrier.

Gene therapy for human disease has been beset by problems. Some encouragement for this approach comes from successful treatment in mouse models of IBD using IL-10 delivered in an adenoviral vector [16]. However, translation of gene therapy into the IBD clinical arena remains a distant prospect.

Conclusions

Although genetics has yet to have a great effect on clinical management of IBD (aside perhaps from TPMT testing), it is already making a major impact on the science of IBD: the prospects are bright for future progress both here and into the clinical arena. Ultimately, although genetics may not give us all the answers, it will at least tell us the right questions to ask.

References

1 Hugot JP, Chamaillard M, Zouali H, *et al.* Association of NOD2 leucine-rich repeat variants with susceptibility to Crohn's disease. *Nature* 2001; **411**: 599–603.

2 Ogura Y, Bonen DK, Inohara N, *et al.* A frameshift mutation in NOD2 associated with susceptibility to Crohn's disease. *Nature* 2001; **411**: 603–6.

3 Lesage S, Zouali A, Cezard J, *et al.* CARD15/NOD2 mutational analysis and genotype-phenotype correlation in 612 patients with IBD. *Am J Hum Genet* 2002; **70**: 845.

4 Rioux JD, Daly MJ, Silverberg MS, *et al.* Genetic variation in the 5q31 cytokine gene cluster confers susceptibility to Crohn disease. *Nat Genet* 2001; **29**: 223–8.

5 Peltekova VD, Wintle RF, Rubin LA, *et al.* Functional variants of OCTN cation transporter genes are associated with Crohn disease. *Nat Genet.* 2004; **36**: 471–5.

6 Ho GT, Nimmo E, Tenesa A, *et al.* Allelic variations of the multidrug resistance gene determine susceptibility and disease behavior in ulcerative colitis. *Gastroenterology* 2005; **128**: 288–9.

7 Satsangi J, Welsh KI, Bunce M, *et al.* Contribution of genes of the major histocompatibility complex to susceptibility and disease phenotype in inflammatory bowel disease. *Lancet* 1996; **347**: 1212–7.

8 Roussomoustakaki M, Satsangi J, Welsh K, *et al.* Genetic markers may predict disease behavior in patients with ulcerative colitis. *Gastroenterology* 1997; **112**: 1845–53.

9 Orchard TR, Thiyagaraja S, Welsh KI, *et al.* Clinical phenotype is related to HLA genotype in the peripheral arthropathies of inflammatory bowel disease. *Gastroenterology* 2000; **118**: 274–8.

10 van Heel DA, Udalova IA, De Silva AP, *et al.* Inflammatory bowel disease is associated with a TNF polymorphism that affects an interaction between the OCT1 and NFκB transcription factors. *Hum Mol Genet* 2002; **11**: 1281–9.

11 Ahmad T, Armuzzi A, Bunce M, *et al.* The molecular classification of the clinical manifestations of Crohn's disease. *Gastroenterology* 2002; **122**: 854–66.

12 Economou M, Trikalinos T, Loizou K, *et al.* Differential effects of NOD2 variants on Crohn's disease risk and phenotype in diverse populations: a metaanalysis. *Am J Gastroenterol* 2004; **99**: 2393–404.

13 Kobayashi K, Chamaillard M, Ogura Y, *et al.* Nod2-dependent regulation of annate and adaptive immunity in the intestinal tract. *Science* 2005; **304**: 731–4.

14 Watanabe T, Kitani A, Murray P, *et al.* NOD2 is a negative regulator of Toll-like receptor 2-mediated T helper type 1 responses. *Nat Immunol* 2004; **5**: 800–8.

15 van Heel D, Ghosh S, Butler M, *et al.* Muramyl dipeptide and toll-like receptor sensitivity in NOD2-associated Crohn's disease. *Lancet* 2005; **365**: 1794–6.

16 Lindsay JO, Ciesielski CJ, Scheinin T, *et al.* Local delivery of adenoviral vectors encoding murine interleukin 10 induces colonic interleukin 10 production and is therapeutic for murine colitis. *Gut* 2003; **52**: 363–9.

25 Probiotics – separating science from snakeoil

FERGUS SHANAHAN & JOHN KEOHANE

LEARNING POINTS

Probiotics

- Not all probiotics are the same; they have variable efficacy in different indications

- While there is evidence for efficacy in animal models of IBD and in human "pouchitis," the role of probiotics as a primary therapy for Crohn's disease or UC is unproven

- There is a critical need for verification of the quality, shelf-life, composition, and stability of many probiotic preparations

- Even if naturally occurring probiotics have suboptimal efficacy in IBD, gentically engineered organisms to deliver anti-inflammatory molecules to the diseased mucosa are promising

Introduction

A probiotic is usually defined as a live microorganism that, when consumed in adequate amounts, confers a health benefit on the host. A prebiotic is a non-digestible food ingredient (frequently an oligosaccharide) that can beneficially influence the health of the host by selectively altering the enteric flora, and a synbiotic is a mixture of pro- and prebiotics. In practice, the definition of probiotics is continually under revision as more is discovered about the mechanism of host–flora interactions. For practical purposes, probiotics are most simply defined in operational terms as commensal organisms that can be harnessed for therapeutic benefit.

Unfortunately, the field of probiotics research has been clouded and probably hindered by exaggerated or unsubstantiated claims for efficacy in a myriad of disorders with little supporting evidence. Simplistic notions of "bowel cleansing" as portrayed in the popular press are conceptually appealing, attractive to patients, and readily exploited commercially. However, the field is beginning to attract rigorous scientific input and two important points have become clear. First, not all probiotics are the same and it is naive to assume that probiotic organisms will behave similarly in different clinical settings. Second, probiotic action is more complex than simply replacing "bad" bacteria with "good" bacteria. Thus, the impact of probiotics or prebiotics is not simply ecologic ("good" for "bad" bacteria) and almost certainly reflects a change in prokaryotic–eukaryotic signaling [1].

The appeal of probiotics to the lay public is the promise of "bugs instead of drugs." The emphasis has generally been on live microorganisms, but with clarification of mechanisms of action and identification of therapeutic probiotic metabolites, a program of "bugs to drugs" discovery may yield a new generation of biologic control agents that will challenge current definitions. For this reason, the more inclusive term *pharmabiotics* may be more useful in the future.

Background and rationale for probiotics in IBD

Disturbances of host–flora interactions have been implicated in the pathogenesis of IBD. Therefore, manipulation of the enteric flora might be anticipated to emerge as a plausible therapeutic option. Comparative studies using germ-free and conventionally colonized animals have established that the intestinal microflora is required for optimal development of mucosal and submucosal structure and function. Regulatory influences of the flora on the intestine range from priming mucosal immunity to promotion of gastrointestinal motility, secretory and absorptive capacity, and also include a variety of metabolic properties such as production of folate and B vitamins. In addition, bacterial colonization of the gut has extra-intestinal effects including the regulation of fat deposition. Collectively, the enteric flora comprises over 400 different bacterial strains, accounts for about 1–2 kg body weight in adult humans, and has a metabolic activity equivalent to a hidden inner organ comparable with that of the liver [1].

It appears that the flora exerts a continual regulatory influence on mucosal homeostasis; disruption of this host–flora dialogue renders the intestine vulnerable to injury. Thus, the bacterial flora may be viewed as an important health asset which occasionally may become a liability by participating in the pathogenesis of IBD in genetically susceptible individuals. It follows from first principles that any strategy that promotes microbial assets and/or offsets liabilities represents a therapeutic option. Therein lies the rationale for probiotic/prebiotics and other forms of therapeutic manipulation of gut flora.

Criteria for selecting a probiotic

Probiotics have traditionally been selected from the genera *Lactobacillus* and *Bifidobacterium*, although other bacteria including *Escherichia coli* and non-bacterial organisms such as *Saccharomyces boulardii* have been selected for probiotic potential. Criteria for selection of microorganisms as candidate probiotics include proliferative capacity and capability of transit and survival within the gastrointestinal tract. This requires relative resistance to acid and bile. Most important are safety criteria. Lactobacilli and bifidobacteria have a long history of usage without hazard. In rare or exceptional circumstances, lactobacilli have been linked with systemic translocation but there appears to be no increased frequency of bacteremia with increased usage of probiotics.

Guidelines for probiotic strain identification and functional characterization have been generated by the Joint Food and Agricultural Organization (FAO) of the United Nations and the World Health Organisation (WHO) [2].

At present, there is no biomarker from *in vitro* studies that reliably predicts function *in vivo* for putative probiotic in any clinical condition. It is unlikely that a single microbial agent or microbial product will be effective in each of the diverse clinical conditions for which probiotic efficacy has been claimed. Furthermore, in light of increasing understanding of pharmacogenomics and nutrigenomics, individual variability in composition of the enteric flora might need to be considered as a determining factor for optimal probiotic strain selection. Without resolution of these pivotal issues, probiotic therapy will struggle to become established in the arena of evidence-based medicine.

Mode of action

Probiotics probably exert their beneficial effects by mimicking normal host–flora interactions [1]. Oral consumption of probiotics is associated with immune engagement and demonstrable systemic immunologic changes [3,4]. Modern techniques, such as laser capture microdissection and gene array analysis of gnotobiotic animals, are now being deployed to probe the molecular events underpinning the regulatory signaling from the lumen and promise to reveal new molecular targets for the design of future therapeutics [5]. Incoming bacterial signals include secreted chemoattractants, such as the formylated peptide f-met-leu-phe, cellular constituents such as lipopolysaccharide and peptidoglycans, and bacterial nucleic acids (CpG DNA). Discrimination of pathogens vs. commensals by the host is mediated, in part, by pattern recognition receptors such as Toll-like receptors (TLRs) which are present on epithelial and immune (dendritic) cells. Engagement of TLRs by ligands from the commensal flora appears to be required for optimal mucosal and immune development and for responses to episodic challenge with pathogens and other forms of injury [6].

Probiotics can also mimic other aspects of the commensal flora including competitive antagonism against pathogens and production of antimicrobial factors such as bacteriocins and other metabolites [7].

Testing the theory – is there evidence for efficacy?

The most compelling evidence for efficacy of probiotics in any clinical condition is in the setting of enteric infections and postantibiotic syndromes where their role is supported by several recent meta-analyses and a favorable Cochrane review [8,9]. There is also a growing body of support for some but not all probiotics in irritable bowel syndrome and this may involve modulation of cytokines [10].

In IBD, there have been many reports showing the prophylactic effects of probiotic feeding in experimental animal models of IBD [1]. In humans with IBD, the most impressive evidence for the role of probiotics has been in patients with pouchitis where the cocktail of eight bacterial strains (VSL3) has been deployed [11,12]. In UC, a strain of *E. coli* Nissl 1917 has been reported to be equivalent in efficacy to mesalazine in maintenance of remission [13]. Efficacy with other agents including a synbiotic in acute UC has also been reported [14]. In patients with Crohn's disease, the role of probiotics is less clear, with recent negative results in the postoperative setting [15]. It seems the inflammatory process may be too aggressive to expect significant efficacy from probiotics as a primary therapy for Crohn's disease.

Problems, pitfalls, and unresolved issues

The interpretation of different studies of probiotics in IBD and other clinical conditions is confounded by the absence of comprehensive comparisons of probiotic performance using different strains in different specific disease states. More importantly, there are several problems and pitfalls that need resolution before guidelines for routine clinical use of probiotics in Crohn's disease or UC can be formulated.

First, the consumer would benefit from stringent regulation of unsubstantiated health claims on labels of some commercially available probiotic products. Second, there is no international standardized system for verification of probiotic product quality in terms of composition, stability, and shelf-life. Indeed, variability in quality may account for some of the apparent discrepancies between clinical experience and reported efficacy in clinical trials for some probiotics. Third, the dose range for humans has not been determined and may vary with different probiotics, in part influenced by survival during gastric transit. In addition, the optimal vehicle and formulation for delivery of probiotics may be an important variable [3], but remains to be defined in many cases. Fourth, variability in composition of the flora throughout the gut confounds the notion that any given strategy for therapeutic manipulation of the enteric flora will be equally effective for diseases that affer-

ent parts of either the small or large bowel. For example, the same probiotic may not be equally suited to different subsets of patients with Crohn's disease, depending on the topographic distribution of the lesions. Fifth, while the use of combinations of probiotic strains may be an appropriate strategy to accommodate different clinical indications and individual variations in host flora, synergy rather than antagonism within any given cocktail of bacteria needs to be demonstrated.

Finally, the use of genetically engineered rather than naturally occurring probiotics has emerged as a plausible strategy to enhance therapeutic efficacy and to deliver anti-inflammatory molecules to the inflamed mucosa. Advantages include direct delivery, avoidance of systemic toxicity, and lower production costs. Proof of principle has already been demonstrated in a murine model of IBD given *Lactococcus lactis* that was engineered to produce either an anti-inflammatory cytokine [16] or trefoil factor to promote healing [17]. Although the use of genetically modified (GM) organisms raises a public health concern, the insertion of the therapeutic transgene into the thymidylate synthase locus means that the GM organism becomes dependent on the enteric microenvironment for a source of thymine or thymidine and this limits its viability when shed in the feces [18]. Controversy surrounding GM foods is widely pervasive, but the concept of engineered probiotics ("turbo probiotics") is likely to be more acceptable, particularly to those who suffer from disabling conditions such as IBD.

References

1 Shanahan F. Pathophysiological basis and prospects for probiotic therapy in inflammatory bowel disease. *Am J Physiol Gastrointest Liver Physiol* 2005; **288**: G417–21.

2 Report of a Joint FAO/WHO Expert Consultation (2001) Health and nutritional properties of probiotics in food including powder milk and live lactic acid bacteria. http://www.fao.org/es/ESN/Probio/report. Pdf

3 Collins JK, Murphy L, Morrissey D, *et al.* A randomised controlled trial of a probiotic *Lactobacillus* strain in healthy adults: assessment of its delivery, transit, and influence on microbial flora and enteric immunity. *Microb Ecol Health Dis* 2002; **14**: 81–89.

4 McCarthy J, O'Mahony L, O'Callaghan L, *et al.* Double blind, placebo controlled trial of two probiotic strains in interleukin 10 knockout mice and mechanistic link with cytokine balance. *Gut* 2003; **52**: 975–80.

5 Hooper LV, Midvedt T, Gordon JI. How host–microbial interactions shape the nutrient environment of the mammalian intestine. *Annu Rev Nutr* 2002; **22**: 283–307.

6 Rakoff-Nahoum S, Paglino J, Eslami-Varzaneh F, Edberg S, Medzhitov R. Recognition of commensal microflora by toll-like receptors is required for intestinal homeostasis. *Cell* 2004; **118**: 229–41.

7 Flynn S, Van Sinderen D, Thornton GM, *et al.* Characterization of the genetic locus responsible for the production of ABP-118, a novel bacteriocin produced by the probiotic bacterium *Lactobacillus salivarius subsp. Salivarius* UCC118. *Microbiology* 2002; **148**: 973–84.

8 Dunne C, Shanahan F. Role of probiotics in the treatment of intestinal infections and inflammation. *Curr Opin Gastroenterol* 2002; **18**: 40–5.

9 Allen SJ, Okoko B, Martinez E, Gregorio G, Dans LF. Probiotics for treating infectious diarrhea. *Cochrane Database Syst Rev* 2004; **2**: CD003048.

10 O'Mahony L, McCarthy J, Kelly P, *et al.* A randomized, placebo-controlled, double blind comparison of the probiotic bacteria *Lactobacillus* and *Bifidobacterium* in irritable bowel syndrome. *Gastroenterology* 2005; **128**: 541–51.

11 Gionchetti P, Rizzello F, Helwig U, *et al.* Prophylaxis of pouchitis onset with probiotic therapy: a double-blind, placebo-controlled trial. *Gastroenterology*. 2003; **124**: 1202–9.

12 Mimura T, Rizzello F, Helwig U, *et al.* Once daily high dose probiotic therapy (VSL#3) for maintaining remission in recurrent or refractory pouchitis. *Gut* 2004; **53**: 108–14.

13 Kruis W, Fric P, Pokrotnies J, *et al.* Maintaining remission of ulcerative colitis with the probiotic *Escherichia coli* Nissle 1917 is as effective as with standard mesalazine. *Gut* 2004; **53**: 1617–23.

14 Furrie E, Macfarlane S, Kennedy A, *et al.* Synbiotic therapy (*Bifidobacterium longum*/Synergy 1) initiates resolution of inflammation in patients with active ulcerative colitis: a randomized controlled pilot trial. *Gut* 2005; **54**: 242–9.

15 Prantrera C, Scribano ML, Falasco G, Andreoli A, Luzi C. Ineffectiveness of probiotics in preventing recurrence after curative resection for Crohn's disease: a randomized controlled trial with *Lactobacillus GG*. *Gut* 2002; **51**: 405–9.

16 Steidler L, Hans W, Schotte L, *et al.* Treatment of murine colitis by *Lactococcus lactis* secreting interleukin-10. *Science* 2000; **289**: 1352–5.

17 Vandenbroucke K, Hans W, Van Huysse J, *et al.* Active delivery of trefoil factors by genetically modified *Lactococcus lactis* prevents and heals acute colitis in mice. *Gastroenterology* 2004; **127**: 502–13.

18 Steidler L, Neirynck S, Huyghebaert N, *et al.* Biological containment of genetically modified *Lactococcus lactis* for intestinal delivery of human interleukin 10. *Nat Biotechnol* 2003; **21**: 785–9.

Medical Treatment: What's Round the Corner?

Worms

DAVID GRUNKEMEIER & R BALFOUR SARTOR

LEARNING POINTS

Worms

- Treatment with *Trichuris suis* ova in UC and Crohn's disease is safe and well tolerated

- Controlled data on efficacy are, as yet, sparse and weak

- Larger controlled studies are required before *T. suis* can be recommended outside clinical trials

- Investigation of the use of helminths to treat IBD may yield other therapeutic species

Introduction

Idiopathic IBD, UC and Crohn's disease, like many immunologically mediated inflammatory disorders, including asthma, rheumatoid arthritis, juvenile onset diabetes, and multiple sclerosis, are primarily conditions of Western industrialized populations with a markedly increased incidence in the second half of the 20th century. These epidemiologic features have fueled speculation that environmental factors may contribute to the pathogenesis of these disorders. The hygiene hypothesis proposes that exposure to ubiquitous infections, including helminths, early in life promotes protective (regulatory) immune responses that prevent onset of pathogenic autoimmune or hypersensitivity processes [1,2]. Administration of a variety of helminths, including *Trichuris suis*, *Trichuris muris*, *Trichinella spiralis*, *Heligmosomoides polygyrus*, *Schistosoma mansoni* eggs and *Hymenolepsis diminuta*, can prevent and

in some cases reverse several experimental Th-1 immune-mediated colitis models (reviewed in Weinstock *et al.* [1]). These observations in preclinical models and a provocative open label pilot study showing potential benefit of *T. suis* in IBD patients has led to considerable interest in a novel therapeutic approach to these disorders [2–6]. *Trichuris suis*, a pig whipworm, transiently colonizes human intestines without replicating or demonstrable adverse effects, making this helminth species an attractive potential therapeutic agent.

Clinical results

Three published clinical trials using *T. suis* for IBD have been performed at the University of Iowa by Summers *et al.* [7]. The first, in 2003 [7], was an open label pilot study that evaluated the effectiveness and safety of helminthic ova in the treatment of active IBD. Seven patients were enrolled: four with Crohn's disease and three with UC. Each patient had their disease for ≥5 years and continued their medications at entry doses throughout the trial. Each patient had active inflammatory disease by endoscopic and laboratory criteria. A single oral dose of 2500 live *T. suis* ova was given, then participants were followed for 12 weeks with repeat routine labs at 2-week intervals. The effect of therapy was determined primarily by responses to a series of questionnaires, including the Inflammatory Bowel Disease Quality of Life questionnaire (IBDQ) [8] and the Crohn's Disease Activity Index (CDAI) [9] or the Simple Clinical Colitis Activity Index (SCCAI) [10] for Crohn's disease or UC, respectively.

Of the seven patients enrolled, three of four Crohn's disease and all three UC patients obtained remission, defined as IBDQ ≥170. The time to remission was nearly 4 weeks, with maximal effects around 8 weeks. However, at the end of the 12-week observation period, two of three Crohn's disease patients and one of the three UC patients who had achieved remission had relapsed. These results suggest a delay in clinical effect of 1 month and only temporary responses. The authors extended the study period in two Crohn's disease and two UC patients by repeating *T. suis* administration every 3 weeks and following patients longer than a year, at which time one Crohn's disease and both UC patients were in prolonged remission.

This pilot study suggests that *T. suis* administration appears to be safe for short- and long-term administration in active IBD. However, the study's limitations preclude generalization to the larger IBD community, because of its uncontrolled nature and the small number of highly selected participants, which excluded stricturing or stenotic Crohn's disease phenotypes, anti-tumor necrosis factor (TNF) treatment, pregnant women, or extremes of age. Additionally, the outcomes were limited to the more subjective measures of the questionnaires, while markers of objective inflammation were either unchanged (C-reactive protein), or not performed (follow-up endoscopy).

Recently, Summers *et al.* [11] published a randomized, double-blinded, placebo-controlled trial of *T. suis* in active UC. Employing intention-to-treat analysis, 54 patients with active UC were randomized to receive either *T. suis* (2500 ova) or placebo orally at 2-week intervals. The primary outcome measure was clinical improvement at 12 weeks, as determined by a decrease of ≥4 in the Ulcerative Colitis Disease Activity Index (UCDAI) [12]. Patients were followed biweekly with the SCCAI, which does not incorporate endoscopic evaluation. Patients continued their concomitant prednisone, 5-ASA agent, and/or 6-mercaptopurine or azathioprine at stable doses. Exclusion criteria were recent medication dose changes, use of antibiotics, cyclosporine or methotrexate, pregnancy, or active infections. At entry, routine laboratory parameters and baseline flexible sigmoidoscopy were performed to assess mucosal inflammation.

A favorable response (decrease in UCDAI ≥4) occurred in 43.3% of ova-treated and 16.7% of placebo-treated subjects ($P = 0.04$), although the mean activity score only decreased from 8.77 to 6.1 in the ova-treated group. The mean score of the responders was 2.8 ± 0.4. Although not significant, responders tended to have total colonic involvement with a shorter disease exacerbation period. However, the number of patients achieving remission (UCDAI ≤2) in the ova-treated group (3/30, 10%) was not significantly different from the placebo group (1/24, 4%). There were no complications or notable side-effects attributed to the *T. suis* ova.

This randomized, controlled study of *T. suis* suggests that administration of ova every other week is safe and induces improvement, after a lag time of approximately 6 weeks, in some patients with UC. However, whether a patient would enjoy long-term benefits is unknown. There were few clinical remissions and disease remained relatively active even in most responders, suggesting that either the optimal dosing regimen or concomitant medication administration has not been identified or that the treatment has only partial benefit.

To evaluate *T. suis* ova safety and efficacy in Crohn's disease, Summer *et al.* [13] performed an open label study involving 29 patients who received 2500 live *T. suis* ova triweekly for 24 weeks. The patients were eligible if they had active Crohn's disease, with a CDAI between 220 and 450 [9], and a small bowel series and colonoscopy documenting disease within the year before enrollment. Concurrent medications, including prednisone, 5-ASA derivatives and/or 6-mercaptopurine or azathioprine at stable doses were allowed. Similar exclusion criteria to the previous studies were employed [7,11]. The participants' mean CDAI was 294, indicating moderate disease activity.

At week 12, 22/29 patients (75.9%) responded (indicated by a decreased CDAI from entry level >100 points or final CDAI <150) and 19/29 (65%) were in remission (CDAI <150). Additionally, at week 24, 23/29 patients (79.3%) responded and 21/29 (72.4%) were in remission. Subset analysis demonstrated a trend for patients using immunosuppressive drugs to have a better response to *T. suis* ova. Conversely, those with prior terminal ileum resection seemed to improve to a lesser degree. There were no reported side-effects of the medication.

This small, open label study suggests efficacy and safety of *T. suis* in the treatment of Crohn's disease. A larger randomized, placebo-controlled trial is warranted to exclude placebo effect.

Conclusions

These three preliminary clinical trials (summarized in Table 26.1) suggest that *T. suis* ova administration is safe

TABLE 26.1 Clinical trials studying use of *Trichuris suis* ova in Crohn's disease (CD) and UC.

Author	Study type	Participants	IBD type	Maximal percent in remission	Maximal percent response	Adverse effects
Summers *et al.* [7]	Pilot open label	7	CD and UC	86%	100%	None
Summers *et al.* [11]	RCT	54	UC	10% (placebo 4%)	43% (placebo 17%)	None
Summers *et al.* [13]	Open label	29	CD	66%* 72%†	76%* 79%†	None

RCT, double-blind, randomized, placebo-controlled trial.
* At 12 weeks.
† At 24 weeks.

and has some therapeutic benefit in active IBD. Also noteworthy is the very high patient compliance level and lack of reported toxicity. However, these studies are far from definitive and multiple questions regarding *T. suis* efficacy and its role in current IBD therapy remain. Only one of these studies was placebo-controlled, and even this had a small number of patients with borderline efficacy ($P = 0.04$) and no induction of remission. While provocative, the Crohn's disease study was small (29 patients) and uncontrolled. The UC and Crohn's disease studies used different treatment intervals (2 vs. 3 week administration, respectively) and the doses were fixed at 2500 ova. The optimal dose, interval, and duration of treatment need to be established. It is not clear whether *T. suis* is the best helminth species for therapy or if non-viable purified worm antigens could be equally effective. Moreover, time to response is relatively slow and benefit is transient after a single dose so that maintenance therapy is required to sustain clinical responses. The participants were highly selected, and the majority was on concomitant traditional IBD therapy. Finally, these studies were performed by a single group that own the patent on this therapeutic approach and must be replicated by independent investigators. The role of helminth administration in IBD treatment has not been established nor have the immunologic mechanisms of protection been elucidated [4]. However, results in Crohn's disease appear particularly promising and should be pursued with a more definitive, larger, blinded trial. If positive results are obtained, it will be important to better understand the mechanisms of therapeutic responses to direct development of optimal strategies to stimulate protective immunity and deviate established pathogenic immune responses.

References

1 Weinstock JV, Summers RW, Elliott DE. Role of helminths in regulating mucosal inflammation. *Springer Semin Immunopathol* 2005; 27: 249–71.

2 Feillet H, Bach JF. Increased incidence of inflammatory bowel disease: the price of the decline of infectious burden? *Curr Opin Gastroenterol* 2004; 20: 560–4.

3 Elliott DE, Summers RW, Weinstock JV. Helminths and the modulation of mucosal inflammation. *Curr Opin Gastroenterol* 2005; 21: 51–8.

4 Mayer L. A novel approach to the treatment of ulcerative colitis: is it kosher? *Gastroenterology* 2005; 128: 1117–9.

5 Moreels TG, Pelckmans PA. Gastrointestinal parasites: potential therapy for refractory inflammatory bowel diseases. *Inflamm Bowel Dis* 2005; 11: 178–84.

6 Korzenik JR. Past and current theories of etiology of IBD: toothpaste, worms, and refrigerators. *J Clin Gastroenterol* 2005; 39: S59–65.

7 Summers RW, Elliott DE, Qadir K, *et al*. *Trichuris suis* seems to be safe and possibly effective in the treatment of inflammatory bowel disease. *Am J Gastroenterol* 2003; 98: 2034–41.

8 Irvine EJ, Feagan B, Rochon J, *et al*. Quality of life: a valid and reliable measure of therapeutic efficacy in the treatment of inflammatory bowel disease. Canadian Crohn's Relapse Prevention Trial Study Group. *Gastroenterology* 1994; 106: 287–96.

9 Best WR, Becktel JM, Singleton JW. Rederived values of the eight coefficients of the Crohn's Disease Activity Index (CDAI). *Gastroenterology* 1979; 77: 843–6.

10 Walmsley RS, Ayres RC, Pounder RE, Allan RN. A simple clinical colitis activity index. *Gut* 1998; 43: 29–32.

11 Summers RW, Elliott DE, Urban JF Jr, Thompson RA, Weinstock JV. *Trichuris suis* therapy for active ulcerative colitis: a randomized controlled trial. *Gastroenterology* 2005; 128: 825–32.

12 Sutherland LR, Martin F, Greer S, *et al*. 5-Aminosalicylic acid enema in the treatment of distal ulcerative colitis, proctosigmoiditis, and proctitis. *Gastroenterology* 1987; 92: 1894–8.

13 Summers RW, Elliott DE, Urban JF Jr, Thompson R, Weinstock JV. *Trichuris suis* therapy in Crohn's disease. *Gut* 2005; 54: 87–90.

27 Smoking and nicotine – poison for Crohn's, potion for colitis?

BRIAN BRESSLER & A HILLARY STEINHART

LEARNING POINTS

Smoking and nicotine

- Smoking is a risk factor for developing Crohn's disease and worsens its outcome

- Stopping smoking improves the course of Crohn's disease

- Onset of UC may be triggered by stopping smoking

- Patients with UC who continue to smoke do better than those who quit

- Transdermal nicotine has some efficacy in active UC but has frequent dose limiting side-effects

Introduction

The influence of cigarette smoking on inflammatory bowel disease is complicated in that, depending on the particular disease, it may have pro-inflammatory or anti-inflammatory effects. The pro-inflammatory effects seen in patients with Crohn's disease can occur by altering cellular and humoral immunity, or by reducing antioxidant capacity and producing oxygen free radicals [1]. In UC, the anti-inflammatory effect can be brought about by increasing mucosal blood flow, or by changing certain cytokine levels [1].

Smoking and Crohn's disease

More than 15 years ago, Calkins [2] performed a meta-analysis of seven Crohn's disease studies, all demonstrating consistent conclusions regarding the negative impact of smoking on Crohn's disease. This meta-analysis concluded that smokers or former smokers were almost twice as likely to have Crohn's disease compared with non-smokers – pooled odds ratio (OR) 2.0 (95% confidence interval [CI] 1.65–2.47) for smokers and OR 1.80 (95% CI 1.33–2.51) for former smokers. Furthermore, the harmful impact of cigarette smoking on the course of Crohn's disease has been shown with respect to both clinical [3] and surgical relapses [4]. Even more concerning, a large Italian cohort study followed IBD patients for a median of 15 years and demonstrated that smoking status contributes significantly to an increased mortality in patients with Crohn's disease [5]. The increased overall mortality was strongly influenced by an increased mortality from gastrointestinal diseases (standardized mortality ratio [SMR] 4.49; 95% CI 1.80–9.25) and lung cancer (SMR 4.00; 95% CI 1.60–8.24).

The genetic determinants of Crohn's disease have been found to be very important in influencing the course of disease and response to treatment in specific groups of patients. These genetic markers are helping us understand the underlying pathophysiology of this disease (see Chapter 27). These facts hold true when dealing with the role of smoking on Crohn's disease. Although a strong association between smoking and Crohn's disease has been shown in most patient populations, studies in both Israel [6] and China [7] have not shown an association between smoking and Crohn's disease. These findings suggest that a genetic predisposition may exist that influences the effect of smoking on Crohn's disease. One of the strongest risk factors for the development of Crohn's disease is the presence of one or more variants of the *CARD15* (NOD2) gene (see Chapter 24). The role of this gene in the pathogenesis of IBD is thought to relate to impaired cellular response to muramyl dipeptide, a component of intracellular peptidoglycans from Gram-negative and Gram-positive bacteria [8]. Smoking has also been shown to have a deleterious effect on function of phagocytes, decreasing their bactericidal and bacteriostatic activity [9]. These similar effects on the ability of phagocytes to deal appropriately with bacterial antigens could, in part, explain the effect of these factors – smoking and *CARD15* – on the risk of developing Crohn's disease.

Smoking cessation and Crohn's disease

Although it appears clear that smoking is bad for Crohn's disease, what is the impact of cessation of smoking in patients with Crohn's disease? Besides the known beneficial effects on cardiovascular disease and cancer prevention, cessation of smoking has been shown to have a beneficial effect on the clinical course of Crohn's disease. In an interventional study, Cosnes *et al.* [10] used counseling and a smoking cessation program in 474 consecutive smokers with Crohn's disease. Only 59 patients (12%) were able to quit smoking for 1 year. These patients were followed up for a median time of 29 months. These quitters had a risk of disease flare that was similar to that of non-smokers and less than that of those who continued to smoke. Furthermore, patients who were able to quit smoking also had less need for steroids and immunosuppressive therapy compared with the smokers. What this trial demonstrated was the positive effect that cessation of smoking has on the natural history of Crohn's disease, and additionally the difficulty that patients have in succeeding with such an intervention, with only 12% succeeding for 1 year. Therefore, clinicians must not only be prepared to advise patients to stop smoking, but they must also provide them with the support they require to reach this very difficult goal. This support may include behavioral or pharmacologic therapy.

Smoking and ulcerative colitis

Advising patients with Crohn's disease to quit smoking is not controversial because this advice has general health benefits and may improve the course of Crohn's disease. The major dilemma, which exists with respect to smoking and IBD, is the potential therapeutic benefit of smoking and nicotine in patients with UC. In the meta-analysis by Calkins [2], nine case–control studies were used to calculate the pooled OR for current smoking compared with non-smoking to be 0.41 (95% CI 0.34–0.48) for the development of UC. They also reported a pooled OR 1.64 (95% CI 1.36–1.98) for former smokers compared with non-smokers for the lifetime risk of developing UC. The course of a patient's UC seems also to be affected by a patient's smoking status. Hospitalization and colectomy rates are less in patients who continue to smoke compared with former smokers [11].

Nicotine and ulcerative colitis

The reason why smoking is beneficial in patients with UC is unknown, but investigators have postulated that nicotine may be responsible for this effect. Multiple studies have been performed to investigate the effect of nicotine in patients with UC.

A Cochrane database review was performed to assess the efficacy and adverse events of transdermal nicotine (15–25 mg/day) for induction of remission in UC [12]. This meta-analysis found transdermal nicotine to be statistically more likely to induce a clinical remission than placebo (OR 2.56; 95% CI 1.02–6.45); moreover, compared with standard therapy (oral prednisone or mesalamine) there was no difference in induction of remission (OR 0.77; 95% CI 0.37–1.60) (Table 27.1). However, when compared with placebo or standard therapy, patients receiving transdermal nicotine were more likely to withdraw from the trials because of adverse events (OR 5.82; 95% CI 1.66–20.47) and were more likely to suffer an adverse event (OR 3.54; 95% CI 2.07–6.08).

According to these results, transdermal nicotine treatment appears to have a role as induction treatment in a selected group of patients who are able to tolerate its side-effects. This may be the population of patients who have recently stopped smoking. Clinical experience suggests that the majority of non-smokers are not able to tolerate the headaches, nausea, and dizziness that frequently occur at the doses required to achieve a clinical benefit. Furthermore, in light of the overall poor safety profile of cigarette smoking it is not unreasonable to help smokers whose UC is in remission to quit smoking with transdermal nicotine treatment. We recommend this with caution, because a randomized, double-blinded study for the maintenance of remission in patients with UC demonstrated no beneficial

TABLE 27.1 Cochrane database review's odds ratios and 95% confidence intervals for clinical remission or clinical improvement with transdermal nicotine compared with placebo or standard medical therapy for patients with UC [11].

	Odds ratio	95% confidence interval
Clinical remission		
Transdermal nicotine vs. placebo	2.56	1.02–6.45
Clinical improvement or remission		
Transdermal nicotine vs. placebo	2.72	1.28–5.81
Clinical remission		
Transdermal nicotine vs. standard therapy	0.77	0.37–1.60

effect of transdermal nicotine over placebo [13]. However, that study did not include current smokers and did not involve smoking cessation.

Outstanding therapeutic questions

Is there a future for nicotine therapy in the treatment of UC? There may be some hope with local nicotine therapy. The rationale behind this is to limit the systemic adverse events seen with transdermal nicotine therapy and to maintain the presumed positive effect of nicotine on UC disease activity. Problems with this form of therapy have been the difficulty in retaining the liquid enemas and the side-effects that still exist because of systemic absorption of nicotine. However, the prevalence of side-effects appears to be less than with the transdermal mode of delivery because approximately 60% of nicotine absorbed from the intestine is converted to cotinine, the major metabolite of nicotine, on first pass through the liver [14].

Clearly there are, and will continue to be, limitations on the use of nicotine for the treatment of UC. Because of the significant and consistent beneficial effect smoking has on UC, alternate mechanisms of cigarette smoke's influence on the pathogenesis of UC should be explored. One component of cigarette smoke, carbon monoxide, has been shown to reduce lipopolysaccharide-mediated secretion of the pro-inflammatory cytokine tumor necrosis factor α (TNF-α) and increase secretion of the anti-inflammatory cytokine interleukin 10 (IL-10) [15]. Carbon monoxide has also been shown to induce heme oxygenase 1, the rate-limiting enzyme in heme metabolism, which is protective against injury in acute and chronic inflammation [16]. Can we deliver a safe dose of carbon monoxide to act as an anti-inflammatory agent in patients with UC? We will have to wait and see.

Conclusion

The relationship between smoking and inflammatory bowel disease has been thoroughly addressed through both classic epidemiologic and clinical approaches. Adding to, and utilizing this knowledge we will hopefully gain further insight into the pathophysiology of IBD, which should lead to better management of this disease.

References

1 Birrenbach T, Bocker U. Inflammatory bowel disease and smoking: a review of epidemiology, pathophysiology, and therapeutic implications. *Inflamm Bowel Dis* 2004; **10**: 848–59.

2 Calkins BM. A meta-analysis of the role of smoking in inflammatory bowel disease. *Dig Dis Sci* 1989; **34**: 1841–54.

3 Timmer A, Sutherland LR, Martin F. Canadian Mesalamine for Remission of Crohn's Disease Study Group. Oral contraceptive use and smoking are risk factors for relapse in Crohn's disease. *Gastroenterology* 1998; **114**: 1143–50.

4 Cottone M, Rosselli M, Orlando A, *et al.* Smoking habits and recurrence in Crohn's disease. *Gastroenterology* 1994; **106**: 643–8.

5 Masala G, Bagnoli S, Ceroti M, *et al.* Divergent patterns of total and cancer mortality in ulcerative colitis and Crohn's disease patients: the Florence IBD study, 1978–2001. *Gut* 2004; **53**: 1309–13.

6 Odes HS, Fich A, Reif A, *et al.* Effect of current cigarette smoking on clinical course of Crohn's disease and ulcerative colitis. *Dig Dis Sci* 2001; **46**: 1717–21.

7 Leong RW, Lau JY, Sung JJ. The epidemiology and phenotype of Crohn's disease in the Chinese population. *Inflamm Bowel Dis* 2004; **10**: 646–51.

8 Inohara N, Ogura Y, Fontalba A, *et al.* Host recognition of bacterial muramyl dipeptide mediated through NOD2: implications for Crohn's disease. *J Biol Chem* 2003; **278**: 5509–12.

9 King TE Jr, Savici D, Campbell PA. Phagocytosis and killing of listeria monocytogenes by alveolar macrophages: smokers versus nonsmokers. *J Infect Dis* 1988; **158**: 1309–16.

10 Cosnes J, Beaugerie L, Carbonnel F. *et al.* Smoking cessation and the course of Crohn's disease: an intervention study. *Gastroenterology* 2001; **120**: 1093–9.

11 Boyko EJ, Perera DR, Koepsell TD, Keane EM, Inui TS.

Effects of cigarette smoking on the clinical course of ulcerative colitis. *Scand J Gastroenterol* 1988; **23**: 1147–52.

12 McGrath J, McDonald JW, Macdonald JK. Transdermal nicotine for induction of remission in ulcerative colitis. *Cochrane Database Syst Rev* 2004; **4**: CD004722.

13 Thomas GA, Rhodes J, Mani V, *et al.* Transdermal nicotine as maintenance therapy for ulcerative colitis. *N Engl J Med* 1995; **332**: 988–92.

14 Benowitz NL, Jacob P III. Metabolism of nicotine to cotinine studied by a dual stable isotope method. *Clin Pharmacol Ther* 1994; **56**: 483–93.

15 Otterbein LE, Bach FH, Alam J, *et al.* Carbon monoxide has anti-inflammatory effects involving the mitogen-activated protein kinase pathway. *Nat Med* 2000; **6**: 422–8.

16 Moore BA, Otterbein LE, Turler A, Choi AM, Bauer AJ. Inhaled carbon monoxide suppresses the development of postoperative ileus in the murine small intestine. *Gastroenterology* 2003; **124**: 377–91.

28 Heparin

AILSA HART & STUART BLOOM

LEARNING POINTS

Heparin

- Heparin has anticoagulant and anti-inflammatory properties

- Controlled trials have shown that low molecular weight heparin does not have a therapeutic role in UC; unfractionated heparin *may* be effective

- Prophylactic heparin is recommended in hospitalized patients with active IBD

Introduction

A therapeutic role for heparin in IBD was suggested over two decades ago. In this chapter, the rationale for using heparin as a treatment for IBD, potential mechanisms of action, and clinical trials using both unfractionated and low molecular weight heparin are discussed.

Rationale for use of heparin in IBD

Several factors have contributed to the rationale for using heparin as a treatment for IBD. There was an early observation that heparin given for incidental deep vein thrombosis to a patient with active UC led to an improvement in bowel symptoms [1]. Second, in the intestinal mucosa of patients with UC, there is histologic evidence of microthrombi within the vasculature [2]. Third, patients with IBD are at

risk of thromboembolism, with a prevalence ranging from 1% to 7% in clinical studies and reaching 39% in autopsy series (see Chapter 57) [3]. Fourth, epidemiologic studies suggest that inherited disorders of coagulation, such as von Willebrand's disease and hemophilia, protect against IBD [4]. Finally, there is evidence that heparin not only has anticoagulant properties, mediated by inhibition of activated coagulation factor X and thrombin, but also anti-inflammatory activities. Heparin interferes with the inflammatory cascade by influencing cell migration, accumulation in tissues and pro-inflammatory cytokine release, and may promote mucosal healing by restoration of growth factors (reviewed in Papa *et al.* [5]). Taken together these factors implicate systemic and mucosal hypercoaguability in IBD pathogenesis and suggest heparin, with its anticoagulant and anti-inflammatory properties, as a potential treatment.

Clinical trials of heparin in IBD

Clinical trials have assessed effects of both unfractionated heparin (UH) and low molecular weight heparin (LMWH) in ameliorating intestinal inflammation. Trial data are summarized in Tables 28.1 (UH) and 28.2 (LMWH).

Unfractionated heparin
Uncontrolled trials
Early studies carried out in the 1980s in over 100 patients with active UC showed that UH used with standard therapy reduced rectal bleeding and colectomy rate [6,7]. After an initial observation of improvement in bowel symptoms in a

TABLE 28.1 Clinical trials of unfractionated heparin in inflammatory bowel disease.

Trial design	Disease	Heparin type	Dose	Comparator	Patient No.	Response to heparin	Response to comparator	P value	Duration	Concomitant Treatment	Adverse events	Reference
Open-label	Ulcerative colitis (steroid-resistant)	UH	30–36 000 IU/day iv or 10 000 U twice daily sc	Nil	10	90%	–	–	6 weeks	Sulfasalazine, reducing steroid	None observed	Gaffney et al. [8]
Open-label	Ulcerative colitis (steroid-resistant)	UH	25–40 000 IU/day iv	Nil	16	75%	–	–	4 weeks	Sulfasalazine	Vaginal bleed (1)	Evans et al. [9]
Open-label	Ulcerative colitis + CD	UH	Iv for 2 weeks (APTT 60s); 12 500 IU twice daily for 6 weeks	Nil	13 UC; 4CD	54% UC 0% CD	–	–	8 weeks	Sulfasalazine	PR bleed requiring blood transfusion (1); colectomy (1)	Folwaczny et al. [10]
Multicenter RCT	Ulcerative colitis	UH	31 456 ± 290 IU/day iv (APTT 1.5–2x control)	Methylpred (0.75–1 mg/kg/day)	25	0%	69%	$P < 0.05$	10 days	Nil	UH – PR bleed (3) Steroid – toxic megacolon (1)	Panes et al. [12]
Single-center RCT	Ulcerative colitis + CD	UH	25–45 000 IU/day iv (APTT 2–3x control) for 5 days; 10 000 IU twice daily sc for 2weeks; 5000 IU twice daily sc for 3 weeks	Hydrocortisone (200 mg four times daily for 5 days); prednisolone 40 mg (reducing course)	17 UC; 3 CD	75%	67%	$P = 0.23$	6 weeks	5-ASA	None observed	Ang et al. [11]

APTT, activated partial thromboplastin time; CD, Crohn's disease; iv, intravenous; PR, per rectum; RCT, randomized controlled trials; sc, subcutaneous; UC ulcerative colitis; UH unfractionated heparin.

TABLE 28.2 Clinical trials of low molecular weight heparin in inflammatory bowel disease.

Trial design	Disease	Heparin type	Dose	Comparator	Patient No.	Response to heparin	Response to comparator	P value	Duration	Concomitant Treatment	Adverse events	Reference
Open-label	Ulcerative colitis (steroid resistant)	Dalteparin	5000 IU twice daily sc	Nil	12	50% remission	–	–	12 weeks	Sulfasalazine	None observed	Torkvist et al. [13]
Open-label	Ulcerative colitis (steroid refractory)	Nandroparin	5.700 IE anti-Xa/0.6 mL twice daily sc	Nil	25	80%	–	–	8 weeks	5-ASA	None observed	Vrij et al. [14]
Open-label	Ulcerative colitis	Enoxaparin	5 mg at weekly intervals	Nil	12	Mean Mayo – 9 ± 1 to 3 ± 2	–	–	12 weeks	5-ASA	Abdominal pain (1); arthralgia (1); edema (1); ↑ ALP	Dotan et al. [15]
Multicenter RCT double-blind, placebo-controlled	Ulcerative colitis (mild to moderate)	Tinzaparin	175 anti-Xa IU/kg/day sc for 2 weeks; 4500 antiXa IU/day sc for 28 days	Placebo	100	31% partial response	39% partial response	NS	6 weeks	5-ASA	PR bleed (1) in placebo	Bloom et al. [16]
Multicenter RCT double-blind, placebo-controlled	Ulcerative colitis	Deligoparin	75 or 125 mg/day sc	Placebo	138	75 mg – 36% 125 mg – 42%	41%	NS	6 weeks	5-ASA	None observed	Korzenik et al. [17]
Multicenter RCT, placebo-controlled	Ulcerative colitis	Dalteparin	5000 IU twice daily sc	Placebo	41	(Not specified)	(Not specified)	NS	8 weeks	5-ASA	None observed	Torkvist et al. [18]

ALP, alkaline phosphatase; 5-ASA, 5-aminosalicylic acid; NS, non-significant; PR, per rectum; RCT, randomized controlled trials; sc, subcutaneous.

UC patient treated with UH for an incidental deep vein thrombosis, Gaffney *et al.* [8] noted that 9/10 UC patients treated with UH achieved clinical remission. Evans *et al.* [9] reported that 12/16 UC patients unresponsive to corticosteroid therapy treated with UH achieved clinical improvement by 4 weeks. Folwaczny *et al.* [10] observed that seven of 13 patients with active UC unresponsive to steroids achieved clinical remission.

Overall, in these uncontrolled studies, UH demonstrated efficacy in the treatment of steroid-resistant UC with a pooled response rate of >70%.

Controlled trials

A prospective, randomized controlled trial comparing UH with conventional steroid treatment in 20 patients with active IBD reported clinical remission in 75% of heparin-treated patients and 67% of steroid-treated patients by 6 weeks. In this trial, endoscopic and histologic improvement was comparable in both groups and no serious adverse events were noted [11].

In contrast, a second randomized controlled trial showed that UH was not beneficial in the treatment of active UC. Panes *et al.* [12] compared UH with steroid treatment in 25 patients with moderate to severe UC. By day 10, 69% of patients in the methylprednisolone group had a significant improvement in clinical disease activity index and eventually achieved remission compared with 0% of the patients treated with UH. In this trial, patients stopped taking 5-aminosalicylic acid (5-ASA) treatments at entry into the study and this, in addition to the short duration of treatment with heparin, may explain the discrepancies between the two randomized controlled trials. It remains possible that heparin is clinically effective in UC when given with concomitant 5-ASA.

Low molecular weight heparin

LMWH represents an attractive alternative to UH in view of the low risk of side-effects, ease of administration, longer half-life, and reduced platelet interactions.

Uncontrolled trials

Six of 12 patients attained clinical remission when treated with dalteparin sodium (Fragmin; Pharmacia & Upjohn) for 12 weeks and 70% of the patients were able to reduce or stop their treatment with steroids [13]. Nadroparine (Fraxiparin; Sanofi) given twice daily in 25 patients with active steroid refractory UC led to clinical, endoscopic, and

histologic improvement in 20 patients [14]. Enoxaparin (Clexane; Aventis Pharma Limited) given at weekly intervals for 12 weeks improved symptoms and endoscopic appearances in 12 patients with active UC [15].

Controlled trials

The largest randomized, placebo-controlled trial of LMWH in the setting of UC used tinzaparin (Innohep; LEO Pharma). Tinzaparin showed no therapeutic benefit compared with placebo in 100 patients with mild to moderately active UC [16]. In addition, the ultra LMWH deligoparin (Incara Pharmaceuticals) showed no benefit over placebo in 138 patients with UC [17]. No clinical benefit was noted with dalteparin sodium in a randomized controlled trial [18].

It may be that differences in therapeutic efficacy between UH and LMWH relate to alterations in anti-inflammatory mechanisms associated with fractionation. Alterations in cell adhesion and release of chemokines from intestinal epithelial cells may be lost with fractionation.

Crohn's disease

Most of the trials have assessed effects of heparin in patients with UC. Only a small number of patients with Crohn's disease have been included in the trials [10,11] and no randomized trials have addressed effects of heparin in Crohn's disease, making it difficult to draw any conclusions about the efficacy of heparin in Crohn's disease.

Extraintestinal manifestations

In uncontrolled studies, UH improved extra-intestinal manifestations of IBD such as erythema nodosum and pyoderma gangrenosum. Beneficial effects of heparin on arthritis in patients with IBD have also been reported [10].

Side-effects

Hemorrhage represents the main concern in treating patients with IBD with heparin. Serious rectal bleeding was noted in 2/13 patients in the open trial reported by Folwaczny *et al.* [10]. No serious side-effects were noted in the study of Ang *et al.* [11]. Three of 12 patients treated with UH in the trial by Panes *et al.* [12] were withdrawn from the study because of increased rectal bleeding. In contrast, there are no reported side-effects related to increased bleeding in clinical trials using LMWH.

Prophylactic heparin in hospitalized patients with IBD

In view of the increased risk of thromboembolic events in IBD [3] and the lack of adverse events related to use of heparin, in particular LMWH, it is recommended that prophylactic LMWH should be given to all hospitalized patients with active IBD (see Chapter 57).

Conclusions

Although initial trials suggested beneficial effects of heparin, these trials have not been fully endorsed by controlled clinical trials, in particular using LMWH. However, it remains possible that the higher molecular weight fractions of unfractionated heparin may have a beneficial immunomodulatory effect in IBD.

References

1 Gaffney PR, O'Leary JJ, Doyle CT, *et al.* Response to heparin in patients with ulcerative colitis. *Lancet* 1991; **337**: 238–9.

2 Dhillon AP, Anthony A, Sim R, *et al.* Mucosal capillary thrombi in rectal biopsies. *Histopathology* 1992; **21**: 127–33.

3 Talbot RW, Heppell J, Dozois RR, Beart RW. Vascular complications of inflammatory bowel disease. *Mayo Clin Proc* 1996; **61**: 140–5.

4 Thompson NP, Wakefield AJ, Pounder RE. Inherited disorders of coagulation appear to protect against inflammatory bowel disease. *Gastroenterology* 1995; **108**: 1011–5.

5 Papa A, Danese S, Gasbarrini A, Gasbarrini G. Review article: potential therapeutic applications and mechanisms of action of heparin in inflammatory bowel disease. *Aliment Pharmacol Ther* 2000; **14**: 1403–9.

6 Zavgorodniy L, Mustgat A. Application of anticoagulants in the complex treatment of ulcerative colitis. *Klin Med* 1982; **60**: 74–80.

7 Zhernakova TV, Kashmenskaya NA, Maltseva IV, *et al.* Haemostasis and heparin therapy in non-specific ulcerative colitis. *Soviet Med* 1984; **2**: 110–3.

8 Gaffney PR, Doyle CT, Gaffney A, *et al.* Paradoxical response to heparin in 10 patients with ulcerative colitis. *Am J Gastroenterol* 1995; **90**: 220–3.

9 Evans RC, Wong VS, Morris AI, Rhodes JM. Treatment of corticosteroid-resistant ulcerative colitis with heparin: a report of 16 cases. *Aliment Pharmacol Ther* 1997; **11**: 1037–40.

10 Folwaczny C, Wiebecke B, Loeschke K. Unfractionated heparin in the therapy of patients with highly active inflammatory bowel disease. *Am J Gastroenterol* 1999; **94**: 1551–5.

11 Ang YS, Mahmud N, White B, *et al.* Randomized comparison of unfractionated heparin with corticosteroids in severe active inflammatory bowel disease. *Aliment Pharmacol Ther* 2000; **14**: 1015–22.

12 Panes J, Esteve M, Cabre E, *et al.* Comparison of heparin and steroids in the treatment of moderate and severe ulcerative colitis. *Gastroenterology* 2000; **119**: 903–8.

13 Torkvist L, Thorlacius H, Sjoqvist U, *et al.* Low molecular weight heparin as adjuvant therapy in active ulcerative colitis. *Aliment Pharmacol Ther* 1999; **13**: 1323–8.

14 Vrij AA, Jansen JM, Schoon EJ, *et al.* Low molecular weight heparin treatment in steroid refractory ulcerative colitis: clinical outcome and influence on mucosal capillary thrombi. *Scand J Gastroenterol Suppl* 2001; **234**: 41–7.

15 Dotan I, Hallak A, Arber N, *et al.* Low-dose low-molecular weight heparin (enoxaparin) is effective as adjuvant treatment in active ulcerative colitis: an open trial. *Dig Dis Sci* 2001; **46**: 2239–44.

16 Bloom S, Kiilerich S, Lassen MR, *et al.* Low molecular weight heparin (tinzaparin) vs. placebo in the treatment of mild to moderately active ulcerative colitis. *Aliment Pharmacol Ther* 2004; **19**: 871–8.

17 Korzenik J, Miner P, Stanton D, *et al.* Multi-centre randomised double-blind placebo-controlled trial of deligoparin for active ulcerative colitis. *Gastroenterology* 2003; **124** (Suppl 1): A67.

18 Torkvist L, Stahlberg D, Bohman L, *et al.* LMWH for the treatment of mild to moderately active steroid refractory/dependent ulcerative colitis: an independent multi-centre randomised controlled study. *Gastroenterology* 2001; **122**: A290.

Medical Treatment: What's Round the Corner?

29 Leukocytapheresis: filtering out the facts

PETER IRVING & DAVID RAMPTON

LEARNING POINTS

Leukocytapheresis for IBD

Pros:

- Novel non-drug strategy
- Apparently effective, safe, and well-tolerated
- Potentially steroid-sparing
- More evidence in UC than Crohn's disease

Cons:

- Randomized controlled data lacking
- Cost
- Resource-intensive

Introduction

Reports describing the successful treatment of active, steroid-resistant IBD with leukocytapheresis first emerged about 10 years ago. In this chapter, we discuss the theory behind using leukocytapheresis to treat IBD, its different forms, the way in which these remove leukocytes, and the indications, efficacy, safety, and possible future role of leukocytapheresis.

Theory

One of the key pathogenic processes in IBD is the loss of the gut's normal tolerance to luminal bacteria, resulting in an inflammatory response with influx into the mucosa of large numbers of neutrophils and monocytes. Removal of activated circulating leukocytes, and their replacement with bone marrow-derived unactivated leukocytes, is therefore a therapeutically attractive principle. Apheresis appears to accomplish this goal; although the overall number of circulating leukocytes may not be decreased by leukocyta-

pheresis, the proportion of neutrophils with an immature phenotype is greatly increased. In addition, decreased production of cytokines and down-regulation of L-selectin expression have been demonstrated after apheresis. Finally, incubation of blood with cellulose acetate beads causes a decrease in neutrophil adhesion to endothelial cells and an increase in neutrophil apoptosis [1].

Systems

Leukocytapheresis involves extracorporeal removal of leukocytes, either by passing venous blood through an adsorptive system, or by centrifugation. Of the two commonly used adsorptive systems, one contains cellulose acetate beads (Adacolumn; Japan Immunoresearch Laboratories, Takasaki, Japan) and the other, a polyester fiber filter (Cellsorba; Asahi Medical Company, Tokyo, Japan). The mechanisms and consequences of leukocyte removal differ between the systems. The cellulose acetate bead column removes approximately 65% of neutrophils, 55% of monocytes, and 2% of lymphocytes from the blood passing through the system; the polyester fiber filter system not only removes leukocytes by adsorption, but also mechanically filters blood cells resulting in the removal from processed blood of almost 100% of neutrophils and monocytes, and 20–60% of lymphocytes [2]. Centrifugation is at least as effective at removing leukocytes as adsorptive columns [3] and also removes a large fraction of lymphocytes. It is of note that leukocytapheresis also removes 20–40% of platelets; activated platelets are not only pro-thrombotic, but also pro-inflammatory and may be important in the pathogenesis of IBD.

The process of performing leukocytapheresis is relatively simple. Vascular access for adsorptive apheresis requires peripheral venepuncture at two sites. Venous blood is drawn from one site at a rate of 30–50 mL/h and passed through the adsorptive system before being returned to the circulation through the other cannula. Sessions usually last for an hour, allowing 2–3 L blood to pass through the adsorptive apparatus. A course of treatment typically comprises 5–10 sessions at weekly intervals. Centrifugation, by contrast, requires only one cannulation site; blood is intermittently withdrawn, centrifuged, and returned to the circulation. Sessions of 1 hour allow processing of 2 L blood.

Evidence

There have been several open trials of the use of leukocytapheresis to treat UC, quoted remission rates varying from 21% to 85% (larger, peer-reviewed trials are summarized in Table 29.1). Although indications for leukocytapheresis vary both between and within studies, the vast majority of patients reported have either steroid-refractory or steroid-dependent disease. However, a study in which a questionnaire was sent to Japanese physicians using the cellulose acetate bead column gives a clearer idea of the efficacy of leukacytapheresis. Data were gathered on 186 patients treated with this system for UC: remission was achieved in 32% and improvement in a further 41% [10].

To date, only two randomized controlled trials have been published in English language, peer-reviewed journals [11]. In the first study, 78 patients were randomly assigned to receive either an increase in their dosage of prednisolone, the magnitude of which varied according to the severity of the disease, or to leukocytapheresis in addition to any therapy that was already being prescribed. Unfortunately, several aspects of the trial, including the heterogeneous clinical characteristics of the patients, the outcome measures used, and the use of total parenteral nutrition in all patients,

make its interpretation difficult. Nevertheless, in this study leukocytapheresis was well tolerated and apparently twice as effective at improving UC as increasing the dose of prednisolone. In the second study, patients were randomised to weekly treatment with either leukocytapheresis or sham treatment (an empty column). Although reported as positive, the paper was statistically flawed; application of the correct test revealed no statistical difference in the main outcome between the two groups. Given, however, that only 19 patients were recruited, this may well represent a type 2 error [12]. Further well-designed, controlled studies of patients with refractory UC are underway and eagerly awaited.

What of leukocytapheresis as either first-line or maintenance therapy in UC? An uncontrolled study has suggested that leukocytapheresis may be effective as a first-line alternative to steroids in steroid-naïve patients [6], while another open study describes 2-weekly to 3-monthly treatment sessions in two steroid-refractory and five steroid-dependent patients [13]. Two patients required colectomy, but remissions of up to 30 months and steroid withdrawal were achieved in others. In addition, several of the studies describe maintenance treatment with leukocytapheresis with varying results; controlled data are also required for these indications.

There is less evidence for the use of leukocytapheresis in Crohn's disease than in UC. The largest study to date (published as an abstract) describes the treatment of 44 patients with Crohn's disease. Remission was achieved in approximately 40% with improvement being seen in a further one-quarter [14].

Safety

Is apheresis safe? In a review of 2000 sessions, half of 92 patients treated with leukocytapheresis experienced

TABLE 29.1 Summary of larger trials of leukocytapheresis for the treatment of active UC. Indications for leukocytapheresis vary between and within studies except where indicated.

Reference	Apheresis	Number of patients	Remission (%)	Improvement (%)
Hanai [4]	Column	39	82	8
Shimoyama [5]	Column	53	21	38
Suzuki [6]*	Column	20	85	0
Sakata [7]	Filter	51	65	18
Amano [8]	Filter	37	48	43
Kohgo [3]†	Centrifugal	50	22	52
Ayabe [9]†	Centrifugal	23	78	N/A

N/A, information not available.
* First-line treatment.
† Failure of conventional therapy.

side-effects at least once (10% of sessions); however, in only 1.5% of sessions did the symptoms require interruption of treatment. Common symptoms were nausea, vomiting, fever, chills, and nasal obstruction, although respiratory distress, palpitations, and chest tightness were also described [15]. In this study, reactions were noted to be more common in the maintenance phase of treatment and were thought to be related to the anticoagulants used.

As with any treatment that modifies leukocyte function, concerns exist about the risk of infection, particularly as the most active leukocytes are removed preferentially. Reassuringly, the available data suggest that infection is not a major problem. Literature from the company marketing Adacolumn suggests that caution should be observed in treating patients with anemia, a hypercoaguable state, or fluid depletion, all of which are common in patients with active IBD. Moreover, all the systems require the use of anticoagulation which may not be risk-free; one trial in which heparin was used therapeutically for UC was stopped prematurely because of serious bleeding in one-quarter of the heparin-treated patients.

Cost

Should the promising early results be confirmed by further well-designed, randomized controlled trials, cost–benefit analyses will become important. Currently, a single session of apheresis using a cellulose acetate column costs approximately £800 ($1400). If apheresis is ever to be used as a primary or maintenance therapy for UC, this cost will need to be reduced. Formal health economic evaluations of leukocytapheresis have not yet been undertaken, but if this approach prevents hospital admission and surgery, keeps people at work, and maintains their quality of life, leukocytapheresis may yet prove to be cost-effective.

Conclusions

The future of leukocytapheresis in the treatment of UC, Crohn's disease, and other inflammatory diseases requires further evaluation. Because of its expense, leukocytapheresis seems unlikely to gain favor as a first-line alternative to steroids in patients with active UC. However, if randomized controlled trials confirm its safety and efficacy, it is likely to become an attractive alternative to cyclosporine, azathioprine, and 6-mercaptopurine.

Clearly, much still needs to be learnt about the efficacy and safety of leukocytapheresis in IBD, as well as its precise indications. Nevertheless, leukocytapheresis may well prove an exciting innovation to patients and gastroenterologists alike.

References

1 Kashiwagi N, Sugimura K, Koiwai H, *et al.* Immunomodulatory effects of granulocyte and monocyte adsorption apheresis as a treatment for patients with ulcerative colitis. *Dig Dis Sci* 2002; 47: 1334–41.

2 Shibata H, Kuriyama T, Yamawaki N. Cellsorba. *Ther Apher Dial* 2003; 7: 44–7.

3 Kohgo Y, Hibi H, Chiba T, *et al.* Leukocyte apheresis using a centrifugal cell separator in refractory ulcerative colitis: a multicenter open label trial. *Ther Apher* 2002; 6: 255–60.

4 Hanai H, Watanabe F, Takeuchi K, *et al.* Leukocyte adsorptive apheresis for the treatment of active ulcerative colitis: a prospective, uncontrolled, pilot study. *Clin Gastroenterol Hepatol* 2003; 1: 28–35.

5 Shimoyama T, Sawada K, Hiwatashi N, *et al.* Safety and efficacy of granulocyte and monocyte adsorption apheresis in patients with active ulcerative colitis: a multicenter study. *J Clin Apher* 2001; 16: 1–9.

6 Suzuki Y, Yoshimura N, Saniabadi AR, *et al.* Selective granulocyte and monocyte adsorptive apheresis as a first-line treatment for steroid naive patients with active ulcerative colitis: a prospective uncontrolled study. *Dig Dis Sci* 2004; 49: 565–71.

7 Sakata H, Kawamura N, Horie T, *et al.* Successful treatment of ulcerative colitis with leukocytapheresis using non-woven polyester filter. *Ther Apher Dial* 2003; 7: 536–9.

8 Amano K, Amano K. Filter leukapheresis for patients with ulcerative colitis: clinical results and the possible mechanism. *Ther Apher* 1998; 2: 97–100.

9 Ayabe T, Ashida T, Kohgo Y. Centrifugal leukocyte apheresis for ulcerative colitis. *Ther Apher* 1998; 2: 125–8.

10 Saniabadi AR, Hanai H, Takeuchi K, *et al.* Adacolumn, an adsorptive carrier based granulocyte and monocyte apheresis device for the treatment of inflammatory and refractory diseases associated with leukocytes. *Ther Apher Dial* 2003; 7: 48–59.

11 Sawada K, Muto T, Shimoyama T, *et al.* Multicenter randomized controlled trial for the treatment of ulcerative colitis with a leukocytapheresis column. *Curr Pharm Des* 2003; 9: 307–21.

12 Sawada K, Kusugami K, Suzuki Y, *et al.* Leukocytapheresis in ulcerative colitis: Results of a multi-center double-blind prospective case-control study with sham apheresis as placebo treatment. *Am J Gastroenterl* 2005; 100: 1362–9.

13 Kondo K, Shinoda T, Yoshimoto H, *et al.* Effective maintenance leukocytapheresis for patients with steroid dependent or resistant ulcerative colitis. *Ther Apher* 2001; 5: 462–5.

14 Ljung Y, Østergaard-Thomsen O, Vatn M, *et al.* Granulocyte, monocyte/macrophage apheresis for IBD in clinical pratice. The Scandinavian experience in 100 patients. *Gut* 2004; 36: A223.

15 Nagase K, Sawada K, Ohnishi K, *et al.* Complications of leukocytapheresis. *Ther Apher* 1998; 2: 120–4.

30 Appendectomy for ulcerative colitis – a therapeutic option?

RICHARD MAKINS & GRAHAM RADFORD-SMITH

LEARNING POINTS

Appendectomy for UC

- UC risk is reduced if appendectomy occurs before age of 20 for confirmed appendicitis or lymphadenitis

- Clinical course of UC is milder after appendectomy

- Appendiceal "skip lesions" are common in distal UC

- Animal models of colitis develop milder disease following appendectomy

Notwithstanding the epidemiologic and animal data, evidence to support therapeutic appendectomy in UC is still limited

---

Introduction

Epidemiology of appendectomy and IBD

Epidemiologic observations have suggested that the appendix may have a role in the pathophysiology of IBD and in particular UC [1]. A prior history of appendectomy is uncommon in patients who develop UC and to a lesser extent in patients who develop Crohn's disease. At least 29 cohort [2] or case–control [3] studies have investigated the relationship between appendectomy and UC; the majority strongly support a protective effect of prior appendectomy against development of UC. Factors that may influence this effect have been investigated in several of these studies, including sex, age at appendectomy, and hygiene. One of two cohort studies [2] included over 200 000 Swedish patients who had undergone appendectomy before the age

of 50. The results demonstrated an incidence–rate ratio (ratio of the incidence rates of UC among appendicectomized patients compared with that of controls) of 0.74 (95% confidence interval [CI] 0.64–0.86) for patients who had an appendectomy. However, this was dependent on the findings at surgery with incidence–rate ratios of 0.73 (95% CI 0.62–0.87) for confirmed appendicitis, 0.48 (95% CI 0.27–0.83) for mesenteric lymphadenitis, but 1.34 (95% CI 0.77–2.38) for non-specific abdominal pain with a histologically normal appendix. Moreover, the inverse relationship between prior appendectomy and development of UC was only maintained if surgery occurred before the age of 20 [2].

The importance of age at appendectomy is strongly supported by two other studies and may also heavily influence findings at surgery as both acute appendicitis and mesenteric adenitis both peak well before the age of 20 years, whereas appendectomy for non-specific abdominal pain is more evenly distributed across a wider age range in males, and peaks later in life in females [4].

Further studies have analyzed the impact of prior appendectomy on the natural history of IBD. Detailed analysis of IBD phenotype demonstrated that prior appendectomy was associated with a delay in disease onset for both UC and Crohn's disease. In addition, in UC, but not in Crohn's disease, the disease was clinically milder in those with prior surgery, as manifested by a reduction in need for immunomodulatory therapy (OR 0.15; 95% CI 0.02–1.15) and proctocolectomy ($P = 0.02$) [3]. These findings have been supported by two independent studies, which demonstrated less frequent episodes of disease activity in patients with previous appendectomy [5,6], and a subsequent reduced risk of colectomy [5].

In contrast, however, appendectomy after an established diagnosis of UC had no significant benefit on admission rates to hospital. A decline in admissions for UC exacerbations after appendectomy was also seen, over a comparable time, in the matched control population of patients with UC and an intact appendix [7].

Mechanisms behind the protective effect of appendectomy – observations in humans

Human studies have thus far been unable to elucidate the mechanisms responsible for the inverse relationship between appendectomy and UC. By having appendectomy as their reference point, the investigations have been unable to differentiate between the immunologic effects of an acute or chronic intra-abdominal inflammatory event (i.e. appendicitis) from the impact of removing a potentially important lymphoid organ early in life (appendectomy) [2]. Very little is known about the pathogenesis of appendicitis. However, several studies have indicated that both genetic and environmental factors contribute to this common disorder [8,9]. Further human studies of appendicitis may well provide clues as to the pathogenesis of UC.

Clues from animal models of IBD

Experimental animal data suggest that the appendix may have a role in the initiation of distal colonic inflammation as is seen in UC. Using the dextran sulphate sodium (DSS) model of colitis in mice, removal of the appendix prior to DSS administration resulted in delayed onset of disease with macroscopically and histologically milder inflammation than was seen when the appendix was left *in situ* [10]. A further study utilized the T-cell receptor knockout mouse model of colitis. These animals spontaneously develop colonic inflammation similar to UC when colonized with normal murine colonic flora. Colitis does not develop in a germ-free environment. Appendectomy prior to bacterial exposure resulted in a significant reduction in the numbers of mice developing colitis, with only 3% at 6 months doing so compared with 80% of controls [11]. However, no experiments have looked at the effect of appendectomy after colitis is established.

The immunologic impact of early appendectomy on the gut has not been studied in humans. In neonatal rabbits, it leads to immunodeficiency with significant reductions in mucosal immunoglobulins IgA, IgG, and IgM, as well as a decrease in antigen-specific immune responses [12]. These observations indicate that at least one protective mechanism offered by early appendectomy may be to render the gut "immunodeficient." The greater impact of appendectomy on UC compared with Crohn's disease may relate specifically to the deficiency in humoral immunity identified by the above experiments in rabbits. However, these observations need to be investigated and confirmed in humans.

Involvement of the appendix in UC

Traditionally, UC has been considered as a continuous disease process extending proximally from the rectum. Discontinuous appendiceal involvement was first described in 1974 [13] and has been demonstrated in 15–86% of colonic resection specimens from patients with UC without cecal involvement [14–16]. Colonoscopic studies have demonstrated cecal inflammation and appendiceal involvement in 75% of patients with isolated distal colonic disease [17], and indicate that this skip lesion is most closely associated with distal UC rather than extensive disease. However, a prospective study of appendectomy for refractory UC indicates that while appendiceal orifice inflammation is highly specific for underlying "appendiceal colitis" (100%), it is insensitive (15%) [18].

It is not possible to establish whether appendiceal involvement precedes and possibly triggers colitis at distant sites, although the appendix is certainly equipped with all the necessary cell lineages to sample, process, and present antigen to both T and B cells, which then migrate to the colonic lamina propria via mesenteric lymph nodes [19,20].

Appendectomy in the treatment of UC

These observations have led to the hypothesis that appendectomy may benefit the clinical course of established UC. Okazaki *et al.* [21] reported the case of a 21-year-old man with a 3-year history of troublesome distal UC and associated periappendiceal inflammation at colonoscopy, who declined standard systemic therapy, and subsequently underwent an appendectomy as a means of limiting inflammation to the distal colon. Two weeks after surgery his bowel habit had improved and by 6 weeks there was marked macroscopic and histologic improvement of his distal colonic mucosa. Consequently, topical therapy was not required.

Radford-Smith et al. [18] described 15 patients with rectosigmoid UC, two of whom had associated endoscopically identifiable appendiceal inflammation. They remained symptomatic despite conventional therapy and went on to have appendicectomies as a potential means of disease modification. Histologic findings confirmed active inflammatory changes in the appendiceal mucosa of 10 patients characterized by a highly activated CD69+ lymphocyte population. The mean follow-up was 20 months. There were significant improvements from baseline in the clinical disease activity index ($P = 0.015$), endoscopic scores ($P = 0.02$), and medication scores ($P = 0.02$) for those patients who had reached the 12-month time point ($n = 10$). The remaining five patients continued on standard therapy and did not undergo colectomy.

Conclusions

There are not yet any controlled data on the potential benefit of appendectomy in large numbers of patients with UC, and the only clinical information comes from individual case reports or open studies. Although appendectomy may represent a novel therapy for patients with poorly controlled distal disease, further study is required before firm conclusions concerning efficacy can be drawn.

References

1 Radford-Smith GL. The role of the appendix and appendectomy in patients with inflammatory bowel disease. *IBD Monitor* 2003; 4: 120–8.

2 Andersson RE, Olaison G, Tysk C, et al. Appendectomy and protection against ulcerative colitis. *N Engl J Med* 2001; 344: 808–14.

3 Radford-Smith GL, Edwards JE, Purdie DM, et al. Protective role of appendectomy on onset and severity of ulcerative colitis and Crohn's disease. *Gut* 2002; 51: 808–13.

4 Kang JY, Hoare J, Majeed A, et al. Decline in admission rates for acute appendicitis in England. *Br J Surg* 2003; 90: 1586–92.

5 Cosnes J, Carbonnel F, Beaugerie L, et al. Effects of appendectomy on the course of ulcerative colitis. *Gut* 2002; 51: 803–7.

6 Naganuma M, Lizuka B, Torii A, et al. Appendectomy protects against the development of ulcerative colitis and reduces its recurrence: results of a multicenter case-controlled study in Japan. *Am J Gastroenterol* 2001; 96: 1123–6.

7 Hallas J, Gaist D, Vach W, et al. Appendectomy has no beneficial effect on admission rates in patients with ulcerative colitis. *Gut* 2004; 53: 351–4.

8 Duffy DL, Martin NG, Mathews JD. Appendectomy in Australian twins. *Am J Hum Genet* 1990; 47: 590–2.

9 Basta M, Morton NE, Mulvihill JJ, et al. Inheritance of acute appendicitis: familial aggregation and evidence of polygenic transmission. *Am J Hum Genet* 1990; 46: 377–82.

10 Krieglstein CF, Cerwinka WH, Laroux FS, et al. Role of appendix and spleen in experimental colitis. *J Surg Res* 2001; 101: 166–75.

11 Mizoguchi A, Mizoguchi E, Chiba C, et al. Role of appendix in the development of inflammatory bowel disease in TCR-α mutant mice. *J Exp Med* 1996; 184: 707–15.

12 Dasso JF, Howell MD. Neonatal appendectomy impairs mucosal immunity in rabbits. *Cell Immunol* 1997; 182: 29–37.

13 Cohen T, Pfeffer RB, Valensi Q. Ulcerative appendicitis occurring as a skip lesion in chronic ulcerative colitis: report of a case. *Am J Gastroenterol* 1974; 62: 151–5.

14 Kroft SH, Stryker SJ, Rao MS. Appendiceal involvement as a skip lesion in ulcerative colitis. *Mod Pathol* 1994; 7: 912–4.

15 Scott IS, Sheaff M, Coumbe A, et al. Appendiceal inflammation in ulcerative colitis. *Histopathology* 1998; 33: 168–73.

16 Groisman GM, George J, Harpaz N. Ulcerative appendicitis in universal and non-universal ulcerative colitis. *Mod Pathol* 1994; 7: 322–5.

17 D'Haens G, Geboes K, Peeters M, et al. Patchy cecal inflammation associated with distal ulcerative colitis: a prospective endoscopic study. *Am J Gastroenterol* 1997; 92: 1275–9.

18 Radford-Smith GL, Eri R, Lumley J, Prentice R, Bryson G. "Targeted" appendectomy for patients with refractory ulcerative colitis. *J Gastroenterol Hepatol* 2003; 18 (Suppl.): B14(29).

19 Bockman DE, Boydston WR. Participation of follicle associated epithelium (fae), macrophages, and plasma cells in the function of appendix. *Scan Electron Microsc* 1982; 3: 1341–50.

20 Sarsfield P, Rinne A, Jones DB, Johnson P, Wright DH. Accessory cells in physiological lymphoid tissue from intestine: an immunohistochemical study. *Histopathology* 1996; 28: 205–11.

21 Okazaki K, Onodera H, Watanabe N, et al. A patient with improvement of ulcerative colitis after appendectomy. *Gastroenterology* 2000; 119: 502–6.

31 Biologic treatments in IBD

RAYMOND D'SOUZA & JAMES LINDSAY

LEARNING POINTS

Biologic treatments in IBD

- Efficacy of a target-specific drug confirms the pathogenic importance of the target molecule in the inflammatory cascade in IBD

- Despite their apparent target specificity, serious unpredicted adverse effects have occurred with some biologics: long-term safety data are essential

- Not all antibodies targeting an individual cytokine are equally effective

- As with infliximab, we shall need to learn how to use new biologics in conjunction with conventional therapy

- Large monoclonal antibodies are likely to be succeeded by small-molecule drugs given orally

---

Introduction

The last decade has seen a huge leap in our understanding of the molecular pathogenesis of IBD. This has allowed a rapid expansion in trials of novel biologic therapies targeting individual steps in the inflammatory cascade. These therapies aim to induce clinical remission in patients resistant to traditional therapies as well as to change the natural history of the disease. However, careful attention to detail is needed in the interpretation of trials of these agents: which groups of patients are being studied, what endpoints are used, and is the mechanism of action clear? We need to ask whether these expensive therapies are safe and cost effective,

and whether they improve quality of life. This chapter discusses recent trials of novel biologic therapies in both Crohn's disease and UC.

Crohn's disease

Although there is debate about the relative role of the innate and acquired immune system in the initial stages of Crohn's disease, the chronic intestinal inflammation that ensues appears to be mediated by apoptosis-resistant Th-1 lymphocytes responding to the enormous antigenic challenge of the intestinal microbiota. T-cell differentiation occurs in response to antigen presentation which is driven by interaction between naïve T lymphocytes and intestinal antigen-presenting cells such as dendritic cells. T-cell differentiation is determined by the cytokine milieu, with interleukin 12 (IL-12) and γ-interferon (IFN-γ) inducing Th-1 differentiation and IL-10 inducing a regulatory T-cell response. Upon activation, Th-1 lymphocytes interact with tissue macrophages and release a range of cytokines and chemokines that lead to both tissue destruction and increased vascular endothelial adhesion molecule expression. This results in leukocyte infiltration of the lamina propria and amplification of the inflammatory response [1]. Clinical trials of biologic therapies that affect each step within this inflammatory cascade have been reported.

Anti-TNF-α therapies

The therapeutic efficacy of antibodies targeting tumor necrosis factor α (TNF-α) was demonstrated by infliximab, the first commercially available biologic therapy for Crohn's disease (see Chapters 17–21). Five further anti-TNF-α

TABLE 31.1 Biologic therapies for Crohn's disease.

Name	Activity	Type	Ig	Route	Effect in Crohn's disease	Reference
Infliximab	Anti-TNF-α	Chimeric	IgG1	IV	Yes: phase III trials in inflammatory and fistulizing disease for induction and maintenance	Chapters 17–21
Adalimumab	Anti-TNF-α	Fully humanized	IgG1	SC	Yes: remission induction in phase II trials, phase III and maintenance awaited. Effective in patients who have lost response to infliximab	5,6
CDP870/ certolizumab	Anti-TNF-α	Humanized	PEGylated Fab' fragment	SC	Modest effect in patients with raised CRP (phase II). Phase III trial (presented at UEGW 2005) demonstrates significant benefit through week 26.	8
CDP571	Anti-TNF-α	95% humanized	IgG4	IV	Modest effect in phase III – no longer in development	4
Etanercept	Anti-TNF-α	Humanized	TNFr (p75) Fc fusion protein	SC	No	2
Onercept	Anti-TNF-α	Recombinant	TNFr (p55) Fc fusion protein	SC	No	3
Natilizumab	Anti-alpha-4 integrin	Fully humanized	IgG4	IV	Yes (phase III) in both inducing remission and maintenance in patients with raised CRP (withdrawn because of safety concerns)	10,11
ABT-874	Anti-IL-12	Humanized	Not documented	SC	Short-lived response but no increased remission rates in phase II trial. Phase III results awaited	13
Fontolizumab	Anti-IFN-γ	Humanized	IgG1	IV	Modest effect in patients with raised CRP. Phase II trial awaited	14
Sargramostim	GM-CSF	Recombinant protein	N/A	IV/SC	Open label trial of 15 patients: response in 80%, remission in 55%. DBPCT of daily SC therapy for 56 days demonstrated a significant increased remission rate although did not meet primary endpoint.	16
MRA	Anti-IL-6R	Humanized	IgG1	IV	Significant benefit in small placebo controlled trial with 80% clinical response and 20% remission rate (no change in endoscopic scores)	17
IL-10	IL-10 protein	Recombinant protein	NA	SC/IV	Modest effect in inducing remission, no benefit in maintenance after surgery	18

IV, intravenous; SC, subcutaneous; CRP, C-reactive protein.
UEGW, United European Gastroanterology Week; DBPCT, double-blind placebo-controlled trial.

antibody therapies have subsequently been developed (Table 31.1), with variable therapeutic effects depending on immunoglobulin backbone, ability to induce apoptosis and immunogenicity. Thus, both etanercept and onercept, which neutralize soluble TNF-α but do not induce mucosal T-cell apoptosis, are ineffective in Crohn's disease [2,3]. Likewise, a phase III, 28-week, placebo-controlled trial of 8-weekly infusions of CDP 571 (IgG4 non-complement-fixing backbone compared with the IgG1 in infliximab) did not reach statistical significance for its primary endpoints of clinical response or remission at 28 weeks [4].

In some patients, the use of infliximab is limited by the production of antibodies to infliximab (ATI) which result in infusion reactions and decreased clinical efficacy. Adalimumab is the first fully humanized monoclonal IgG1 anti-TNF-α antibody, which also induces T-cell apoptosis. Initial open label studies demonstrated a modest therapeutic efficacy in patients who have either lost response or developed hypersensitivity to infliximab, although most patients required dose escalation [5]. A phase II, placebo-controlled, dose-ranging trial of two subcutaneous injections of adalimumab in 299 patients with active disease demonstrated a significant clinical response compared with placebo at the higher doses [6]. The results of a phase III maintenance trial should be available soon. It will be important to assess the number of patients who required a dose escalation and monitor the levels of anti-drug antibodies in order to define more clearly the efficacy and cost-effectiveness of adalimumab compared with infliximab.

An initial dose-ranging study of a single infusion of CDP870 certolizumab (Table 31.1) in 92 patients found no difference compared with placebo in the primary endpoint of clinical response at week 4 [7]. In a larger trial (PRECiSE I) of 292 patients receiving three infusions, certolizumab again failed to reach significance in its primary endpoint of clinical response at week 12, although it did demonstrate efficacy at week 10 [8]. However, in the 41% of patients who had an elevated C-reactive protein (CRP) at baseline, certolizumab showed a significant response compared with placebo at all time points. This highlights the need to ensure that patients entering clinical trials have definite evidence of active disease. The phase III (PRECiSE II) trial (presented at UEGW 2005) demonstrates significant benefit of Certolizumab/CDP-870 (400 mg sc every week) over placebo in maintenance of remission of Crohn's disease through week 26 in patients who initially responded to remission induction using 400 mg at 0.2 and 4 weeks.

Selective adhesion molecule antagonists

Antibodies to alpha-4 integrins, which mediate leukocyte migration into the intestinal mucosa, have proved therapeutic in animal models. Several large trials of natalizumab (Table 31.1) in patients with active disease and as a maintenance therapy have been reported. As with CDP870, the phase II trial comparing two infusions of natalizumab with placebo failed to reach significance for its primary endpoint of clinical remission at week 6 [9]. However, there was a significant difference between active drug and placebo at other time points and a more impressive response to therapy in the subgroup of patients with a raised CRP. Preliminary reports of the phase III trials, ENACT-1 and ENACT-2, which importantly included patients who had previously been treated with anti-TNF-α agents suggest a significant advantage over placebo in clinical response and quality of life [10]. The subgroup of patients who had previously received but not responded to infliximab also showed a significant response to natalizumab [11]. Unfortunately, further trials have been suspended after case reports of patients developing progressive multifocal leukoencephalopathy after receiving natalizumab for Crohn's disease as well as for multiple sclerosis for which they had previously also been given interferon-β [12].

Alternative cytokine therapies

Strategies designed to inhibit Th-1 T-cell differentiation such as anti-IL-12 and anti-IFN-γ antibodies have proven effective in animal models. In patients with Crohn's disease, a phase II trial of seven weekly injections of ABT-874, a humanized anti-IL-12 antibody, demonstrated a significant increase in initial response compared with placebo although this benefit was lost by week 12 [13]. Furthermore, the drug did not lead to an increase in disease remission compared with placebo. Likewise, initial abstract reports of the anti-IFN-γ antibody, fontolizumab, have not been promising, although efficacy was noted in patients with a raised CRP [14]. A follow-up study of 34 patients (87% with a raised CRP) receiving four doses of fontolizumab demonstrated a response in 80%, but a much lower remission rate [15]. Open label trials of antibodies to the IL-6 receptor and sargramostim (granulocyte-macrophage colony-stimulating factor, GM CSF) have shown positive results. Furthermore, a recent placebo controlled trial of GM CSF demonstrated a significant increase in patients entering disease remission, although, it did not reach its primary endpoint of disease response at day 56 [16,17].

Therapies designed to promote the immunoregulatory effects of the mucosal immune system such as IL-10 have not demonstrated clinical efficacy as a primary therapy or as a maintenance strategy after surgically induced remission. Ongoing work will determine whether direct delivery of immunoregulatory therapy to the inflamed mucosa proves more effective [18].

Ulcerative colitis

Clinical trials of biologic therapies in UC are less well-advanced than in Crohn's disease and no such therapy is licensed for use in this condition. This may reflect less clarity in our understanding of the molecular pathogenesis of UC, or perhaps that surgery offers an effective cure such that the expense of biologic therapies is not justified. However, as in Crohn's, there is an excess of apoptosis-resistant lymphocytes and also raised levels of cytokines such as TNF-α, IFN-γ, IL-5, and IL-13 [19].

Several trials of infliximab for chronic active and steroid-refractory UC have been published (see Chapter 20). There are no published placebo-controlled trials for the other anti-TNF-α antibodies, although a modest short-lived response after a single infusion of CDP571 was reported in an open trial [20]. However, a recent controlled study suggests efficacy in UC for an orally administered topically acting small molecular weight compound, RDP58, which inhibits TNF-α production [21].

Limited data from a phase I trial demonstrating clinical efficacy with visilizumab, an anti-CD-3 antibody that induces apoptosis in activated lymphocytes, seems to suggest that, as in Crohn's disease, apoptosis induction will be a key factor in efficacy for UC [22]. A total of 53 patients who had previously failed intravenous steroids have now been treated, with a 60% response rate which is maintained for up to 90 days [23].

Therapies that target the IL-2 pathway have also shown promise in UC. In an open trial of 10 patients with chronic active UC, two infusions of daclizumab, an IgG1 humanized anti-CD25 (IL-2Ra) antibody, led to improvement in clinical, endoscopic, and quality of life scores at 8 weeks [24]. Likewise, basiliximab, a chimeric monoclonal antibody to IL-2R, demonstrated clinical benefit and reversed steroid resistance in an open trial of 30 patients, although the murine component of this antibody may induce immunogenicity with repeated use [25].

Several topical biologic strategies have been investigated in refractory distal UC. Alicaforsen, an enema containing an antisense inhibitor to the adhesion molecule ICAM-1 has been compared with both placebo and mesalamine enemas in two phase II trials [26]. This therapy appears to be at least as effective as mesalamine enemas although it reaches its maximum benefit after 6 weeks. Finally, there has been interest in growth factors that expedite mucosal restitution as a therapy for UC. Epidermal growth factor (EGF),administered as an enema together with mesalamine, produced remission at 4 weeks in 10/12 patients compared with 1/12 patients treated with mesalamine plus placebo [27]. However, the concern that EGF may up-regulate proto-oncogenes needs to be excluded before use of these therapies becomes widespread.

Conlusions

It is now a decade since the efficacy of anti-TNF-α therapy in Crohn's disease was first reported. Despite the large number of clinical trials driven by investment from the pharmaceutical industry, infliximab remains the only licensed biologic therapy in IBD. However, it is likely that it will be joined by other anti-TNF-α antibodies in the near future. Despite evidence of benefit in patients with definite intestinal inflammation, the adhesion molecule therapies need to prove their safety before they reach the marketplace. Further clinical trials of the alternative cytokine therapies are required to compare their clinical effects and investigate the benefits and safety of combination therapies.

Several lessons have been learnt that should be applied to future research and development programs. It is essential to delineate the mechanism of action of a potential therapeutic strategy before launching large clinical trials, careful selection criteria are required to ensure that patients have active disease, and it is important to consider the route of administration to ensure that the biologic agent reaches its therapeutic target. As well as demonstrating enhanced therapeutic efficacy over traditional therapies, novel biologics must be shown to be safe; this requires long-term follow-up from trials and meticulous adverse event reporting as the new generation of therapies enters clinical practice. Finally, it is likely that, in the foreseeable future, biologics currently requiring injection or infusion will be succeeded by a new generation of small molecular weight agents which, when given orally, will target specific pathophysiologic pathways.

References

1 Sartor RB. Innate immunity in the pathogenesis and therapy of IBD. *J Gastroenterol* 2003; **38**: 43–7.

2 Sandborn WJ, Hanauer SB, Katz S, *et al.* Etanercept for active Crohn's disease: a randomised, double-blind placebo-controlled trial. *Gastroenterology* 2001; **121**: 1088–94.

3 Rutgeerts P, Lemmens L, Van Assche G, *et al.* Treatment of active Crohn's disease with onercept (recombinant human

soluble p55 tumour necrosis factor receptor): results of a randomised, open-label, pilot study. *Aliment Pharmacol Ther* 2003; **17**: 185–92.

4 Sandborn WJ, Feagan BG, Radford-Smith G, *et al*. CDP571, a humanised monoclonal antibody to tumour necrosis factor alpha, for moderate to severe Crohn's disease: a randomized, double blind, placebo controlled trial. *Gut* 2004; **53**: 1485–93.

5 Papadakis KA, Shaye OA, Vasiliauskas EA, *et al*. Safety and efficacy of adalimumab (D2E7) in Crohn's disease patients with an attenuated response to infliximab. *Am J Gastroenterol* 2005; **100**: 75–9.

6 Hanauer SB, Sandborn WJ, Rutgeerts P, *et al*. Human Anti-Tumor Necrosis Factor Monoconal Antibody (Adalimumab) in Crohn's disease: the CLASSIC-I Trial. *Gastroenterology* 2006; **130**(2): 323–33.

7 Winter TA, Wright J, Ghosh S, *et al*. Intravenous CDP870, a PEGylated Fab′ fragment of a humanized antitumour necrosis factor antibody, in patients with moderate-to-severe Crohn's disease: an exploratory study. *Aliment Pharmacol Ther* 2004; **20**: 1337–46.

8 Schreiber S, Rutgeerts P, Fedorak RN, *et al*. A randomized, placebo–controlled trial of certolizumab pegol (CDP870) for treatment of Crohn's disease. Gastroenterology 2005; **129**(3): 807–18.

9 Ghosh S, Goldin E, Gordon FH, *et al*. Natalizumab for active Crohn's disease: Natalizumab Pan-European Study Group. *N Engl J Med* 2003; **348**: 24–32.

10 Sandborn WJ, Colombel JF, Enns R, *et al*. Natalizumab induction and maintenance therapy for Crohn's disease. *N Engl J Med* 2005; **353**: 1912–25.

11 Sandborn WJ, Colombel JF, Enns R, *et al*. Efficacy assessment of natalizumab in patients with Crohn's disease and prior history of anti-TNF therapy: results from ENACT-1. *Gastroenterology* 2004: **126** (Suppl): A583.

12 Van Assche G, Van Ranst M, Sciot R, *et al*. Progressive multi-focal leukoencephalopathy after natalizumab therapy for Crohn's disease. *N Engl J Med* 2005; **353**: 362–8. Epub 2005 Jun 9.

13 Mannon PJ, Fuss IJ, Mayer L, *et al*. Anti-interleukin-12 antibody for active Crohn's disease. *N Engl J Med* 2004; **351**: 2069–79.

14 Reinisch W, Hommes DW, Von Assche G, *et al*. A dose-escalating placebo-controlled double-blind, single-dose and multi-dose, safety and tolerability study of fontolizumab, a humanised anti-interferon-gamma antibody, in patients with moderate-to-severe Crohn's disease. **Gut** 2006. Epub 2006, Feb 21.

15 de Villers W, Katz S, Salzberg B, *et al*. Chronic dosing of Fontolizumab (huzaftm), a humanized anti IFN-gamma antibody, in patients with moderate to severe Crohn's disease. *Gastroenterology* 2005; **128**: A720.

16 Korzenik JR, Dieckgraefe BK, Valentine JF, *et al*. Sargramostim for active Crohn's disease. *N Engl J Med* 2005; **352**: 2193–201.

17 Ito H, Takazoe M, Fukuda Y, *et al*. A pilot randomised trial of a human anti-interleukin-6 receptor monoclonal antibody in active Crohn's disease. *Gastroenterology* 2004; **126**: 989–96.

18 Lindsay JO, Hodgson HJF. The immunoregulatory cytokine Interleukin-10: a therapy for Crohn's disease. *Aliment Pharmacol Ther* 2001; **15**: 1709–16.

19 Peppelenbosch MP, van Deventer SJ. T cell apoptosis and inflammatory bowel disease. *Gut* 2004; **53**: 1556–8.

20 Evans RC, Clarke L, Heath P, *et al*. Treatment of ulcerative colitis with an engineered human anti-TNF alpha antibody CDP571. *Aliment Pharmacol Ther* 1997; **11**: 1031–5.

21 Travis S, Yap LM, Hawkey C, *et al*. RDP Investigators Study Group. RDP58 is a novel and potentially effective oral therapy for ulcerative colitis. *Inflamm Bowel Dis* 2005; **11**: 713–9.

22 Plevy S, Salzberg B, van Assche G, *et al*. A humanized anti-CD3 monoclonal antibody, visilizumab, for treatment of refractory ulcerative colitis: results of a phase I study. *Gastroenterology* 2004; **126**: A-75, Abstract 579.

23 Targan S, Salzberg B, Mayer L, *et al*. A Phase II study: multiple dose levels of vizulizimab are well tolerated and produce rapid and sustained improvement in ulcerative colitis patients refractory to treatment with iv steroids (IVSR-UC). *Gastroenterology* 2005; **128**: A493.

24 Van Assche G, Dalle I, Noman M, *et al*. A pilot study on the use of the humanised anti-interleukin-2 receptor antibody daclizumab in active ulcerative colitis. *Am J Gastroenterol* 2003; **98**: 369–76.

25 Creed TJ, Norman MR, Probert CS, *et al*. Basiliximab (anti-CD25) in combination with steroids may be an effective new treatment for steroid-resistant ulcerative colitis. *Aliment Pharmacol Ther* 2003; **18**: 65–75.

26 Miner P, Nichols T, Schwartz H, *et al*. A phase 2 trial to assess the safety and efficacy of two dose formulations of alicoforsen enema compared with 4 g mesalamine enema for acute ulcerative colitis. *Gastroenterology* 2005; **128**: A491.

27 Sinha A, Nightingale J, West K, *et al*. Epidermal growth factor enemas with oral mesalamine for mild-to-moderate left-sided ulcerative colitis or proctitis. *N Engl J Med* 2003; **349**: 350–7.

32 Stem cell transplantation for IBD

PAUL FORTUN & CHRISTOPHER HAWKEY

Introduction

The concept that hematopoietic stem cell transplantation (HSCT) might offer a potential for cure in Crohn's disease arose serendipitously, with observations that patients undergoing bone marrow transplantation for other disease experienced improvement and sometimes complete remission of their Crohn's.

The proposed rationale for the efficacy of HSCT is that it replaces the genetic predisposition to Crohn's disease. This relies on the premises that Crohn's is an immunomediated, even autoimmune disease, and that resetting the immune system will exempt it from environmental triggers at a later date. These issues are reviewed largely in relation to Crohn's disease, given that difficult UC has a relatively straightforward cure with surgery.

Crohn's disease as an immunomediated disease

The phenotypic expression of Crohn's disease is the result of an interaction between genetic and environmental factors, and this interaction is mediated by the immune system. Specific mutations, such as those of the *NOD2* (*CARD15*) gene (see Chapter 24), increase the risk of Crohn's disease, but require environmental factors, such as smoking, early hygiene, diet, and the luminal microbial environment, for disease expression.

While the mechanisms by which interactions between genetic and environmental factors lead to Crohn's disease are unclear, it involves a loss of immune tolerance to commensal bacteria in the gastrointestinal tract, characterized by an overactive Th-1 immune response [1,2]. As well as abnormal cell-mediated immunity and defects in regulatory T-cell function, IBD demonstrates features of an autoimmune disease [3], including, for example, perinuclear antineutrophil cytoplasmic antibodies (pANCA) in UC, and antibodies against *Saccharomyces cerevisiae* (ASCA) in Crohn's disease.

Given that bone marrow and stem cell transplantation have been beneficial in other diseases characterized by loss of immune tolerance [4], it is possible that these procedures could be of value in Crohn's disease.

Effect on coincident IBD of HSCT given for other diseases

The first report of a patient with Crohn's disease who underwent allogeneic bone marrow transplant for lymphoma was in 1993 [5]. The patient's Crohn's disease improved, although reported follow-up was only 6 months. Since then, at least 20 patients with IBD (including one patient with UC) have been reported who underwent HSCT for indications such as leukemia, lymphoma, and breast cancer (Table 32.1).

One of the more impressive outcomes occurred in a patient with CD from the age of 9 years needing substantial treatment for 7 years [12]. Following an autologous HSCT for non-Hodgkin's lymphoma there was no clinical or laboratory evidence of Crohn's disease recurrence in the next 7 years [10].

In a series from Seattle [6], 3/5 patients whose Crohn's disease was active before allogeneic transplantation for leukemia achieved remission for up to 10 years despite discontinuation of immunosuppression.

In a recent German series, seven patients with Crohn's disease and four with UC for a median of 10 (range 0.5–22) years had a post-transplant follow-up of 34 (range 3–117) months [9]. Six patients had active disease at conditioning. Ten patients went into remission following transplantation (three had early symptoms, with findings of atypical histology, cytomegalovirus [CMV] colitis, and graft-versus-host disease [GVHD]).

Our experience of a 41-year-old patient with diffuse colonic Crohn's disease for 16 years prior to autologous HSCT for follicular lymphoma was informative. Colonoscopy before transplantation showed patchy inflammatory changes compatible with mild active Crohn's disease. Following transplantation he went into remission from his lymphoma and his bowel symptoms ceased, allowing

TABLE 32.1 Summary of hematopoietic stem cell transplantation (HSCT) for patients with incidental Crohn's disease (italic type) and primarily for Crohn's disease (bold type).

Reference	Number	Type of HSCT	Indication	Outcome	Follow-up	Comment
Lopez-Cubero [6]	6	Allogeneic	*Leukemia*	4/6 remission	6–15 years 1/6 died 1/6 surgery	
Soderholm [7]	1	Allogeneic	*AML*	Remission	5 years	Regular endoscopic follow-up
Drakos [[5]	1	Autologous	*NHL*	Remission	6 months	Diarrhea post-BMT
Castro [8]	2F (1CD, 1UC)	Autologous	*Breast cancer*	Both off Rx; CD mild colitis on FU colonoscopy	2 years	High-dose chemo + HSCT CD had PMC
Ditschkowski [9]	11	Autologous	*Leukemia and MDS*	10 remissions 1 died pulmonary fungal infection	34 months Pre HSCT	Chemo and RT
Kashyap [10]	1	Autologous	*NHL*	Remission	7 years	
Kreisel [11]	1	Autologous	**CD**	Clinical +	9 months histologic improvement	"Prophylactic" steroids and MTX
Scime [12]	1	Autologous	**CD**	Clinical remission	5 months	Clinical, endoscopic and histologic improvement
Oyama [13]	12	Autologous	**CD**	Sustained remission in 11/12 patients	7–37 months	Clinical, endoscopic and histologic improvement

AML, acute myeloid leukaemia; BMT, bone marrow transplantation; CD, Crohn's disease; F, female; FU, follow up; MDS, myelodysplastic syndrome; MTX, methotrexate; NHL, non-Hodgkin's lymphoma; PMC, Pseudomembranous colitis; RT, radiotherapy; Rx, treatment.

stoppage of all immunosuppressive drugs. Eighteen months after transplantation, colonoscopy showed no evidence of Crohn's disease macro- or microscopically.

It must be stressed that two of the reported patients with leukemia and Crohn's disease died. One had CMV enteritis after autologous HSCT, but died of pulmonary fungal infection [9]. Another developed *Clostridium difficile*-induced colitis and intestinal GVHD, and died of septicemia 3 months after allogeneic HSCT [6]. In the same series, one of the six patients had a relapse of their Crohn's disease at the site of an ileocolonic anastamosis 1.5 years after allogeneic HSCT.

It is not possible to determine whether this mortality would also accrue in patients for whom Crohn's disease was the sole indication for bone marrow transplant. The reported infectious enteritides can occur in patients with Crohn's disease on immunosuppression, raising the concern that they may be particularly likely after HSCT. Overall, however, most patients (19/22) entered remission, sometimes prolonged (15 years). This has led to burgeoning interest in performing HSCT primarily for Crohn's disease.

HCST specifically for Crohn's disease

Apart from case reports (Table 32.1) [11,12], the only series reported on HSCT for Crohn's disease as the primary indication has been a phase I study [13] of 12 patients with refractory Crohn's disease (median Crohn's Disease Activity Index [CDAI] 291). All had failed treatment with corticosteroids, mesalamine, thiopurines, and infliximab; half had received methotrexate. Eleven entered "sustained" remission (median follow-up 18 months, range 7–37 months). One patient, a smoker, had recurrence of Crohn's disease at 15 months.

Unresolved issues and controversies

Safety

The decision to employ this therapy involves a comparison between the expected morbidity and mortality of severe non-responsive Crohn's disease and of HSCT. The estimated mortality of Crohn's disease varies in early series from 6% to 13% [14,15]. More recent series, however, have found no increase in mortality [16], suggesting improvements in treatment and surveillance, or a confounding variable in the earlier series in the form of increased deaths being due to smoking [17]. Proponents of HSCT for

Crohn's disease point out that the mortality for severe cases as a subset may be in the range of 10% [18], giving a favorable trade-off against autologous HSCT (mortality 2–5%) [18]. The substantial morbidity of Crohn's disease must also feature in the equation.

Although, reassuringly, Burt *et al.* [19] report that over 70 HSCTs have been performed for autoimmune diseases without any transplant-related mortality (TRM), the TRM for all autoimmune diseases has been 8.6% in other registry data, compared with an expected mortality of the diseases themselves of 1–3% [20].

Mechanism of action of HSCT

There is uncertainty about which component of this complex therapy (Table 32.2) is responsible for the response. It is possible that autologous HSCT simply allows more intense immunosuppression, with the role of the stem cell reinfusion to shorten the neutropenic interval. Disease improvement is seen with most patients after HSC mobilization alone [12,13], and for other autoimmune diseases it has been argued that the conditioning regime alone will suffice without stem cell infusion [21]. HSCT may simply enable immunosuppression to be more intense with subsequent long-term benefit arising through reinstated immunoregulation. It is therefore essential, prior to subjecting the patient to HSCT, that there is a period of optimization of current management or, as previously advocated, review in the form of a second opinion [22].

In addition, some patients who underwent HSCT for indications other than Crohn's disease also had chemotherapy, while the Chicago series all received prophylactic antibiotic regimens which could have some efficacy against Crohn's disease [20].

Recently, interesting insights into previously unsuspected mechanisms by which stem cell transplantation could affect the gut have emerged. In both animal and patient studies, sex-mismatched transplants have been given, enabling donor cells to be identified by immunohistochemical staining for the Y chromosome. These have shown that a population of myofibroblasts derived from the donor populates the intestinal mucosa, particularly in the subepithelial segment [23]. In addition, bone-marrow derived cells have been shown to have a role in neovasculogenesis [24]. Given the importance of myofibroblasts in orchestrating the function of epithelial cells, these data suggest a mechanism other than one targeted at immunosuppression that could beneficially reset patient functions,

TABLE 32.2 Comparison of autologous vs. allogeneic hematopoietic stem cell transplantation (HSCT) in Crohn's disease (CD).

Autologous	Allogeneic
Procedure	
Mobilization: cyclophosphamide, G-CSF,	High-dose immunoablative therapy (e.g. cyclophosphamide)
↓	Total body irradiation
Leukopheresis	↓
↓	HSCT from HLA matched donor, (usually sibling)
Conditioning: cyclophosphamide, ATG, methylprednisolone, G-CSF	
↓	
HSCT	
Safety	
Stronger myeloablative regimen	Increased morbidity (e.g. GVHD) and mortality
Efficacy	
Potential for relapse	Potentially ablates bone marrow
Outcome	
Increasing evidence for achieving remission	Dramatic remission possible, but two reported fatalities
Evidence	
Sustained remission in 11/12 patients, non-randomized trial	Favorable short-term responses reported for CD

ATG, antithymocyte globulin; G-CSF, granulocyte colony-stimulating factor; GVHD, graft-versus-host disease; HLA, human leukocyte antigen.

for example enhancing barrier function. One therapeutic modality for the future may be therefore to be more selective, with "mini-transplantation" of healing allogeneic mesenchymal stem cells by non-myeloablative HSCT [20].

Autologous vs. allogeneic transplantation

(Table 32.2)

What are we trying to achieve: total ablation or merely resetting the immune system? Allogeneic transplantation could completely replace the genetic predisposition to Crohn's disease in circulating leukocytes, whereas autologous transplantation might work by clearing the body of committed lymphocyte clones, restoring the status quo of being predisposed to Crohn's disease but not suffering from it. In practice, total immune ablation is probably not feasible, even with allogeneic HSCT and the graft-versus-autoimmune (GVA) effect. The final outcome is probably a dynamic balance between tolerance and immunity [20], so that resetting by autologous HSCT should suffice. An important premise for the feasibility of autologous HSCT is that "autoimmunity is learned and not genetically pre-ordained" [4].

Autologous HSCT is generally regarded as safer and less complicated than allogeneic HSCT and therefore preferable for autoimmune diseases [4]. However, there is a theoretical increased potential for relapse after reinfusion

of unmanipulated autologous stem cells. This may be reduced by T lymphocyte depletion, for example by CD34+ cell selection.

Allogeneic HSCTs for Crohn's disease have usually been from human leukocyte antigen (HLA) matched siblings, or occasionally HLA-matched unrelated donors [6]. This carries the potential risk of transferring the genetic predisposition to Crohn's disease, for example through the *NOD2/CARD15* gene. Indeed, there have been reports of acquired Crohn's colitis [25] and UC [26], although in the case of suspected genetic transfer of Crohn's disease risk, testing for the 30 known *NOD2/CARD15* mutations was negative.

As a further safety issue, both donor and recipient *NOD2/CARD15* mutations have been associated with increased transplant-related mortality and GVHD after allogeneic HSCT [27].

Conclusions

HSCT shows promise in offering a cure for Crohn's disease. Proof of concept studies are required to determine how resetting of the immune balance is achieved. HSCT may be appropriate for a subset of patients with severe Crohn's disease in whom the trade-off of risk versus benefit might favor this intensive treatment.

References

1 Banias G, Sugawara K, Pagnini C, Cominelli F. The Th1 immune pathway as a therapeutic target in Crohn's disease. *Curr Opin Investig Drugs* 2003; **4**: 1279–86.

2 Watts DA, Satsangi J. The genetic jigsaw of inflammatory bowel disease. *Gut* 2002; **50** (Suppl 3): 31–6.

3 Wen Z, Fiocchi C. Inflammatory bowel disease: autoimmune or immune-mediated pathogenesis? *Clin Dev Immunol* 2004; **11**: 195–204.

4 Burt RK, Traynor AE. Haematopoietic stem cell transplantation: a new therapy for autoimmune disease. *Stem Cells* 1999; **17**: 366–72.

5 Drakos PE, Nagler A, Or R. Case of Crohn's disease in bone marrow transplantation. *Am J Hematol* 1993; **43**: 157–8.

6 Lopez-Cubero SO, Sullivan KM, McDonald GB. Course of Crohn's disease after allogeneic marrow transplantation. *Gastroenterology* 1998; **114**: 433–40.

7 Soderholm JD, Malm C, Juliusson G, Sjodhl R. Long-term endoscopic remission of Crohn's disease after autologous stem cell transplantation for acute myeloid leukaemia. *Scand J Gastroenterol* 2002; **37**: 613–6.

8 Castro J, Benich HI, Smith L, *et al.* Prolonged clinical remission in patients (pts) with inflammatory bowel disease (IBD) after high dose chemotherapy (HDC) and autologous blood stem cell transplantation. *Blood* 1996; **88**: 133A.

9 Ditschkowski M, Einsele H, Schwerdtfeger R, *et al.* Improvement of inflammatory bowel disease after allogeneic stem cell transplantation. *Transplantation* 2003; **75**: 1745–7.

10 Kashyap A, Forman SJ. Autologous bone marrow transplantation for non-Hodgkin's lymphoma results in long-term remission of coincidental Crohn's disease. *Br J Haematol* 1998; **103**: 651–2.

11 Kreisel W, Potthoff K, Bertz H, *et al.* Complete remission of Crohn's disease after high-dose cyclophosphamide and autologous stem cell transplantation. *Bone Marrow Transplant* 2003; **32**: 337–40.

12 Scime R, Cavallaro AM, Tringali S, *et al.* Complete clinical remission after high-dose immune suppression and autologous hematopoietic stem cell transplantation in severe Crohn's disease refractory to immunosuppressive and immuno-modulator therapy. *Inflamm Bowel Dis* 2004; **10**: 892–4.

13 Oyama R, Craig RM, Traynor AE, *et al.* Autologous haematopoietic stem cell transplantation in patients with refractory Crohn's disease. *Gastroenterology* 2005; **128**: 552–63.

14 Farmer RG, Whelan G, Fazio VW. Long-term follow-up of patients with Crohn's disease: relationship between clinical pattern and prognosis. *Gastroenterology* 1985; **88**: 818–25.

15 Cooke WT, Mallas E, Prior P, Allan RN. Crohn's disease: course, teatment and long term prognosis. *Q J Med* 1980; **49**: 363–84.

16 Munkholm P, Langholz E, Davidsen M, Binder V. Intestinal cancer risk and mortality in patients with Crohn's disease. *Gastroenterology* 1993; **105**: 1716–23.

17 Masala G, Bagnoli S, Ceroti M, *et al.* Divergent patterns of total and cancer mortality in ulcerative colitis and Crohn's disease patients: the Florence IBD study 1978–2001. *Gut* 2004; **53**: 1309–13.

18 Craig RM. Autologous haematopoietic stem cell transplant for Crohn's disease. *Autoimmun Rev* 2002; **1**: 244–9.

19 Burt RK, Traynor A, Craig R, Marmont AM. The promise of haematopoietic stem cell transplant for autoimmune diseases. *Bone Marrow Transplant* 2003; **31**: 521–4.

20 Barkholt L, Lofberg R. Resetting the immune system in refractory Crohn's disease: is autologous hematopoietic stem cell transplantation the way forward? *Gastroenterology* 2005; **128**: 786–8.

21 Brodsky RA, Petri M, Smith BD, *et al.* Immunoablative high-dose cyclophosphamide without stem-cell rescue for refractory, severe autoimmune disease. *Ann Intern Med* 1998; **129**: 1031–5.

22 Hawkey CJ, Snowdon JA, Lobo A, *et al.* Stem cell transplantation for inflammatory bowel disease: practical and ethical issues. *Gut* 2000; **46**: 869–72.

23 Brittan M, Hunt T, Jeffery R, *et al.* Bone marrow derivation of pericryptal myofibroblasts in the mouse and human small intestine and colon. *Gut* 2002; **50**: 752–7.

24 Brittan M, Chance V, Elia G, *et al.* A regenerative role for bone marrow following experimental colitis: contribution to neovasculogenesis and myofibroblasts. *Gastroenterology* 2005; **128**: 1984–95.

25 Sonwalker SA, James RM, Ahmad T, *et al.* Fulminant Crohn's colitis after allogeneic stem cell transplant. *Gut* 2003; **52**: 1518–21.

26 Spiers AS. Ulcerative colitis after bone-arrow transplantation for acute leukaemia. *N Engl J Med* 1984; **311**: 1259.

27 Dickinson AM, Middleton PG, Rocha V, Gluckman E, Holler E, Eurobank members. Genetic polymorphisms predicting the outcome of bone marrow transplants. *Br J Haematol* 2004; **127**: 479–90.

Medical Treatment:
What's Round the Corner?

Complementary and alternative therapy –
the way forward or a step back?

LOUISE LANGMEAD & DAVID RAMPTON

LEARNING POINTS

Complementary therapy

- Complementary medicine, particularly herbal therapy, is widely used by patients with IBD

- There is limited controlled evidence indicating efficacy of aloe vera, wheat grass juice, *Boswellia serrata*, traditional Chinese medicines, and bovine colostrum in IBD

- Natural therapies are not necessarily safe: fatal hepatic and irreversible renal failure have occurred with some preparations and interactions with conventional drugs are potentially dangerous

- There is a need for further controlled clinical trials of the potential efficacy of complementary and alternative approaches in IBD, together with enhanced legislation to maximize their quality and safety

Introduction

The term complementary and alternative medicine (CAM) denotes theories and practices in medicine that deviate from the conventional. The combined term comprises a heterogeneous range of diagnostic and therapeutic procedures ranging from traditional practices such as acupuncture, traditional Chinese medicine, Ayurvedic medicine, homeopathy, and herbal medicine, to more modern complementary practices including aromatherapy and reflexology. What constitutes CAM changes with the passage of time and as our realization of its efficacy and mechanisms

of action in certain settings increases. A decade ago, for example, probiotic therapies would have been categorized as a CAM approach. With the knowledge that they may have a therapeutic effect in IBD, however (see Chapter 25), probiotics are now considered a mainstream option.

CAM tends to be excluded from the realms of established scientific medicine. Indeed, much information about its possible effectiveness is anecdotal or historical, the view often being taken that the use of a particular approach by successive generations of people in a range of different societies and cultures must indicate that it works. There has been far too little well-designed research into the potential efficacy and safety of CAM in human disease in general, and in IBD in particular.

CAM is discussed in this book because the approaches used are new to the management of IBD, and because of the rapidly increasing use by patients of this modality in the Western world. Doctors and other medical staff can no longer ignore the potential benefits and dangers of CAM; it will not go away.

Current usage of CAM

Recent surveys have shown a steadily increasing impact of CAM in the West over recent decades, with up to 50% of people now using some form, most commonly herbal remedies [1,2]. In developing countries, the usage is even more widespread [3]. The extensive use of CAM in IBD is likely to be related to its chronic and refractory nature [4] and has been linked with poor quality of life in relation to psychosocial function [5].

TABLE 33.1 Complementary and alternative therapies claimed to have benefit in IBD.

Approach	Disease	Trial design	Outcome	Reference
Non-herbal				
Acupuncture	Active Crohn's	Randomized, single-blind, controlled	Improvement	[10]
Acupuncture with moxibustion	Active UC	Comparative	Similar to Western treatment	[11]
Bovine colostrum enemas	Active UC	Randomized, double-blind, controlled	Better than placebo	[18]
Herbal				
Jian Pi Ling tabs, RSF-FS enemas	Active UC	Randomized controlled	Better than oral 5-ASA	See [8]
Kui jie qing enemas	Active UC	Controlled	Better than 5-ASA, pred	See [8]
Yukui tang tabs, herbal decoction enemas	Active UC	Controlled	Better than pred	See [8]
Germinated barley	Active UC	Open	Improvement of active disease	[13,14]
	Inactive UC	Comparative	Better maintenance than conventional treatment	[15]
Aloe vera gel	Active UC	Randomized, double-blind, controlled	Better than placebo	[9]
Wheat grass juice	Active UC	Randomized, double-blind, controlled	Better than placebo	[16]
Boswellia serrata	Active UC	Controlled	Similar to sulfasalazine	[17]
	Active Crohn's	Controlled	Similar to 5-ASA	[18]
Curcumin	Active proctitis	Open	Improvement	[18]
	Active Crohn's			

5-ASA, 5-aminosalicylate; pred, prednisolone.

Efficacy of CAM in IBD

Trial design

One of the principal challenges relating to assessment of the potential efficacy of CAM in IBD, or any other illness, is trial design [6,7]. In particular, it is very difficult to devise a suitable control arm for use in blinded trials of approaches such as acupuncture, hypnotherapy, and even herbal therapies in which the test remedy has a characteristic flavor, smell, or appearance. However, concerns that the already substantial placebo response in conventional clinical trials in IBD (see Chapter 22) might be still higher in trials utilizing CAM approaches have been allayed by the limited data available [7–9].

Herbal remedies

Reported trials using herbal therapies in IBD relate almost always to UC rather than Crohn's disease.

Studies reported in Chinese literature refer to the treatment of UC with various herbal remedies, but often only abstracts are available in English (Table 33.1) [8]. Such studies have usually employed conventional therapy with steroids and sulfasalazine as the control, but were generally not clearly randomized or blinded. The same applies to open-label Japanese trials suggesting efficacy for a germinated barley foodstuff, given as a putative prebiotic [13,14]. In a comparative study, this preparation also appeared effective and safe as maintenance treatment for UC [15].

In contrast, a randomized, double-blind, controlled study showed that aloe vera gel, given for 4 weeks to patients with moderately active UC, produced a clinical response in significantly more patients than did placebo; rectal mucosal histologic appearances also improved after aloe vera [9]. In a trial of similar design, wheat grass juice orally [16] was reported to reduce disease activity to a greater extent than did placebo in patients with active disease. In a comparative trial undertaken in India, the effect of the gum resin from *Boswellia serrata* in moderately active UC was compared with sulfasalazine [17]; remission was achieved in over 75% of both study groups. An extract of *Boswellia serrata*, H15, had at least similar efficacy to mesalazine in a randomized, double-blind trial in patients with active Crohn's disease [18]. Lastly, in a recent pilot study, curcumin, the yellow pigment of the curry spice, turmeric, was reported to be beneficial when given orally to five patients with proctitis and five with Crohn's disease [19].

Other CAM modalities

In a single-blind, controlled trial, acupuncture reduced Crohn's Disease Activity Index (CDAI) and improved general well-being in patients with Crohn's disease to a greater extent than did insertion of needles into non-acupuncture points [10]. A comparative study from China suggested, furthermore, that acupuncture with moxibustion (in which heat is added by burning herbs over the acupuncture site) was as effective as conventional Western therapy in UC [11]. Finally, enemas containing bovine colostrum were superior to placebo in a controlled trial in patients with active distal UC [12]. We are unaware of any other trials of CAM in patients with IBD.

Possible modes of action of CAM

One barrier to the acceptance of CAM by conventional doctors has been the apparent lack of any scientific explanation for its possible efficacy. Indeed, types of CAM such as acupuncture have been based on historical and cultural constructs often entirely unfamiliar to the majority of Western clinicians. Recently, however, mechanisms by which some of these modalities may work have become increasingly apparent. For example, it is now clear from the emerging field of psychoneuroimmunology (see Chapter 35) that neuronal connections between the brain and the enteric nervous system, and in turn with the immune and inflammatory cells in the lamina propria, could mediate any anti-inflammatory gastrointestinal effects of modalities such as acupuncture and hypnotherapy.

In relation to herbal remedies, the problem is different. Unpurified herbal preparations contain a huge range of biologically active compounds [8], some of which may have beneficial and others adverse effects. Extensive work

of varying quality, clinical relevance, and accessibility has suggested that, *in vitro* at least, individual chemicals derived from a variety of plants may have antibacterial, antioxidant, anticytokine, antispasmodic, and neuromodulatory actions [8]. It is clearly difficult, however, to extrapolate from a knowledge of the chemical composition and activities *in vitro* of an extract from a given plant to its possible efficacy (or safety) *in vivo*. This will depend on a number of factors including the amounts of individual constituents in the extract (which may vary with the plant's origin and the method of preparation of the extract), interactions between individual constituents, and their pharmacokinetics, of which little is known in most instances.

Side-effects of CAM in IBD

Direct toxicity

Contrary to widespread popular belief, "natural" does not mean safe. While it is unlikely that therapies such as reflexology will have direct adverse effects, the same cannot be said of herbal therapies, toxicity from which has included fatal liver and renal failure [7,8]. Unfortunately, there are limited formal data on the incidence even of acute severe side-effects such as these, and knowledge of possible longer term sequelae such as mutagenicity and carcinogenicity is even more scanty.

Toxic effects have also been associated with the deliberate inclusion of prescription medicines in some, particularly traditional Chinese, herbal preparations: these have included corticosteroids, fenfluramine, and glibenclamide [20]. Other toxic products found in some preparations have included mercury, arsenic, lead, human placenta (with a risk of transmitting hepatitis C or HIV), and bat excreta [20].

Drug interactions

The interaction of herbal therapies with conventional drugs needs further clarification. In the context of UC, however, St. John's Wort reduces blood levels of cyclosporine by enhancing the activity of cytochrome p450 enzymes [8].

Indirect adverse effects

Perhaps more importantly, use of CAM may be complicated by indirect adverse effects. For example, patients initially consulting alternative practitioners may suffer from misdiagnosis. Others may delay or forego appropriate conventional options in favor of ineffective unconventional ones.

Conclusions

Complementary and alternative medicine: the way forward or a step back? Systematic and comprehensive screening of the plant kingdom for potentially beneficial new anti-inflammatory agents is well worthwhile: indeed, many pharmaceutical companies have been aware of this for some years and are undertaking just such a search. In any event, patients have already made their decision: complementary and alternative medicine is here to stay.

This being so, it is up to doctors and clinical scientists to sort the wheat from the chaff. Despite the difficulties associated with evaluating CAM, it is essential that further efforts are made to assess scientifically the efficacy and safety of, at least, those therapies that are most frequently used. Herbal preparations, in particular, should require licensing by an independent national body in order to improve their quality and safety and to ensure that claims of efficacy are validated by controlled trials. The general public, pharmacists, and doctors need to be aware of the direct and indirect risks associated with use of complementary and alternative therapies of all types.

Despite these caveats, the words of Herbert Spencer (1820–1903) should be heeded in this context: "There is a principle which is a bar against all information, which is proof against all argument and cannot help but keep man in everlasting ignorance, which is condemnation without investigation."

References

1 Eisenberg DM, Davis RB, Ettner SL, *et al.* Trends in alternative medicine use in the United States, 1990–97: results of a follow up national survey. *JAMA* 1998; **280**:1569–75.

2 Zollman C, Vickers A. ABC of complementary medicine: users and practitioners of complementary medicine. *BMJ* 1999; **319**: 836–8.

3 Bodeker G. Lessons on integration from the developing world's experience. *BMJ* 2001; **322**: 164–7.

4 Hilsden RJ, Scott CM, Verhoef MJ. Complementary medicine use by patients with inflammatory bowel disease. *Am J Gastroenterol* 1998; **93**: 697–701.

5 Langmead L, Chitnis M, Rampton DS. Use of complementary therapy by patients with IBD may indicate psychosocial distress. *Inflamm Bowel Dis* 2002; **8**: 174–9.

6 Mason S, Tovey P, Long AF. Evaluating complementary medicine: methodological challenges of randomised controlled trials. *BMJ* 2002; **325**: 832–4.

7 Koretz RL, Rotblatt M. Complementary and alternative medicine in gastroenterology: the good, the bad and the ugly. *Clin Gastroenterol Hepatol* 2004; **2**: 957–67.

8 Langmead L, Rampton DS. Review article: herbal treatment in gastrointestinal and liver disease: benefits and dangers. *Aliment Pharmacol Ther* 2001; **15**: 1239–52.

9 Langmead L, Feakins RM, Goldthorpe S, *et al.* Randomised, double-blind, placebo-controlled trial of oral aloe vera gel for active ulcerative colitis. *Aliment Pharmacol Ther* 2004; **19**: 739–47.

10 Joos S, Brinkhaus B, Maluche C, *et al.* Acupuncture and moxibustion in the treatment of active Crohn's disease: a randomised controlled study. *Digestion* 2004; **69**: 131–9.

11 Yang C, Yan H. Observation of the efficacy of acupuncture and moxibustion in 62 cases of chronic colitis. *J Tradit Chin Med* 1999; **19**: 111–4.

12 Khan Z, MacDonald C, Wicks AC, *et al.* Use of the 'nutriceutical', bovine colostrums, for the treatment of distal ulcerative colitis: results from an initial study. *Aliment Pharmacol Ther* 2002; **16**: 1917–22.

13 Kanauchi O, Mitsuyama K, Homma T, *et al.* Treatment of ulcerative colitis patients by long-term administration of germinated barley food stuff: multi-centre open trial. *Int J Mol Med* 2003; **12**: 701–4.

14 Kanauchi O, Suga T, Tochihara M, *et al.* Treatment of ulcerative colitis by feeding with germinated barley food stuff: first report of a multi-centre open controlled trial. *J Gastroenterol* 2002; **37** (Suppl 14): 67–72.

15 Hanai H, Kanauchi O, Mitsuyama K, *et al.* Germinated barley foodstuff prolongs remission in patients with ulcerative colitis. *Int J Mol Med* 2004; **13**: 643–7.

16 Ben-Arye E, Goldin E, Wengrower D, *et al.* Wheat grass juice in the treatment of active distal ulcerative colitis: a randomised double-blind placebo-controlled trial. *Scand J Gastroenterol* 2002; **37**: 444–9.

17 Gupta I, Parihar A, Malhotra P, *et al.* Effects of *Boswellia serrata* gum resin in patients with ulcerative colitis. *Eur J Med Res* 1997; **2**: 37–43.

18 Gerhardt H, Seifert F, Buvari P, Vogelsang H, Repges R. Therapy of active Crohn's disease with Boswellia extract H15. *Z Gastroenterol* 2001; **39**: 11–7 (in German).

19 Holt PR, Katz S, Kirshoff R. Curcumin therapy in inflammatory bowel disease: a pilot study. *Dig Dis Sci* 2005; **50**: 2191–3.

20 Anonymous. Safety of traditional Chinese medicines and herbal remedies. *Curr Probl Pharmacovigilance* 2004; **30**: 10–11.

EAMONN QUIGLEY

LEARNING POINTS

Functional problems

- Evidence accumulates for low-grade mucosal and muscularis inflammation in irritable bowel syndrome (IBS)

- Inflammation in inflammatory bowel disease (IBD) may disrupt intestinal motor and sensory systems and alter gut function

- Patients with IBS and IBD may, at times, share similar symptoms

- Confusion between IBS and IBD is most likely to occur when IBD is "subclinical" or in apparent remission

- Upper gastrointestinal symptoms in the IBD patient are more likely to be caused by reflux or functional dyspepsia than IBD

Introduction

In the past, inflammatory bowel disease (IBD) and irritable bowel syndrome (IBS) were regarded as such distinct and separate entities that they were never even considered in the same context. We now recognize, not only that they may coexist and that IBD patients may have a predilection to IBS-type symptoms, but that mucosal inflammation may be an important phenomenon in IBS. How things have changed!

Theory

Recent interest in a putative role for inflammation in IBS, coupled with experimental evidence for important interactions between inflammation and gut muscle and nerve,

have rekindled an examination of relationships between IBS and IBD. Few would propose that these disorders represent one and the same disease process; what we know of their respective natural histories, genetics, immunology, pathophysiology, and pathology renders such a proposal a non-starter. However, recent information suggests that lessons derived from research and clinical experience in one disorder may cast light on enigmas and clinical challenges in the other. Interactions with the "internal" or luminal environment appear important in both; it is now not unreasonable to suggest that IBD and IBS represent dysfunctional responses to luminal antigens, whether presented by the indigenous or an aberrant flora. In IBD, in particular, there is abundant evidence to indicate a central role for the gut flora in the initiation and perpetuation of the inflammatory process.

Evidence to support a role for luminal factors in IBS can be garnered from three main sources: the role of prior infection in the initiation of IBS; the suggestion that chronic, low-grade inflammation is common in IBS; and, finally, and most contentious, reports of alterations in the gut flora in IBS. The concept of post-infectious IBS (P-I IBS), long-recognized by clinicians, is now well established and supported by several prospective and retrospective studies [1]. There is also compelling evidence for a role for low-grade inflammation in IBS [2]. In one study of 77 IBS patients, 31 demonstrated microscopic inflammation and eight fulfilled criteria for lymphocytic colitis [3]. Among the group with "normal" histology, immunohistology revealed evidence of immune activation in all. That IBS patients may be predisposed to an – albeit contained – inflammatory response to luminal triggers is also supported by findings of a reduced frequency of the high-producer phenotype for the anti-inflammatory cytokine interleukin-10 (IL-10) [4] and by the documentation of a reversal of the normal ratio between IL-10 and the pro-inflammatory cytokine IL-12 [5]. The finding, in one study, of low-grade infiltration of lymphocytes in the myenteric plexus in 9/10 patients with severe IBS provides evidence for the extension of the inflammatory process beyond the confines of the mucosal compartment [6].

Dysmotility and visceral hypersensitivity are widely believed to be foremost in the pathogenesis of symptoms in IBS [7]; both also occur in IBD. IBD provides considerable evidence for a role for inflammation in motor dysfunction; there is, indeed, a suggestion that some of the motor abnormalities associated with IBD [8] may persist following apparent resolution of inflammation, thus providing one potential explanation for why some IBD patients' disease could evolve into an IBS-type syndrome during periods of remission. This intriguing suggestion is supported by studies associating IBS-type symptoms with impaired quality of life among IBD patients in remission [9,10]. Another example of a potential interaction between IBS and IBD was recently presented by Shen *et al.* [11]. Among 61 patients who developed symptoms suggestive of pouchitis following ileal pouch-anal anastomoses for UC, 26 failed to achieve diagnostic criteria for pouchitis and were described as suffering from the irritable pouch syndrome (IPS). Observations from experimental studies indicate that chronic inflammation may lead to changes in the phenotype of both smooth muscle and enteric neurons, to the extent that they can assume immunologic functions, leading to a self-perpetuating cycle of interactions between inflammatory cells and the enteric neuromuscular apparatus, per se. These changes have been noted in the context of inflammation limited to the mucosa, even at sites remote from the inflammation [12].

It has been suggested that visceral hypersensitivity is highly specific for IBS [7]. While visceral sensation has received little attention in IBD, in general, the potential role of sensory dysfunction is amply exemplified by acute proctitis where rectal compliance is reduced and the rectum is hypersensitive, factors that contribute to the symptoms of urgency and tenesmus which are the hallmarks of this disorder [13].

Clinical dilemmas

The interactions between IBS and IBD may impinge on

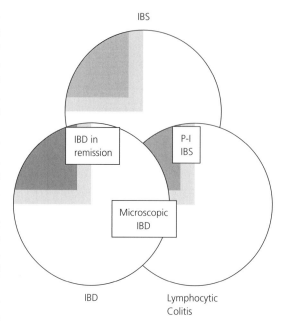

FIG 34.1 Potential relationships between irritable bowel syndrome (IBS) and inflammatory bowel disease (IBD). PI-IBS, post-infective IBS.

clinical practice and present significant diagnostic and therapeutic challenges, both at initial presentation and during follow-up (Fig. 34.1).

At the time of initial evaluation, the following clinical presentations may present a diagnostic challenge.

Chronic abdominal pain and constipation-predominant IBS

Here, IBD and IBS may both be considered in the differential diagnosis. It must be emphasized, however, that chronic abdominal pain, *in the absence of* any alteration of bowel habit or of any evidence of systemic upset is an exceptionally rare manifestation of IBD and cannot, by definition, be regarded as IBS [14]. Other causes, or in the absence of any evidence of an "organic" cause, functional abdominal pain should be considered. In the absence of evidence of episodes of acute or subacute obstruction, the diagnosis of chronic intestinal pseudo-obstruction should, in general, not be considered.

Similarly, it must also be stressed that the likelihood of missing IBD in a young female with the typical symptoms of constipation-predominant IBS, *in the absence of* diarrhea, systemic upset, or any of the physical or laboratory findings characteristic of Crohn's disease, is rare. For these reasons, the yield of small bowel X-rays and colonoscopy in these populations is as close to zero as makes no clinical difference [14].

My personal view is that colonoscopy is *not* indicated in either of these scenarios and could well be regarded as inappropriately invasive.

Chronic diarrhea or diarrhea-predominant IBS

This clinical context is completely different from those described above and the threshold for investigation much lower. Diagnoses such as IBD, celiac disease, and disaccharide intolerance should always be considered in a patient who truly presents with chronic persistent diarrhea.

As ever in clinical medicine, attention to the patient's history and an awareness of the clinical context are of critical importance in the approach to the patient at initial presentation. The attentive and aware clinician should be able to avoid performing unnecessary, invasive, and distressful procedures.

Established IBD

There is, to my mind, more potential for diagnostic confusion in the follow-up of patients with established IBD. The following scenarios may present special challenges.

Altered bowel habit

The recurrence, or persistence of, altered bowel habit, associated with abdominal discomfort, in the patient with IBD who has been in apparent remission.

In Crohn's disease, in particular, there are many potential causes, other than active disease, for diarrhea (see Chapter 46) and associated abdominal cramps. Once these have been eliminated, and clinical and laboratory evaluations provide no evidence of disease activity, IBS may be considered. It is of interest that systemic markers of inflammation have been shown to be elevated to a similar extent in IBD in remission, and in diarrhea-predominant IBS [15]. It should be remembered, especially in areas of high prevalence, that coincidental celiac disease may generate similar symptoms.

Development of upper gastrointestinal symptoms

Esophageal symptoms

In this context it must be remembered that gastro-oesophageal reflux disease (GORD) is a much more likely explanation for heartburn, chest pain, or regurgitation in a patient with IBD than esophageal Crohn's disease. If empiric treatment does not resolve the issue, endosocopy will.

Dyspeptic symptoms

Symptoms suggestive of delayed gastric emptying may arise in IBD for a number of reasons. Clearly, antroduodenal Crohn's may actually obstruct the gastric outlet. Furthermore, gastric emptying delay has also been documented in patients with active IBD, and especially Crohn's disease, in the absence of actual involvement of the foregut [8]. Finally, there is no reason why patients with IBD should be regarded as immune from the development of functional or non-ulcer dyspepsia. In each of these instances, attention to clinical details, basic laboratory assessment and, where doubt persists, endoscopy should resolve the dilemma.

References

1 Spiller RC. Postinfectious irritable bowel syndrome. *Gastroenterology* 2003; **124**: 1662–71.

2 Collins SM. A case for an immunological basis for irritable bowel syndrome. *Gastroenterology* 2002; **122**: 2078–80.

3 Chadwick VS, Chen W, Shu D, *et al*. Activation of the mucosal immune system in irritable bowel syndrome. *Gastroenterology* 2002; **122**: 1778–83.

4 Gonsalkorale WM, Perrey C, Pravica V, Whorwell PJ, Hutchinson IV. Interleukin 10 genotypes in irritable bowel syndrome: evidence for an inflammatory component. *Gut* 2002; **52**: 91–3.

5 O'Mahony L, McCarthy J, Kelly P, *et al*. Lactobacillus and bifidobacterium in irritable bowel syndrome: symptom responses and relationship to cytokine profiles. *Gastroenterology* 2005; **128**: 541–51.

6 Tornblom H, Lindberg G, Nyberg B, Veress B. Full-thickness biopsy of the jejunum reveals inflammation and enteric neuropathy in irritable bowel syndrome. *Gastroenterology* 2002; **123**: 1972–79.

7 Quigley EMM. Current concepts of the irritable bowel syndrome. *Scand J Gastroenterol* 2003; **38**(Suppl 237): 1–8.

8 Quigley EM. Irritable bowel syndrome (IBS) and inflammatory bowel disease (IBD): inter-related diseases? *Chin J Dig Dis* 2005; **6**: 122–32.

9 Isgar B, Harmann M, Kaye MD, Whorwell PJ. Symptoms of irritable bowel syndrome in ulcerative colitis in remission. *Gut* 1983; **24**: 190–2.

10 Simren M, Axelsson J, Gillberg R, *et al*. Quality of life in inflammatory bowel disease in remission: the impact of IBS-like symptoms and associated psychological factors. *Am J Gastroenterol* 2002; **97**: 389–96.

11 Shen B, Achkar J-P, Lashner BA, *et al.* Irritable pouch syndrome: a new category of diagnosis for symptomatic patients with ileal pouch-anal anastomosis. *Am J Gastroenterol* 2002; **97**: 972–7.

12 Geboes K, Collins S. Structural abnormalities of the nervous system in Crohn's disease and ulcerative colitis. *Neurogastroenterol Motil* 1998; **10**: 189–202.

13 Rao SSC, Read NW, Davison PA, Bannister JJ, Holdsworth CD. Anorectal sensitivity and responses to rectal distension in patients with ulcerative colitis. *Gastroenterology* 1987; **93**: 1270–5.

14 Brandt LJ, Locke GR, Olden K, *et al.* An evidence-based approach to the management of irritable bowel syndrome in North America. *Am J Gastroenterol* 2002; **97**(Suppl): S1–S26.

15 Poullis AP, Zar S, Sundaram KK, *et al.* A new, highly sensitive assay for C-reactive protein can aid the differentiation of inflammatory bowel disorders from constipation- and diarrhea-predominant functional bowel disease. *Eur J Gastroenterol Hepatol* 2002; **14**: 409–12.

35 Psychological stress: something to worry about?

JOEL E D MAWDSLEY & DAVID RAMPTON

LEARNING POINTS

Psychological stress

- Experimental stress can contribute to initiation and reactivation of gastrointestinal inflammation in animal models of colitis

- Recent studies suggest that chronic stress and adverse life events can cause relapse in patients with IBD

- In addition to pro-inflammatory effects, stress can worsen symptoms such as stool frequency

- There are few trials of the efficacy of stress reduction therapy in IBD and these have produced mixed results

Introduction

Psychological stress is frequently reported as worsening IBD and recent advances in the concept of psychoneuroimmunology have given scientific plausibility to this possibility. In this chapter we review whether psychological stress is able to worsen gastrointestinal inflammation in both humans with IBD and animal models of colitis. We briefly discuss the mechanisms by which this might occur and review the evidence to support therapeutic interventions based on stress reduction.

The stress response and psychoneuroimmunology

Stress can be defined as any threat to an organism's homeostasis, whether physical (physiological) or perceived (psychological). The stress response seeks to maintain homeostasis and is mediated via two interconnected effector pathways: the hypothalamic–pituitary–adrenal axis (HPA) and the autonomic nervous system (ANS). The gut also has its own rich nerve supply, the enteric nervous system (ENS), which conventionally has been thought to control the motility, exocrine, and endocrine functions of the gastrointestinal tract and to communicate with the ANS to form the "brain–gut axis."

Psychoneuroimmunology is the study of the mechanisms by which behavioral factors and central nervous system (CNS) function can influence inflammation and the immune system at both systemic and local tissue levels. Many of the neuropeptides of the HPA axis, ANS, and ENS can bind to lymphocytes and other inflammatory cells via specific receptors, leading to alterations in structure and function. The overall effects of stress on the immune system are complex and depend on both the intensity and duration of the stressor.

Psychological stress and adverse life events in IBD

Several case studies have suggested that psychological stress can both exacerbate symptoms and precipitate relapse in IBD but, being retrospective, these are inevitably subject to recall bias. Well-designed, prospective investigations of psychological stress and life events as causative factors for relapse in IBD are difficult to perform. They require a long study period to allow a sufficient number of relapses to occur to test for correlation, and a high degree of patient compliance for the collection of detailed diary records of life events and stress and gastrointestinal symptoms. There are often confounding changes in medication during the study period. Many of the clinical scoring systems commonly used to assess IBD activity contain variables, such as stool frequency, which are known to be affected adversely by stress but which do not necessarily reflect a worsening of inflammation.

The results of early studies of the relationship between stress, depression, and disease activity in IBD are mixed, but more recent analyses, where meticulous attempts have been made to address these methodologic problems, have found a positive association. Levenstein et al. [1], in a prospective cohort study of 62 patients with ulcerative colitis (UC), found that 90% of patients who scored in the upper tertile of the Perceived Stress Questionnaire (PSQ) experienced a relapse in the subsequent 2 years as compared with 44% in the lower tertile. A score in the upper tertile of the PSQ was also predictive of mucosal abnormalities in patients with UC who reported no symptoms. Bitton et al. [2] found the number of stressful life events in the preceding month to be a risk factor for relapse in a 1-year prospective study of 60 patients with UC. In a 2-year prospective study of 18 patients with Crohn's disease, Mardini et al. [3] found depression and less so life events to be predictors of relapse. Mittermaier et al. [4] reported that patients with inactive IBD had a significantly increased chance of relapse during the following 18 months if their score on the Beck's Depression Inventory was raised. Two smaller studies have suggested that daily stress may also exacerbate the symptoms of IBD [5,6].

Lastly, in many therapeutic trials of IBD, placebo response rates, which relate not only to subjective measures but also to objective measures such as the degree of mucosal inflammation seen at endoscopy, are as high as 30–40%. This provides further, albeit indirect, evidence to suggest that changes in psychological state can affect disease activity.

Experimental psychological stress and gastrointestinal immune and inflammatory function in humans with IBD and animal models of colitis

There are limited data available on the effects of acute experimental stress on the mucosal inflammatory response in humans. Immersion of the hand in ice cold water increased the luminal jejunal concentration of the mast cell mediators tryptase and histamine in both healthy volunteers and patients with food allergy [7]. Repeated sessions of the same stressor increased the number of activated mast cells seen by electron microscopy in mucosal biopsies from healthy controls and even more so in patients with quiescent Crohn's disease and UC [8]. In patients with quiescent UC who underwent a modified dichotomous listening test, there was an increase in the concentration of tumor necrosis factor α (TNF-α) in perimucosal fluid and in the production of reactive oxygen metabolites by rectal mucosal biopsies [9].

There is better evidence in animal models of colitis to suggest that both acute and chronic experimental stress can contribute to the initiation and reactivation of gastrointestinal inflammation. Rats subjected to restraint stress, a model of acute stress, for the 4 days prior to the induction of colitis by 2,4,6-trinitrobenzenesulfonic acid (TNBS) developed an increased mucosal inflammatory response compared with those given TNBS alone [9]. Restraint stress in the absence of any other co-stimuli caused a partial reactivation of mucosal inflammation in rats that had recovered from TNBS colitis 6 weeks previously; there was an increase in colonic myeloperoxidase, although there were no inflammatory changes detectable by light microscopy. Restraint stress also lowered the dose of TNBS required to reactivate fully colitis in mice that had recovered from TNBS colitis 8 weeks previously [10]. This susceptibility was transferable between mice by a population of CD4-rich lymphocytes taken from spleen and mesenteric lymph nodes, suggesting that stress-induced reactivation is dependent on the presence of key immune cells [11]. Adult rats that had undergone previous prolonged maternal separation, a model of chronic stress and depression, were more susceptible to the effects of acute stress, experiencing a greater severity of dextran sulfate-induced colitis when subjected to a series of inescapable foot shocks, than controls [13].

Putative mechanisms by which stress might increase gastrointestinal inflammation

Altered hypothalamic–pituitary–adrenal axis function

Normally, in both animals and humans, stimulation of the HPA arm of the stress response leads to the release of cortisol which has a principally anti-inflammatory action. LEW/N

TABLE 35.1 Summary of trials of stress reduction therapy in IBD.

Reference	Intervention	Patients	Outcome
Schwarz [18]	Cognitive behavioral therapy, muscle relaxation	11 patients with IBD	No improvement in IBD symptoms
Keller [19]	Psychotherapy	108 patients with CD	No reduction in number or severity of relapses over 2 years
Milne [20]	Stress management program	80 patients with CD	Reduced CDAI over next year
Garcia-Vega [21]	Stress management program	45 patients with CD	Reduced IBD symptoms over next year

CD, Crohn's disease; CDAI, Crohn's Disease Activity Index.

rats have a reduced corticotropin-releasing factor (CRF) content of the hypothalamus and consequently exhibit a markedly decreased corticosterone response to stressful stimuli. They also show an increased susceptibility to TNBS-induced colitis in the presence of coexisting restraint stress [14].

There is evidence that HPA axis function may be altered in humans with IBD and thus predispose to stress-induced increases in disease activity. Straub *et al.* [15] found a reduced level of HPA axis stimulation, as measured by serum cortisol, compared with sympathetic tone, as indicated by serum levels of neuropeptide Y, in patients with IBD compared with controls.

Increased intestinal permeability and altered bacterial–mucosal interactions

Increased permeability and altered bacterial–mucosal interactions in response to stress may allow greater exposure of antigens to the underlying mucosal immune system, driving the inflammatory response. Both chronic and acute stress in rats have been shown to increase jejunal and colonic permeability to inert marker molecules, such as mannitol and Cr-EDTA, and to antigenic proteins such as horse radish peroxidase (HRP). Repeated water-avoidance stress increased the phagocytic uptake of killed *Escherichia coli* into follicle-associated epithelium (FAE) in mice [16]. The application of noradrenaline increased the adherence of *E. coli* 0157 to murine cecal mucosa and led to increased internalization of *Salmonella choleraesuis* and *E. coli* 0157 in isolated porcine Peyer's patches [17].

Many of these stress-induced changes are dependent on the presence of mast cells, and mucosal mast cell degranulation is likely to be a key process in mediating the inflammatory effects of stress on the gastrointestinal tract.

Therapeutic implications

Despite these advances in our understanding of the relationship between psychological stress and IBD, most stress reduction therapy remains unformalized, and studies of its efficacy in patients with IBD are few. There are a wide variety of psychotherapeutic interventions that could be assessed, making standardization difficult. Because of the nature of the intervention these trials are difficult to perform in a blinded controlled manner and, as already discussed, with placebo rates of up to 40%, any genuine therapeutic effect can be hard to detect. Of those trials that have been reported, the results are conflicting (Table 35.1) and further studies are required before a view can be taken as to whether any form of stress reduction therapy may benefit patients with IBD.

Conclusions

There is now good evidence in both humans with IBD and animal models of colitis that stress can act as a causative factor in provoking disease relapse. However, there is as yet little evidence to support therapeutic interventions based on stress reduction.

References

1 Levenstein S, Prantera C, Varvo V, *et al.* Stress and exacerbation in ulcerative colitis: a prospective study of patients enrolled in remission. *Am J Gastroenterol* 2000; **95**: 1213–20.
2 Bitton A, Sewitch MJ, Peppercorn MA, *et al.* Psychosocial determinants of relapse in ulcerative colitis: a longitudinal study. *Am J Gastroenterol* 2003; **98**: 2203–8.

3 Mardini HE, Kip KE, Wilson JW. Crohn's disease: a two-year prospective study of the association between psychological distress and disease activity. *Dig Dis Sci* 2004; **49**: 492–7.

4 Mittermaier C, Dejaco C, Waldhoer T, *et al.* Impact of depressive mood on relapse in patients with inflammatory bowel disease: a prospective 18-month follow-up study. *Psychosom Med* 2004; **66**: 79–84.

5 Greene BR, Blanchard EB, Wan CK. Long-term monitoring of psychosocial stress and symptomatology in inflammatory bowel disease. *Behav Res Ther* 1994; **32**: 217–26.

6 Garrett VD, Brantley PJ, Jones GN, McKnight GT. The relation between daily stress and Crohn's disease. *J Behav Med* 1991; **14**: 87–96.

7 Santos J, Saperas E, Nogueiras C, *et al.* Release of mast cell mediators into the jejunum by cold pain stress in humans. *Gastroenterology* 1998; **114**: 640–8.

8 Farhadi A, Keshavarzian A, Van de Kar LD, *et al.* Heightened responses to stressors in patients with inflammatory bowel disease. *Am J Gastroenterol* 2005; **100**: 1796–804.

9 Mawdsley J, Rampton DS. Acute psychological stress increases rectal mucosal an LPS-stimulated whole blood release of TNF-alpha in patients with inactive ulcerative colitis. *Gut* 2006; **55** (abstract in print).

10 Gue M, Bonbonne C, Fioramonti J, *et al.* Stress-induced enhancement of colitis in rats: CRF and arginine vasopressin are not involved. *Am J Physiol* 1997; **272**: G84–91.

11 Collins SM, McHugh K, Jacobson K, *et al.* Previous inflammation alters the response of the rat colon to stress. *Gastroenterology* 1996; **111**: 1509–15.

12 Qiu BS, Vallance BA, Blennerhassett PA, Collins SM. The role of CD4+ lymphocytes in the susceptibility of mice to stress-induced reactivation of experimental colitis. *Nat Med* 1999; **5**: 1178–82.

13 Milde AM, Enger O, Murison R. The effects of postnatal maternal separation on stress responsivity and experimentally induced colitis in adult rats. *Physiol Behav* 2004; **81**: 71–84.

14 Million M, Tache Y, Anton P. Susceptibility of Lewis and Fischer rats to stress-induced worsening of TNB-colitis: protective role of brain CRF. *Am J Physiol* 1999; **276**: G1027–36.

15 Straub RH, Herfarth H, Falk W, Andus T, Scholmerich J. Uncoupling of the sympathetic nervous system and the hypothalamic-pituitary-adrenal axis in inflammatory bowel disease? *J Neuroimmunol* 2002; **126**: 116–25.

16 Velin AK, Ericson AC, Braaf Y, Wallon C, Soderholm JD. Increased antigen and bacterial uptake in follicle associated epithelium induced by chronic psychological stress in rats. *Gut* 2004; **53**: 494–500.

17 Green BT, Lyte M, Kulkarni-Narla A, Brown DR. Neuromodulation of enteropathogen internalization in Peyer's patches from porcine jejunum. *J Neuroimmunol* 2003; **141**: 74–82.

18 Schwarz SP, Blanchard EB. Evaluation of a psychological treatment for inflammatory bowel disease. *Behav Res Ther* 1991; **29**: 167–77.

19 Keller W, Pritsch M, Von Wietersheim J, *et al.* Effect of psychotherapy and relaxation on the psychosocial and somatic course of Crohn's disease: main results of the German Prospective Multicenter Psychotherapy Treatment study on Crohn's Disease. *J Psychosom Res* 2004; **56**: 687–96.

20 Milne B, Joachim G, Niedhardt J. A stress management programme for inflammatory bowel disease patients. *J Adv Nurs* 1986; **11**: 561–7.

21 Garcia-Vega E, Fernandez-Rodriguez C. A stress management programme for Crohn's disease. *Behav Res Ther* 2004; **42**: 367–83.

36 Drugs to avoid

PAUL COLLINS & JONATHAN RHODES

LEARNING POINTS

Drugs to avoid

- Most drugs are well-tolerated in IBD

- Some but not all studies have suggested that NSAIDs, acetaminophen (paracetamol), oral contraceptives, antidiarrheal agents, antibiotics, oral iron supplements, and isotretinoin may exacerbate IBD

- Absolute avoidance of particular drugs by patients with IBD cannot be recommended on existing evidence

- However, important drug interactions such as allopurinol with thiopurines must be avoided

Introduction

The etiology of IBD remains incompletely understood but involves an interplay of genetic predisposition and environmental factors. Environmental factors that have been implicated as precipitants include drugs that are commonly used in patients with IBD. Some of these drugs are freely available without prescription.

Analgesics and anti-inflammatories

Troublesome musculoskeletal symptoms can accompany IBD (see Chapter 54). Non-steroidal anti-inflammatory drugs (NSAIDs) can be effective in managing painful arthropathies, but have been implicated in precipitating flares of IBD.

NSAIDs inhibit cyclo-oxygenase, the key regulator of prostaglandin synthesis. Prostaglandins are important mediators of the inflammatory response in IBD and their concentrations in tissue correlate with disease activity. Cyclo-oxygenase (COX) exists in two isoforms: the con-

stitutively expressed COX-1, and the inducible isoform COX-2. Prostaglandins appear to have a protective effect in colitis. Prostaglandin E_2 (PGE_2), for example, inhibits lipopolysaccharide-induced tumor necrosis factor α (TNF-α) production and nitric oxide synthesis. Non-selective COX inhibition leads to development of colitis in the interleukin-10 knockout murine model of colitis with a concomitant reduction of PGE_2 levels [1].

Case reports have documented disease flares after NSAID exposure with four reports of relapse after repeat exposure [2]. Fifteen epidemiologic studies of IBD relapse following NSAID exposure were identified in a recent systematic review of the literature [2]. An association was demonstrated in six studies, but was significant in only two. In one cohort study of 669 patients with IBD, a relative risk of relapse following NSAID use in a 5-year period was calculated as 1.95 (95% confidence interval [CI] 1.15–3.29) [3]. However, studies of the risk of NSAID use in IBD patients have been hampered by small sample sizes and methodology problems and there is an inconsistency in the results. There are only limited data regarding the use of COX2 inhibitors in IBD but no advantage of COX2 inhibitors over conventional NSAIDs has been demonstrated (see Chapter 37). The reason for analgesic use is not documented in many cases, raising the possibility that the analgesic use might have reflected increased symptoms prior to a disease flare.

It has become accepted practice to avoid NSAID use in IBD even though the evidence for this is inconsistent. Moreover, IBD patients may occasionally require NSAIDs to obtain adequate management of painful arthropathies that can accompany their disease. In these circumstances it seems reasonable to advise patients to take a relatively mild NSAID such as ibuprofen while informing them about the possible theoretical increased risk of relapse (see Chapter 54).

TABLE 36.1 Drugs associated with precipitation or worsening of IBD.

NSAIDs	Idiosyncratic relapse of IBD in some patients
Oral contraceptive use	Associated with development of Crohn's disease
Antidiarrheal agents	Can precipitate toxic megacolon in severe colitis
Narcotic analgesia	Risk of narcotic dependence
Antibiotics	Causal link with Crohn's disease not established
Iron	Theoretical risk of pro-inflammatory effect
Isotretinoin	Cases of disease flare described

NSAIDs, non-steroidal anti-inflammatory drugs.

Acetaminophen (paracetamol) is also not free from suspicion. In a large case–control study, Dominitz et al. [4] looked at 1940 patients with IBD. They failed to demonstrate an association between NSAID use and flares of IBD, but showed a significant association between acetaminophen use and relapse (odds ratio 1.57; 95% CI 1.21–1.31). In a case–control study by Rampton et al. [5] relapse was more common in patients using analgesics, an effect that appeared largely related to acetaminophen use. Potential mechanisms by which this may occur include the role of acetaminophen as a weak inhibitor of prostaglandin synthesis. It has also been postulated that acetaminophen has a direct toxic effect on colonic mucosa, particularly in patients with UC [6]. Acetaminophen is a phenol and is detoxified by sulfation. The colonic epithelium expresses a phenol sulfotransferase whose activity has been shown to be reduced in UC [7]. However, in patients with Crohn's and UC, acetaminophen has no effect on fecal calprotectin levels (a marker of inflammation), whereas naproxen and nabumetone increase fecal calprotectin [8]. Acetaminophen is often prescribed in preference to NSAIDs in patients with IBD as a safe alternative but there does appear to be weak evidence that acetaminophen use may be related to flares of IBD (Table 36.1).

IBD and oral contraceptives

Oral contraceptives have been implicated in the development of Crohn's disease, but any association with UC has been much less strong [9]. Higher prevalence of oral contraceptive use has been observed in female populations with colonic Crohn's compared with women in the general population [10]. A relative risk (adjusted for smoking) of developing Crohn's disease of 1.44 (95% CI 1.12–1.86) has been calculated in a meta-analysis of oral contraceptive use in an IBD population [11]. It has been suggested that women with more active disease may wish to avoid pregnancy and will therefore be more likely to use some form of birth control and this may be a confounding factor in some of these studies. However, it should be noted that absorption of the oral contraceptive may be unreliable in patients with extensive small intestinal disease.

A possible mechanism by which oral contraceptives may precipitate Crohn's is by a thrombogenic effect with multifocal infarction [12]. This may be relevant to the association between smoking and Crohn's disease. It should also be noted that active Crohn's disease represents a moderate risk for venous thrombosis (see Chapter 57) and that this risk will presumably be increased further by concomitant usage of oral contraceptives.

Case reports of colonic Crohn's associated with oral contraceptive use have tended to be cases of non-granulomatous colitis; this has led to speculation that oral contraceptive use may predispose to a non-granulomatous colitis indistinguishable from colonic Crohn's [10].

Thus, although oral contraceptives can generally be safely used in mild to moderate IBD, alternative forms of birth control should be considered in women with more severe Crohn's disease.

Other drugs and their use in IBD

Antidiarrheals (loperamide and codeine) are generally safe in Crohn's disease. However, use of these agents can have a deleterious effect in active severe colitis, and has been implicated in the development of toxic megacolon [13]. Moreover, they have been shown not to reduce stool frequency in active UC.

Addiction to **narcotic analgesics** has been identified as a potential problem in IBD patients. Narcotic dependence in patients with no current active bowel disease is more common amongst Crohn's patients and is associated with psychiatric morbidity [14]. Although in the acute setting, narcotic analgesia may rarely be required, it should be viewed as a temporary measure only.

An association between **antibiotic use** and subsequent development of Crohn's disease has been reported [15]. It is not clear whether this association is an example of reverse causality (e.g. in a prodromal phase of Crohn's there will be increased contact with medical services and increased prescription of medications including antibiotics). A causal link has not been established and further study will be required. Conversely, a number of relatively small studies have reported beneficial effects of antibiotics such as metronidazole, ciprofloxacin, and clarithromycin in Crohn's disease.

Anemia commonly complicates inflammatory bowel disease and **iron** supplementation may be required in up to 65% of patients (see Chapter 38) [16]. Oral iron has been shown to be associated with a condition resembling Crohn's disease in IL-10 knockout mice. In murine models of IBD, microscopic signs of inflammation have been seen following iron supplementation [16]. Mechanisms by which iron may exert an inflammatory effect include generation of reactive oxygen species, activation of NF-κB and via an alteration of T-cell dependent immune response. Whether this translates into a clinically significant effect on IBD in humans is not clear and a retrospective analysis of iron supplementation in IBD failed to demonstrate a worsening of disease activity [17].

Isotretinoin, a synthetic retinoid used in the treatment of acne vulgaris, may act as a trigger for IBD. Although safely used in many patients with IBD, cases of flares of disease on treatment with recurrence on rechallenge with the drug have been described [18]. An internet newsgroup site [19] also cites unreported cases of IBD precipitated by isotretinoin. It has been speculated that isotretinoin may induce this effect by stimulation of killer T-cells, disturbing epithelial tissue growth or disruption of glycoprotein synthesis [19]. Consideration should be given to withdrawal of isotretinoin in patients with flares of IBD while on this medication.

Conclusions

Despite described associations between commonly prescribed medications and IBD, most drugs are tolerated well by IBD patients. There may be an idiosyncratic reaction between NSAIDs and IBD with precipitation of relapse. The association between oral contraceptive use and IBD is less strong. Other commonly used drugs may have an adverse effect on IBD, but absolute avoidance of particular drugs in IBD cannot be recommended on existing evidence.

References

1 Berg DJ, Zhang J, Weinstock JV, *et al.* Rapid development of colitis in NSAID-treated IL-10-deficient mice. *Gastroenterology* 2002; **123**: 1527–42.

2 Forrest K, Symmons D, Foster P. Systematic review: is ingestion of paracetamol or non-steroidal anti-inflammatory drugs associated with exacerbations of inflammatory bowel disease? *Aliment Pharmacol Ther* 2004; **20**: 1035–43. (Review.)

3 Aalykke C, Hallas J, Lauritsen K. Role of NSAID use in inflammatory bowel disease: a 5-year follow-up study. *Gastroenterology* 2000; **118**: A869.

4 Dominitz JA, Koepsell TD, Boyko EJ. Association between analgesic use and inflammatory bowel disease (IBD) flares: a retrospective cohort study. *Gastroenterology* 2000; **118**: A581.

5 Rampton DS, McNeil NI, Sarner M. Analgesic ingestion and other factors preceding relapse in ulcerative colitis. *Gut* 1983; **24**: 187–9.

6 Ramakrishna BS, Roberts-Thomson IC, Pannall PR, Roediger WE. Impaired sulphation of phenol by the colonic mucosa in quiescent and active ulcerative colitis. *Gut* 1991; **32**: 46–9.

7 Langmann T, Moehle C, Mauerer R, *et al.* Loss of detoxification in inflammatory bowel disease: dysregulation of pregnane X receptor target genes. *Gastroenterology* 2004; **127**: 26–40.

8 Smale S, Sigthorsson G, Foster R, Forgacs I, Bjarnason I. NSAIDs and relapse of IBD. *Gastroenterology* 2002; **122**: A23.

9 Boyko EJ, Theis MK, Vaughan TL, Nicol-Blades B. Increased risk of inflammatory bowel disease associated with oral contraceptive use. *Am J Epidemiol* 1994; **140**: 268–78.

10 Rhodes JM, Cockel R, Allan RN, *et al.* Colonic Crohn's disease and use of oral contraception. *BMJ* 1984; **288**: 595–6.

11 Godet PG, May GR, Sutherland LR. Meta-analysis of the role of oral contraceptive agents in inflammatory bowel disease. *Gut* 1995; **37**: 668–73.

12 Wakefield AJ, Sawyerr AM, Hudson M, Dhillon AP, Pounder RE. Smoking, the oral contraceptive pill, and Crohn's disease. *Dig Dis Sci* 1991; **36**: 1147–50.

13 Brown JW. Toxic megacolon associated with loperamide therapy. *JAMA* 1979; **241**: 501–2.

14 Edwards JT, Radford-Smith GL, Florin TH. Chronic narcotic use in inflammatory bowel disease patients: prevalence and clinical characteristics. *J Gastroenterol Hepatol* 2001; **16**: 1235–8.

15 Card T, Logan RF, Rodrigues LC, Wheeler JG. Antibiotic use and the development of Crohn's disease. *Gut* 2004; **53**: 246–50.

16 Oldenburg B, Koningsberger JC, Van Berge Henegouwen GP, Van Asbeck BS, Marx JJ. Iron and inflammatory bowel disease. *Aliment Pharmacol Ther* 2001; **15**: 429–38.

17 de Silva AD, Mylonaki M, Rampton DS. Oral iron therapy in inflammatory bowel disease: usage, tolerance, and efficacy. *Inflamm Bowel Dis* 2003; **9**: 316–20.

18 Godfrey KM, James MP. Treatment of severe acne with isotretinoin in patients with inflammatory bowel disease. *Br J Dermatol* 1990; **123**: 653–5.

19 Prokop LD. Isotretinoin: possible component cause of inflammatory bowel disease. *Am J Gastroenterol* 1999; **94**: 2568.

37 NSAIDs and COX-2 selective agents: cause or cure of pain in IBD?

INGVAR BJARNASON & DAVID SCOTT

LEARNING POINTS

NSAIDs and COX-2 selective agents

- Conventional NSAIDs and COX-2 selective agents are effective anti-inflammatory analgesics in IBD

- Although non-selective NSAIDs are tolerated in the short term by most patients with IBD, they cause clinical relapse in approximately one-quarter within a week

- COX-2 selective agents do not increase intestinal inflammation and appear safe in the short term

- NSAID-induced relapse of IBD is a result of dual inhibition of COX-1 and COX-2

Introduction

Non-steroidal anti-inflammatory drugs (NSAIDs) are one of the most successful groups of drugs, reflecting their efficacy and perceived clinical need. Their use is limited by adverse reactions, especially upper gastrointestinal toxicity. When the cyclo-oxygenase-2 enzyme (COX-2) was identified, the development of new NSAIDs focused on producing drugs that specifically target COX-2. This new generation of anti-inflammatory drugs – the so-called COX-2 selective drugs – cause less gastrointestinal toxicity than conventional NSAIDs, but their overall benefits are less certain following the withdrawal of rofecoxib and valdecoxib because of their cardiovascular toxicity.

Need for anti-inflammatory analgesics in IBD

Patients with UC and Crohn's disease frequently require anti-inflammatory analgesics over and above the healthy population because of peripheral arthritis, sacroiliitis, ankylosing spondylitis, and osteoporosis-related fractures [1]. However, there has been a sustained interest in the possibility that NSAIDs may worsen or precipitate clinical disease activity in patients with IBD. It has even been suggested that NSAIDs may in some cases cause a colitis [2], which may closely resemble IBD [3].

Mechanism of action of NSAIDs

Prior to 1990 there was a consensus that NSAIDs inhibited the "COX enzyme" and that this inhibition accounted for both their therapeutic benefits and side-effects, which were perceived to be predominantly gastric and renal [4]. In the 1990s a new dogma arose suggesting that the inhibition of COX-2 accounted for most of the therapeutic effects of NSAIDs while inhibition of COX-1 accounted for their gastric side-effects. Publications emphasized the "constitutively expressed enzyme (COX-1) carrying out housekeeping" functions while COX-2 was only expressed in the kidney and at sites of inflammation. The development and marketing of COX-2 specific drugs was based on this simple message and the promise of maintaining, if not improving, efficacy with fewer gastric side-effects. However, this argument is far too simplistic because COX-1 knockout mice, in which there is no naturally occurring COX-1 enzyme, do not show upper gastrointestinal damage [5,6], and COX-2 deficient mice have normal pain perception and inflammatory reactions. Indeed, current evidence shows that both the adverse and therapeutic effects require dual inhibition of both of the COX enzymes and that the damage caused by conventional NSAIDs is increased when they act topically.

Regardless of the possibility that the drugs were successfully developed and marketed on such an incorrect concept about the reasons for their enhanced safety, there is no doubt that the COX-2 selective agents have analgesic and anti-inflammatory properties comparable to those of conventional NSAIDs in rheumatic patients. Their efficacy in treating joint symptoms in patients with IBD and the various arthritides (where COX-2 is up-regulated) is not in doubt. Furthermore, as COX-2 is up-regulated in the diseased bowel of patients with IBD, it was even thought possible that the COX-2 selective agents might be therapeutic for IBD itself.

Early observational studies

Early reports suggested that intestinal inflammation and symptoms in patients with UC improved with conventional NSAID treatment [7]. However, most subsequent studies, albeit not all [8,9], suggest that NSAIDs may be one of the causes of clinical relapse of IBD [10–15]. One problem in interpreting these studies is that a large number are case reports and others are retrospective surveys; in both cases the temporal relationships between disease activity and drug ingestion is not always clear. Furthermore, patients with IBD are at risk of spontaneous clinical relapse of their disease [16].

Descriptive reporting has not clarified the position with the COX-2 selective agents. Some reports describe exacerbations of IBD with the use of celecoxib and rofecoxib [17–19], while others consider they are safe [20].

Prospective studies with COX-2 selective agents and conventional NSAIDs in IBD

Sandborn *et al.* [21] administered placebo vs. celecoxib (200 mg twice daily) for 2 weeks to 220 patients with quiescent UC who had symptomatic arthralgias. Clinical exacerbation of disease was defined using the Mayo Clinic score and an endoscopic score. The relapse rate did not differ significantly between the two groups (3% and 4% in the celecoxib and placebo groups, respectively). This study suggests that celecoxib is safe in the short term in patients with IBD.

A separate study assessed the prevalence of clinical relapse with conventional NSAIDs [22]. Patients with quiescent IBD (Crohn's disease and UC) were given acetaminophen (paracetamol) ($n = 26$) or conventional NSAIDs including naproxen ($n = 32$), diclofenac ($n = 29$), and indometacin ($n = 22$) for 4 weeks. The non-selective NSAIDs were associated with a 17–28% clinical relapse rate within 9 days of ingestion while acetaminophen was safe. In order to elucidate the mechanism of this detrimental effect, the study was expanded to assess intestinal inflammation, as assessed by fecal calprotectin concentrations, before and during treatment of five groups of 20 patients with quiescent IBD with acetaminophen, naproxen (topical effect, COX-1, and COX-2 inhibitor), nabumetone (COX-1 and COX-2 inhibitor), nimesulide (selective COX-2 inhibitor without a significant topical action), and low-dose aspirin (selective COX-1 inhibition). The results showed that no patient had an early relapse on acetaminophen, nimesulide, or aspirin while 20% of those on naproxen and nabumetone relapsed. These clinical relapses were associated with escalating intestinal inflammatory activity and appear to be brought about by dual inhibition of the COX enzymes, as occurs in relation to NSAID-induced gastrointestinal damage in patients without IBD [22].

Conclusions: conventional NSAIDs or COX-2 in IBD?

All NSAIDs cause some cardiovascular toxicity. For example, population studies show an increased risk of death from cardiovascular problems attributed to ibuprofen, although this appears to be a result of hypertensive adverse events [23] rather than myocardial infarction [24]. However, it is clear that some COX-2 drugs, specifically rofecoxib, cause an increased rate of cardiovascular morbidity and mortality. The data about other COX-2 drugs, when used at recommended doses, are less clear-cut, although regulatory bodies have advised they should not be given to patients with pre-existing cardiovascular disease.

The data in patients with IBD show that most patients tolerate short-term treatment with conventional NSAIDs. However, COX-2 selective agents are better tolerated than conventional NSAIDs when taken short term, although unfortunately they do not reduce intestinal inflammation.

Low-dose aspirin, so commonly used for cardiovascular prophylaxis, also appears to be well tolerated in patients with IBD. The mechanism that underlies the NSAID-induced relapse of IBD appears the same as that causing gastro-intestinal damage in patients with rheumatic disorders.

References

1 Smale S, Natt RS, Orchard T, Russell AS, Bjarnason I. Spondylarthropathy and inflammatory bowel disease. *Arthritis Rheum* 2001; **44**: 2728–36.

2 Bjarnason I, Hayllar J, Macpherson AJ, Russell AS. Side effects of nonsteroidal anti-inflammatory drugs on the small and large intestine. *Gastroenterology* 1993; **104**: 1832–47.

3 Gleeson MH, Davis AJ. Non-steroidal anti-inflammatory drugs, aspirin and newly diagnosed colitis: a case–control study. *Aliment Pharmacol Ther* 2003; **17**: 817–25.

4 Vane JR. Towards a better aspirin. *Nature* 1994; **367**: 215–6.

5 Langenbach R, Morham SG, Tiano HF, *et al.* Prostaglandin synthase 1 gene disruption in mice reduced arachidonic acid-induced inflammation and indomethacin-induced gastric ulceration. *Cell* 1995; **83**: 483–92.

6 Sigthorsson G, Simpson RJ, Walley M, *et al.* COX-1 and 2, intestinal integrity and pathogenesis of NSAID-enteropathy in mice. *Gastroenterology* 2002; **122**: 1913–23.

7 Campieri M, Franchi LGA, Bazzocchi G, *et al.* Prostaglandins, indomethacin and ulcerative colitis. *Gastroenterology* 1980; **78**: 193.

8 Bonner GF, Walczak M, Kitchen L, Bayona M. Tolerance of nonsteroidal antiinflammatory drugs in patients with inflammatory bowel disease. *Am J Gastroenterol* 2000; **95**: 1946–8.

9 Bonner G, Fakhri A, Vennamaneni SR. A long-term cohort study of nonsteroidal anti-inflammatory drug use and disease activity in outpatients with inflammatory bowel disease. *Inflamm Bowel Dis* 2004; **10**: 751–7.

10 Rampton DS, Sladen GE. Relapse of ulcerative proctocolitis during treatment with NSAID. *Postgrad Med J* 1981; **57**: 297–99.

11 Rampton DS, Sladen GE. Prostaglandin synthesis inhibitors in ulcerative colitis: flurbiprofen compared with conventional treatment. *Prostaglandins* 1981; **21**: 417–25.

12 Rampton DS, McNeil MI, Sarner M. Analgesic ingestion and other factors preceding relapse in ulcerative colitis. *Gut* 1983; **24**: 187–9.

13 Kaufmann HJ, Taubin HL. Nonsteroidal anti-inflammatory drugs activate quiescent inflammatory bowel disease. *Ann Intern Med* 1987; **107**: 513–6.

14 Felder JB, Korelitz BI, Rajapakse R, *et al.* Effects of non-steroidal antiinflammatory drugs on inflammatory bowel disease: a case–control study. *Am J Gastroenterol* 2000; **95**: 1949–54.

15 Evans JM, McMahon AD, Murray FE, McDevitt DG, MacDonald TM. Non-steroidal anti-inflammatory drugs are associated with emergency admission to hospital for colitis due to inflammatory bowel disease. *Gut* 1997; **40**: 619–22.

16 Tibble J, Sigthorsson G, Fagerhol M, Bjarnason I. Surrogate markers of intestinal inflammation are predictive for relapse in patients with inflammatory bowel disease. *Gastroenterology* 2000; **119**: 15–22.

17 Bonner GF. Exacerbation of inflammatory bowel disease associated with the use of celecoxib. *Am J Gastroenterol* 2001; **96**: 1306–8.

18 Gornet JM, Hassani Z, Modiglian R, Lemann M. Exacerbation of Crohn's colitis with severe colonic hemorrhage in a patient on rofecoxib. *Am J Gastroenterol* 2002; **97**: 3209–10.

19 Matuk R, Crawford J, Abreu MT, *et al.* The spectrum of gastrointestinal toxicity and effect on disease activity of selective cyclooxygenase-2 inhibitors in patients with inflammatory bowel disease. *Inflamm Bowel Dis* 2004; **10**: 352–6.

20 Mahadevan U, Loftus EV, Tremaine WJ, Sandborn WJ. Safety of selective cyclooxygenase-2 inhibitors in inflammatory bowel disease. *Am J Gastroenterol* 2003; **97**: 910–4.

21 Sandborn WJ, Stenson WF, Brynskov J, *et al.* Safety of celecoxib in patients with ulcerative colitis in remission: a randomized, double-blind placebo-controlled study. *Am J Gastroenterol* 2004; **99**: S257. (Abstract 794)

22 Takeuchi K, Smale S, Premshand P, *et al.* Prevalence and mechanism of nsaid-induced clinical relapse in patients with inflammatory bowel disease. (Unpublished data).

23 Lipworth L, Friis S, Blot WJ, *et al.* A population-based cohort study of mortality among users of ibuprofen in Denmark. *Am J Ther* 2004; **11**: 156–63.

24 Garcia Rodriguez LA, Varas-Lorenzo C, Maguire A, Gonzalez-Perez A. Nonsteroidal antiinflammatory drugs and the risk of myocardial infarction in the general population. *Circulation* 2004; **109**: 3000–6.

Part 4 Common Clinical Challenges: Beyond the Text Book

38 Iron replacement – is it safe and effective?

STEFANIE KULNIGG & CHRISTOPH GASCHE

LEARNING POINTS

Iron replacement

- Iron deficiency is characterized by ferritin <30 µg/L, transferrin saturation <16%, and reduced mean cell volume and mean cell hemoglobin [1]; anemia is defined by Hb <12 and ≤13.5 g/dL in women and men, respectively.
- Iron deficiency anemia is common and clinically important in IBD
- Many patients with IBD tolerate oral iron supplementation poorly
- Intravenous replacement therapy with iron sucrose infusions is both safe and effective

Introduction

Iron is an essential nutrient for all living cells. It is a cofactor for enzymes in the mitochondrial respiration chain, in the citric acid cycle and in DNA synthesis. It is also the central molecule for binding and transporting oxygen within hemoglobin and myoglobin. Anemia is a common complication in IBD. Up to one-third of patients suffer from anemia that may impact on their quality of life through symptoms such as fatigue, impaired cognitive function, and loss of libido. Moreover, effects on education and work can cause lasting damage to social and professional development. Anemia-associated dyspnea and tachycardia may even necessitate hospitalization and blood transfusions.

Anemia in IBD

Iron deficiency and anemia of chronic disease are the most common causes of inadequate erythropoiesis in IBD. Vitamin B_{12} or folate deficiency, drug-induced bone marrow suppression (by 6-mercaotopurine, azathioprine, sulfasalazine, or rarely 5-aminosalicylic acid), and auto-immune hemolysis may also occasionally contribute to IBD-associated anemia.

Iron metabolism

Iron deficiency is the most common nutritional deficiency in IBD. Iron homeostasis is regulated solely through iron uptake in the duodenum and upper jejunum. Active iron excretion does not occur in cellular organisms; therefore, limitation of iron uptake is the only regulatory mechanism to protect cells from toxic iron overload. Daily, 1–2 mg iron are absorbed from the diet and a similar amount is lost through cell debris from the skin and intestine. Even in severe iron deficiency, no more than 40 mg/day can be absorbed [2]. After absorption, iron is bound to transferrin, and transported via the circulation to the organs. There, diferric transferrin binds to the transferrin receptor with high affinity and undergoes endocytosis, thereby providing iron for cellular needs. Intracellular iron is stored in ferritin.

Iron deficiency anemia in IBD

Overt intestinal bleeding, as well as chronic (obscure) bleeding cause loss of red cells and thereby of iron, which may exceed the limits of iron absorption. Moreover, in Crohn's disease of the duodenum or upper jejunum, iron absorption may be impaired [3]. More commonly, the combination of reduced dietary intake, anti-acidic drug therapy, and continuous intestinal blood loss through ulcerated mucosal surfaces leads to a negative iron balance. Whether it has resulted in anemia or not, iron deficiency should be treated. For example, an average sized male Crohn's patient with hemoglobin 13.2 g/dL, transferrin saturation 7%, and ferritin 27 μg/L has a mean deficit of at least 700 mg iron which should receive appropriate attention and therapy.

Iron deficient erythropoiesis is commonly detected through microcytosis and red cell hypochromia. If this occurs in the presence of abundant iron stores (high ferritin levels), and there is no concurrent hemoglobinopathy, it is a result of functional iron deficiency: the erythroblast is iron deficient (because of low transferrin saturation) while iron is kept in the reticuloendothelial system.

Anemia of chronic disease in IBD

The production of pro-inflammatory cytokines within inflamed bowel segments perpetuates not only the inflammatory reaction within the bowel, but has systemic effects on bone marrow stem cells, resulting in anemia of chronic disease. The pathogenesis of anemia of chronic disease is similar whatever the underlying condition (e.g. rheumatoid arthritis, IBD, chronic infection, or malignancy); circulating γ-interferon, interleukins IL-1 and IL-6, and tumor necrosis factor α (TNF-α) directly suppress erythropoiesis and reduce red blood cell life span [4]. Functional iron deficiency also prevents efficient erythropoiesis in this condition.

Iron replacement

Oral iron preparations

Generally oral iron preparations contain iron as ferrous salts (e.g. ferrous sulfate, ferrous gluconate, ferrous fumarate). Enteric-coated ferrous salt formulations should not be prescribed, because they may release their iron content beyond the sites of maximal iron absorption; enteric preparations may also impact upstream of strictures in small bowel Crohn's, leading to a risk of local ulceration and obstruction. Oral iron preparations are cheap and convenient to take (Table 38.1). However, patient compliance may limit their usefulness: although some studies have shown the contrary [5,6], it is widely believed that compliance is poor in patients with IBD because of gastrointestinal side-effects such as nausea, bloating, abdominal pain, and diarrhea. This may be an IBD-specific problem because non-IBD patients tend to complain of constipation. Iron may even increase

TABLE 38.1 Oral vs. intravenous iron replacement.

Oral (ferrous iron) Iron salts	Intravenous (ferric iron) Iron sucrose
Pros	
Cheap	Independent of enteral absorption capacity
Easy administration route	Good compliance Fast iron replacement (up to 500 mg per infusion)
Cons	
Gastrointestinal side-effects	Infusion setting
Activation of intestinal inflammation	Expense
Low bioavailability	

IBD activity [7], possibly because of iron-catalyzed formation of reactive oxygen species in the gut lumen. Indeed, iron supplements have been shown to have a pro-inflammatory effect in animal models of colitis [8]. Finally, despite oral supplementation, in IBD-associated anemia continuous blood loss often exceeds the capacity of enteral iron absorption, resulting in further drops in hemoglobin levels [9].

Intravenous iron preparations

Historically, intravenous iron was formulated as iron dextran. Because of the high risk of anaphylactic reactions (caused by the dextran compound), this formulation should no longer be used. This occasionally fatal adverse event has led to prejudice against other safer and equally effective intravenous iron formulations, such as iron sucrose and iron gluconate, which do not cause anaphylaxis. Iron gluconate, which is only available in a few countries, however, is potentially toxic because of its labile nature. The iron bound within it can be released rapidly to plasma proteins such as transferrin. If transferrin is oversaturated, ionic iron may cause endothelial damage resulting in capillary leak syndrome and hypovolemia [10]. Doses not exceeding 125 mg per infusion are therefore recommended [11].

Iron sucrose (former iron saccharate) is available in most countries and has the lowest risk of side-effects and is best given as a dilute solution (in NaCl 0.9%). Iron sucrose is partially taken up by apotransferrin (transferrin without iron) but also by the cells of the reticuloendothelial system. Repeated doses of 200–300 mg per infusion are well tolerated and safe [12–14]; however, in iron deficiency anemia single doses up to 500 mg (max 7 mg/kg) may be given. In some countries a test dose is recommended, but true anaphylactic reactions with iron sucrose have never been reported. In our hands thousands of infusions have been given without significant side-effects [15,16]. Iron sucrose should not, however, be administered if the transferrin saturation is above 50%, during severe bacterial infection (e.g. pneumonia, abscess) or if the patient suffers from toxic megacolon.

The individual iron requirement can be calculated according to Ganzoni's formula [17]:

Total iron deficit (mg) = body weight (kg) × 0.24 × (target hemoglobin (150 g/L) – actual hemoglobin g/L) + 500 mg (for iron depot if body weight >35 kg)

Intramuscular or subcutaneous routes of parenteral iron administration are obsolete, because of their many side-effects and limited efficacy.

If iron infusions fail to increase hemoglobin, the addition of erythropoietin can be effective. Combination therapy is typically needed in patients whose anemia is predominantly related to chronic disease. When iron and erythropoietin are used in combination, virtually all patients with IBD-associated anemia can be successfully treated. Target hemoglobin levels should be within the normal range.

Conclusions

Careful consideration of iron replacement in IBD is important because iron deficiency is a common problem. Unfortunately, it is frequently underdiagnosed and under-treated. Some of this is because of doctors' ignorance of its clinical importance, and some is because of the short-comings of oral iron replacement. The recent introduction of intravenous iron sucrose has significantly changed this scenario: adequate amounts of iron can now be delivered safely within a short period of time without significant gastrointestinal side-effects. With a severity-adjusted treat-ment regimen, virtually all patients can be successfully treated within a 4–8 week period. Thus, we believe that iron sucrose is the medication of choice for iron replace-ment in patients with IBD.

References

1 Weiss G, Goodnough LT. Anemia of chronic disease. *N Engl J Med* 2005; **352**: 1011–23.

2 Finch C. Regulators of iron balance in humans [see com-ments]. *Blood* 1994; **84**: 1697–702.

3 Bartels U, Pedersen NS, Jarnum S. Iron absorption and serum ferritin in chronic inflammatory bowel disease. *Scand J Gastroenterol* 1978; **13**: 649–56.

4 Gasche C. Anemia in IBD: the overlooked villain. *Inflamm Bowel Dis* 2000; **6**: 142–50.

5 de Silva AD, Mylonaki M, Rampton DS. Oral iron therapy in inflammatory bowel disease: usage, tolerance, and efficacy. *Inflamm Bowel Dis* 2003; **9**: 316–20.

6 Schroder O, Mickisch O, Seidler U, et al. Intravenous iron sucrose versus oral iron supplementation for the treatment of iron deficiency anemia in patients with inflammatory bowel disease: a randomized, controlled, open-label, multicenter study. *Am J Gastroenterol* 2005; **100**: 2503–9.

7 Erichsen K, Hausken T, Ulvik RJ, et al. Ferrous fumarate deteriorated plasma antioxidant status in patients with Crohn disease. *Scand J Gastroenterol* 2003; **38**: 543–8.

8 Carrier J, Aghdassi E, Platt I, Cullen J, Allard JP. Effect of oral iron supplementation on oxidative stress and colonic inflammation in rats with induced colitis. *Aliment Pharmacol Ther* 2001; **15**: 1989–99.

9 Schreiber S, Howaldt S, Schnoor M, et al. Recombinant erythropoietin for the treatment of anemia in inflammatory bowel disease. *N Engl J Med* 1996; **334**: 619–23.

10 Zanen AL, Adriaansen HJ, van Bommel EF, Posthuma R, Th de Jong GM. 'Oversaturation' of transferrin after intravenous ferric gluconate (Ferrlecit®) in haemodialysis patients. *Nephrol Dial Transplant* 1996; **11**: 820–4.

11 Silverstein SB, Rodgers GM. Parenteral iron therapy options. *Am J Hematol* 2004; **76**: 74–8.

12 Gasche C, Lomer MCE, Cavill I, Weiss G. Iron, anaemia, and inflammatory bowel diseases. *Gut* 2004; **53**: 1190–7.

13 Chandler G, Harchowal J, Macdougall IC. Intravenous iron sucrose: establishing a safe dose. *Am J Kidney Dis* 2001; **38**: 988–91.

14 Schroder O, Schrott M, Blumenstein I, et al. A study for the evaluation of safety and tolerability of intravenous high-dose iron sucrose in patients with iron deficiency anemia due to gastrointestinal bleeding. *Z Gastroenterol* 2004; **42**: 663–7.

15 Bodemar G, Kechagias S, Almer S, Danielson BG. Treatment of anaemia in inflammatory bowel disease with iron sucrose. *Scand J Gastroenterol* 2004; **39**: 454–8.

16 Gasche C, Dejaco C, Waldhoer T, et al. Intravenous iron and erythropoietin for anemia associated with Crohn disease: a randomized, controlled trial. *Ann Intern Med* 1997; **126**: 782–7.

17 Ganzoni AM. [Intravenous iron-dextran: therapeutic and experimental possibilities.] *Schweiz Med Wochenschr* 1970; **100**: 301–3.

39 Hepatitis B and C viruses – how do they affect management of IBD?

GRAHAM R FOSTER & ALICK N S NKHOMA

Introduction

Chronic infection with hepatotropic viruses – either hepatitis B (HBV) or hepatitis C (HCV) – is common and many patients with IBD will have past or ongoing infection. In this chapter we discuss the relationship between viral hepatitis and IBD before reviewing the complex interactions between the different treatments for these disorders.

IBD and chronic viral hepatitis

Patients with IBD have a higher risk of acquiring HBV or HCV infection, with a prevalence of up to 25% in one series [1]. The risk is related to greater exposure to surgery, blood transfusion, and endoscopy [1,2], and may be higher in Crohn's disease than UC [1]. Cell-mediated immunity driven by Th-1 cytokines is a feature of Crohn's disease, while UC may be Th-2 cytokine-driven [3]. In HCV infection, Th-2 type immune responses may contribute to the development of chronic infection [4]; however, no studies examining the natural history of chronic infection with hepatotropic viruses in conjunction with IBD have been performed.

Effect of treatment of IBD on viral hepatitis

The treatment of IBD in patients with viral hepatitis raises the question of what effects immunomodulatory drugs have on hepatic infection (Table 39.1).

Anti-TNF antibodies

Infliximab has been observed to reactivate latent HBV in rheumatoid arthritis and Crohn's disease [5]. Thus, patients with low level replication of HBV (i.e. HBsAg-positive, HBeAg-negative disease with normal liver function tests [LFTs]) are at risk of disease reactivation, and even patients with past infection (i.e. anti-HBc positive) may suffer from disease recurrence following anti-tumor necrosis factor (TNF) therapy. Although there is not yet proven evidence

TABLE 39.1 Effects of drugs used in the treatment of IBD on liver function and on viral replication in chronic viral hepatitis.

Drug class	Drug-induced hepatitis	Abnormal transaminases (ALT/AST)	Viral replication
Corticosteroids	Unlikely	No	Increased
Anti-TNF antibodies	Unlikely	No	Increased
Aminosalicylates	Possible	Possible	No effect
Thiopurines	Possible	Possible	Increased
Cyclosporine	Rare	Rare	Increased
Methotrexate	Possible	Possible	Increased

ALT, alanine aminotransferase; AST, aspartate aminotransferase; TNF, tumor necrosis factor.

of benefit, the authors advocate that such patients should receive prophylactic lamivudine to prevent disease reactivation. Indeed, this therapy has been shown to be beneficial in patients receiving chemotherapy for lymphoma [6].

The effects of anti-TNF therapy on patients with chronic HCV infection have not been studied, but a transient increase in viremia is likely.

Corticosteroids

As with anti-TNF therapy, patients with past exposure to HBV (i.e. anti-HBc-positive) or low level disease (HBsAg-positive, HBeAg-negative with normal LFTs) are at risk of disease reactivation when given corticosteroids for their IBD, and prophylactic therapy with lamivudine should be used. In patients with ongoing HBV-related disease (i.e. HBeAg-positive or HBeAg-negative with high level viremia), viral activation with an increase in liver inflammation (disease "flares") may be associated with changes in the immunologic responses to HBV, and is often precipitated by immunosuppressive therapy. Such patients should be reviewed before initiating steroid therapy and consideration given to treatment with lamivudine or alternative antiviral agents such as adefovir.

In patients with chronic HCV infection (i.e. antibody positive with viral RNA detectable in serum by sensitive molecular assays), steroids may increase HCV viremia with widespread infection of hepatocytes. Paradoxically, this increase in viremia is associated with a reduction in hepatic inflammation and a decrease in transaminase activity, presumably indicating that some of the liver inflammation associated with chronic HCV infection is brought about by the antiviral immune response. However, in patients with renal transplants, this reduction in hepatic inflammation is associated with an increase in the rate of fibrosis progression

[7,8]. At present there are no effective direct inhibitors of HCV replication and prophylactic antiviral therapy is not possible. Steroids should therefore be used with extreme caution in patients with chronic HCV infection and the normalization of LFTs should *not* be interpreted as benign.

Thiopurines

In common with many immunosuppressive drugs, azathioprine and mercaptopurine may induce both disease recurrence and reactivation in patients with past or current chronic HBV infection. As outlined above, prophylactic lamivudine is probably wise, although evidence of benefit is lacking.

Studies of isolated thiopurine therapy in patients with chronic HCV infection have not been performed. In renal transplantation patients, immunosuppression with both azathioprine and corticosteroids paradoxically decreases serum aminotransferases and increases both viremia and the rate of fibrosis progression. It is probable that isolated thiopurine therapy will have similar effects, and in patients with coexisting chronic HCV infection and IBD the dose used should be minimized and the drug discontinued as soon as possible. Indeed, it may be wise to consider regular liver biopsies (e.g. every 3 years) in IBD patients with chronic HCV infection receiving long-term azathioprine. Biopsy-proven fibrosis progression should prompt a review of the therapeutic options and consideration should be given to alternative treatments.

An additional problem associated with thiopurines in patients with chronic viral hepatitis is that the drug itself is hepatotoxic [9,10]. Thus, in patients with chronic viral hepatitis who are receiving thiopurines, an increase in the severity of the hepatitis should not be ascribed to the viral infection until drug-related hepatotoxicity has been excluded by liver biopsy.

Other immunosuppressive drugs

Methotrexate is directly hepatotoxic and also causes antiviral specific cytotoxic T-cell depletion resulting in decreased hepatitis B viral clearance [5]. When used with infliximab in rheumatoid arthritis, methotrexate has been shown to reactivate hepatitis B [5]; because the same effect is likely in IBD, patients with markers of HBV infection should receive prophylactic lamivudine while on methotrexate.

Cyclosporine, a calcineurin inhibitor that prevents clonal expansion of T-cell subsets, may reduce killing of viral infected cells and thereby reactivate viral hepatitis. Although direct evidence of benefit is – once again – lacking, lamivudine prophylaxis should be considered in patients with ongoing or past HBV infection if cyclosporine is to be used.

5-Aminosalicylates

The topical nature of their action prevents significant effects of 5-aminosalicylate (5-ASA) drugs on hepatotropic viruses, but they can induce chronic hepatitis [11]. Therefore, changes in liver inflammation should be investigated by liver biopsy and not attributed to any underlying viral hepatitis.

Comments

Although very few studies have addressed the effects of IBD-associated immunosuppression on concurrent viral hepatitis, conclusions can be drawn from studies of other diseases.

Immunosuppressant-treated patients with active chronic hepatitis B infection may have a deterioration in liver function and should be given a direct antiviral agent to prevent disease progression. In this context, lamivudine appears to be effective and safe. However, long-term lamivudine in patients with high level viral replication may cause viral mutations leading to disease reactivation and even hepatic decompensation. It is therefore important to ensure that these patients receive regular virologic monitoring so that the development of viral resistance can be identified and resolved by changing to an alternative drug, such as adefovir. For patients previously exposed to HBV (anti-HBc-positive) and in those with low level HBV viremia (HBsAg-positive, HBeAg-negative with normal LFTs and viral loads <10^5), prophylaxis with lamivudine is prudent to reduce the risk of viral reactivation. These patients are probably at low risk of developing viral resistance but long-term monitoring of the viral load is nevertheless advised.

For patients with chronic HCV infection and IBD, prolonged immunosuppressive therapy may increase viremia and the risk of cirrhosis. Unfortunately, effective drugs to combat this are not yet available and the clinician is left with the invidious task of monitoring the patient's decline.

In addition to the effects of immunosuppressive drugs on viral replication and virus-induced liver damage, it should be remembered that many of the drugs widely used in the treatment of IBD are themselves hepatotoxic. Prompt investigation of any change in the severity of the hepatitis is important; without this, it is unwise to attribute any changes to the effects of therapy on viral replication.

Use of interferon for treatment of viral hepatitis in IBD patients

The type I interferons are potent antiviral and immuno-stimulatory cytokines which are used widely in chronic HCV and often in chronic HBV infection. The immunomodulatory effects of the type I interferons are complex, ill-understood, and contradictory. In patients with multiple sclerosis, β-interferon (IFN-β) is used to suppress inflammation but the same cytokine has also been used successfully as an immunostimulant to treat patients with viral hepatitis. In Europe and the USA, IFN-α is used to treat viral hepatitis but its effects are similar to those of IFN-β (i.e. it has both immunostimulatory and immunoinhibitory effects). It is believed that the context and dose of the type I interferons have a major effect on the outcome of therapy but their contradictory effects make it impossible to predict their impact in patients with autoimmune disorders – a good case can be made both for beneficial and harmful effects! A few contradictory reports have studied the impact of interferon therapy in patients with IBD – one small study reported that the drug was safe in patients with both UC and Crohn's disease [12], while others have described relapse and exacerbation of UC [13–15]. One study to evaluate the efficacy of interferon in UC suggested that the drug was safe but not effective [16]. Thus, the safety and efficacy of interferon therapy in patients with IBD is unclear.

In patients with chronic HBV infection, where effective alternatives such as lamivudine and adefovir exist it is wise to avoid interferon. For patients with chronic HCV infection and IBD, therapy with interferon is best avoided but if there is biopsy-proven fibrosis progression it is reasonable to try a course of a pegylated interferon and ribavirin. However, the patient should be monitored closely and warned that therapy may exacerbate their bowel disease.

Conclusions

We recommend that patients with IBD should have viral hepatitis screening. Patients with chronic HBV infection needing immunosuppression should receive carefully supervised lamivudine or adefovir; those with inactive or past HBV infection should be given prophylactic lamivudine. In the absence as yet of effective therapeutic options, patients with chronic HCV infection who require immunosuppression for their IBD should be monitored using 3-yearly liver biopsies.

The safety of IFN-α in patients with IBD is not yet known. It can be avoided in hepatitis B by use of other agents, and, when necessary in hepatitis C, should be used with caution.

References

1 Biancone L, Pavia M, Del Vecchio BG, *et al*. Hepatitis B and C virus infection in Crohn's disease. *Inflamm Bowel Dis* 2001; 7: 287–94.

2 Longo F, Hebuterne X, Tran A, *et al*. [Prevalence of hepatitis C in patients with chronic inflammatory bowel disease in the region of Nice and evaluation of risk factors.] *Gastroenterol Clin Biol* 2000; 24: 77–81.

3 Fiocchi C. Inflammatory bowel disease: etiology and pathogenesis. *Gastroenterology* 1998; 115: 182–205.

4 Kamal SM, Rasenack JW, Bianchi L, *et al*. Acute hepatitis C without and with schistosomiasis: correlation with hepatitis C-specific CD4(+) T-cell and cytokine response. *Gastroenterology* 2001; 121: 646–56.

5 Ostuni P, Botsios C, Punzi L, Sfriso P, Todesco S. Hepatitis B reactivation in a chronic hepatitis B surface antigen carrier with rheumatoid arthritis treated with infliximab and low dose methotrexate 1. *Ann Rheum Dis* 2003; 62: 686–7.

6 Simpson ND, Simpson PW, Ahmed AM, *et al*. Prophylaxis against chemotherapy-induced reactivation of hepatitis B virus infection with lamivudine. *J Clin Gastroenterol* 2003; 37: 68–71.

7 Zylberberg H, Nalpas B, Carnot F, *et al*. Severe evolution of chronic hepatitis C in renal transplantation: a case control study. *Nephrol Dial Transplant* 2002; 17: 129–33.

8 Toz H, Ok E, Yilmaz F, *et al*. Clinicopathological features of hepatitis C virus infection in dialysis and renal transplantation. *J Nephrol* 2002; 15: 308–12.

9 Menor C, Fernandez-Moreno MD, Fueyo JA, *et al*. Azathioprine acts upon rat hepatocyte mitochondria and stress-activated protein kinases leading to necrosis: protective role of *N*-acetyl-L-cysteine. *J Pharmacol Exp Ther* 2004; 311: 668–76.

10 Kontorinis N, Agarwal K, Gondolesi G, *et al*. Diagnosis of 6-mercaptopurine hepatotoxicity post liver transplantation utilizing metabolite assays. *Am J Transplant* 2004; 4: 1539–42.

11 Deltenre P, Berson A, Marcellin P, *et al*. Mesalazine (5-aminosalicylic acid) induced chronic hepatitis. *Gut* 1999; 44: 886–8.

12 Cottone M, Magliocco A, Trallori G, *et al*. Clinical course of inflammatory bowel disease during treatment with interferon for associated chronic active hepatitis. *Ital J Gastroenterol* 1995; 27: 3–4.

13 Wenner WJ Jr, Piccoli DA. Colitis associated with alpha interferon? *J Clin Gastroenterol* 1997; 25: 398–9.

14 Yasumori K, Aramaki T, Mizuta Y, *et al*. [Exacerbation of ulcerative colitis and chronic hepatitis by the treatment with interferon for chronic hepatitis B.] *Nippon Shokakibyo Gakkai Zasshi* 1995; 92: 1066–70.

15 Mitoro A, Yoshikawa M, Yamamoto K, *et al*. Exacerbation of ulcerative colitis during alpha-interferon therapy for chronic hepatitis C. *Intern Med* 1993; 32: 327–31.

16 Tilg H, Vogelsang H, Ludwiczek O, *et al*. A randomised placebo controlled trial of pegylated interferon alpha in active ulcerative colitis. *Gut* 2003; 52: 1728–33.

40 Pregnancy: what drugs can we use?

THEA THOMAS & ELSPETH ALSTEAD

LEARNING POINTS

In pregnancy

- In pregnancy IBD is associated with increased risk to the fetus

- Aminosalicylates are safe in conventional doses, but folic acid supplementation should be given with sulfasalazine

- Methotrexate is teratogenic, and should only be prescribed for women using reliable forms of contraception after full discussion of the risks. Termination should be discussed in the early stages of pregnancy

- Azathioprine and 6-mercaptopurine are probably safe

- In treating active IBD, steroids are safe, and cyclosporine carries less risk than emergency surgery

- Limited data suggest that anti-TNF antibodies are safe

- All decisions should be made after full discussion of the evidence available and its limitations

Introduction

Inflammatory bowel disease (IBD) affects people of all ages including during their reproductive years. Women frequently voice concerns about fertility, the effect of their disease on pregnancy, and adverse effects of drug treatments [1]. In this chapter we review the available evidence about the safety of drugs commonly used to treat IBD.

Effects of IBD on fertility

Fertility does not seem to be affected in women with UC other than those who have had surgery [2,3]. In contrast, active Crohn's disease does impair fertility [2]. Women with Crohn's disease are known to have a delayed age of first pregnancy after the diagnosis [4]. In addition, women with Crohn's have fewer children than might be expected after diagnosis with a higher rate of failure to conceive (42% vs. 28%) [5].

Effects of IBD on pregnancy outcome

Most woman with inactive IBD can expect to have a normal pregnancy. However, in women with IBD, particularly Crohn's, there is thought to be an increased risk of preterm birth and small babies, and the cesarean section rate is higher [6]. The best indicators of outcome of pregnancy are thought to be related to disease activity and complications, particularly in Crohn's. If conception occurs in patients with active IBD, the disease is likely to stay active during the ensuing pregnancy [2]. There is evidence to suggest that Crohn's disease activity is slightly lower during pregnancy. This improvement may be related in part to a reduction in tobacco consumption during this period [7].

Drug treatment during pregnancy

It can be difficult to decide between continuing and stopping maintenance therapy during pregnancy. Although some maintenance drugs are known to be teratogenic, there is increasing evidence that others are safe in pregnancy. These risks therefore need to be weighed up against those associated with an acute exacerbation, and the risk of emergency surgery, which carries a 60% chance of fetal loss [8]. Ideally, discussion between the physician, mother, and partner should begin before conception and otherwise, as early as possible during the pregnancy. All decisions must be made on an individual basis. At this stage, advice about folic acid supplementation and diet should also be given.

Aminosalicylates

Aminosalicylates have been used in pregnancy for many years and are generally safe. They are poorly absorbed and there is little placental transport from mother to fetus. They may be used in pregnancy either as maintenance treatment or for the induction of remission (as in non-pregnant patients).

Although there is no evidence directly related to sulfasalazine, concern has been raised about the safety of folic acid antagonists in pregnancy in terms of neural tube defects and other anomalies, principally cardiovascular defects and cleft palate [9]. Folic acid supplementation should be strongly advised around conception, and a change to an alternative aminosalicylate considered.

Mesalazine is safe in a dosage of less than 3 g/day [10]. However, high-dose mesalazine has been associated with interstitial nephritis in a newborn infant and is therefore inadvisable during pregnancy [11].

Aminosalicylates are excreted in breast milk in small amounts. No harmful effects have been observed from breast feeding while the mother is taking sulfasalazine or conventional doses of mesalazine (<3 g/day).

Corticosteroids

Corticosteroids are well tolerated in pregnancy and their use has not been associated with abnormal fetal outcomes. Although they cross the placental barrier there is no convincing evidence of teratagenicity in humans. Neonatal adrenal insufficiency, a theoretical complication of maternal steroid use, is exceptionally rare, and reports of intrauterine growth retardation are at least in part thought to be caused by the underlying disease. Corticosteroids are therefore indicated in moderate to severely active disease as for non-pregnant patients [12]. Rectal preparations may be used until the third trimester unless there is specific concern about miscarriage or premature delivery.

Corticosteroids are poorly excreted in breast milk. If possible, a 4-hour delay after oral dosing should be observed. In practical terms, breast feeding appears to be safe in patients on corticosteroids [8].

Azathioprine and 6-mercaptopurine

Azathioprine and 6-mercaptopurine have no effect on human interstitial cell function or gametogenesis in the dosage used in clinical practice. They do not interfere with folic acid metabolism. There has never been any demonstration of teratogenicity of these agents in human pregnancy. There is extensive experience of the use of azathioprine in transplant recipients and patients with rheumatologic disorders, with no evidence of adverse outcomes. There is limited data relating to the use of these agents in pregnant patients with IBD [13,14]. Only one study has suggested an increase in perinatal mortality, congenital malformations, and pre-term birth and it concluded that more data was required to establish whether the associations were causal or confounding [15]. Therefore, if after full discussion it is deemed essential to maintain remission, it is reasonable to continue the treatment with a thiopurine.

Although the manufacturers advise patients not to breast feed while taking azathioprine or 6-mercaptopurine, there is extensive clinical experience of mothers taking these agents with no apparent adverse effects.

Although continued treatment with a thiopurine is probably safe in pregnancy and breast feeding, in view of the side-effects and complications that may arise with their initiation, it is advisable not to commence thiopurine treatment during pregnancy.

Cyclosporine

Cyclosporine is a potent immunosuppressant with significant incidence of serious side-effects in any patient (see Chapter 16). However, it has not been associated with increased adverse effects on the fetus. The risks to the mother include neurologic, renal and hepatic toxicity and, particularly in the third trimester, fluid overload (see Chapter 14). This makes its use limited to patients with fulminant colitis not responding to steroids in order to avoid colectomy [16,17], which is said to carry a 60% chance of fetal loss [8].

Methotrexate

Methotrexate is mutagenic and teratogenic and is contraindicated in pregnancy or anyone considering pregnancy. In addition, patients commencing methorexate treatment should be advised to use reliable contraception throughout and for 6 months after their course of treatment. If conception occurs, there is a high risk of serious neural tube defects. If termination of pregnancy cannot be contemplated, high-dose folic acid therapy should be administered for the remainder of pregnancy [18].

Anti-TNF antibodies

Post marketing surveillance of patients treated with infliximab has identified 59 pregnancies in patients before conception or during pregnancy. There was no increase in miscarriage. Two complications of pregnancy were reported: one premature birth and one child born with Fallot's tetralogy. This outcome was no different from that expected from the general population [19].

A recent retrospective study looking at the effects of infliximab on pregnancy and fetal outcome suggests that the benefits of infliximab in achieving a response and maintenance of remission in mothers with Crohn's disease outweigh the risks to the fetus of exposure to the drug. In this study of 10 women, all 10 pregnancies ended in live births, three infants were premature, and one had low birth weight; none had congenital malformations, intrauterine growth retardation or small for gestational age parameters [20]. Therefore, although more data are required, there is no theoretical or actual evidence of adverse effect.

Antibiotics

There are theoretical concerns about mutagenicity with metronidazole; however, this drug has been used extensively in the treatment of bacterial vaginosis in pregnancy and has been shown to be safe [21]. There are no data regarding the effects of longer courses of metronidazole such as used in the treatment of Crohn's disease (see Chapter 10).

Despite their theoretical risks, ciprofloxacin and other quinolones have been used in pregnancy without any evidence of congenital or musculoskeletal abnormalities [22]. Again there is no evidence about their safety with long-term use.

Conclusions

It is important to discuss all the issues relating to the management of IBD in pregnancy with the mother and her partner, preferably before conception is attempted. Topics should include: the evidence available about disease activity and complications during pregnancy and the possible effects on the fetus of an unwell mother; the background incidence of congenital abnormalities for any pregnancy; the limited evidence about the safety of drugs; and the methodologic difficulties of obtaining such evidence. Some women contemplating or already having achieved pregnancy may decide to discontinue drug treatment, despite advice that it may be better to continue [23].

References

1 Alstead EM, Nelson-Piercy C. Inflammatory bowel disease in pregnancy. *Gut* 2003; **52**: 159–61.

2 Hudson M, Flett G, Sinclair TS, *et al.* Fertility and pregnancy in inflammatory bowel disease. *Int J Gynaecol Obstet* 1997; **58**: 229–37.

3 Olsen KO, Juul S, Berndtsson I, *et al.* Ulcerative colitis: female fecundity before diagnosis, during disease and after surgery compared to a population sample. *Gastroenterology* 2002; **122**: 15–9.

4 Larzilliere I, Beau P. Chronic inflammatory bowel disease and pregnancy: case control study. *Gastroenterologie Clin Biol* 1998; **22**: 1056–60.

5 Mayberry JF, Weterman IT. European survey of fertility and pregnancy in women with Crohn's disease: a case control study by European collaborative group. *Gut* 1998; **27**: 821–5.

6 Kornfield D, Cnattinguis S, Ekbom A. Pregnancy outcome in women with inflammatory bowel disease: a population based cohort study. *Am J Obstet Gynaecol* 1997; **177**: 942–6.

7 Agret F, Cosnes J, Hassani Z, *et al.* Impact of pregnancy on the clinical activity of Crohn's disease. *Aliment Pharmacol Ther* 2005; **21**: 509.

8 Alstead EM. (2004) Inflammatory bowel disease in pregnancy. *Gastroenterology Update* (Ed. J. Mayberry). Radcliffe Publishing Ltd, 215–24

9 Hernandez-Diaz S, Werler MM, Walker AM, *et al.* Folic acid antagonists during pregnancy and the risk of birth defects. *N Engl J Med* 2000; **343**: 1608–14.

10 Diav-Citrin O, Park YH, Veerasuntharam G, *et al.* The safety of mesalazine in human pregnancy: a prospective controlled cohort study. *Gastroenterology* 1998; **114**: 23–8.

11 Colombel JF, Brabant G, Gubler MC, *et al.* Renal insufficiency in infant: side effect of prenatal exposure to mesalazine? *Lancet* 1994; **344**: 620–1.

12 Mogadem M, Dobbins WO, Korelitz BI, *et al.* Pregnancy and inflammatory bowel disease: effect of sulfasalazine and corticosteroids on foetal outcome. *Gastroenterology* 1981; **80**: 72–6.

13 Alstead EM, Ritchie JR, Lennard Jones JE, *et al.* Safety of azathioprine in inflammatory bowel disease. *Gastroenterology* 1990; **99**: 443–6.

14 Francella A, Dayan A, Rubin P, *et al*. 6-Mercaptopurine is safe therapy for child bearing patients with inflammatory bowel disease: a case control study. *Gastroenterology* 1996; **110**: 909.

15 Norgard B, Pedersen L, Fonager K, Rasmussen SN, Sorensen HT. Azathiaprine, mercaptopurine and birth outcome: a population based cohort study. *Aliment Pharmacol Ther* 2003; **17**: 827–34.

16 Radomski JS, Ahlswede BA, Jarrell BE, *et al*. Outcomes of 500 pregnancies in 335 female kidney, liver and heart transplant recipients. *Transplant Proc* 1995; **27**: 1089–90.

17 Bermas BL, Hill JA. Effects of immunosuppressive drugs during pregnancy. *Arthritis Rheum* 1995; **38**: 1722–32.

18 Donnerfield AE, Pastuszak A, Noah JS, *et al*. Methotrexate exposure prior to and during pregnancy. *Teratology* 1994; **49**: 79–81.

19 Katz JA, Litchenstein GR, Keenan GF, *et al*. Outcome of pregnancy in women receiving remicade (infliximab) for the treatment of Crohn's disease and rheumatoid arthritis. *Gastroenterology* 2001; **120**: A69.

20 Mahadevan U, Kane S, Sandborn WJ, *et al*. Intentional infliximab during pregnancy for induction or maintenance of remission in Crohn's disease. *Aliment Pharmacol Ther* 2005; **21**: 733–8.

21 Piper JM, Mitchell EF, Ray WA. Prenatal use of metronidazole and birth defects: no association. *Obstet Gynaecol* 1993; **82**: 348–52.

22 Berkovitch M, Pastuszak A, Gazarian M. Safety of the new quinolones in pregnancy. *Obstet Gynaecol* 1994; **84**: 535–8.

23 Connell W, Miller A. Treating inflammatory bowel disease during pregnancy: risks and safety of therapy. *Drug Saf* 1999; **21**: 311–23.

41 How to prevent growth failure in children

JUTTA KÖGLMEIER & NICK CROFT

LEARNING POINTS

Growth failure in children with IBD

- Accurate and regular measurement of height, weight, pubertal stage, and bone age is mandatory
- Crossing the centiles on growth charts or a reduction in height velocity (centile or SDS/Z score) are the most useful measurements of growth failure
- Growth failure frequently complicates the clinical course of children with IBD and can occur prior to gastrointestinal symptoms; it is more common in Crohn's disease than UC
- Catch-up growth will occur only if addressed before puberty begins
- Improving nutrition and controlling disease activity, with minimal use of steroids, is the best way of maximizing growth

---

Introduction

Growth failure is a common, serious complication in children with IBD and is often accompanied by delayed puberty. This can have a serious impact on the self-esteem of the adolescent patient and diminish final adult height. The aim of this chapter is to define growth failure, discuss the underlying pathologic mechanisms and therapeutic options, and to highlight potential consequences if left untreated.

What is growth failure?

There is no widely accepted definition of growth failure.

Monitoring of growth is carried out either by interpreting single measurements of height or by calculating the height velocity (over a period of not less than 3 months). Both height alone and height velocity can be compared with age- and sex-matched peers in the form of centiles (on charts) or standard deviation (SDS)/Z scores.

Single measurements of height do not allow for children of small families expected to be less than (for example) the third centile. Equally, a tall child, who fails to grow, can be missed using single measurements if he/she is on (for example) the 75th centile. Thus, it is vital to measure the children regularly and follow the progress of their height using growth charts or centiles (or SDS/Z scores). It is also helpful to measure parents to predict the genetic growth potential from the mid-parental height.

To interpret growth information it is vital to assess pubertal stage and bone age. The growth velocity of a prepubertal child with IBD (with delayed puberty) must be interpreted with caution when compared to his/her age-matched peers who are pubertal and expected to be growing rapidly. Similarly, a delayed bone age may allow an individual child a longer growth period than his/her age-matched peers and so allow catch-up growth.

Measuring the final adult height is undoubtedly an important measure in the context of academic research and assessing the outcome of interventions, but is of no use in the clinical management of growing children [1].

The importance of regularly and accurately measuring growth, and how poorly it is carried out outside pediatric clinics, has been highlighted previously [2].

How common is growth failure?

Growth impairment has been shown prior to diagnosis, at diagnosis, and after diagnosis of IBD.

In countries regularly documenting children's height it has been possible to show that growth faltering precedes the diagnosis of IBD in up to 90% of patients with Crohn's disease and less commonly in UC [3,4]. The majority of children with prediagnosis growth failure were prepubertal and 20–40% of them continued to have severe linear growth retardation with a height below the third centile during the subsequent clinical course [3].

The majority of adults with childhood onset IBD have heights between the 5th and 97th centile, but the distribution is skewed towards the lower centiles, resulting in a final height below the 5th centile in 7–30% of cases [3].

What causes growth failure?

Growth failure in IBD is thought to be a consequence of some or all of the following: poor nutrition (resulting from inadequate intake); a direct consequence of the inflammatory process on bone growth; and the growth suppressing effects of treatments, specifically steroids.

Insulin-like growth factor-1 (IGF-1) production from the liver is stimulated by growth hormone (GH). IGF-1 then binds to receptors in the growth plate chondrocytes to stimulate growth [3]. Children with IBD secrete normal levels of GH, but their plasma IGF-1 concentration is reduced, suggesting insensitivity of the liver to GH. There is also evidence in animal models of the direct inhibitory effects of interleukin 6 (IL-6), tumor necrosis factor (TNF), IL-1, and other inflammatory cytokines on growth [3]. In an animal model of colitis it has been estimated that approximately 60% of growth failure was a result of nutritional deprivation and 40% to inflammation [5]. Some of these growth-related effects can be reversed using IL-6 antibody [6].

In male children, jejunal involvement in Crohn's disease and disease extent are associated with reduced height [7]. Steroid use, particularly if used in early puberty, causes stunting of growth [8].

Management of growth failure

Auxology

All children with IBD should have their height, weight, pubertal staging, and bone age measured on a regular basis by people trained in auxologic techniques. Weight should be recorded at every visit, height every 3–4 months, pubertal stage and bone age at least once a year. In the absence of gastrointestinal symptoms, a reduction in growth velocity

can be the first sign of disease relapse and alert the physician to modify the child's management.

Medical therapy

The principles of minimizing growth failure are to keep the disease under control using as few steroids as possible. This can be achieved using enteral nutrition to get the subject into remission and immunosuppressants, surgery, and biologics such as infliximab to maintain remission in chronic relapsing disease.

In children with active Crohn's disease, a 6-week course of exclusive **enteral nutrition**, using either polymeric or elemental formulae, leads to remission in 70–80% of patients, a success rate similar to that in steroids [9]. In a randomized study, children receiving steroids had a lower growth velocity than those treated with an elemental diet [10]. Thus, steroids should be considered as a second-line therapeutic option, particularly in children with documented growth failure.

A 6-week course of a polymeric diet in children with Crohn's disease reduced inflammation and increased plasma IGF-1 before significantly improving their nutritional status, suggesting that the growth-enhancing effects of enteral nutrition are related to reduction of inflammation rather than poor nutrition [11]. Whether the feed is polymeric or elemental probably does not matter as both have been shown to be effective. Although enteral nutrition does not induce remission in UC, it is important in children with significant weight loss.

Preventing disease relapse is particularly important to maximize the growth potential of children and adolescents. Continuing supplemental nutrition to maintain remission and enhance growth has been proposed; however, no quality studies have been performed in this area. In a retrospective study, the use of overnight feeding in underweight patients appeared to reduce relapse rates and improve linear growth [12].

5-Aminosalicylate preparations are widely prescribed for children with Crohn's disease but there are no studies demonstrating reduction of relapse rates or improvement of growth. In UC, such therapy may enhance growth by reducing the need for steroids.

In children with Crohn's disease, **azathioprine or 6-mercaptopurine** reduce relapse rates [13]. Whether their early use is advantageous in the long-term management of growth problems in IBD has not been established.

Infliximab has shown potential for the management of growth failure in the presence of ongoing active disease

[14]. The growth-enhancing effect of infliximab may be exerted through reduction of systemic inflammation and by prevention of the growth-inhibiting effects of TNF on the growth plate.

Surgical treatment of localized disease can be very effective at enhancing growth, and is most effective in the prepubertal period [15].

Why is attention to growth important?

Catch-up growth will occur only before the closure of the epiphyseal plate; early detection and management of growth failure is therefore essential before puberty begins. A reduced growth velocity is a sign of poorly controlled IBD and demands prompt intensification of therapy. Failure to take such action can lead to delayed puberty and diminished stature; both can have a significant negative impact on the psychological health of adolescents and young adults [16].

References

1 Sawczenko A, Ballinger AB, Croft NM, Sanderson IR, Savage MO. Adult height in patients with early onset of Crohn's disease. *Gut* 2003; **52**: 454–5.

2 Ghosh S, Drummond HE, Ferguson A. Neglect of growth and development in the clinical monitoring of children and teenagers with inflammatory bowel disease: review of case records. *BMJ* 1998; **317**: 120–1.

3 Ballinger AB, Camacho-Hubner C, Croft NM. Growth failure and intestinal inflammation. *Q J Med* 2001; **94**: 121–5.

4 Hildebrand H, Karlberg J, Kristiansson B. Longitudinal growth in children and adolescents with inflammatory bowel disease. *J Pediatr Gastroenterol Nutr* 1994; **18**: 165–73.

5 Ballinger AB, Azooz O, El Haj T, Poole S, Farthing MJ. Growth failure occurs through a decrease in insulin-like growth factor 1 which is independent of undernutrition in a rat model of colitis. *Gut* 2000; **46**: 694–700.

6 Azooz O, Farthing MJG, Ballinger A. Interleukin-6 (IL-6) contributes to suppression of linear growth associated with intestinal inflammation. *Gastroenterology* 2001; **118**: A62.

7 Sawczenko A, Ballinger AB, Savage MO, Croft NM, Sanderson IR. Delay in diagnosis and jejunal involvement predispose to growth failure in Crohn's disease. *Arch Dis Child* 2003; **88** (Suppl 1): A8.

8 Escher JC, Croft NM, European Collaborative Research Group on Budesonide in Paediatric IBD. Budesonide versus prednisolone for the treatment of active Crohn's disease in children: a randomized, double-blind, controlled, multicentre trial. *Eur J Gastroenterol Hepatol* 2004; **16**: 47–54.

9 Heuschkel RB, Walker-Smith JA. Enteral nutrition in inflammatory bowel disease of childhood. [Review] [21 refs]. *JPEN J Parenter Enteral Nutr* 1999; **23** (5 Suppl): S29–S32.

10 Sanderson IR, Udeen S, Davies PS, Savage MO, Walker-Smith JA. Remission induced by an elemental diet in small bowel Crohn's disease. *Arch Dis Child* 1987; **62**: 123–7.

11 Bannerjee K, Camacho-Hubner C, Babinska K, *et al.* Anti-inflammatory and growth-stimulating effects precede nutritional restitution during enteral feeding in Crohn disease. *J Pediatr Gastroenterol Nutr* 2004; **38**: 270–5.

12 Wilschanski M, Sherman P, Pencharz P, *et al.* Supplementary enteral nutrition maintains remission in paediatric Crohn's disease. *Gut* 1996; **38**: 543–8.

13 Markowitz J, Grancher K, Kohn N, Lesser M, Daum F. A multicenter trial of 6-mercaptopurine and prednisone in children with newly diagnosed Crohn's disease. *Gastroenterology* 2000; **119**: 895–902.

14 Borrelli O, Bascietto C, Viola F, *et al.* Infliximab heals intestinal inflammatory lesions and restores growth in children with Crohn's disease. *Dig Liver Dis* 2004; **36**: 342–7.

15 Beattie RM, Camacho-Hubner C, Wacharasindhu S, *et al.* Responsiveness of IGF-I and IGFBP-3 to therapeutic intervention in children and adolescents with Crohn's disease. *Clin Endocrinol (Oxf)* 1998; **49**: 483–9.

16 Stephens M, Batres LA, Ng D, Baldassano R. Growth failure in the child with inflammatory bowel disease. *Semin Gastrointest Dis* 2001; **12**: 253–62.

42 Predicting outcome in severe UC

SIMON TRAVIS

LEARNING POINTS

Predicting outcome in severe UC

- Be objective: use a validated predictive index (e.g. C-reactive protein (CRP) >45 mg/L or stool frequency >8/day) on the third day of intensive therapy for severe UC

- Make contingency plans: call the surgeons and stoma therapist on day 3 if the index indicates a high likelihood of colectomy

- Make a decision at this early stage: augment therapy (e.g. start cyclosporine) unless clearly responding to steroids

- Involve the patient: discuss contingency plans early

- Recognize limitations: 85% of partial responders on day 7 will come to colectomy within 10 years

- Delays in decision making increase morbidity and mortality

Introduction

The response to intensive treatment of severe UC with steroids has remained unchanged for almost 50 years. In the landmark paper by Truelove and Witts in 1955 [1], 41% went into remission, 27% made a partial response, and 32% deteriorated during admission and either needed colectomy or died. In 2001, a nationwide prospective survey of 116 patients with severe UC treated in 29 UK hospitals, 41% had a complete and 31% a partial response, while 28% went on to have a colectomy [2]. The only appreciable difference in outcome from the 1955 study was that no patient died. It is easy to forget that the mortality in severe attacks

of UC has declined from approximately 75% for first attacks in 1933 [3], to 7% after the introduction of steroids in 1955 [3], to <1% in specialist centers today [4].

There remain two principal clinical dilemmas in managing severe UC: how to identify at an early stage those who are likely to need colectomy, and when to start rescue medical therapy in time so that surgery, if it becomes necessary, is not inappropriately delayed. The two are not mutually exclusive and demand the most taxing clinical judgment. As therapeutic options increase (e.g. cyclosporine, infliximab, or visilizumab) (see Chapters 16, 20, 31), so too does the opportunity for medical indecision making. When surgery is deferred, outcome deteriorates. Only a single patient need die as a result of complications caused by operating too late to negate the benefits of medical therapy. This is illustrated by a courageous report in 2001, from a British District General Hospital where general physicians managed severe UC [5]. Out of 32 episodes of severe UC in 25 patients from 1994–2000, six patients died, giving a mortality of 24% (identical to the placebo group mortality in the 1955 trial [3]). All who had surgery were treated for 10 days or more before colectomy. This is manifestly unacceptable, but it would be surprising if similar events were not occurring unreported in other hospitals without specialist input. This is the impetus behind a national audit of morbidity and mortality among inpatients with UC (and Crohn's disease), commencing in the UK in 2006.

Simple, objective measures are therefore needed to aid decision making. Patients usually report feeling better after intensive treatment with steroids and intravenous fluid is started [6], but this is in comparison to how unwell they felt before admission. They naturally want to avoid colectomy.

Physicians frequently collude, because they too are keen to avoid the irrevocable decision for colectomy. As a consequence, studies have attempted to develop predictive indices. The importance of using one of these indices increases as medical options proliferate.

Factors that predict the need for colectomy can be broadly divided into radiologic, clinical, biochemical, and genetic.

Radiologic criteria

Radiologic criteria include the presence of colonic dilatation >5.5 cm (associated with a 75% need for colectomy), or mucosal islands on a plain abdominal radiograph (75% colectomy) [7]. The presence of an ileus (indicated by three or more small bowel loops of gas) was associated with colectomy in 73% in a retrospective study [8], but only 50% in a prospective study from the same institution [4]. The depth of colonic ulceration after gentle air insufflation identified 42/49 patients with deep ulcers that were associated with the need for colectomy [9], but this is not widely used in clinical practice.

Clinical markers

Clinical markers depend on the objective measures of stool frequency or temperature. A stool frequency >12/day on day 2 was associated with 55% colectomy [7], while a frequency >8/day on day 3 of intensive treatment predicted colectomy in 85% on that admission [4]. This latter measure has been validated: a frequency >4 and CRP >25 mg/L on day 3 (or when stool frequency × 0.14 CRP ≥8 on day 3: "Swedish index") predicted colectomy in 75% [10].

Biochemical markers

Biochemical markers include C-reactive protein (CRP), albumin and pH. An erythrocyte sedimentation rate (ESR) >75 or a pyrexia >38°C on admission have been associated with a five- to ninefold increase in the need for colectomy in a prospective study of 67 patients [11]. In this study, lack of response to steroids was predicted by <40% reduction in stool frequency within 5 days. Nevertheless, indices that provide relative values are not that clinically useful. Patients (and their doctors) prefer to know an absolute estimate of the likelihood of colectomy, rather than relative measures.

Genetic markers

Genetic markers (see Chapter 24) are still in their infancy. Between 1 and 3% of the general population express HLA DRB1*103, while 16% of those who have colectomy express this haplotype [12]. Furthermore, a polymorphism in the gene for the multidrug resistance (*MDR-1*) efflux pump, which is associated with drug resistance in chemotherapy, is also associated with steroid resistance and therefore colectomy in UC [13]. It will be immediately apparent, however, that although genetic polymorphisms have the potential to predict the outcome of disease in an individual from the time of diagnosis, they cannot be used for decision making when colectomy threatens.

Conclusion

Of all these, the simple measures of CRP >45 mg/L and stool frequency 3–8/day, or a stool frequency >8/day on day 3 [4] have become a useful guide. The alternative "Swedish index" has been used as a threshold (index ≥8) for randomizing patients to biologic therapy (infliximab) [14]. The figures are easy to remember, simple to apply, and define an approach to treatment. At the very least, patients meeting these criteria should have a joint consultation with physician and surgeon, as well as being introduced to a stomatherapist by way of contingency planning. Treatment with intravenous 2 mg/kg cyclosporine should also be considered at that stage, if cyclosporine has not already been commenced as monotherapy on admission. Because cyclosporine works rapidly (usually 48–96 hours), the patient can be prepared for possible surgery in a timely manner, so that emergency colectomy and the need for a stoma does not come out of the blue. This contingency planning helps patients come to terms with the possibility of medical failure. Far too frequently surgeons are asked to see a patient, who has already been in hospital for a week or more, on a Friday evening when the stomatherapist has gone home for the weekend.

Indices exist to be applied, as a threshold for triggering appropriate action at an early stage. This means surgical consultation and assessment by a stomatherapist *in addition to* augmenting medical treatment. The CRP and stool frequency criteria are neither immutable nor always reproduced. Other criteria may do as well, but must be as simple. The importance is to have objective measures of response integrated into the clinical strategy, so that patients with severe UC are not blighted by prevarication. At the end of the day it helps to know that 15/49 patients who had an incomplete response to medical therapy just 7 days after starting intensive treatment (as judged by a stool frequency >3/day or with visible blood in their stools) had a 40% chance of needing colectomy within 6 months and 85%

chance of colectomy over the next decade, compared with 32% in those who responded completely to medical therapy [15]. This should inform discussion with patients.

References

1 Truelove SC, Witts LJ. Cortisone in ulcerative colitis: final report on a therapeutic trial. *BMJ* 1955; **ii**: 1041–8.

2 Hawthorne AB, Travis SPL and the BSG IBD Clinical Trials Network. Outcome of inpatient management of severe ulcerative colitis: a BSG IBD Clinical Trials Network Survey. *Gut* 2002; **50**: A16.

3 Hardy TL, Bulmer E. Ulcerative colitis. *BMJ* 1933; **ii**: 812–5.

4 Travis SPL, Farrant JM, Ricketts C, *et al*. Predicting outcome in severe ulcerative colitis. *Gut* 1996; **38**: 905–10.

5 Stenner JMC, White P, Gould SR. Audit of the management of severe ulcerative colitis in a DGH. *Gut* 2001; **48**: A87.

6 Dunckley P, Jewell DP. Management of acute severe colitis. *Best Pract Res Clin Gastroenterol* 2003; **17**: 89–103.

7 Lennard-Jones JE, Ritchie JK, Hilder W, Spicer CC. Assessment of severity in colitis: a preliminary study. *Gut* 1975; **16**: 579–84.

8 Chew CN, Nolan DJ, Jewell DP. Small bowel gas in severe ulcerative colitis. *Gut* 1991; **32**: 1535–7.

9 Almer S, Bodemar G, Franzen L, *et al*. Use of air enema radiography to assess depth of ulceration during acute attacks of ulcerative colitis. *Lancet* 1996; **347**: 1731–5.

10 Lindgren SC, Flood LM, Kilander AF, *et al*. Early predictors of glucocorticoid treatment failure in severe and moderately severe attacks of ulcerative colitis. *Eur J Gastroenterol Hepatol* 1998; **10**: 831–5.

11 Benazzato L, D'Inca R, Grigoletto F, *et al*. Prognosis of severe attacks in ulcerative colitis: effect of intensive medical treatment. *Dig Liver Dis* 2004; **36**: 461–6.

12 Roussomoustakaki M, Satsangi J, Welsh K, *et al*. Genetic markers may predict disease behavior in patients with ulcerative colitis. *Gastroenterology* 1997; **112**: 1845–53.

13 Ho GT, Nimmo ER, Tenesa A, *et al*. Allelic variations of the multidrug resistance gene determine susceptibility and disease behavior in ulcerative colitis. *Gastroenterology* 2005; **128**: 288–96.

14 Järnerot G, Hertervig E, Friis-Liby I, *et al*. Infliximab as rescue therapy in severe to moderately severe ulcerative colitis: a randomized placebo-controlled study. *Gastroenterology* 2005; **128**: 1805–11.

15 Bojic D, Al-Ali M, Jewell DP, Travis SPL. Long term outcome following intensive treatment for severe ulcerative colitis *Gut* 2005; **54**: A155.

43 Refractory proctitis

ANNE BALLINGER & RICHARD MAKINS

LEARNING POINTS

Refractory proctitis

In patients with apparently refractory proctitis, it is essential to:

- Confirm the diagnosis: exclude other causes of proctitis and rectal bleeding

- Optimize conventional therapy with 5-ASA, steroids, and/or immunosuppressive drugs

- Address contributory factors such as proximal constipation, poor drug adherence, and psychosocial issues

- Be open to therapies with a limited evidence-base such as topical acetarsol and lidocaine, and complementary approaches

- For some patients surgery is needed

Introduction – optimal treatment of ulcerative proctitis

At diagnosis approximately one-third of patients with UC will have disease limited to the rectum. Topical 5-aminosalicyclic acid (5-ASA) is superior to topical corticosteroids for improvement and induction of remission whether assessed by symptoms, endoscopic appearances, or histology [1,2]. In addition, topical 5-ASA is superior to oral preparations [2]. The combination of oral and rectal ASA is superior to rectal ASA alone. Many patients with limited disease will already be taking maintenance oral ASA drugs and in the remainder a decision regarding combination treatment (and therefore the extra cost) has to be made on a case by case basis [3].

A suppository is the best choice of preparation for treatment of proctitis as it remains confined to the rectum (i.e. a high concentration of drug at the site that matters) and, unlike foam and liquid enemas, does not spread proximally beyond the rectum [4]. In a dose–response study of topical Pentasa enema, 65% of patients were markedly improved at 8 weeks using 1 g/day, with no benefit at higher doses [5]. Combination treatment with topical 5-ASA and topical steroids is superior to either agent alone and is used in patients who do not respond to single drug treatment [6]. Adding in an oral 5-ASA treatment and a tapering dose of corticosteroids is usually the next step for the non-responders.

Refractory proctitis

There is no strict definition for refractory proctitis and few studies have specifically addressed the definition or prevalence. In one small study of 40 patients, five (12.5%) continued to have symptoms after 8 weeks of oral and topical steroids with the later addition of mesalazine enemas for non-responders [7]. In some of this group there will be proximal extension of disease such that suppositories are no longer a suitable preparation. In follow-up studies, 16–20% of patients with ulcerative proctitis have proximal extension of disease at 5 years and 4% overall have disease extending beyond the splenic flexure [8,9]. Colonoscopy should therefore be performed in patients with refractory disease. As well as assessment of disease extent, colonoscopy and biopsy will exclude conditions other than colitis that are mimicking the symptoms of active colitis (e.g. colorectal cancer, infection, solitary rectal ulcer syndrome, reduced rectal compliance).

Compliance with drug treatment may also be a factor in symptom resolution. Although this has not specifically been

TABLE 43.1 Summary of management considerations in patients with refractory proctitis.

Proximal extension of disease beyond the rectum
Ingestion of drugs that exacerbate colitis, e.g. non-steroidal anti-inflammatory drugs
Poor compliance with medication
Disease other than colitis presenting with similar symptoms
Laxatives for proximal constipation
Alternative medical therapy (as discussed in the text)
Surgery

assessed in this group of patients, overall non-compliance with medication may be as high as 41% in all patients with IBD [10]. The inflamed rectum may lead to alterations in colonic motility with prolonged transit through uninvolved colon. There is no evidence that proximal constipation is associated with refractory disease but in some patients laxative treatment (e.g. a sachet of Movicol) is associated with resolution of colitic symptoms. The considerations that must be taken into account in the management of patients with apparent refractory colitis are summarized in Table 43.1. In addition, a full discussion with the patient will enable them to understand the need for prolonged treatment in some cases, the likely outcome of treatment, and the variety of treatments that may be need to induce a remission.

The evidence base for effective alternative therapies to 5-ASA and corticosteroids in refractory distal UC is small. Patients with severe disease may need admission to hospital for treatment with intravenous **steroids** and/or **cyclosporine**.

Treatment with **local anesthetics** was introduced on the basis that blockade of some neurally mediated events, such as epithelial proliferation, vascular congestion, and effects on immune cells may be beneficial. Treatment with 2% lidocaine enemas 20 mL twice daily resulted in symptom relief and mucosal healing in 83% of patients with proctosigmoiditis after treatment for 6–34 weeks [11]. Two-thirds of patients were resistant to previous therapy. Many presented with recurrent symptoms in the year after treatment was stopped, illustrating the need for maintenance treatment, including azathioprine, in patients who have had an episode of refractory proctitis.

Transdermal **nicotine** is superior to placebo for induction of remission in patients with UC. In patients with distal colitis, nicotine patches in combination with oral mesalazine was superior to combined therapy with oral and rectal mesalazine [12]. In two small open label studies, nicotine enemas, 6 mg/day for 4 weeks, produced clinical

improvement in 54–71% of patients unresponsive to first-line therapy [13,14].

Acetarsol suppositories (250 mg twice daily for 4 weeks) induced clinical and sigmoidoscopic remission in 9/10 patients with refractory proctitis [15]. Maximal blood and urine arsenic concentrations occurred within the first week and fell to pretreatment values by 4 weeks. **Epidermal growth factor** (EGF) is a potent mitogenic peptide and stimulates repair of damaged mucosa. EGF enemas (5 µg in 100 mL) induced clinical remission in 10/12 (83%) patients with active left-sided colitis after 2 weeks of therapy compared with only 8% of the control group [16]. Both groups were also treated with oral 5-ASA and the very low placebo response was still apparent at 12 weeks. There have been no larger, published, placebo-controlled studies since this pilot study. **Aloe vera** is superior to placebo in patients with mild to moderate colitis (see Chapter 33). Although this treatment has not been specifically assessed in patients with refractory disease, it is a safe and well-tolerated treatment and may have some benefit in this group of patients.

Leukocytapheresis (see Chapter 29) has not been specifically assessed in patients with refractory proctitis or distal colitis but an open label study in patients with active distal colitis showed clinical remission in 21/30 patients (70%) after five aphereses [17]. **Immunoglobulin G, interleukin-10, topical cyclosporine, bismuth** and **short-chain fatty acid enemas** have been assessed in distal colitis but the studies are either too small to make meaningful conclusions or there has been no benefit of treatment [18].

Appendicectomy has also been advocated for refractory distal colitis, particularly when peri-appendiceal "skip lesions" are identified at colonoscopy. As yet, however, data are only available from individual case reports or small case series. (see Chapter 30).

Conclusions

Patients with refractory proctitis can be very difficult to treat. Management principles include confirming the diagnosis, optimizing standard conventional therapy, and then, when necessary, trying less well-established new therapies. Despite these measures, in a small proportion of patients with proctitis, there will be no alternative, in the end, to panproctocolectomy. Keeping the patient fully informed of the nature of their disorder, and discussing with them its therapeutic alternatives, is, as in other IBD contexts, of central importance.

References

1 Marshall JK and Irvine EJ. Rectal corticosteroids versus alternative treatments in ulcerative colitis: a meta-analysis. *Gut* 1997; **40**: 775–81.

2 Cohen RD, Woseth DM, Thisted RA, Hanauer SB. A meta-analysis and overview of the literature on treatment options for left-sided ulcerative colitis and ulcerative proctitis. *Am J Gastroenterol* 2000; **95**: 1263–76.

3 Brown J, Haines S, Wilding IR. Colonic spread of three rectally administered mesalazine (Pentasa) dosage forms in healthy volunteers as assessed by gamma scintigraphy. *Aliment Pharmacol Ther* 1997; **11**: 685–91.

4 Safdi M, DeMicco M, Sninsky C, *et al.* A double-blind comparison of oral versus rectal mesalamine versus combination therapy in the treatment of distal ulcerative colitis. *Am J Gastroenterol* 1997; **92**: 1867–71.

5 Hanauer SB. Dose-ranging study of mesalamine (PENTASA) enemas in the treatment of acute ulcerative proctosigmoiditis: results of a multicentered placebo-controlled trial. The US PENTASA Enema Study Group. *Inflamm Bowel Dis* 1998; **4**: 79–83.

6 Mulder CJJ, Fockens P, Meijer JWR, *et al.* Beclomethasone dipropionate (3 mg) versus 5-aminosalicyclic acid (2 g) versus the combination of both (3 mg/2 g) as retention enemas in active ulcerative proctitis. *Eur J Gastroenterol Hepatol* 1996; **8**: 549–53.

7 Travis SPL, Dannatt E, McGovern DPB, *et al.* Managed care for distal ulcerative colitis: preliminary results. *Gut* 2001; **48** (Suppl): A87.

8 Meucci G, Vecchi M, Astegiano M, *et al.* The natural history of ulcerative proctitis: a multicenter, retrospective study. Gruppo di Studio per le Malattie Infiammatorie Intestinali (GSMII). *Am J Gastroenterol* 2000; **95**: 469–73.

9 Ayres RC, Gillen CD, Walmsley RS, Allan RN. Progression of ulcerative proctosigmoiditis: incidence and factors influencing progression. *Eur J Gastroenterol Hepatol* 1996; **8**: 555–8.

10 Sewitch MJ, Abrahamowicz M, Barkun A, *et al.* Patient non-adherence to medication in inflammatory bowel disease. *Am J Gastroenterol* 2003; **98**: 1535–44.

11 Bjorck S, Dahlstrom A, Johansson L, Ahlman H. Treatment of the mucosa with local anaesthetics in ulcerative colitis. *Agents Actions* 1992; Spec No: C60–72.

12 Guslandi M, Frego R, Viale E, Testoni PA. Distal ulcerative colitis refractory to rectal mesalamine: role of transdermal nicotine versus oral mesalamine. *Can J Gastroenterol* 2002; **16**: 293–6.

13 Sandborn WJ, Tremaine WJ, Leighton JA, *et al.* Nicotine tartrate liquid enemas for mildly to moderately active left-sided ulcerative colitis unresponsive to first-line therapy: a pilot study. *Aliment Pharmacol Ther* 1997; **11**: 663–71.

14 Green JT, Thomas GA, Rhodes J, *et al.* Nicotine enemas for active ulcerative colitis: a pilot study. *Aliment Pharmacol Ther* 1997; **11**: 859–63.

15 Forbes A, Britton TC, House IM, Gazzard BG. Safety and efficacy of acetarsol suppositories in unresponsive proctitis. *Aliment Pharmacol Ther* 1989; **3**: 553–6.

16 Sinha A, Nightingale J, West KP, *et al.* Epidermal growth factor enemas with oral mesalamine for mild-to-moderate left-sided ulcerative colitis or proctitis. *N Engl J Med* 2003; **349**: 350–7.

17 Yamamoto T, Umegae S, Kitagawa T, *et al.* Granulocyte and monocyte adsorptive apheresis in the treatment of active distal ulcerative colitis: a prospective, pilot study. *Aliment Pharmacol Ther* 2004; **20**: 783–92.

18 Travis SPL, The management of refractory distal colitis. *Proc R Coll Physicians Edinb* 2001; **31**: 222–8.

44 CMV co-infection – does it matter?

DAAN HOMMES

Introduction

It is estimated that approximately 15% of all patients suffering from UC will eventually require hospitalization [1], with risk of progressing to a toxic (fulminant) colitis and/or a toxic megacolon. Cytomegalovirus (CMV) infection is frequently diagnosed during severe attacks of UC, but its significance for disease severity is unknown. A critical appraisal of nine case series and 33 case reports addressing the role of CMV in IBD patients did not lead to definitive conclusions regarding its pathogenic role [2]. Unanswered questions that remain are:

1 Which patients are at risk?

2 Is CMV reactivation caused by the level of immunosuppressive therapy?

3 Does CMV infection affect the clinical course of disease?

CMV replication in outpatients with IBD

To address these complex questions, we prospectively assessed evidence for CMV infection in a large cohort of our IBD patients. It is common clinical practice to assess mucosal CMV involvement in IBD patients either by demonstration of inclusion bodies on hematoxylin and eosin (H&E) staining or by immunohistochemical methods. Systemic viremia can be detected using a quantitative detection of CMV by polymerase chain reaction (PCR). Recently, a novel CMV PCR assay has been introduced and validated for the detection and quantitation of CMV DNA in human fecal specimens [3]. Not only does this test provide quantitative assessment of viral load, suitable for monitoring of antiviral therapy, but it also avoids repeated invasive endoscopy with biopsies.

Using serology and quantitative fecal and blood CMV analysis, we studied CMV replication in outpatients with active and quiescent IBD. CMV seropre-valence (immunoglobulin G [IgG]) was determined in 108 patients, 52 with UC and 56 with Crohn's disease (Table 44.1). Thirty-seven percent of UC patients and 63% of Crohn's disease patients tested positive for CMV IgG antibodies, none had

TABLE 44.1 Clinical characteristics and outcome of cytomegalovirus (CMV) tests (serology, polymerase chain reaction [PCR] on blood and fecal samples) of 108 IBD consecutive patients visiting the outpatient clinic.

Outpatient clinic (n = 108)	Ulcerative colitis		Crohn's disease	
	Seropositive (n = 19)	Seronegative (n = 33)	Seropositive (n = 35)	Seronegative (n = 21)
Male/female	10/9	18/15	7/28	6/15
Age (range)	49 (25–77)	43 (25–73)	40 (22–66)	44 (22–70)
Disease duration	7.4 years	9.2 years	14.2 years	8.2 years
Disease localization	7 pancolitis 10 left-sided 2 proctitis	11 pancolitis 17 left-sided 4 proctitis	14 small bowel 14 large bowel 7 both	10 small bowel 7 large bowel 4 both
Surgical history	1 pt	0	6 pts	9 pts
Comedication				
None	2	3	7	3
Mesalazine	15	27	8	4
Steroids	3	9	8	5
Azathioprine	4	9	6	8
Methotrexate	–	–	7	3
Infliximab	–	–	2	2
Disease activity				
Remission/active	12/7	18/7	14/21	7/14
CMV (PCR)				
Positive blood test	1/19*	All negative	All negative	All negative
Positive fecal test	2/19†	All negative	All negative	All negative

* One patient tested positive for CMV both in blood and stool sample. She had a history of a pancolitis, but was in clinical remission at the time of sample collection and was not on immunosuppressive therapy.
† One patient tested positive for CMV only in the fecal specimen. He had pancolitis, was in remission at the time of sample collection and was not on immunosuppressive therapy.

detectable IgM antibodies. Forty-eight percent of the UC and 73% of the Crohn's disease patients were on immunosuppressive therapy. Twenty-seven percent of UC and 63% of Crohn's disease patients had moderately active disease at the time of sample collection, but there was no relation between disease activity and CMV seropositivity. No CMV copies were detected in blood and/or stool specimens of the 54 IgG negative patients. Despite the use of immunosuppressive therapy in 30/54 seropositive patients, evidence of CMV replication was detected in only two (see Table 44.1 for details).

CMV reactivation in inpatients with acute severe UC

Seventeen patients were hospitalized in our hospital, 2000–2003, for a severe episode of UC (Table 44.2). Patients were given i.v. prednisolone (50 mg/day), and if no response was seen within 7 days, cyclosporine i.v. was added (4 mg/kg/day). If patients did not respond within 6 days after initiation of cyclosporine, surgery was proposed. In this series (Table 44.2), 9/17 patients (53%) required cyclosporine. Overall, 11/17 patients (65%) eventually responded to medical therapy. In sharp contrast to quiescent or mild to moderate active UC patients (see above), CMV seroprevalence in severely ill, hospitalized patients was 71% (vs. 37% in UC outpatients). At the time of admission, increased fecal CMV copies were present in 75% of seropositive patients (range 1000–130 000 C/mL), and in 42% of these patients this was accompanied by systemic viremia (range 1100–24 000 C/mL). Generally, CMV copy numbers detected in fecal samples were higher than those measured

TABLE 44.2 Characteristics and clinical outcome of patients hospitalized for severe ulcerative colitis.

Patients hospitalized (n = 17)	Ulcerative colitis	
	CMV seropositive (n = 12)	CMV seronegative (n = 5)
Male/female	6/6	4/1
Age (range)	46 (33–87)	33 (21–50)
Disease duration	8.8 years	6.6 years
Disease localization	4 left-sided 8 pancolitis	2 left-sided 3 pancolitis
Medication on admission	1 none 8 mesalasine 5 azathioprine 6 corticosteroid 1 tacrolimus	0 none 1 mesalasine 1 azathioprine 4 corticosteroid
Disease activity* (range)	15.8 (13–18)	16.4 (13–18)
Medication during hospitalization	6 i.v. steroids only 6 i.v. steroids then cyclosporine	2 i.v. steroids only 3 i.v. steroids then cyclosporine
Outcome	8 complete remission 0 partial remission 4 colectomy	2 complete remission 1 partial remission 2 colectomy
CMV measurements *CMV replication at admission (PCR)* Blood (range copies/ml) Feces (range copies/ml)	 5/12 (1100–24 000) 9/12 (1000–130000)	 All negative All negative
CMV replication during treatment (PCR) Blood (range copies/ml) Feces (range copies/ml)	 9/12 (1000–26 000) 12/12 (12 000–180 000)	 All negative All negative
Ganciclovir therapy Clinical remission Colectomy	 5/12 3/5	 2/5 Not applicable

* Disease activity scores according to the modified Truelove & Witts scale; complete remission is defined as score <4.

in blood samples (Table 44.2). Treatment with intravenous steroids and cyclosporine was clearly associated with an increase in CMV copies in both feces and blood samples. Antiviral therapy was initiated in 5/10 patients with increased CMV copies in both blood and in stool samples: however, successful CMV eradication was not associated with clinical benefit in all patients, 2/5 needing colectomy.

Discussion

It seems that there is no increase in CMV seroprevalence in IBD out-patients when compared with a healthy control population. In CMV seropositive UC patients with quiescent or mild to moderate disease activity, even when treated with oral steroids or immunosuppressives, no apparent CMV replication occurs. However, UC patients hospitalized for severe relapse show an increased seroprevalence and, in our experience, during the course of treatment, all seropositive patients have detectable CMV copy numbers as assessed by PCR analysis. Intravenous steroids and cyclosporine were shown to further increase CMV copy numbers in both fecal and blood samples in severely ill patients. Induction of clinical remission using steroids alone, or in combination with cyclosporine, resulted in the spontaneous disappearance of detectable CMV in several patients. Ganciclovir treatment successfully eradicated CMV infection in five patients but was not able to prevent colectomy in two.

Systemic viral load lags behind the fecal CMV load, suggesting a "spill" into the circulation when local viral loads exceed a certain critical threshold. This phenomenon has also been observed in seronegative recipients of renal transplants from seropositive donors receiving immuno-suppressive drugs, in whom CMV viremia can be detected within 2–4 weeks after the transplantation [4]. In both instances, it is likely that a higher level of immunosup-pression further hampers cellular immunity against CMV. Hence, our data indicate that latent CMV is reactivated in severely inflamed mucosa from seropositive UC patients receiving immunosuppressives, that immunosuppression further promotes replication of CMV, and that systemic CMV viremia is a spillover of local viral replication.

How is CMV reactivated in the diseased gut? Probable candidates for CMV latency in the gut are endothelial cells and monocytes. Indeed, CMV inclusions were identified in endothelial cells in colonic tissue specimens of UC patients [5]; this was confirmed by immunohistochemical stain-ing [6,7]. Furthermore, it is likely that latently infected circulating monocytes and dendritic cells migrate to sites of inflammation and differentiate into permissive cells supporting active replication [8–11].

It has been suggested that the pro-inflammatory cytokine, tumor necrosis factor α (TNF-α), is one of the key factors responsible for reactivation of CMV in latently infected cells [12–15]. TNF-α may induce viral reactivation by stimulating the activity of the IE (immediate early) enhancer/promoter via activation of NF-κB, initiating IE1 and IE2 gene expression essential for viral replication [16]. NF-κB itself is up-regulated by a wide variety of cytokines reported in mucosal specimens of active UC patients, including IL-1, IL-18, and TNF-α [17]. NF-κB can also be activated by bacterial products signaling through Toll-like receptors which in turn are highly expressed by epithelial and lamina propria mononuclear cells in UC [18]. In fact, recently it was proposed that NF-κB could serve as a poten-tial target for inhibition of CMV reactivation [19].

Conclusions

In conclusion, CMV replication during a severe attack of UC does matter. The two key factors that determine replication in latently infected hosts are: (i) the severity and

extent of inflammation; and (ii) the degree of immuno-suppression. Although in our series antiviral therapy in patients who failed medical therapy did not always improve clinical outcome, it remains to be determined whether coadministration of antiviral therapy during intense im-munosuppressive treatment induces more rapid healing, and influences clinical outcome (e.g. length of treatment, hospital stay, duration of response). Especially if antiviral therapy is initiated early in the disease course, the effect could be beneficial. At present, we have adopted the treat-ment algorithm of initiating antiviral therapy when systemic CMV infection becomes manifest, alongside immunosup-pressive therapy. A double-blind, placebo-controlled study to investigate the efficacy of antiviral therapy in fulminant UC is currently under way in Europe.

References

1 Edwards FC, Truelove SC. The course and prognosis of ulcer-ative colitis. *Gut* 1963; **41**: 299–315.

2 Hommes DW, Sterringa G, van Deventer SJ, Tytgat GN, Weel J. The pathogenicity of cytomegalovirus in inflam-matory bowel disease: a systematic review and evidence-based recommendations for future research. *Inflamm Bowel Dis* 2004; **10**: 245–50.

3 Boom R, Sol C, Weel J, *et al.* Detection and quantitation of human cytomegalovirus DNA in faeces. 2000; **84**: 1–14.

4 Rentenaar RJ, Gamadia LE, Hoek van der N, *et al.* Develop-ment of virus-specific CD4+ T cells during primary cytome-galovirus infection. *J Clin Invest* 2000; **105**: 541–8.

5 Eyre-Brook IA, Dundas S. Incidence and clinical significance of colonic cytomegalovirus infection in idiopathic inflamma-tory bowel disease requiring colectomy. *Gut* 1986; **27**: 1419–25.

6 Roberts WH, Sneddon JM, Waldman J, *et al.* Cytomegalovirus infection of gastrointestinal endothelium demonstrated by simultaneous nucleic acid hybridization and immunohisto-chemistry. *Arch Pathol Lab Med* 1989; **113**: 461–4.

7 Roberts WH, Hammond S, Sneddon JM, *et al. In situ* DNA hybridization for cytomegalovirus in colonoscopic biopsies. *Arch Pathol Lab Med* 1988; **112**: 1106–9.

8 Soderberg-Naucler C, Fish KN, Nelson JA. Reactivation of latent human cytomegalovirus by allogeneic stimulation of blood cells from healthy donors. *Cell* 1997; **91**: 119–26.

9 Koffron A, Varghese T, Hummel M, *et al.* Immunosuppression is not required for reactivation of latent murine cytomegalo-virus. *Transplant Proc* 1999; **31**: 1395–6.

10 Kondo K, Kaneshima H, Mocarski ES. Human cytomegalovirus latent infection of granulocyte-macrophage progenitors. *Proc Natl Acad Sci USA* 1994; **91**: 1879–83.

11 Soderberg-Naucler C, Nelson JY. Human cytomegalovirus latency and reactivation: a delicate balance between the virus and its host's immune system. *Intervirology* 1999; **42**: 314–21.

12 Stein J, Volk HD, Liebenthal C, *et al*. Tumour necrosis factor alpha stimulates the activity of the human cytomegalovirus major immediate early enhancer/promoter in immature monocytic cells. *J Gen Virol* 1993; **74**: 2333–8.

13 Docke WD, Prosch S, Fietze E, *et al*. Cytomegalovirus reactivation and tumour necrosis factor. *Lancet* 1994; **343**: 268–9.

14 Fietze E, Prosch S, Reinke P, *et al*. Cytomegalovirus infection in transplant recipients: the role of tumor necrosis factor. *Transplantation* 1994; **58**: 675–80.

15 Hummel M, Zhang Z, Yan S, *et al*. Allogeneic transplantation induces expression of cytomegalovirus immediate-early genes *in vivo*: a model for reactivation from latency. *J Virol* 2001; **75**: 4814–22.

16 Mocarski ES, Kemble GW, Lyle JM, *et al*. A deletion mutant in the human cytomegalovirus gene encoding IEI (491aa) is replication defective due to a failure in autoregulation. *Proc Natl Acad Sci USA* 1996; **93**: 1321–6.

17 Neurath MF, Becker C, Barbulescu K. Role of NF-κB in immune and inflammatory responses in the gut. *Gut* 1998; **43**: 856–60.

18 Cario E, Podolsky DK. Differential alteration in intestinal epithelial cell expression of toll-like receptor 3 (TLR3) and TLR4 in inflammatory bowel disease. *Infect Immun* 2000; **68**: 7010–7.

19 Prosch S, Wuttke R, Kruger DH, *et al*. NF-κB: a potential therapeutic target for inhibition of human cytomegalovirus (re)activation? *Biol Chem* 2002; **383**: 1601–9.

45 Treatment of oral Crohn's disease

CARLO NUNES, MICHAEL ESCUDIER & JEREMY D SANDERSON

LEARNING POINTS

Oral Crohn's disease

- True oral Crohn's disease is rare

- The pediatric and young adult populations are most commonly affected

- Oral manifestations of Crohn's must be distinguished from true oral Crohn's

- Oral manifestations such as aphthous ulcers are often a consequence of active inflammation elsewhere in the gut, or to hematinic deficiency

- Dietary manipulation is the preferred treatment in children and young adults

- Topical treatment with 5-ASA, corticosteroids, or tacrolimus is well tolerated and can be effective

- Use of immunosuppressant therapy resembles that used for intestinal Crohn's disease

- Surgical treatment is reserved for severe fibrotic lip enlargement

Introduction

Oral Crohn's disease represents a particular challenge in the management of IBD, not least because it is uncommon and presents to a variety of specialists including dental practitioners. In general, therefore, experience of the condition is limited outside specialist centers.

No study has assessed the prevalence of true oral Crohn's disease. Clinical practice suggests it is no higher than 1% of existing Crohn's disease cases. Conversely, the prevalence rates of oral manifestations in Crohn's disease may be as high as 20% [1]. The disease is more common in the pediatric and young adult population when minor nutritional deficiencies and orofacial disfigurement may have significant consequences on growth and psychosocial development, respectively. Indeed, the morbidity and psychosocial impact of oral Crohn's disease is generally under-recognized.

The term "oral Crohn's disease" is confusing as patients may present with typical orofacial lesions without any intestinal involvement. This group is probably best defined under the umbrella term orofacial granulomatosis (OFG) [2]. While OFG may precede the onset of gut Crohn's disease by a number of years, the condition can clearly exist as a separate entity confined to the orofacial region, and includes some cases of sarcoidosis, tuberculosis, and the Melkersson–Rosenthal syndrome [3,4].

Oral manifestations of Crohn's disease vs. oral Crohn's disease

It is important to distinguish oral Crohn's/OFG from other more common oral manifestations of Crohn's disease. These include aphthous ulceration, angular cheilitis, glossitis, and oral candidosis. Many of these features are considered secondary to the effects of active inflammation elsewhere or to hematinic deficiency [5]. Crops of oral aphthous ulceration tend to occur in association with Crohn's disease flares and improve with induction of remission. True oral Crohn's disease/OFG, however, presents typically with lip swelling and lip fissures, and may involve a variety of sites around the oral cavity with resulting gingivitis, deep linear

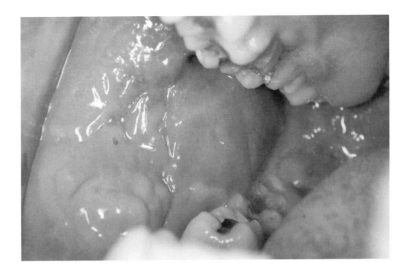

FIG 45.1 Oral Crohn's disease: buccal cobblestoning and mucosal tags.

oral sulcus ulceration, buccal cobblestoning and nodularity, and mucosal tags (Fig. 45.1). Floor of mouth involvement in the region of the salivary gland duct orifices presents with a classic "staghorn" appearance. The tongue is involved less commonly and the soft and hard palate even more rarely [1].

Diagnosis

The diagnosis of oral Crohn's disease is confirmed by typical histologic changes on biopsy. The presence of non-caseating epithelioid granulomas forms the mainstay of diagnosis but other typical features include lymphoedema of the corium with prominent lymphatics and collections of lymphocytes. Granulomas may be deep seated and revealed only on further sectioning of the original sample [6].

An initial work-up should also include swabs of any lip fissures or angular cheilitis, because superimposed infection, particularly staphylococcal, is common. Likewise, saliva samples may reveal *Candida* requiring specific treatment. Outside the oral cavity, the work-up should consist of biochemical and hematologic assessment including hematinics (iron markers, folate, and vitamin B_{12}). In our experience, endoscopic assessment of the gastrointestinal tract is not necessary routinely in patients presenting with OFG and should be guided by the presence or absence of gut symptoms. Low-grade, granulomatous inflammation is frequently present in the upper or lower gastrointestinal tract in those without gut symptoms but there is little to

suggest that identification of such changes alters the approach to treatment of the mouth [7].

Treatment

The management of oral Crohn's disease/OFG mirrors the approach used for IBD in general. Hence, treatment can be broadly divided into general, dietary, topical, systemic, and surgical therapy. Likewise, treatment may be aimed at induction or maintenance of remission. Also, treatment needs to be decided according to whether there is oral disease alone or whether there is simultaneous active gut disease.

Ideally, a multidisciplinary approach consisting of an oral/dental surgeon, gastroenterologist, dietitian, and, possibly, a psychologist is required. Treatment may not be needed if symptoms and signs are mild or remit spontaneously. Long-term follow-up suggests that OFG, like IBD, often runs a chronic course over years with periods of exacerbations requiring specific therapy [8]. Inevitably, the evidence base for particular therapies is limited; the treatment of oral Crohn's disease/OFG is largely based on small non-randomized trials and anecdotal case reports.

General

Non-specific oral lesions (e.g. aphthous stomatitis, glossitis, and *Candida*) often indicate hematinic and/or nutritional deficiencies. These include vitamin B_{12}, folate and iron deficiency, and, in more severe cases, malnutrition requiring appropriate calorie supplementation. Infected lip fissures and angular cheilitis should be treated with topical anti-biotics (e.g. Fucidin). Poor dentition is not infrequent, particular in those with significant gut Crohn's disease and perhaps contributed to by corticosteroids, and attention to diet and oral hygiene is therefore required.

Diet

Investigations of hypersensitivity to food allergens, particularly cinnamon aldehyde and benzoates, have strengthened the notion that an abnormal response to dietary antigens plays a substantial part in the pathogenesis of OFG, perhaps more so than in gut Crohn's disease [9]. Benzoates are a preservative in many foods, while cinnamon aldehyde is used as flavoring in soft – particularly fizzy – drinks, chewing gum, ice cream, cakes, toothpaste, and mouthwashes. The beneficial effects of a cinnamon- and benzoate-free diet were first reported from the Glasgow Dental Hospital [9]. This type of exclusion diet is therefore now recommended as the first-line approach in mild to moderate cases with minimal or no coexistent gut disease. Exclusive enteral nutrition has also been successful and can be tried where an exclusion diet has failed or where coexistent active gut Crohn's disease is present, especially small bowel disease in children and young adults.

Topical

Patients with mild oral disease may benefit from topical therapy, with remission reported in up to 50% of cases without evident gut involvement [10]. For lip swelling in particular, topical mesalazine (Topasa) and tacrolimus have been used with success and can be used also at other sites in the oral cavity [11]. However, intraoral disease is better treated with topical steroid mouthwashes such as betamethasone (Betnesol). Intralesional injection of steroid (triamcinolone) may be of benefit but this is usually short term and best reserved for acute localized swelling. A delayed-release triamcinolone injection appears to reduce lip swelling and lead to disease-free periods for up to 19 months [12]. Adjunctive antiseptic/analgesic mouthwashes may also help.

Systemic

A stepwise approach is preferred with systemic therapy reserved for patients who have failed topical therapy or who require systemic therapy for concomitant bowel involvement. The systemic regimen used resembles that of gut Crohn's and consists of corticosteroids, thiopurines,

methotrexate, and infliximab. Some specialists have also suggested that thalidomide may have a particular role in this setting [13].

Although one might speculate as to possible beneficial effects on oral disease through amelioration of coexistent gut disease, oral aminosalicylates are ineffective. In acute flares and more severe oral disease, systemic corticosteroids are effective [14]. The dosage (prednisolone 40–60 mg/day) is similar to that used for gut Crohn's disease and a standard tapering regimen with complete withdrawal is recommended. Steroid-dependence or steroid-resistance should prompt the introduction of steroid-sparing immunosuppressive therapy. Azathioprine or 6-mercaptopurine should be used first in this setting and the regimen and monitoring should be as in other cases of IBD. Methotrexate (15–25 mg/week orally) may be used in those who are unable to tolerate thiopurines but experience is limited and anecdotal experience suggests that the drug may be more difficult to tolerate because of adverse effects on the oral mucosa. The successful use of thalidomide has also been reported in those who have failed conventional immunosuppressive therapy [13]. The dose used to achieve a clinical response varies from 50–300 mg/day. However, whether thalidomide has long-term benefit is unclear and its toxicity in women (and men) of child bearing age severely restricts its use.

Anecdotal success has been reported with infliximab, perhaps especially for those with intraoral disease failing on immunosuppression [15]. Resistant isolated chronic lip swelling appears unresponsive. Otherwise, the approach to using infliximab should be identical to that for active gut Crohn's disease.

Surgery

Persistent orofacial swelling, particularly gross lip swelling may cause serious cosmetic and psychological problems. It may also interfere with the ability to eat and speak. Surgical reduction of severely thickened fibrotic lips is sometimes appropriate and can be regarded as akin to the resection of inactive fibrotic stricturing disease in the gut. However, careful evaluation of the lip is required to exclude active inflammation or infection prior to recommending such an approach.

Conclusions

Oral Crohn's disease is rare but may have a profound

effect on the quality of life of affected individuals. In view of the limited data available, an evidence-based treatment strategy is lacking. However, knowledge of how to combine established treatment regimens for intestinal Crohn's disease with therapeutic measures unique to inflammation in the oral cavity should lead to improved treatment of this difficult condition. As with many other specialist settings, the best outcome is achieved with a multidisciplinary approach.

References

1 Basu MK, Asquith P. Oral manifestations of inflammatory bowel disease. *Clin Gastroenterol* 1980; **9**: 307–21.

2 Wiesenfield D, Ferguson MM, Mitchell DN, *et al.* Orofacial granulomatosis: a clinical and pathological analysis. *Q J Med* 1985; **54**: 101–13.

3 Eveson JW. Granulomatous disorders of the oral mucosa. *Semin Diagn Pathol* 1996; **13**: 118–27.

4 Challacombe SJ. Oro-facial granulomatosis and oral Crohn's disease: are they specific diseases and do they predict systemic Crohn's disease? *Oral Dis* 1997; **3**:127–9.

5 Halme L, Meurman JH, Laine P, *et al.* Oral findings in patients with active or inactive Crohn's disease. *Oral Surg Oral Med Oral Pathol* 1993; **76**: 175–81.

6 Field EA, Tyldesley WR. Oral Crohn's disease revisited: a 10-year review. *Br J Oral Maxillofac Surg* 1989; **27**: 114–23.

7 Sanderson JD, Barnard K, Shirlaw P, *et al.* The oral and intestinal features of oro-facial granulomatosis. *Gastroenterology* 1999; **116**: A811.

8 Plauth M, Jenss H, Meyle J. Oral manifestations of Crohn's disease. *J Clin Gastroenterol* 1991; **13**: 9–37.

9 Wray D, Rees SR, Gibson J, Forsyth A. The role of allergy in oral mucosal diseases. *Q J Med* 2000; **93**: 507–11.

10 Plauth M, Jenss H, Meyle J. Oral manifestations of Crohn's disease: an analysis of 79 cases. *J Clin Gastroenterol* 1991; **13**: 29–37.

11 Hodgson T, Hegarty A, Porter S. Topical tacrolimus and Crohn's disease. *J Pediatr Gastroentrol Nutr* 2001; **33**: 633.

12 Mignogna MD, Fedele S, Russo LL, *et al.* Effectiveness of small-volume, intralesional, delayed-release triamcinolone injections in orofacial granulomatosis: a pilot study. *J Am Acad Dermatol* 2004; **51**: 265–8.

13 Hegarty A, Hodgson T, Porter S. Thalidomide for the treatment of recalcitrant oral Crohn's disease and orofacial granulomatosis. *Oral Surg Oral Med Oral Pathol Oral Radiol Endod* 2003; **95**: 576–85.

14 Tyldesley WR. Oral Crohn's disease and related conditions. *Br J Oral Surg* 1979; **17**: 1–9.

15 Mahadevan U, Sandborn WJ. Infliximab for the treatment of orofacial Crohn's disease. *Inflamm Bowel Dis* 2001; **7**: 38–42.

46 Pathophysiologic approach to treatment of diarrhea in Crohn's disease

HENRY J BINDER

LEARNING POINTS

Diarrhea in Crohn's disease

- Diarrhea is a frequent symptom in Crohn's disease and multiple pathogenetic processes may be responsible

- Pathogenic mechanisms include:
  - mucosal inflammation
  - bile and fatty acid-mediated secretion
  - bacterial overgrowth
  - lactose intolerance
  - short bowel syndrome

- Identification of the principal contributing factor(s) in each patient makes possible specific and successful therapy of their diarrhea

Introduction

Diarrhea is an important symptom of patients with Crohn's disease. Multiple pathogenic processes may be responsible for the diarrhea that occurs in Crohn's disease, and its successful treatment often depends on the **pathophysiologic** process that is responsible for this diarrhea. Because the fundamental etiology(s) of Crohn's disease are not known and no *specific* therapies for Crohn's disease are available, it is critical to establish the pathogenic mechanism(s) that are responsible for the diarrhea in patients with Crohn's disease as the initial step to initiating potentially successful therapy.

Multiple different pathophysiologic processes can explain the diarrhea of Crohn's disease. These include: inflamma-

tion; steatorrhea; bile acids; stasis and bacterial overgrowth; lactose intolerance; and short bowel syndrome.

Inflammation

The primary pathogenic process in Crohn's disease is chronic inflammation and diarrhea is often secondary to ongoing intestinal inflammation. Thus, the multiple inflammatory intermediates associated with this inflammation may induce diarrhea by virtue of their effects on intestinal epithelial cells, enteric neurons, lamina propria cells (e.g. mast cells), and/or myofibroblasts. Most often the common denominator of these inflammatory mediators is their ability to change intestinal electrolyte movement by increasing one or more second messenger (i.e. cAMP, cGMP, and/or Ca) levels in intestinal enterocytes.

Recent studies have emphasized the roles of pro-inflammatroy cytokines such as tumor necrosis factor α (TNF-α), and γ-interferon (IFN-γ) as well as of one or more eicosanoids. Thus, it is not unlikely that the therapeutic effects of infliximab, a monoclonal antibody to TNF-α, include a reversal of the changes in ion transport that occur secondary to TNF-α. Similarly, evidence exists that 5-aminosalicylates (5-ASA) and glucocorticosteroids inhibit synthesis of secretory prostaglandins.

Steatorrhea

Diarrhea in patients with Crohn's disease may also be secondary to steatorrhea. Diarrhea in patients with steatorrhea is due to stimulation of fluid and electrolyte secretion by non-absorbed fatty acids in the large (and possibly small) intestine. Treatment of the diarrhea in this setting is dependent upon successful treatment of steatorrhea; this in turn is dependent on identification of the mechanism(s) responsible for steatorrhea. If the cause cannot be corrected, effective treatment is still possible with a reduced-fat diet.

Dietary lipid, exclusively in the form of triglycerides, requires several steps for normal digestion and absorption: pancreatic lipolysis; micelle formation by intraduodenal conjugated bile acids; uptake and re-esterification by small intestine; and chylomicron formation prior to exit from enterocytes via lymphatics. In Crohn's disease, steatorrhea may occur as a result of:

1 A reduced intraduodenal concentration of conjugated bile acids secondary to ileal dysfunction (see below)

2 Inadequate small intestinal surface area usually as a result of prior intestinal resections but also with recurring inflammation in the remaining small intestine

3 Stasis and bacterial overgrowth (see below)

Bile acids

Changes in normal bile acid physiology may also cause diarrhea in Crohn's disease. Bile acids are synthesized in the liver from cholesterol and excreted into the duodenum in bile; required in the duodenum for the formation of mixed micelles (see above); and absorbed primarily in the ileum by an active transport process, although smaller amounts are absorbed in the jejunum and colon by ionic and non-ionic diffusion. The amount of bile acids lost in stool each day is matched by the amount that is synthesized by the liver. Ileal inflammation and/or resection can interrupt the enterohepatic circulation of bile acids in Crohn's disease; this results in an increase in bile acids entering the colon and consequent induction of active chloride-induced fluid secretion and diarrhea. These fecal bile acid losses will be compensated by increased hepatic synthesis of bile acids. Cholestyramine, an anion (i.e. bile acid) binding resin, can be effective in such patients with diarrhea. However, with increasing ileal dysfunction and bile acid losses, the liver cannot continually compensate to maintain the bile acid pool size. The latter then will be reduced, resulting in a decrease in intraduodenal bile acid concentrations. As a consequence, there is **both** diarrhea and steatorrhea, and cholestyramine becomes ineffective because the diarrhea is due to both bile acids and fatty acids. Indeed, under these

TABLE 46.1 Features that characterize bile acid (BA) and fatty acid diarrhea.

Characteristic	Bile acid	Fatty acid
Length of ileal resection	Small	Large
Ileal BA absorption	↓	↓↓
Fecal BA output	↑	↑↑
Fecal BA loss compensated by hepatic synthesis	Yes	No
BA pool size	Normal	↓
Duodenal BA concentration	Normal	↓
Steatorrhea	None or mild	Yes (>20 g/day)
Responds to low fat diet	No	Yes
Responds to cholestyramine	Yes	No

circumstances, binding of bile acids by cholestyramine potentially results in a further reduction of the bile acid pool size and a worsening of steatorrhoea. A low-fat diet may be the only effective therapy. The differences that occur following a relatively small (bile acid) and large (fatty acid) intestinal resection are contrasted in Table 46.1. Following resection in Crohn's disease, inflammation may be present in the remaining intestine so that anti-inflammatory therapy may also be effective (see above).

Stasis and bacterial overgrowth

Steatorrhea in Crohn's disease may also be a result of stasis and bacterial overgrowth syndrome. In non-Crohn's disease patients, stasis syndromes may occur either as a result of anatomic stasis with so-called blind loops (e.g. jejunal diverticula) or functional stasis (e.g. scleroderma). In Crohn's disease, there are **three** potential clinical settings in which stasis syndromes may occur:

1 fistulazation

2 strictures

3 an absence of the ileocecal valve (i.e. post-ileocolonic resection) with bacterial colonization of the distal small intestine

The manifestations of stagnant bowel syndrome are diarrhea, steatorrhea, and macrocytic anemia resulting from bacterial deconjugation of conjugated to unconjugated bile acids and utilization of cobalamin (vitamin B_{12}), respectively.

Lactase deficiency

Milk or lactose intolerance in such patients may represent

either primary or secondary lactase deficiency. There is a significant incidence of primary lactase deficiency in several ethnic groups who also have an increased incidence of Crohn's disease (e.g. Ashkenazi Jews), while secondary lactase deficiency may result from either absent or inflamed small intestinal mucosa. It is, therefore, important to consider the possibility that the diarrhea in a patient with Crohn's disease is not solely due to the Crohn's disease but is caused, at least in part, by primary lactase deficiency.

Short bowel syndrome

Crohn's disease may require multiple intestinal resections resulting in short bowel syndrome (see Chapter 47). In these patients, additional pathophysiologic events may be present which require specific treatment. Diarrhea in patients with short bowel syndrome can be due to steatorrhea; inadequate intestinal surface area; increased gastric acid secretion; and lactose intolerance. Enhanced gastric acid and volume secretion is likely to be mediated by the absence of one or more intestinal hormones (e.g. secretin) that inhibit gastric acid secretion. Proton pump inhibitors may reduce diarrhea by reducing the volume of fluid entering the small intestine. A low intraduodenal pH can also result in steatorrhea secondary to inactivation of lipase and precipitation of bile acids. Thus, treatment of patients with short bowel syndrome who have sufficient intestinal surface area such that total parenteral nutrition is not required will include a low-fat, lactose-free diet and a proton-pump inhibitor. If such individuals have also had a resection of the ileocolonic junction, intermittent use of an antibiotic

(e.g. tetracycline, metronidazole) for bacterial overgrowth may be also helpful.

Conclusion

Each patient with Crohn's disease who presents with diarrhea needs to undergo a careful assessment of its likely pathogenesis. Such an approach allows therapy to be directed specifically at the relevant pathophysiological mechanism(s) and thereby maximizes the chance of obtaining an improvement in at least this aspect of the patient's symptoms.

Further reading

Ammons HV, Phillips SF: Inhibition of colonic water and electrolyte absorption by fatty acids in man. *Gastroenterology* 1973; **65**: 744–9.

Binder HJ. Nutrient-induced diarrhea. In: Field M (ed.) *Textbook of Diarrheas*. Elsevier Science Publishing, 1991: 159–72.

Binder HJ. Disorders of absorption. In: *Harrison's Principles of Internal Medicine*, 16th edn. New York: McGraw Hill, 2004: 1763–76.

Fine KD, Schiller LR. AGA technical review on the evaluation and management of chronic diarrhea. *Gastroenterology* 1999; **116**: 1464–86.

Kalha KS, Sellin JH. Physiologic consequences of surgical treatment for inflammatory bowel disease. In: *Inflammatory Bowel Disease*. Philadelphia, PA: Saunders, 2004: 316–32.

McJunkin B, Fromm H, Sarva RP, Amin P. Factors in the mechanism of diarrhea in bile acid malabsorption: fecal pH – a key determinant. *Gastroenterology* 1981; **80**: 1454–64.

Mekhjuan JS, Phillips SF, Hofmann AF. Colonic secretion of water and electrolytes induced by bile acids: perfusion studies in man. *J Clin Invest* 1971; **50**: 1569–77.

Common Clinical Challenges: Beyond the Text Book

47 Short bowel

JEREMY NIGHTINGALE

LEARNING POINTS

Short bowel

- The presence or absence of a colon defines the management of patients with a short bowel

- The management of a high output stoma (jejunostomy or ileostomy) starts with restricting oral hypotonic fluid and giving a glucose-saline solution (90–120 mmol/L sodium). Loperamide before meals and gastric antisecretory drugs may help. Magnesium supplements are often needed

- A liquid sip or enteral feed for patients with a jejunostomy needs to be of low osmolality (100 mOsm/kg and sodium concentration 100 mmol/L)

- Hypomagnesemia is treated by correcting dehydration, oral magnesium oxide, and 1-α cholecalciferol

- Jejunum-colon patients on an oral diet need a high-energy diet rich in polysaccharides and low in oxalate

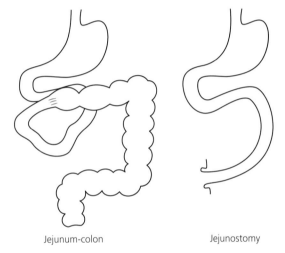

Jejunum-colon   Jejunostomy

FIG 47.1 Types of patient with a short bowel.

What is a short bowel?

Human small intestine varies from 3.5 to 8.0 m in length. After a small bowel resection, it is therefore more important to refer to the length of bowel remaining than the length removed. Women generally have a shorter small intestine than men, perhaps explaining why a short bowel is more common in women. Patients having a small intestinal resection can be classified into those with jejunum in continuity with a functioning colon (jejunum-colon) and those with an end jejunostomy (jejunostomy) (Fig. 47.1). Problems of a short bowel occur when less than 200 cm small intestine remains leading to reduced intestinal absorption so that macronutrient and/or water and electrolyte supplements are needed to maintain health and/or growth (Table 47.1) [1].

TABLE 47.1 Guide to bowel length and long-term fluid/nutritional support needed by patients with a short bowel [13].

Jejunal length (cm)	Jejunum-colon	Jejunostomy
0–50	PN	PN + PS
51–100	ON	PN + PS*
101–150	None	ON + OGS
151–200	None	OGS

OGS, oral (or enteral) glucose/saline solution; ON, oral (or enteral) nutrition; PN, parenteral nutrition; PS, parenteral saline (+/– magnesium).

* At 85–100 cm may need PS only.

Reasons for a short bowel in IBD

Short bowel is most commonly caused by Crohn's disease [2], patients normally having undergone multiple intestinal resections [2]. Moreover, patients with a high enterocutaneous fistula or an enteroenteral internal fistula may need the same management as a patient with a short bowel.

A jejunostomy rarely occurs after a colectomy for UC although it can result if there are complications (e.g. sepsis, fistula, or ileoanal pouch failure).

Physiology of a short bowel

Gastric emptying may be increased in patients with a jejunostomy and <100 cm of remaining small bowel [3]. Those with an intact colon, however, have normal gastric emptying, perhaps because of high circulating levels of two hormones produced by the terminal ileum and colon: peptide YY (PYY) and glucagon-like peptide-2 (GLP-2), which primarily reduce gut transit and stimulate small bowel mucosal growth, respectively [4,5]. Over time, these hormones may cause functional and structural adaptation allowing the absorptive function of patients with jejunum-colon, but not of those with a jejunostomy, to improve.

In addition, gastric acid hypersecretion occurs in animals after major jejunal resections, although evidence of this in humans remains anecdotal. However, in patients with a jejunostomy, losses of 0.5 L saliva, 2.0 L gastric acid, and 1.5 L pancreatico-biliary secretions can occur. Such fluid has a sodium concentration of approximately 100 mmol/L.

Finally, as most patients with a short bowel have lost their terminal ileum, they are at risk of vitamin B_{12} deficiency.

Clinical assessment

Knowledge of the length of residual small bowel allows predictions of the long-term need for fluid and nutritional support (Table 47.1).

Water, sodium, and magnesium

Dehydration is common in patients with a jejunostomy and may result in thirst, hypotension, and prerenal failure. Daily monitoring allows its detection as indicated by an abrupt fall in body weight, postural systolic hypotension (>10 mmHg), low urine volume (<400 mL/24 h), random urinary sodium concentration <10 mmol/L or, if severe, by rising serum creatinine and urea.

Magnesium depletion is common in patients with a high stomal or stool output. A serum value <0.6 mmol/L may cause jerky movements and tremor, and <0.2 mmol/L convulsions.

Nutrition

Undernutrition is suggested by a body mass index <18.5 kg/m^2, percentage weight loss of >10%, and/or a mid-arm muscle circumference <19 cm in women or <21 cm in men [6].

Management

After a resection resulting in a short bowel, nutritional and fluid support are given early. Parenteral nutrition used initially, even when enough bowel is thought to remain, helps wound healing and ileus recovery, and prevents vitamin and mineral deficiencies. Proton pump inhibitors for up to 6 months may prevent gastric acid hypersecretion. If a patient cannot be stabilized with an oral diet, supplemental enteral feeding may be used: the use of percutaneous endoscopic gastrostomy (PEGs) in Crohn's disease is safe and not associated with long-term problems [7]. Both types of patient are likely to need long-term vitamin B_{12} treatment.

Jejunum-colon

Undernutrition and diarrhea (steatorrhea), may develop in the months after resection. If possible, an oral diet is preferred, but, due to malabsorption, patients may need to consume twice as much as a normal person. Unabsorbed long-chain fatty acids arriving in the colon increase transit, reduce water and sodium absorption, and are toxic to bacteria, thereby reducing carbohydrate fermentation and energy salvage; they also bind calcium and magnesium. A low-fat diet has therefore been recommended. However, fat is rich in energy and low in volume, contains essential fatty acids and makes food palatable and its excessive restriction should be avoided if possible. In addition, unabsorbed carbohydrate is fermented in the colon and helps salvage energy [8], so a diet high in polysaccharides and low in oxalate (see below) is recommended. If undernutrition persists or worsens, or if diarrhea is unmanageable, parenteral nutrition may be necessary; however, as fluid balance is not usually a major problem, it may only be needed 2–4 times a week.

Calcium oxalate renal stones

Jejunum-colon patients have a 25% chance of developing calcium oxalate renal stones [2]; less common is nephrocalcinosis leading to chronic renal failure. The underlying etiology of increased colonic absorption of dietary oxalate may result from fat malabsorption (luminal free fatty acids bind calcium causing oxalate otherwise itself bound to calcium to become soluble and thus absorbable), bile salt malabsorption (causing increased colonic permeability to oxalate), reduced bacterial degradation of oxalate, pyridoxine or thiamine deficiency, and hypocitraturia. Patients at risk should avoid dehydration and take a low oxalate diet by avoiding spinach, rhubarb, beetroot, nuts, chocolate, tea, wheat bran, and strawberries. Other possible measures include reducing dietary fat or replacing it with medium-chain triglycerides, increasing dietary calcium, or giving oral cholestyramine to bind bile salts [9].

Jejunostomy

The proportion of energy, nitrogen, and fat absorbed from the diet remains constant so a diet high in energy is necessary. However, hyperosmolar feeds (as in an elemental diet) cause water to diffuse into the bowel lumen and be lost via the stoma and should be avoided. It is also important to keep the sodium concentration in liquid feeds to 100 mmol/L or to add sodium chloride to food. Thus, the ideal sip or enteral feed consists of large molecules (polysaccharide, protein, and long-chain triglycerides) with an osmolality approximating 300 mOsm/kg and a sodium concentration of 100 mmol/L. If the volume of feed needed to maintain nutrition causes excessive stomal output, parenteral fluid may be needed [10].

Management of a high output stoma

High output stomas (usually >2 L/day) occur not only with jejunostomies but also in 17% of ileostomies [11]. They cause dehydration rapidly, especially in hot weather; patients need to comply with treatment at all times.

The first step in management is to exclude other causes of high output such as intra-abdominal sepsis, partial or intermittent bowel obstruction, infective enteritis, sudden drug withdrawal (steroids or opiates), prokinetic drug use (metoclopramide), or recurrent Crohn's.

Equilibrium is restored with intravenous normal saline (2–4 L/day) to reduce thirst. The patient is kept "nil by mouth" initially and soon realizes that their output is driven by their oral intake. Over 2–3 days, intravenous saline is gradually withdrawn while food and restricted oral fluids are reintroduced. The amount of oral hypotonic fluid (which increases stomal sodium and fluid loss) is restricted to <500 mL/day, increasing to a liter over the first week.

Patients are encouraged to sip a glucose-saline drink (90–120 mmol/L sodium) such as the WHO cholera solution without potassium (20 g glucose, 3.5 g sodium chloride, and 2.5 g sodium bicarbonate in 1 L of cold tap water).

If the above is not adequate, drugs to reduce motility may be given. Loperamide (2–8 mg half an hour before food) is preferred to codeine phosphate (30–60 mg before food) as it is neither sedative nor addictive, and does not affect pancreatico-biliary secretions: a powdered preparation in a capsule is ideal as tablets may pass through the remaining intestine unchanged. For patients with a very high output (>4 L/day), oral omeprazole 40 mg/day will reduce gastric acid secretion and, if adequately absorbed, is as effective as octreotide.

Hypomagnesemia is treated by correcting dehydration (so preventing secondary hyperaldosteronism, which retains sodium in the kidney at the expense of potassium and magnesium), giving oral magnesium oxide, or 1-α cholecalciferol (avoiding hypercalcemia) and, if undernutrition is not a major problem, reducing dietary fat.

Some patients will not maintain hydration with the above measures and thus will require intravenous or subcutaneous saline.

Other complications

Gallstones

Gallstones are common (45%), particularly in men [2], and probably result from gallbladder stasis. Methods to promote gallbladder contraction include intravenous amino acids, enteral feeds, cholecystokinin (CCK) injections and nonsteroidal anti-inflammatory drugs (NSAIDs). In addition, bile composition may be changed by NSAIDs or ursodeoxycholic acid, and by reducing the formation of lithogenic secondary bile acids by either accelerating bowel transit or by inhibiting bowel bacteria (e.g. with metronidazole). Some units advocate prophylactic cholecystectomy whenever a large resection of small intestine is performed [12].

Confusion

Specific causes of confusion in patients with a short bowel include hypomagnesemia (see above), thiamine deficiency, D-lactic acidosis and hyperammonemia. Wernicke–Korsakoff psychosis responds rapidly to large doses of thiamine.

D-lactic acidosis occurs only in patients with a preserved colon and is probably due to colonic microflora degrading fermentable carbohydrate to form D-lactate. This is absorbed but not metabolized, resulting in metabolic acidosis with a large anion gap. Treatment involves restricting mono- and oligosaccharides and encouraging the intake of more slowly digestible polysaccharides (starch), thiamine supplements, and broad-spectrum antibiotics. Rarely, the patient needs to fast while receiving parenteral nutrition.

Hyperammonemia occurs because the amount of intestine remaining is inadequate to manufacture enough citrulline to detoxify ammonia in the urea cycle. This is a problem if there is concomitant renal impairment, preventing excretion of the excess ammonia. Giving arginine (an intermediary in the urea cycle) corrects the hyperammonemia [13].

Surgical treatments

Surgical attempts to slow intestinal transit or increase the surface area for absorption have been used, with favorable results reported from the reversal of a 10-cm segment of small intestine [14].

Intestinal transplantation

Small bowel transplantation is becoming increasingly successful. However, as the quality of life and survival of patients needing long-term home parenteral nutrition is good, small bowel transplantion is considered only in patients with irreversible progressive liver disease, loss of venous access, recurrent central line sepsis, or unable to manage parenteral nutrition [13].

Potential new medical treatments

Cholylsarcosine, a synthetic conjugated bile acid resistant to deconjugation, has been used and may increase energy absorption by approximately 170 kcal/day [15]. In one of four randomized, placebo-controlled studies using growth hormone to stimulate mucosal growth, a small improvement in nutrient absorption occurred. Plasma levels of GLP-2, which causes villus growth, are low in patients with a jejunostomy; subcutaneous GLP-2 has been shown to increase nutrient absorption [15].

Conclusions

The surgical therapy of IBD may result in a short bowel. In patients with a jejunostomy, fluid losses dominate the clinical situation, while in those with jejunum-colon progressive undernutrition and diarrhea are the greatest problems. With appropriate treatment most patients can be managed with an oral or enteral regimen.

References

1 Nightingale JMD. Introduction. Definition and classification of intestinal failure. In: Nightingale JMD (ed.). *Intestinal Failure*. Greenwich Medical Media, 2001: xix–xx.

2 Nightingale JMD, Lennard-Jones JE, Gertner DJ, Wood SR, Bartram CI. Colonic preservation reduces the need for parenteral therapy, increases the incidence of renal stones but does not change the high prevalence of gallstones in patients with a short bowel. *Gut* 1992: **33**: 1493–7.

3 Nightingale JMD, Kamm MA, van der Sijp JRM, *et al*. Disturbed gastric emptying in the short bowel syndrome: evidence for a "colonic brake". *Gut* 1993; **34**: 1171–6.

4 Nightingale JMD, Kamm MA, van der Sijp JRM, *et al*. Gastrointestinal hormones in the short bowel syndrome: PYY may be the 'colonic brake' to gastric emptying. *Gut* 1996; **39**: 267–72.

5 Jeppesen PB, Hartmann B, Thulesen J, *et al*. Elevated plasma glucagon-like peptide 1 and 2 concentrations in ileum-resected short bowel patients with a preserved colon. *Gut* 2000; **47**: 370–6.

6 Nightingale JMD, Walsh N, Bullock ME, Wicks AC. Comparison of three simple methods for the detection of malnutrition. *J R Soc Med* 1996; **89**: 144–8.

7 Nightingale JMD. Gastrostomy placement in patients with Crohn's disease. *Eur J Gastroenterol Hepatol* 2000; **12**: 1073–5.

8 Nordgaard I, Hansen BS, Mortensen PB. Colon as a digestive organ in patients with short bowel. *Lancet* 1994; **343**: 373–6.

9 Tomson CRV. Nephrocalcinosis and nephrolithiasis. In: Nightingale JMD (ed.). *Intestinal Failure*. Greenwich Medical Media, 2001: 227–42.

10 Nightingale JMD. Management of a high output jejunostomy. In: Nightingale JMD (ed.). *Intestinal Failure*. Greenwich Medical Media, 2001: 375–92.

11 Baker ML, Nightingale JMD. Management of high output stomas. *Gut* 2004; **53** (suppl 3): A72.

12 Byrne MF, Murray FE. Gallstones. In: Nightingale JMD (ed.). *Intestinal Failure*. Greenwich Medical Media, 2001: 213–26.

13 Nightingale JMD, Woodward J, Small bowel/Nutrition Committee of BSG. BSG Guidelines on the Management of Patients with a Short Bowel. *Gut* (in press)

14 Thompson JS. Surgery for patients with a short bowel. In: Nightingale JMD (ed.). *Intestinal Failure*. Greenwich Medical Media, 2001: 515–27.

15 Nightingale JMD. The medical management of intestinal failure: methods to reduce the severity. *Proc Nutr Soc* 2003; **62**: 703–10.

48 Management of internal fistulae

DAVID RAMPTON

LEARNING POINTS

Internal fistulae

- There is a paucity of controlled data on which to base recommendations for treatment of internal fistulae in Crohn's disease

- Management should be undertaken by an experienced IBD medical-surgical team.

- All patients require assessment of the relevant anatomy, of disease activity, and of their nutritional status

- Fluid and electrolyte, and nutritional deficiencies should be corrected promptly

- In contrast to perianal fistulae, internal fistulae respond poorly to drugs and surgery is often required

- 6-Mercaptopurine may be efficacious, the effects of infliximab are unimpressive but need further study, and steroids may worsen outcome.

Introduction

Internal fistulae are fistulae that connect two bowel loops, or connect the intestine with the skin or other internal organs. In relation to Crohn's disease, they specifically exclude perianal fistulae. Internal fistulae occur in 5–15% of all patients with Crohn's [1], and in approximately one-third of patients requiring surgery [2]; the most common are enterocolonic, enteroenteric, enterocutaneous, and enterovesical. The prognosis of Crohn's disease complicated by fistulae is that of penetrating disease, nearly half of affected patients needing surgery within a year of diagnosis, and one-third needing repeat surgery in 10 years in one large early series [1].

The aim of this chapter is to outline, with particular reference to pharmacologic treatment, management of patients with this often challenging complication of Crohn's disease; for full reviews see Levy and Tremaine [3] and Present [4]. At the outset, it should be emphasized that the literature contains no controlled data on which to base therapeutic decisions, the few controlled studies to date on treatment of patients with fistulous Crohn's having been focused primarily on patients with perianal disease [5–7].

Investigations

As in other patients presenting with Crohn's disease, prompt assessment of relevant disease anatomy, disease activity, and nutritional status are essential if rational management decisions are to be taken.

Anatomy

Relevant anatomy is delineated using contrast radiology (e.g. barium follow-through, fistulogram), endoscopy, abdominal computed tomography (CT) scan, and/or magnetic resonance imaging [8]; selection of the most appropriate test, and their subsequent interpretation, is best undertaken in close collaboration with a specialist gastrointestinal radiologist (see also Chapter 4). Information required includes the length and complexity of fistulae, the sites they connect, the presence of any associated abscess, the presence of any obstructing stricture downstream of the fistula, and the length of residual uninvolved intestine.

Disease activity

Formal clinical indices such as the Crohn's Disease Activity Index (CDAI) are rarely used outside clinical trials, and in most situations clinical assessment is backed up by laboratory measures of inflammation such as serum hemoglobin, platelet count, erythrocyte sedimentation rate (ESR), C-reactive protein, and albumin. A high neutrophil count may indicate associated sepsis.

Nutritional status

Some patients with internal fistulae are severely malnourished and/or fluid depleted, and rapid evaluation of their nutritional status and fluid and electrolyte balance is mandatory [9]. This involves both clinical (e.g. body-mass index, mid-arm circumference) [10], and laboratory measures (e.g. serum hemoglobin, hematinics, albumin, urea, creatinine, electrolytes, calcium, magnesium, zinc, vitamin D). Patients with enterocutaneous fistulae should have their fistula output measured. Those patients with a high output, which are usually proximal, are at particular risk of fluid, electrolyte, and nutritional depletion.

Principles of treatment

Asymptomatic internal fistulae

Internal fistulae found incidentally (e.g. on barium follow-through examination), and unassociated with symptoms, usually require no specific therapy beyond that given for the indication for which the imaging was requested [3].

Symptomatic internal fistulae (Fig. 48.1)

Management of these patients should be undertaken by a multidisciplinary team comprising, for example, a medical gastroenterologist and a colorectal surgeon with special interests in IBD, nutrition team, specialist IBD nurse, stoma therapist, and radiologist. Malnourished and/or fluid and electrolyte-depleted patients need prompt restoration of their deficiencies [9]. While in patients with high output proximal fistulae, total parenteral nutrition may be necessary, in those with distal small bowel or colonic fistulae, enteral feeding is usually sufficient (see Chapter 22). Antibiotics may be indicated in patients with concurrent small bowel overgrowth or sepsis; percutaneous drainage may be necessary in patients with defined collections. Prescription of steroids should be minimized in view of the high incidence of complications associated with their use in patients with complex Crohn's disease (see Chapter 9). Specific pharmacologic options and the principles of surgery in patients failing to respond to medical therapy are discussed below.

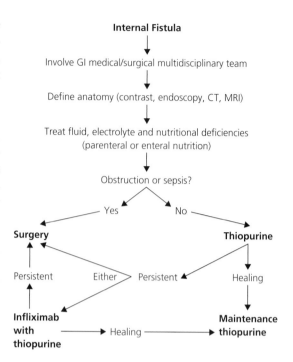

FIG 48.1 Algorithm for management of internal fistula in Crohn's disease. Note that none of the recommendations is based on controlled evidence. CT, computed tomography; GI, gastrointestinal; MRI, magnetic resonance imaging.

Medical therapy of internal fistulae in Crohn's disease

Limitations of evidence

There is no formal controlled evidence on which to found recommendations about therapy of *internal* fistulae in Crohn's, the only data available deriving from small retrospective or open-label evaluations and from controlled trials focused on perianal disease [5–7]. Controlled trials are made very difficult by the small numbers of patients with internal fistulae treated even in large specialist centers. Furthermore, study end-points have inevitably been imperfect. Closure or reduced drainage from an enterocutaneous fistula, for example, may be associated with development of an abscess rather than improvement.

Uncontrolled reports

Uncontrolled reports have claimed efficacy in treatment of internal fistulae using metronidazole [11], 6-mercaptopurine [12], methotrexate [13], cyclosporine [14–16], and octreotide [17]. Confidence in the veracity of these reports, however, has to be tempered by their open-label and often retrospective nature, by the use in several of combinations of drugs, and by the fact that in all but two of these series the number of patients treated was less than 10.

In the largest of these studies, apparently not yet published in full, use of 6-mercaptopurine together with antibiotics and an aminosalicylate was associated with closure of enterovesical fistulae in 13/31 (42%) patients, 67% patients avoiding surgery over a mean follow-up of 8 years [12]. Prior use of steroids significantly worsened response to this treatment (see Chapter 9).

Infliximab

Several studies of varying design have reported on the effects of infliximab in patients with internal fistulae, but none has shown unequivocal benefit.

In the original controlled report of the efficacy of infliximab in fistulous Crohn's disease, 90% of patients had perianal rather than internal fistulae, and results in the latter group of patients cannot be extracted from the published data [5]. In the subsequent maintenance study (ACCENT II), the vast majority of patients again had perianal disease [18]. However, in this study, 22/39 (58%) patients with internal fistulae, and 16/25 (64%) of those with rectovaginal fistulae responded to the initial infusions of infliximab given at 0, 2, and 6 weeks. *Post hoc* analysis published separately showed that approximately half of rectovaginal fistulae were still closed after 14 weeks, maintenance of closure being slightly longer (median 46 weeks) in patients on infliximab than in those given placebo (33 weeks) [6].

Uncontrolled studies have suggested that infliximab may be more effective in healing perianal than internal fistulae in Crohn's disease, and have given far less encouraging results in relation to internal fistulae than those extractable from the ACCENT II trial. In one, infliximab healed almost 80% of perianal fistulae but only 40% of enterocutaneous and 15% of rectovaginal fistulae [19]. In another tiny but intriguing report, three infliximab infusions given to four patients with internal fistulae, of whom two also had perianal fistulae, healed both the perianal but none of the internal fistulae [20]. Lastly, a retrospective case note review showed that of 17 patients given infliximab for internal fistulae, only two had complete healing, the other 15 needing or declining surgery because of an inadequate response [21].

Available evidence on the efficacy of infliximab in the treatment of internal fistulae is thus inadequate. Because many patients with internal fistulae have accompanying intra-abdominal sepsis, use of infliximab cannot be recommended at present except in rare patients in whom sepsis has been excluded or eradicated, and in whom all other medical and surgical therapeutic options have been exhausted.

Tacrolimus

A controlled trial has shown that tacrolimus is effective, if not entirely safe, for the treatment of fistulous Crohn's disease [7]. However, as in the infliximab controlled trials [5,6], most patients had perianal disease, and it is not possible to confirm from the paper whether or not this drug is effective in internal fistulae.

Surgery

Internal fistulae that fail to heal on medical therapy need surgical intervention. Risk factors include the presence of distal obstruction, the fistula arising from a grossly diseased segment of bowel, and a short tract between skin and bowel in patients with enterocutaneous fistulae [22]. Details of the necessary surgery are beyond the scope of this chapter, but principles include preoperative optimization of nutritional status, drainage of any associated abscess, resection of diseased bowel, and repair of the fistula itself. How prior use of drugs such as steroids and infliximab affects the need for, and outcome of surgery is discussed elsewhere (see Chapters 9 and 21).

Conclusions

All patients need to be cared for by an experienced multidisciplinary team. Meticulous attention needs to be paid to defining the relevant anatomy, and to assessing and correcting any fluid and nutritional deficits. Because of the relative rarity of symptomatic internal fistulae, there have been no controlled trials to confirm or refute the efficacy of specific medical therapy. Until or unless such data become available, patients not requiring immediate surgery because of sepsis or obstruction should be started on a thiopurine; infliximab may be worth a short trial in those not responding and in whom sepsis and alternative treatment options have been excluded. A high proportion of patients will fail to respond to medical treatment and come eventually to surgery. Throughout their illness, and particularly in view of the increasing complexity of the various therapeutic options, patients should be kept fully informed about their progress and participate in decisions about their treatment.

References

1 Greenstein AJ, Sachar DB, Pasternack BS, Janowitz HD. Re-operation and recurrence in Crohn's colitis and ileocolitis: crude and cumulative rates. *N Engl J Med* 1975; **293**: 685–90.

2 Michelassi F, Stella N, Balestracci T, *et al.* Incidence, diagnosis and treatment of enteric and colorectal fistulae in patients with Crohn's disease. *Ann Surg* 1993; **218**: 660–6.

3 Levy C, Tremaine WJ. Management of internal fistulas in Crohn's disease. *Inflamm Bowel Dis* 2002; **8**: 106–11.

4 Present DH. Crohn's fistula: current concepts in management. *Gastroenterology* 2003; **124**: 1629–35.

5 Present DH, Rutgeerts P, Targan S, *et al.* Infliximab for the treatment of fistula in patients with Crohn's disease. *N Engl J Med* 1999; **340**: 1398–405.

6 Sands BE, Anderson FH, Bernstein CN, *et al.* Infliximab maintenance therapy for fistulising Crohn's disease. *N Engl J Med* 2004; **350**: 876–85.

7 Sandborn WJ, Present DH, Isaacs KL. Tacrolimus for the treatment of fistulas in patients with Crohn's disease: a randomised, placebo-controlled trial. *Gastroenterology* 2003; **125**: 380–8.

8 Rubesin SE, Scotiniotis I, Birnbaum BA, Ginsberg GG. Radiologic and endoscopic diagnosis of Crohn's disease. *Surg Clin North Am* 2001; **81**: 39–70.

9 Song HK, Buzby GP. Nutritional support for Crohn's disease. *Surg Clin North Am* 2001; **81**: 103–15.

10 Nightingale JM, Walsh N, Bullock ME, Wicks AC. Three simple methods of detecting malnutrition on medical wards. *J R Soc Med* 1996; **89**: 144–8.

11 Jakobovits J, Schuster MM. Metronidazole therapy for Crohn's disease and associated fistulae. *Am J Gastroenterol* 1984; **79**: 533–40.

12 Wheeler SC, Marion J, Present DH. Medical therapy, not surgery, is the appropriate first line treatment of Crohn's enterovesical fistula. *Gastroenterology* 1998; **114**: A1113.

13 Mahadevan U, Marion JF, Present DH. Fistula response to methotrexate in Crohn's disease: a case series. *Aliment Pharmacol Ther* 2003; **18**: 1003–8.

14 Hanauer SB, Smith MB. Rapid closure of Crohn's disease fistulas with continuous intravenous cyclosporine A. *Am J Gastroenterol* 1993; **88**: 646–9.

15 Present DH, Lichtiger S. Efficacy of cyclosporine in treatment of fistula of Crohn's disease. *Dig Dis Sci* 1994; **39**: 374–80.

16 Egan LJ, Sandborn WJ, Tremaine WJ. Clinical outcome following treatment of refractory inflammatory and fistulising Crohn's disease with intravenous cyclosporine. *Am J Gastroenterol* 1998; **93**: 442–8.

17 Lavy A, Yassin K. Octreotide for enterocutaneous fistulas of Crohn's disease. *Can J Gastroenterol* 2003; **17**: 555–8.

18 Sands BE, Blank MA, Patel K, *et al.* Long term treatment of rectovaginal fistulas in Crohn's disease: response to infliximab in the ACCENT II study. *Clin Gastroenterol Hepatol* 2004; **2**: 912–20.

19 Parsi MA, Lashner BA, Achkar J-P, Connor JT, Brzezinski A. Type of fistula determines response to infliximab in patients with fistulous Crohn's disease. *Am J Gastroenterol* 2004; **99**: 445–9.

20 Miehsler W, Reinisch W, Kazemi-Shirazi L, *et al.* Infliximab: lack of efficacy on perforating complications in Crohn's disease. *Inflamm Bowel Dis* 2004; **10**: 36–40.

21 Poritz LS, Rowe WA, Koltun WA. Remicade does not abolish the need for surgery in fistulizing Crohn's disease. *Dis Colon Rectum* 2002; **45**: 771–5.

22 Pettit SH, Irving MH. The operative management of fistulous Crohn's disease. *Surg Gynaecol Obstet* 1988; **167**: 223–8.

49   What is indeterminate colitis?

GARRET CULLEN & DIARMUID O'DONOGHUE

LEARNING POINTS

Indeterminate colitis

- Accounts for approximately 10% of IBD

- Is a clinical, endoscopic, radiologic, and histologic diagnosis

- May evolve to become UC or Crohn's disease

- May be identified by the absence of serologic markers associated with UC or Crohn's

- Is a valid diagnosis representing part of the spectrum of IBD

Introduction

Indeterminate colitis (IC) is a term applied to the 10–15% of cases of IBD in which a diagnosis of UC or Crohn's disease cannot be established [1]. As the disease evolves, more than 50% will be reclassified as either UC or Crohn's disease, with the majority being diagnosed as UC [2]. Price first used the term IC in 1978 when he described diagnostic difficulties in a series of colectomy specimens from patients with a diagnosis of UC [3]. Initially, the term was used when the diagnosis could not be established in colectomy specimens but is now frequently employed in reference to endoscopic appearances and colonic biopsies.

Given the lack of defined diagnostic criteria and a universally accepted definition of IC, it is inevitable that incidence and prevalence differ between studies. Population based studies have demonstrated an average annual incidence ranging from 1.6 to 2.4/100 000. Prevalence of IC may change dramatically after surgery and evaluation of the colectomy specimen [4]. While the medical management of IC differs little from that of Crohn's disease or UC, its diagnosis impacts significantly on surgical treatment. Decisions such as the timing and type of surgery, including ileal pouch anal anastamosis (IPAA), are highly dependent on the type of IBD.

Clinical dilemmas

When IBD is confined to the large bowel it is not surprising that difficulties will arise in making a firm distinction between Crohn's disease and UC. A diagnosis of Crohn's disease is easy to support in the presence of perianal disease, rectal sparing, or true skip lesions. On the other hand, continuous friable mucosa extending proximally from the anorectal margin is suggestive of UC.

Pitfalls may arise, however, especially in previously treated patients. Medical treatment of UC can lead to a patchy resolution of inflammation and give the appearance of Crohn's disease. The use of 5-aminosalicylate (5-ASA) enemas can result in a normal rectum in well-documented UC [5]. Immunomodulatory drugs (azathioprine, infliximab) can produce mucosal healing in Crohn's disease. It is also worth noting that bowel preparation compounds (sodium phosphate) can cause mild colitis and even aphthoid ulceration [6].

Variations in the pattern and extent of disease in UC can lead to diagnostic difficulties. A number of patients with distal colitis may have patchy inflammation at the appendiceal orifice, ascending colon, and/or cecum (cecal patch). This may give the false impression of a skip lesion leading to a change in diagnosis to Crohn's disease or IC. Biopsy of the terminal ileum may be helpful as it is usually uninvolved with a cecal patch.

Terminal ileal inflammation resulting from backwash ileitis in UC may also lead to a false diagnosis of Crohn's disease. Patchy right-sided inflammation has been shown to be of little clinical relevance and is only of importance to prevent false diagnosis of skip lesions [7]. The difficulty in correctly classifying IBD is highlighted by the large study from Cleveland where it was noted that just over 4% of all patients undergoing IPAA for UC were found to have developed Crohn's disease [8].

Pathologic dilemmas

A pathologic distinction between various forms of IBD can, likewise, be difficult and controversial. Differentiation can be problematic even when the entire colon is available for study [3]. This is compounded when surgery has been performed for fulminant disease. Nicholls and Wells [9] suggested that the diagnosis of IC is more likely to occur in the setting of an acutely inflamed colon. Macroscopic features are of limited value in the acutely inflamed colon, with linear ulceration and fissures being common and not indicative of Crohn's disease [10]. Intensive corticosteroid treatment in fulminant disease may lead to the histologic appearance of IC [11].

Thus, it is not surprising that the small endoscopic biopsies can be inconclusive. The finding of granulomas, submucosal inflammation, and fissure ulcers will all point to Crohn's disease but their absence does not necessarily signify UC. It is inevitable that there will be a degree of variability in diagnosis between different pathologists and clinicians. Some pathologists are more willing to accept a greater degree of variation in patterns seen in UC while others are more sensitive to changes seen in Crohn's disease. In such situations, IC will be less commonly diagnosed. Farmer et al. [12] demonstrated that a diagnosis of IC was more likely to be made by a pathologist with a specialist interest in gastroenterology.

Serologic markers

Perinuclear antineutrophil cytoplasmic antibodies (pANCA) and anti-Saccharomyces cervisiae antibodies (ASCA) have been suggested as a method of differentiating UC from Crohn's disease (see Chapter 3). p-ANCA has a specificity approaching 90% in UC but its sensitivity (40–60%) limits its usefulness. Joossens et al. [13] suggested that these markers might be of use in categorizing IC. Those with negative serology were more likely to retain their diagnosis of IC.

Other forms of colitis

One of the great strengths of a diagnosis of IC is that it should alert us to the possibility of other diagnoses. Infectious colitis must be considered in the acute setting and may easily be confused as UC. The patchy inflammation, thumbprinting, and a cobblestone appearance often seen in ischemic colitis can be mistaken for Crohn's disease.

The importance of a carefully taken drug history is demonstrated by the way non-steroidal inflammatory drug (NSAID) colitis or ileocolitis can mimic Crohn's disease with its patchy distribution and even stricture formation [14] (see Chapter 37). Diverticular disease associated colitis (DDAC) can mimic Crohn's disease (see Chapter 61). It is imperative that the pathologist be aware that diverticula were seen endoscopically.

Conclusions

Considerable debate remains as to whether IC is an independent form of colitis, a distinct type of IBD, or a "wait and see" diagnosis that will eventually be classified as UC or Crohn's disease. Studies of the serologic markers pANCA and ASCA have raised the possibility that IC may be a separate clinicopathologic entity.

Specific clinical situations such as fulminant colitis, treatment effects, biopsy sampling errors, and interobserver variation in histology reporting all influence the diagnosis in IBD. The clinician must also be aware of other conditions that may mimic IBD.

For the most part, IC seems to behave more like UC than Crohn's disease. In cases where treatment decisions must be made based on the diagnosis, it is important to identify features of Crohn's disease that would preclude a specific treatment. This is especially so where surgery is being considered. Issues surrounding ileal pouch anal anastamosis in IC are dealt with in the following chapter.

The diagnosis of IC should not be considered a failure; it is a valid diagnosis when available information does not permit a confident diagnosis of Crohn's disease or UC.

References

1 Guindi M, Ridell RH. Indeterminate colitis. *J Clin Pathol* 2004; 57: 1233–44.

2 Moum B, Vatn MH, Ekbom A, *et al*. Inflammatory bowel disease: re-evaluation of the diagnosis in a prospective population based study in southeastern Norway. *Gut* 1997; **40**: 328–32.

3 Price AB. Overlap in the spectrum of non-specific inflammatory bowel disease: colitis indeterminate. *J Clin Pathol* 1978; **31**: 567–77.

4 Kangas E, Matikainen M, Matilla J. Is "indeterminate colitis" Crohn's disease in the long-term follow-up? *Int Surg* 1994; **79**: 120–3.

5 Kim B, Barnett JL, Kleer CG, *et al*. Endoscopic and histological patchiness in treated ulcerative colitis. *Am J Gastroenterol* 1999; **94**: 3258–62.

6 Driman DK, Preiksaitis HG. Colorectal inflammation and increased cell proliferation associated with oral sodium phosphate bowel preparation solution. *Hum Pathol* 1998; **29**: 972–8.

7 Mutinga M, Farraye F, Wang H, *et al*. Clinical significance of right-sided colonic inflammation in patients with left sided chronic ulcerative colitis. *Gastroenterology* 2001; **120**: A450.

8 Schmidt CM, Lazenby AJ, Hendrickson RJ, *et al*. Preoperative terminal ileal and colonic resection histopathology predicts risk of pouchitis in patients after ileoanal pull-through procedure. *Ann Surg* 1998; **227**: 654–62.

9 Nicholls RJ, Wells AD. Indeterminate colitis. *Baillieres Clin Gastroenterol* 1992; **6**: 105–12.

10 Swan NC, Geoghegan JG, O'Donoghue DP, *et al*. Fulminant colitis in inflammatory bowel disease: detailed pathologic and clinical analysis. *Dis Colon Rectum* 1998; **41**: 1511–5.

11 Rudolph WG, Uthoff SM, McAuliffe TL, *et al*. Indeterminate colitis: the real story. *Dis Colon Rectum* 2002; **45**: 1528–34.

12 Farmer M, Petras RE, Hunt LE, *et al*. The importance of diagnostic accuracy in colonic inflammatory bowel disease. *Am J Gastroenterol* 2000; **95**: 3184–8.

13 Joossens S, Reinisch W, Vermeire S, *et al*. The value of serologic markers in indeterminate colitis: a prospective follow up study. *Gastroenterology* 2002; **122**: 1242–7.

14 Evans JM, McMahon AD, Murray FE, *et al*. Non-steroidal anti-inflammatory drugs are associated with emergency admission to hospital for colitis due to inflammatory bowel disease. *Gut* 1997; **40**: 619–22.

50 Pouches for indeterminate colitis?

LAURA HANCOCK & NEIL MORTENSEN

Introduction

Restorative proctocolectomy with ileal pouch-anal anastomosis (IPAA) for patients with indeterminate colitis (IC) is controversial. In this chapter we outline the reasons for this clinical dilemma, review the evidence, and discuss the role of pouch surgery in patients with IC.

Restorative proctocolectomy with IPAA is the treatment of choice for patients with UC and familial adenomatous polyposis coli that ultimately require surgery. The procedure removes the diseased bowel, preserves sphincter function, and avoids the need for permanent ileostomy. Since the initial description of pouch surgery by Parks *et al.* in 1978 [1], technical modifications have been made and surgical expertise has advanced so that the procedure can now be performed safely for UC with a low complication rate and a 10% pouch failure rate long term [2].

Patients with Crohn's disease have been widely regarded as unsuitable candidates for pouch surgery because of the risk of recurrence of disease in the ileal reservoir. Un-suspected Crohn's disease is a leading cause of pouch failure and has been recorded in up to 45% of patients who have undergone inadvertent IPAA [3]. Regimbeau *et al.* [4] published more favorable results in which 41 patients underwent IPAA, of whom 26 had a preoperative diagnosis of colonic Crohn's disease, with no history of perianal or small bowel disease. Crohn's disease-related complications occurred in 35% at 10 years with a low pouch excision rate of 10% at 10 years. Nevertheless, most surgeons still regard complications of pouch surgery in Crohn's disease to be unacceptably high and it remains a contraindication to pouch construction. A proportion of patients with IC will ultimately turn out to have Crohn's disease with a potentially adverse outcome with IPAA. This leads to the inevitable question – are pouches appropriate in patients with a diagnosis of indeterminate colitis? To answer this dilemma the evidence must be considered.

Evidence

The Mayo Clinic have performed three assessments of pouch outcome for IC over the last 10 years [2,5,6]. The most recent publication reviewed 82 patients with IC and 1437 patients with UC who underwent an IPAA between 1981 and 1985 with a median follow-up approaching 7 years [2]. Patients with IC had significantly more episodes of pelvic sepsis (17% IC vs. 7% UC; $P < 0.01$), pouch fistula (31% IC vs. 9% UC; $P < 0.001$), and pouch failure (27% IC vs. 11% UC; $P < 0.001$). The most important cause of pouch failure in patients with IC was fistula, sepsis, or both. Fifteen percent of the patients with IC compared with 2% of the patients with UC ultimately had their diagnosis changed to Crohn's disease. An atypical distribution of inflammation

TABLE 50.1 Summary of published outcomes of ileoanal pouch surgery in patients with indeterminate colitis.

Reference	Year	IC patients (n)	IC pouch failure (%)	UC patients (n)	UC pouch failure (%)	Median follow-up (months)
Pezim [5]	1989	25	8	489	4	38
Koltun [7]	1991	18	28	235	0.4	40
Atkinson [8]	1994	16	19	158	5	–
McIntyre [6]	1995	71	19	1232	8	56
Marcello [9]	1997	42	12	499	2	–
Yu [2]	2000	82	27	1437	11	83
Delaney [10]	2001	115	3.4	1399	3.5	53
Pishori [11]	2004	13	0	285	2.1	40

IC, indeterminate colitis.

(skip lesions and rectal sparing) was identified more frequently in patients who were eventually diagnosed with Crohn's disease but this did not achieve statistical significance. IC patients who did not convert to Crohn's disease had a clinical outcome that was equivalent to UC with 85% having functioning pouches at 10 years. Functional outcomes were comparable in all three groups (Table 50.1).

The largest published series to date of patients who have undergone IPAA for IC is from the Cleveland Clinic [10]. Between 1983 and 1999, 115 patients who had IPAA for IC and 1399 for UC were identified after re-evaluation of the pathology. There was no significant difference in the overall IPAA failure rate: 3.4% for IC patients and 3.5% for UC patients. However, like the Mayo experience, they observed a higher complication rate in the IC group compared with the UC group with a significantly higher frequency of pelvic abscess (8.7% IC vs. 2.2% UC; $P < 0.05$) and perianal fistula (7.0% IC vs. 2.6% UC; $P < 0.01$). The median stool frequency was the same for both IC and UC. There was an increased incidence of conversion to a diagnosis of Crohn's disease in the IC patients (6% IC vs. 1.3% UC) but this was considerably lower than that observed at the Mayo Clinic although a shorter follow-up period of 4 years is noted. IC patients had a slightly but significantly lower Cleveland Global Quality of Life Score compared with UC although when asked 93.3% of patients with IC would be happy to undergo IPAA again, compared with 97.9% patients who had UC.

Most authors agree that the complication rates of IPAA are higher in patients with IC compared with patients with UC. A higher pouch failure rate has also been observed in the IC patients with the exception of those described by Delaney et al. [10] and more recently Pishori et al. [11] who

demonstrated no difference in failure rates. Functional outcomes are equivalent after IPAA for IC and UC. More patients with IC convert to a diagnosis of Crohn's disease than those with an initial diagnosis of UC. The question is therefore, are the complication and failure rates acceptable such that it is reasonable to perform pouch surgery in patients with IC? We believe that pouch surgery is a suitable alternative to total proctocolectomy and permanent ileostomy in patients with IC but there are several issues that should be considered prior to recommending pouch surgery in order to optimize patient outcome.

Patient selection

When considering pelvic pouch surgery every effort must be made to differentiate between UC and Crohn's disease. When all the distinguishing features of Crohn's disease and UC have been considered, there will still be approximately 10% of IBD specimens in which the pathologic diagnosis remains in doubt and these are labeled as IC [12]. Price [12] made the point that differentiation is particularly difficult when the colectomy is performed for acute severe colitis because of the depth of the inflammatory infiltrate within the wall of these specimens. In this situation, earlier mucosal biopsies should be reviewed to help refine the diagnosis.

When faced with a pathologic diagnosis of IC it is essential to put the histology into the context of the clinical, radiologic, and endoscopic findings as a complete review can often reclassify the patient into having either UC or Crohn's disease. Wells et al. [13] from St Mark's examined the case records of 46 patients with IC and combined the pathology with preoperative clinical information and radiologic reports. On that basis, 19 patients were reclassified to probable

Crohn's disease, 11 to probable UC, and 16 remained as having IC. Crohn's disease did not develop over a median of 10 years of follow-up in those patients who continued to be classified as having IC after extensive investigation [13].

Serologic markers such as anti-*Saccharomyces cerevisiae* antibody (ASCA) and perinuclear antineutrophil cytoplasmic antibody (p-ANCA) (see Chapter 3) have also shown some promise as a method of improving diagnostic accuracy [14]. Furthermore, advances in the genetic classification of the IBD may lead to a combination of molecular and immunologic markers being used as diagnostic tools in the future.

Conclusions

Patients who have any clinical manifestations of Crohn's disease, specifically patients with a past or present history of perineal sepsis, fissure, or fistula should not be considered as candidates for pouch surgery. If, after careful assessment, the patient cannot be classified as having UC or Crohn's disease and surgery is required, the options are total proctocolectomy and permanent ileostomy or IPAA. Patients should be provided with information regarding the potential complications and outcomes of both procedures so that they can participate in the decision process. A staged procedure involving an initial subtotal colectomy and ileostomy allows a full assessment of the pathologic, clinical, radiologic, and endoscopic findings. If the diagnosis remains as IC following colectomy, a completion proctectomy and ileoanal pouch can be offered providing that the patient is well informed and fully accepts the risks.

References

1 Parks AG, Nicholls RJ. Proctocolectomy without ileostomy for ulcerative colitis. *BMJ* 1978; **2**: 85–8.

2 Yu CS, Pemberton JH, Larson D. Ileal pouch-anal anastomo-sis in patients with indeterminate colitis: long-term results. *Dis Colon Rectum* 2000; **43**: 1487–96.

3 Sagar PM, Dozois RR, Wolff BG. Long-term results of ileal pouch-anal anastomosis in patients with Crohn's disease. *Dis Colon Rectum* 1996; **39**: 893–8.

4 Regimbeau JM, Panis Y, Pocard M, *et al.* Long-term results of ileal pouch-anal anastomosis for colorectal Crohn's disease. *Dis Colon Rectum* 2001; **44**: 769–78.

5 Pezim ME, Pemberton JH, Beart RW Jr, *et al.* Outcome of 'indeterminant' colitis following ileal pouch-anal anastomo-sis. *Dis Colon Rectum* 1989; **32**: 653–8.

6 McIntyre PB, Pemberton JH, Wolff BG, Dozois RR, Beart RW Jr. Indeterminate colitis: long-term outcome in patients after ileal pouch-anal anastomosis. *Dis Colon Rectum* 1995; **38**: 51–4.

7 Koltun WA, Schoetz DJ Jr, Roberts PL, *et al.* Indeterminate colitis predisposes to perineal complications after ileal pouch-anal anastomosis. *Dis Colon Rectum* 1991; **34**: 857–60.

8 Atkinson KG, Owen DA, Wankling G. Restorative proctoco-lectomy and indeterminate colitis. *Am J Surg* 1994; **167**: 516–8.

9 Marcello PW, Schoetz DJ Jr, Roberts PL, *et al.* Evolutionary changes in the pathologic diagnosis after the ileoanal pouch procedure. *Dis Colon Rectum* 1997; **40**: 263–9.

10 Delaney CP, Remzi FH, Gramlich T, Dadvand B, Fazio VW. Equivalent function, quality of life and pouch survival rates after ileal pouch-anal anastomosis for indeterminate and ulcerative colitis. *Ann Surg* 2002; **236**: 43–8.

11 Pishori T, Dinnewitzer A, Zmora O, *et al.* Outcome of patients with indeterminate colitis undergoing a double-stapled ileal pouch-anal anastomosis. *Dis Colon Rectum* 2004; **47**: 717–21.

12 Price AB. Overlap in the spectrum of non-specific inflamma-tory bowel disease: 'colitis indeterminate'. *J Clin Pathol* 1978; **31**: 567–77.

13 Wells AD, McMillan I, Price AB, Ritchie JK, Nicholls RJ. Natural history of indeterminate colitis. *Br J Surg* 1991; **78**: 179–81.

14 Joossens S, Reinisch W, Vermeire S, *et al.* The value of serologic markers in indeterminate colitis: a prospective follow-up study. *Gastroenterology* 2002; **122**: 1242–7.

Common Clinical Challenges: Beyond the Text Book

51 Colitis-associated cancer: what's the risk to your patients?

JAYNE EADEN

LEARNING POINTS

Colitis-associated cancer

- Risk factors for colitis-associated cancer include:
  - Dysplasia
  - Disease duration
  - Disease extent
  - Sclerosing cholangitis
  - Young age at diagnosis
  - Family history of colorectal cancer
  - Inflammation and endoscopic appearances
  - Folate deficiency
- Colectomy is the only certain way of preventing colitis-associated cancer
- Further evidence is required to confirm the protective effects of:
  - 5-aminosalicylate (5-ASA)
  - Ursodeoxycholic acid

Introduction

The first case of adenocarcinoma complicating UC was reported in 1925. Since that time the role of cancer surveillance in the management of colitis has been a subject of controversy for a number of reasons. Some patients are at greater risk of developing colorectal cancer (CRC). It is important that gastroenterologists are aware who these patients are in order that surveillance is conducted appro-

priately and patients can make an informed decision on whether they wish to undergo surveillance. This chapter covers the epidemiology of cancer in IBD including the magnitude of the risk and the risk factors. The aim is to provide practical pointers for the management of such patients.

Duration and extent of disease

Although it is undisputed that patients with long-term UC have an increased risk of CRC, its magnitude has been difficult to estimate. Early publications were mostly case reports, and formal epidemiologic studies came from referral centers with their inherent selection biases. Later, population-based studies covering defined geographic areas were reported. A meta-analysis of 116 published studies reporting a colonic cancer risk in UC showed the risk for *any* patient with colitis is 2% at 10 years, 8% at 20 years, and 18% after 30 years of disease [1]. Because the risk increases with time, it is recommended in the British Society of Gastroenterology (BSG) guidelines that the surveillance interval be shortened with increasing duration of disease (Fig. 51.1) [2].

The risk of CRC in Crohn's disease has been even more contentious. Early studies included patients with colonic resections, some included patients with small bowel disease and others did not adjust for duration of disease. The risks reported from studies that represent the "at risk population" (i.e. those with long-standing, unresected, and extensive colonic Crohn's disease) give increased estimates. However, even without adjusting for the potential biases, the largest population-based study demonstrated a CRC

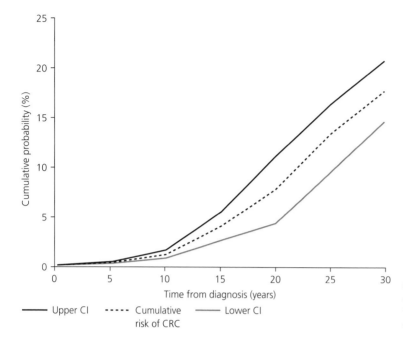

FIG 51.1 Cumulative risk of developing colorectal cancer in UC [1]. CI, confidence interval; CRC, colorectal cancer.

risk that is equal to the risk seen in UC patients [3]. In fact, absolute cumulative colon cancer frequencies for UC and Crohn's disease have been found to be almost identical: 8% for UC and 7% for Crohn's disease after 20 years of disease [4]. In summary, Crohn's colitis should raise the same concerns regarding cancer risk, as does UC.

The other major factor increasing the cancer risk is extent of disease. Most cancers arise in patients with subtotal or pancolitis. There is general agreement that there is little or no increased risk associated with proctitis [5] while left-sided colitis carries an intermediate cancer risk [6].

Primary sclerosing cholangitis

Several studies have indicated that patients with concomitant primary sclerosing cholangitis (PSC) may be at a higher risk of colorectal neoplasia although others have suggested the clinical significance of this risk may be low. A meta-analysis has determined that PSC increases the risk fourfold [7]. In addition, the risk of cancer remains even after liver transplantation, with an incidence of approximately 1% per person per year [8]. Because these patients are at a vastly increased risk it is recommended that they have annual colonoscopy from the time that PSC is diagnosed [2].

Age at onset of colitis

There has been some debate as to whether patients with onset of colitis early in life have an increased risk compared with older patients. However, the most recent data found that the cumulative cancer risk in patients with extensive colitis is 40% in patients in whom the disease started before the age of 15 years and 25% in patients developing colitis between 15 and 39 years [6]. Thus, surveillance in adolescents must be based on the duration of the illness, not their chronologic age.

Family history of colorectal cancer

A positive family history of sporadic CRC is a risk factor for colon cancer in the general population. Recent evidence suggests this may also have an impact in patients with UC. A case–control study found that a family history of sporadic colon cancer was twice as common in colitis patients with CRC compared with UC controls matched for extent and duration of colitis [9]. More research has shown the relatives of patients with *both* IBD and CRC have an 80% increased risk of CRC [10]. However, the evidence does not suggest a common genetic link between IBD and CRC.

Inflammation and endoscopic appearance of the colon

Previously the severity and frequency of colitis attacks did not appear to confer an increased cancer risk. However, recent evidence has emerged indicating that CRC is more likely to develop if there is ongoing inflammation in the colon, albeit at a microscopic level [11]. Investigators have also noticed a higher than expected frequency of malignant neoplasms in perianal fistulae, excluded segments, and strictures in patients with Crohn's disease [12].

The BSG guidelines [2] state that during surveillance colonoscopy extra biopsies should be taken from dysplasia-associated lesions or masses (DALMs), irregular plaques, villiform elevations, ulcers and strictures as they may often harbor neoplastic lesions [13,14].

Dysplasia

Dysplasia is recognized to be premalignant but the likelihood of progression to cancer is difficult to predict (see Chapter 52). It is generally accepted that a DALM or high grade dysplasia (HGD) has a high propensity for malignancy [15]. More controversy occurs when low grade dysplasia (LGD) in flat mucosa is found at colonoscopy. A literature review found that 29% of such patients showed progression at some time to HGD, DALM, or cancer [15]. More recent data indicate that the 5-year predictive value for HGD or cancer in patients with LGD is 53% [16]. The Leeds group found that HGD or cancer developed in only 10% of their patients diagnosed with LGD [17]. However, their findings are likely to be due to the unreliable diagnosis of LGD caused by high rates of inter- and intraobserver variation amongst pathologists in the study.

The effect of medication

A higher CRC risk may be related to folate deficiency, which can occur as a result of competitive inhibition, for example by sulfasalazine. If patients are maintained on this aminosalicylate it may be wise to supplement their diet with folic acid [18].

While most concur that there appears to be an increased risk of CRC in patients with IBD, population-based studies in Scandinavia have shown the opposite [19,20]. This lack of increased risk may be secondary to their long-standing and widespread policy of regular anti-inflammatory therapy

with aminosalicylates. Many gastroenterologists are now using aminosalicylates as chemopreventive agents as the evidence for their benefit is mounting and cannot be ignored [21].

Data are also emerging on the chemopreventive potential of other agents in IBD such as ursodeoxycholic acid in PSC patients, folate, and calcium. These have recently been reviewed but more studies are needed to fully define their role [22].

Initial worries about immunosuppressants such as azathioprine and mercaptopurine leading to an increased CRC risk seem to be unfounded.

Miscellaneous

Gastrointestinal microflora have been implicated in the pathogenesis of IBD and colon tumorigenesis. In addition, colitis-associated cancer in interleukin 10 (IL-10) knockout mice has been reduced by 40% by feeding such mice with probiotics [23]. This area is interesting but requires further study before any conclusions can be reached.

A trend towards a preventive effect for smoking has been demonstrated in two studies but obviously smoking could not be recommended to patients [11,24]!

Conclusions

Perhaps the risk factors outlined above could be utilized in future to modify colonoscopic surveillance for individual patients according to their particular risk. This may allow a reduction in the number of colonoscopies needed in those at lower risk.

References

1 Eaden JA, Abrams K, Mayberry JF. The risk of colorectal cancer in ulcerative colitis: a meta-analysis. *Gut* 2001; **48**: 526–35.

2 Eaden JA, Mayberry JF. Guidelines for screening and surveillance of asymptomatic colorectal cancer in patients with inflammatory bowel disease. *Gut* 2002; **51**: v10–12

3 Bernstein CN, Blanchard JF, Kliewer E, Wajda A. Cancer risk in patients with inflammatory bowel disease: a population based study. *Cancer* 2001; **91**: 854–62.

4 Gillen CD, Walmsley RS, Prior P, Andrews HA, Allan RN. Ulcerative colitis and Crohn's disease: a comparison of the colorectal cancer risk in extensive colitis. *Gut* 1994; **35**: 1590–2.

5 Langholz E, Munkholm P, Davidsen M, Binder V. Colorectal cancer risk and mortality in patients with ulcerative colitis. *Gastroenterology* 1992; **103**: 1444–51.

6 Ekbom A, Helmick C, Zack M, Adami HO. Ulcerative colitis and colorectal cancer: a population-based study. *N Engl J Med* 1990; **323**: 1228–33.

7 Soetniko RM, Lin OS, Heidenreich PA, Young HS, Blackstone MO. Increased risk of colorectal neoplasia in patients with primary sclerosing cholangitis and ulcerative colitis: a meta-analysis. *Gastrointest Endosc* 2002; **56**: 48–54.

8 Loftus EV Jr, Aguilar HI, Sandborn WJ, *et al.* Risk of colorectal neoplasia in patients with primary sclerosing cholangitis and ulcerative colitis following orthotopic liver transplantation. *Hepatology* 1998; **27**: 685–90.

9 Nuako KW, Ahlquist DA, Mahoney DW, *et al.* Familial predisposition for colorectal cancer in chronic ulcerative colitis: a case–control study. *Gastroenterology* 1998; **115**: 1079–83.

10 Askling J, Dickman PW, Karlen P, *et al.* Colorectal cancer rates among first-degree relatives of patients with inflammatory bowel disease: a population-based study. *Lancet* 2001; **357**: 262–6.

11 Rutter M, Saunders B, Wilkinson K, *et al.* Severity of inflammation is a risk factor for colorectal neoplasia in ulcerative colitis. *Gastroenterology* 2004; **126**: 451–9.

12 Connell WR, Sheffield JP, Kamm MA, *et al.* Lower gastrointestinal malignancy in Crohn's disease. *Gut* 1994; **35**: 347–52.

13 Blackstone MO, Riddell RH, Rogers G, Levin B. Dysplasia-associated lesion or mass (DALM) detected by colonoscopy in long-standing ulcerative colitis: an indication for colectomy. *Gastroenterology* 1981; **80**: 366–74.

14 Rutter MD, Saunders BP, Wilkinson KH, *et al.* Cancer surveillance in longstanding ulcerative colitis: endoscopic appearances help predict cancer risk. *Gut* 2004; **53**: 1813–6.

15 Bernstein CN, Shanahan F, Weinstein WM. Are we telling patients the truth about surveillance colonoscopy in ulcerative colitis? *Lancet* 1994; **343**: 71–4.

16 Ullman T, Croog V, Harpaz N, Sachar DB, Itzkowitz S. Progression of flat low-grade dysplasia to advanced neoplasia in patients with ulcerative colitis. *Gastroenterology* 2003; **125**: 1311–9.

17 Lim CH, Dixon MF, Vail A, *et al.* Ten year follow up of ulcerative colitis patients with and without low grade dysplasia. *Gut* 2003; **52**: 1127–32.

18 Lashner BA, Provencher KS, Seidner DL, Knesebeck A, Brzezinski A. The effect of folic acid supplementation on the risk for cancer or dysplasia in ulcerative colitis. *Gastroenterology* 1997; **112**: 29–32.

19 Jess T, Winther KV, Munkholm P, Langholz E, Binder V. Intestinal and extra-intestinal cancer in Crohn's disease: follow-up of a population-based cohort in Copenhagen County, Denmark. *Aliment Pharmacol Ther* 2004; **19**: 287–93.

20 Rubio CA, Befrits R, Ljung T, Jaramillo E, Slezak P. Colorectal carcinoma in ulcerative colitis is decreasing in Scandinavian countries. *Anticancer Res* 2001; **21**: 2921–4.

21 Eaden JA. Aminosalicylates for the chemoprevention of colorectal cancer in patients with inflammatory bowel disease. *Semin Inflamm Bowel Dis* 2004; **3**: 1–7.

22 Croog VJ, Ullman TA, Itzkowitz SH. Chemoprevention of colorectal cancer in ulcerative colitis. *Int J Colorectal Dis* 2003; **18**: 392–400.

23 O'Mahony L, Feeney M, O'Halloran S, *et al.* Probiotic impact on microbial flora, inflammation and tumour development in IL-10 knockout mice. *Aliment Pharmacol Ther* 2001; **15**: 1219–25.

24 Pinczowski D, Ekbom A, Baron J, Yuen J, Adami HO. Risk factors for colorectal cancer in patients with ulcerative colitis: a case–control study. *Gastroenterology* 1994; **107**: 117–20.

Common Clinical Challenges: Beyond the Text Book

52 What to do with dysplasia, DALMs, and adenomas

MATT RUTTER

LEARNING POINTS

Dysplasia, DALMs, and adenomas

- Most dysplastic lesions are macroscopically detectable

- Endoscopic resectability of dysplastic masses determines prognosis – terminology is less important

- Expert histologic assessment is crucial – a second opinion is often advisable

- The prognosis of low grade dysplasia is uncertain, but may not be as bad as previously suspected

Introduction

The management of dysplasia in colitis is controversial. There are no randomized, controlled trials to assist the clinician, and most of the data on which decisions are based have come from retrospective studies subject to bias. The natural history of dysplasia is poorly understood, and often curtailed by surgery or endoscopic resection. Review of the literature is also hampered by evolving definitions for dysplasia-associated lesions/masses (DALMs) and by the reclassification of colorectal dysplasia in colitis in 1983 [1].

Nevertheless, when faced with a histology report describing dysplasia in colitis, the clinician has to make an urgent and important decision either to advise an immediate and life-changing panproctocolectomy or to continue surveillance, potentially putting the patient at risk of a fatal colorectal cancer.

Reassuringly, recent data have provided us with a greater understanding of colorectal dysplasia, allowing a more rational approach to dysplasia management (Fig. 52.1).

Dysplasia proximal to colitic extent

It is well established that dysplastic lesions detected proximal to the extent of colitis can safely be considered to be sporadic adenomas, resected endoscopically, and the patient placed on standard non-colitic adenoma surveillance protocols [2,3].

Dysplasia within an area of colitis

Two important steps should be taken before a management decision is made for a patient with dysplasia.

Step 1 – review histology

The histologic diagnosis and grading of dysplasia in colitis is subjective. It can be extremely difficult to discriminate between dysplastic changes and regenerative changes of inflammation. Studies have demonstrated high levels of interobserver variation, even amongst experts [4]. Performing surveillance colonoscopies during remission, thereby minimizing inflammatory changes (but without undue delay of the surveillance procedure), can aid discrimination. Nevertheless, the first step in the management of dysplasia should be to have the specimen reviewed by a second experienced histopathologist.

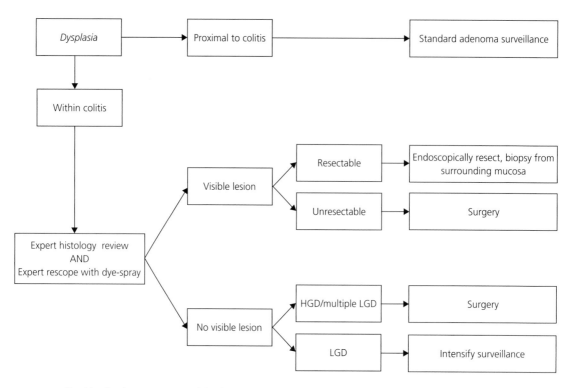

FIG 52.1 Algorithm for the management of dysplasia in colitis. HGD, high grade dysplasia; LGD, low grade dysplasia.

Step 2 – repeat colonoscopy

If dysplasia has been confirmed, the colonoscopy should be repeated by a colonoscopist experienced in colitis surveillance. A careful examination with pancolonic dye spraying should be performed where possible, as there is evidence from prospective trials that this increases the detection of synchronous dysplastic lesions [5,6]. Dye spraying also aids delineation of dysplastic areas, reducing the chance of incomplete excision of lesions.

Once these two steps have been performed, the clinician is in a position to make a more evidence-based decision on optimal dysplasia management.

Dysplastic masses

Contrary to popular belief, the majority of dysplastic lesion in colitis are macroscopically visible, although the appearance can be varied and subtle [7,8]. Early retrospective studies suggested that patients with such lesions carried a high risk of cancer, and colectomy has been advocated [2]. However, more recent prospective studies have demon-

strated that many lesions can be endoscopically resected [9,10]. One long-term follow-up study showed that although just over 50% of patients with endoscopically resected dysplastic lesions in UC developed further lesions, this incidence was no higher than that of non-colitic patients with sporadic adenomas and only one cancer occurred (in a patient with established primary sclerosing cholangitis) [11].

Categorization of dysplastic masses into DALMs, adenoma-like masses, and sporadic adenomas is arbitrary as there are no clear-cut endoscopic, histologic, or immunohistochemical discriminators. Thus, ultimately, the key factor for management of a dysplastic mass is whether the lesion can be removed endoscopically in its entirety. Dye spraying aids delineation of the lesion edge, and biopsies should always be taken from around the resected margin to ensure there is no residual dysplastic tissue. Where endoscopic resection is complete, the prognosis is excellent [7,10,11]. However, surgery is mandated for lesions that cannot be endoscopically resected as such lesions usually harbor malignancy [7].

Endoscopically invisible dysplasia

Dysplasia that is endoscopically invisible even after dye spraying is relatively rare, and needs to be discriminated from the clinical scenario of dysplasia being detected in an apparently random (non-targeted) biopsy, but where in reality the biopsy was targeted towards a visible lesion not documented on the endoscopy report. This demonstrates the importance of careful documentation of all surveillance biopsies and, where doubt exists, pancolonic dye spraying may help clarify whether a visible lesion is present.

Where genuinely endoscopically invisible dysplasia does occur, it poses an additional problem for the clinician as it cannot be reliably resected endoscopically. Clinical management mainly depends on the grade of dysplasia and its natural history.

High grade dysplasia

Many studies have reported a high incidence of colorectal cancer being discovered at colectomy performed for high grade dysplasia, or developing over a relatively short time-frame in patients declining surgery. Bernstein et al.'s [12] review of 10 prospective UC surveillance studies reported a 42% cancer risk at immediate colectomy. These data are compelling evidence for the detection of endoscopically invisible high grade dysplasia being an indication for immediate panproctocolectomy.

Low grade dysplasia

The natural history and management of low grade dysplasia is more controversial. This is in part because of the histologic difficulties distinguishing between true dysplasia and regenerative changes, with consequent wide variation in its reported incidence. Histologic review by an expert pathologist is important to reduce the risk of over-reporting of dysplasia.

Bernstein et al.'s [12] review reported that colorectal cancer was present in the surgical specimen of 19% of patients with low grade dysplasia undergoing immediate colectomy. Furthermore, 16–29% of patients with untreated low grade dysplasia progressed to DALM, high grade dysplasia, or cancer. On the basis of these and similar data [3], many centers advocate panproctocolectomy after the detection of low grade dysplasia. However, more recent studies have reported a more favorable prognosis, with progression to either high grade dysplasia or cancer occurring in 3.3–10.3% of patients at 10 years' follow-up, and have advocated continued surveillance [13,14].

On balance, provided the colon has been carefully re-examined by an experienced colonoscopist using pancolonic dye spray, intensified surveillance appears to be a reasonable management strategy, although it is prudent to discuss the option of prophylactic colectomy with the patient. The detection of multiple synchronous or metachronous areas of colorectal dysplasia should perhaps sway the clinician towards performing a colectomy. Additional considerations include other risk factors for cancer such as primary sclerosing cholangitis, the patient's age, and comorbidity.

Conclusions

The management of colorectal dysplasia in colitis remains controversial. However, recent data have improved our understanding of its natural history, and recent improvements in endoscopic detection and polypectomy techniques now permit more patients to avoid colectomy. Terminology for dysplastic masses such as DALMs are unhelpful and may distort clinical management; endoscopic resectability is the key factor in decision making. Any management decision should be postponed until expert histologic and colonoscopic reassessment has been performed, and patients' other risk factors and wishes need to be taken into consideration.

References

1 Riddell RH, Goldman H, Ransohoff DF, et al. Dysplasia in inflammatory bowel disease: standardized classification with provisional clinical applications. *Hum Pathol* 1983; **14**: 931–68.

2 Blackstone MO, Riddell RH, Rogers BH, Levin B. Dysplasia-associated lesion or mass (DALM) detected by colonoscopy in long-standing ulcerative colitis: an indication for colectomy. *Gastroenterology* 1981; **80**: 366–74.

3 Connell WR, Lennard-Jones JE, Williams CB, et al. Factors affecting the outcome of endoscopic surveillance for cancer in ulcerative colitis [see comments]. *Gastroenterology* 1994; **107**: 934–44.

4 Melville DM, Jass JR, Morson BC, et al. Observer study of the grading of dysplasia in ulcerative colitis: comparison with clinical outcome. *Hum Pathol* 1989; **20**: 1008–14.

5 Kiesslich R, Fritsch J, Holtmann M, et al. Methylene blue-aided chromoendoscopy for the detection of intraepithelial neoplasia and colon cancer in ulcerative colitis. *Gastroenterology* 2003; **124**: 880–8.

6 Rutter MD, Saunders BP, Schofield G, et al. Pancolonic indigo carmine dye spraying for the detection of dysplasia in ulcerative colitis. *Gut* 2004; **53**: 256–60.

7 Rutter MD, Saunders BP, Wilkinson KH, *et al.* Most dysplasia in ulcerative colitis is visible at colonoscopy. *Gastrointest Endosc* 2004; **60**: 334–9.

8 Morson BC, Pang LS. Rectal biopsy as an aid to cancer control in ulcerative colitis. *Gut* 1967; **8**: 423–34.

9 Engelsgjerd M, Farraye FA, Odze RD. Polypectomy may be adequate treatment for adenoma-like dysplastic lesions in chronic ulcerative colitis [see comments]. *Gastroenterology* 1999; **117**: 1288–94.

10 Rubin PH, Friedman S, Harpaz N, *et al.* Colonoscopic polypectomy in chronic colitis: conservative management after endoscopic resection of dysplastic polyps. *Gastroenterology* 1999; **117**: 1295–300.

11 Odze RD, Farraye FA, Hecht JL, Hornick JL. Long-term follow-up after polypectomy treatment for adenoma-like dysplastic lesions in ulcerative colitis. *Clin Gastroenterol Hepatol* 2004; **2**: 534–41.

12 Bernstein CN, Shanahan F, Weinstein WM. Are we telling patients the truth about surveillance colonoscopy in ulcerative colitis? *Lancet* 1994; **343**: 71–4.

13 Lim CH, Dixon MF, Vail A, *et al.* Ten year follow up of ulcerative colitis patients with and without low grade dysplasia. *Gut* 2003; **52**: 1127–32.

14 Rubio CA, Befrits R. Low-grade dysplasia in flat mucosa in ulcerative colitis. *Gastroenterology* 2004; **126**: 1494–5.

Part 5 Managing IBD Outside the Gut

53 Pyoderma gangrenosum

ANA PAULA CUNHA & FERNANDO TAVARELA VELOSO

LEARNING POINTS

Pyoderma gangrenosum

- Pyoderma gangrenosum occurs in 1–2% of patients with IBD

- It is a painful, nodular lesion that rapidly enlarges and ulcerates

- The clinical course is usually independent of the underlying IBD and colectomy is rarely beneficial

- Corticosteroids are generally effective, but cyclosporine is also a good therapeutic option when systemic steroids are contraindicated or unsuccessful

- Infliximab has emerged recently as the most potent therapy

Introduction

Pyoderma gangrenosum (PG) is an uncommon, idiopathic, autoimmune-mediated inflammatory condition, characterized by ulcerative skin lesions (Fig. 53.1), affecting 1–2% of patients with IBD [1].

The most prevalent clinical variant is classic PG, which is characterized by the occurrence of nodules and pustules that rapidly enlarge and ulcerate. Histopathology usually shows signs of chronic ulceration and a neutrophilic vascular reaction infiltrating the dermis. Because there is no specific test, the diagnosis can be difficult, only being established when the clinical and histopathologic pictures are consistent with PG, and other pustular or ulcerative dermatoses have been excluded. Most patients have an associated systemic disease, generally autoimmune inflammatory

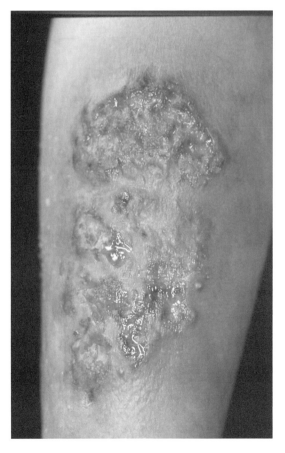

FIG 53.1 Typical ulcerative skin lesion seen in pyoderma gangrenosum.

conditions, such as IBD, seronegative arthritis, and connective tissue disorders, or hematological problems, such as myelodysplastic and lymphoproliferative diseases [2].

Management of PG continues to be a therapeutic challenge and usually requires aggressive local and systemic therapy. The identification and control of the underlying systemic disease is also extremely important.

In early or mild forms of PG, local wound care and topical agents are beneficial. However, severe disease shows a minimal response to local treatment, and systemic therapies, mainly antibiotics and immunomodulators, are required.

Many reasons make it difficult to create protocols for the management of PG, such as the differences between patients, the lack of randomized studies, and the complexity of the pathogenic mechanisms involved, which are not yet well defined.

Topical treatment

Topical treatment used to be limited to wound care and local steroids. However, several topical drugs have been described recently as being effective [3].

Corticosteroids

Successful treatment with topical and intralesional injection of corticosteroids has been described for many years [3].

Tacrolimus (FK 506)

Because of its lipophilic and hydrophobic structure, this potent immunosuppressant agents, which act by calcineurin inhibition, penetrate the ulcer-surrounding tissue resulting in a good topical effect. Tacrolimus, as a 0.03% or 0.1% ointment, is described as being effective [4].

Nicotine

Topical nicotine, used both as a cream or gum, is reportedly effective in PG [5].

Collagen matrices

Autologous or heterologous collagen matrices work by creating a scaffold for fibroblastic proliferation and production of new collagen, as well as for aggregation of platelets and coagulation factors to promote hemostasis. Some case reports suggest these matrices as a treatment option in PG [6].

Surgery

Although local surgery is generally best avoided, some patients have been successfully treated with skin grafts while under immunosuppressive therapy [7].

Systemic treatment

Immunosuppressive therapies including systemic steroids and cyclosporine have been, until recently, the most commonly used treatments. However, within the last few months, the only placebo-controlled trial to have been undertaken in patients with PG has confirmed the efficacy of infliximab, and this is likely to become first-line therapy (Fig. 53.2) [8, 9, 10].

Corticosteroids

High-dose systemic glucocorticoids have historically been the mainstay of PG therapy, because of their potent immunosuppressive and anti-inflammatory properties; in some cases, pulsed methylprednisolone therapy results in rapid regression of lesions. However, serious side-effects are associated with prolonged steroid therapy (see Chapter 9), and alternative or adjunctive therapies must always be considered. As soon as disease control has been achieved, the introduction of a corticosteroid-sparing agent is recommended (see below).

Cyclosporine

When systemic steroids are contraindicated or unsuccessful, cyclosporine has until recently been the best choice. Nephrotoxicity and hypertension are its main adverse effects. PG usually responds to initial oral doses greater than 3 mg/kg/day, with maintenance therapy at 3 mg/kg/day, generally for no more than 10 months. Significant improvement is expected within 3 months of initiation of therapy. Some patients may require low-dose maintenance therapy, but others tolerate complete withdrawal of the drug [2].

Other systemic agents, used either as monotherapy or as steroid-sparing drugs, have been used (see below). However, most of them provide incomplete long-term responses or are associated with important side-effects after chronic administration; these include an increased incidence of infections and lymphoproliferative diseases.

Azathioprine

Azathioprine is generally safe when used carefully and is well-tolerated, although it can cause myelosuppression

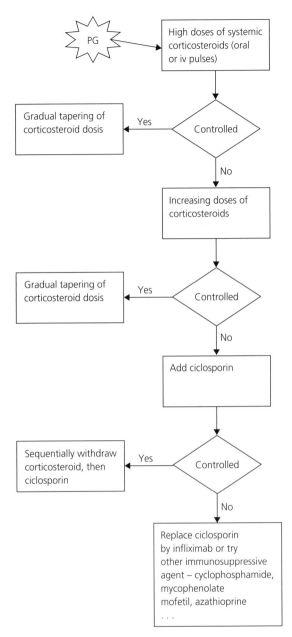

FIG 53.2 Systemic treatment algorithm for pyoderma gangrenosum. PG, pyoderma gangrenosum.

and hepatotoxicity. The usual dose of azathioprine is 2–3 mg/kg/day. It can be used in PG, usually after other therapies have failed and in combination with systemic steroids [2].

Mycophenolate mofetil

This ethyl-ester of mycophenolic acid selectively inhibits inosine monophosphate dehydrogenase in the purine synthesis pathway. It has potent cytostatic effects on both T and B lymphocytes. The usual dose in recalcitrant PG is 2 g/day, generally in addition to systemic steroids or cyclosporine. Known side-effects include gastrointestinal, genitourinary, and neurologic disturbances [9].

Tacrolimus (FK 506)

Successful use of tacrolimus in steroid- and cyclosporine-resistant PG has been reported with doses of 0.1–0.3 mg/kg/day [10], but careful monitoring of blood levels is essential if the risk of serious side-effects is to be minimized.

Cyclophosphamide

Cyclophosphamide is an alkylating agent with potentially serious side-effects, such as leukopenia and thrombocytopenia. The recommended dose is 2 mg/kg/day, either orally with gradual tapering, or iv pulse dosing [11].

Infliximab

Recent studies suggest that infliximab, 5 mg/kg as an intravenous infusion, at 0, 2, and 8 weeks, is safe and effective in IBD-associated pyoderma gangrenosum [8,9,10] and is now the drug of choice. The more common side-effects are infusion related and cutaneous reactions [1,12,13] (see Chapters 17–19).

Other systemic therapeutic approaches

High-dose immunoglobulin

Intravenous immunoglobulins are increasingly used in inflammatory and autoimmune diseases. In PG, clinical benefit with 0.4 g/kg/day for 5 days has been described [14].

Colchicine

Antimitotic, anti-inflammatory, and immunomodulating properties of colchicine may account for its beneficial effects in PG. It inhibits polymerization of tubulin dimers to microtubules and interferes with neutrophil chemotaxis and phagocytosis. At low doses, generally 1–2 mg/day, this drug is effective and well tolerated by most patients [15].

Dapsone

Dapsone has been effective in a long list of inflammatory

cutaneous diseases. It interferes with the cytotoxic system and inhibits both lysosomal enzyme activity and generation of 5-lipoxygenase products in polymorphonuclear leukocytes. The main adverse effects are hemolysis and methemoglobinemia, particularly in patients with glucose-6-dehydrogenase deficiency and when used in doses greater than 50 mg/day.

Conclusions

No specific therapy is consistently effective in patients with PG. The response to different drugs is unpredictable and some patients have disease refractory to all treatment. However, with the emergence of newer drugs, particularly infliximab, we now have more therapeutic options for recalcitrant cases.

References

1 Regueiro M, Valentine J, Plevy S, *et al.* Infliximab for treatment of pyoderma gangrenosum associated with inflammatory bowel disease. *Am J Gastroenterol* 2003; **98**: 1821–6.

2 Vidal D, Puig L, Gilaberte M, Alomar A. Review of 26 cases of classical pyoderma gangrenosum: clinical and therapeutic features. *J Dermatol Treat* 2004; **15**: 146–52.

3 Wenzel J, Gerdsen R, Phillipp-Dormston W, Bieber T, Uerlich M. Topical treatment of pyoderma gangrenosum. *Dermatology* 2002; **205**: 221–3.

4 Khurrum M, Marquez H, Nogueras J, Weiss EG, Wexner SD. Topical tacrolimus (FK 506) in the treatment of recalcitrant parastomal pyoderma gangrenosum associated with Crohn's disease: report of two cases. *Colorectal Dis* 2004; **6**: 250–3.

5 Patel GK, Rhodes JR, Evans B, Holt PJA. Sucessful treatment of pyoderma gangrenosum with topical 0.5 nicotine cream. *J Dermatol Treat* 2004; **15**: 122–5.

6 Farris DR, Schutzer PJ, Don PC, Silverberg NB, Weinberg JM. Resolution of pyoderma gangrenosum after therapy with lyophilized bovine collagen matrix. *Dermatology* 2003; **206**: 284–5.

7 Vereecken P, Wautrecht JC, De-Dobbeller G, Heenen M. A case of pyoderma gangrenosum stabilized with lymecycline, topical benzoyl peroxide and treated by autograft. *Dermatology* 1997; **195**: 50–1.

8 Grange F, Djilali-Bouzina F, Weiss AM, *et al.* Corticosteroid-resistant pyoderma gangrenosum associated with Crohn's disease: rapid cure with infliximab. *Dermatology* 2002; **205**: 278–80.

9 Lee MR, Cooper AJ. Mycophenolate mofetil in pyoderma gangrenosum. *J Dermatol Treat* 2004; **15**: 303–7.

10 Weichert G, Sauder DN. Efficacy of tacrolimus (FK 506) in idiopatic treatment-resistant pyoderma gangrenosum. *J Am Acad Dermatol* 1998; **39**: 648–50.

11 Reynoso-von-Drateln C. Intravenous cyclophosphamide pulses in pyoderma gangrenosum: an open trial. *J Rheumatol* 1997; **24**: 689.

12 Zaccagna A, Baertone A, Puiatti P, *et al.* Anti-tumor necrosis factor alfa monoclonal antibody (infliximab) for the treatment of pyoderma gangrenosum associated with Crohn's disease. *Eur J Dermatol* 2003; **13**: 258–60.

13 Brooklyn TN, Shetty A, Bowden J, *et al.* Infliximab for the treatment of pyoderma gangrenosum: a randomised, double blind placebo controlled trial. *Gut* 2005; **54** (Suppl 2): A23.

14 Dirschka T, Kastner U, Behrens S. Successful treatment pyoderma gangrenosum with intravenous human immunoglobulin. *J Am Acad Dermatol* 1998; **39**: 789–90.

15 Kontochristopoulos GJ, Stavropoulos PG, Gregoriou S, Zakopoulou N. Treatment of pyoderma gangrenosum with low-dose colchicine. *Dermatology* 2004; **209**: 233–6.

Part 5 Managing IBD Outside the Gut

54 Arthritides – helping the joints without harming the gut

HORACE WILLIAMS & TIM ORCHARD

> **LEARNING POINTS**
>
> **Arthritides**
>
> - Arthritis is the most common extraintestinal manifestation of IBD
>
> - Treatment is largely symptomatic, but because of their adverse effects on the gut, NSAIDs should be used sparingly
>
> - Large joint arthritis usually responds to treatment of the underlying IBD
>
> - Small joint polyarthritis is more problematic and may require long-term treatment with immuno-modulators, including methotrexate and infliximab

Introduction

Joint problems are the most common extraintestinal manifestation of IBD. Two clinical patterns are recognized: axial disease and peripheral arthritis. Ankylosing spondylitis occurs in 3–6% of patients with IBD; radiologic evidence of isolated sacroiliitis, which may be asymptomatic, is more common (up to 43%) [1]. Peripheral arthritis affects between 5 and 20% of IBD patients and has been classified into two types [2]. Type 1 is a pauciarticular arthritis, usually associated with *active* bowel disease (and hence responds to treatment of the bowel disease), while type 2 is a polyarthritis, which tends to run a course independent of the bowel disease. In some patients the arthritis may be more debilitating than the underlying gut disease, and it often requires separate treatment.

Peripheral arthritis associated with IBD is not erosive or deforming, and so the aims of treatment are to gain symptomatic control without upsetting the underlying bowel disease. In axial disease symptom control is important, but minimizing disease progression is also important. Unfortunately, many of the pharmacologic interventions available have gastrointestinal side-effects and must be used with care. We discuss the current treatment options for IBD joint disease, the newer agents available, and promising developments for the future. It is recommended that both a gastroenterologist and a rheumatologist manage all patients with significant joint disease (Table 54.1).

TABLE 54.1 Clinical features of IBD arthritis.

Peripheral arthritis	
Type 1	<5 joints affected
	Parallels bowel disease
	Attacks <10 weeks' duration
Type 2	≥5 joints affected
	Independent of bowel disease
	Duration of months to years
Axial disease	
Ankylosing spondylitis	Identical to idiopathic AS
	Usually unrelated to bowel disease
Sacroiliitis	May be asymptomatic

AS, ankylosing spondylitis.

Treatment algorithm for arthritis associated with IBD[1]	
1 nd line	• Physical therapies • Intra-articular joint injection • Simple analgesia
2 nd line	• NSAIDs if gut disease quiescent (with caution) • Sulfasalazine • Mesalazine, (Pentasa® preparation) (possible benefit) • Methotrexate (possible benefit)
3 rd line	• Infliximab

FIG 54.1 Treatment algorithm for arthritis associated with IBD. COX-2 inhibitors considered elsewhere.

Physical therapies

Physical therapies are of particular importance to patients with ankylosing spondylitis, the intention being to prevent deformities of the spine and subsequent respiratory compromise and disability (Fig. 54.1) [3]. Exercise programs should emphasize deep breathing, spinal exercises, and swimming. They have no effects on the bowel. There is little evidence to help predict which patients will develop progressive ankylosing spondylitis, and spinal exercises should probably be recommended to all patients who have evidence of axial disease (sacroiliitis), irrespective of whether it appears to be progressive or is symptomatic. Conversely, exercises may be helpful in patients with back pain who are HLA-B27 positive, even in the absence of positive spinal imaging.

The management of peripheral arthritis may involve resting the affected joint and using a walking stick or splint to relieve the pressure on it. An exercise regimen should still be instituted, however, to maintain a normal range of movement and prevent muscle wasting.

Analgesia and NSAIDS

Relief of pain is the mainstay of treatment for all forms of IBD-associated arthritis, but due to the potential effects of non-steroidal anti-inflammatory drugs (NSAIDs) on the gut, simple analgesics such as acetaminophen (paracetamol) should be used if possible. Compound analgesics such as co-dydramol may be used if required, but compounds containing codeine may cause constipation, and thereby exacerbate difficult distal UC.

NSAIDs are the initial treatment of choice in idiopathic ankylosing spondylitis and are effective in peripheral arthritis, but there is evidence that they cause exacerbations of IBD and consequent hospitalization [4,5]. Bonner *et al.* [6], following their study of outpatients, have suggested that patients with quiescent or mildly active IBD are less susceptible to flares caused by NSAIDs than those with already active disease.

While NSAIDs are not contraindicated in IBD patients, they should be avoided in type 1 arthritis as it is usually self-limiting and responds to treatment of the bowel disease. They may be used with caution in axial disease and type 2 peripheral arthritis, but should be stopped if the bowel disease worsens.

The use of COX-2 inhibitors in patients with IBD is considered in Chapter 37, but may not confer any advantage over non-selective NSAIDs.

Corticosteroids: intra-articular and systemic

Intra-articular injection of steroid and a local anesthetic such as lidocaine is effective in the treatment of peripheral arthritis [1,3] and is probably under-used. It can be of particular use in patients with type 1 arthritis to alleviate symptoms until their joints improve with treatment of their bowel disease. Injection of the sacroiliac joints under imaging guidance may benefit patients with ankylosing spondylitis refractory to other therapy [7], but the benefit may be short-lived. Such local treatments do not appear detrimental to the gut.

Arthritis alone is not normally an indication for systemic corticosteroids but these may be indicated for concurrent IBD, and may be tried if other treatments fail in persistent arthritis. In this case, smaller doses than those used for treating IBD may be effective (e.g. prednisolone 10–15 mg). Ankylosing spondylitis usually responds poorly to oral steroids [7].

Sulfasalazine and mesalazine

Early trials of sulfasalazine suggested a beneficial effect on both axial and peripheral disease but later, larger studies have shown responses in peripheral arthritis only [8,9].

Sulfasalazine remains the second-line drug of choice in active spondyloarthropathy, and can also be used to treat UC and Crohn's colitis.

The efficacy of sulfasalazine in arthritis has been ascribed to the sulfapyridine moiety of the drug and neither the Asacol® (Procter and Gamble) nor the Salofalk® (Dr Falk Pharma) preparation of mesalazine (5-ASA) has been shown to have positive effects on joint disease [10]. The possibility of a change from mesalazine to sulfasalazine in IBD patients with arthritis has therefore been suggested [1]. However, trials of the Pentasa® (Ferring) preparation in spondyloarthropathy have shown statistically significant improvements in clinical, physical, and laboratory measures of joint disease activity, indicating that it is a valid treatment option [11]. It has been hypothesized that the release of Pentasa in the proximal small bowel (the other two preparations being released more distally) could have a role in the apparent difference in their efficacy in relieving joint symptoms.

However, these trials have been small, and further evaluation is required to determine whether the differences in efficacy between sulfasalazine and between the different 5-ASA compounds is related to their actions in the gut or in the joint. In the meantime, an empirical change of 5-ASA compound to sulfasalazine or Pentasa in patients with severe joint disease would appear reasonable.

Methotrexate, azathioprine, and cyclosporine

While methotrexate has become a first-line treatment for rheumatoid arthritis, and is also used in IBD, evidence for its use in the spondyloarthropathies is limited. Several open label trials have suggested that there may be some benefit; other placebo-controlled studies have been less positive [7]. Nonetheless, it is still used by many rheumatologists in this context. It remains an option for the treatment of active IBD and ankylosing spondylitis although data on its efficacy are not available. In patients with active gut disease (particularly Crohn's disease) requiring immune suppression together with severe arthritis, methotrexate may be the immunosuppressant of choice ahead of azathioprine, but again this is an empirical approach and is not backed by trial evidence.

Azathioprine and cyclosporine are widely used for the treatment of IBD but there is no evidence as to their efficacy in peripheral arthritis or spondyloarthropathy.

Infliximab

The use of infliximab in the treatment of Crohn's disease and ankylosing spondylitis has become well established, and there are now studies to support its efficacy in the management of spondyloarthropathy associated with Crohn's disease.

A recent trial evaluated infliximab in 24 such patients who received repeated infusions for a period of 12–18 months [12]. Infliximab significantly improved both gastrointestinal and articular symptoms; peripheral arthritis, axial disease, and enthesitis were all effectively controlled. In the control group, treatment was with standard Crohn's therapy including steroids and azathioprine. These improved bowel disease and peripheral arthritis (especially type 1) but had little effect on axial and enthesitic pain.

In patients with active Crohn's disease and arthritis, including axial disease which can be difficult to treat, infliximab is an attractive option. Whether it will have long-term effects on the progression of spondylitis has yet to be investigated.

Possible future treatments

Thalidomide

Several trials of thalidomide have suggested benefits in the treatment of active, refractory Crohn's disease; in the largest, 14/22 patients who completed the trial had a significant decrease in the Crohn's disease activity index [13]. In a study of 30 male patients with refractory ankylosing spondylitis, 80% of the 26 patients who completed the trial had a positive clinical response [14].

Thalidomide may in future have a part to play in managing patients with active joint and bowel disease uncontrolled by other agents, although its toxicity and the side-effect of fatigue are likely to limit its use.

Bisphosphonates

Intravenous pamidronate has recently been investigated as a treatment for ankylosing spondylitis. A Canadian controlled study [15] of 84 patients compared a 60-mg dose given monthly for 6 months with a 10-mg dose (placebo was not used as pamidronate is recognized to cause transient arthralgia and myalgia after the initial dose which may compromise effective patient blinding). In the 60 mg group significant improvements were found in the commonly used indices of disease activity and functional ability.

Patients with enteropathic ankylosing spondylitis may benefit from bisphosphonate treatment in the future; a positive effect on reduced bone mineral density in IBD patients would also be expected.

Conclusions

The management of IBD-associated arthritis should begin with physiotherapy and simple analgesia. NSAIDs may be cautiously tried, but should be avoided in peripheral arthritis associated with active gut disease. They should be stopped at the earliest sign of worsening gastrointestinal symptoms. Intra-articular steroid injections may be effective; systemic steroid therapy is not usually required for arthritis alone.

The use of sulfasalazine is well established, but the Pentasa formulation of mesalazine may also have positive effects on spondyloarthritis as well as in IBD. There is inconclusive evidence for the use of methotrexate, but anecdotally it remains an option for the treatment of active IBD and arthritis.

Infliximab has potent effects in the treatment of active IBD, axial and peripheral arthritis.

Future treatments for the arthritides of IBD may include thalidomide for treatment-refractory cases, and bisphosphonates.

References

1 Fornaciari G, Salvarini C, Beltrami M, *et al.* Musculoskeletal manifestations in inflammatory bowel disease. *Can J Gastroenterol* 2001; **15**: 399–403.

2 Orchard TR, Wordsworth BP, Jewell DP. Peripheral arthropathies in inflammatory bowel disease: their articular distribution and natural history. *Gut* 1998; **42**: 387–91.

3 Levine JB, Lukawski-Trubish D. Extraintestinal considerations in inflammatory bowel disease. *Gastroenterol Clin North Am* 1995; **24**: 633–46.

4 Felder JB, Korelitz BI, Rajapakse R, *et al.* Effects of non-steroidal antiinflammatory drugs on inflammatory bowel disease: a case–control study. *Am J Gastroenterol* 2000; **95**: 1949–54.

5 Evans JM, McMahon AD, Murray FE, *et al.* Non-steroidal anti-inflammatory drugs are associated with emergency admission to hospital for colitis due to inflammatory bowel disease. *Gut* 1997; **40**: 619–22.

6 Bonner GF, Walczak M, Kitchen L, Bayona M. Tolerance of nonsteroidal anti-inflammatory drugs in patients with inflammatory bowel disease. *Am J Gastroenterol* 2000; **95**: 1946–8.

7 Dougados M, Dijkmans B, Khan M, *et al.* Conventional treatments for ankylosing spondylitis. *Ann Rheum Dis* 2002; **61**: 40–50.

8 Clegg DO, Reda DJ, Abdellatif M. Comparison of sulfasalazine and placebo for the treatment of axial and peripheral articular manifestations of the seronegative spondyloarthropathies: a Department of Veterans Affairs cooperative study. *Arthritis Rheum* 1999; **42**: 2325–9.

9 Dougados M, van der Linden S, Leirisalo-Repo M, *et al.* Sulfasalazine in the treatment of spondyloarthropathy: a randomised, multicenter, double-blind, placebo-controlled study. *Arthritis Rheum* 1995; **38**: 618–27.

10 Van Denderen JC, van der Horst-Bruinsma IE, Bezemer PD, Dijkmans BA. Efficacy and safety of mesalazine (Salofalk®) in an open study of 20 patients with ankylosing spondylitis. *J Rheumatol* 2003; **30**: 1558–60.

11 Thomson GT, Thomson BR, Thomson KS, Ducharme JS. Clinical efficacy of mesalamine in the treatment of the spondyloarthropathies. *J Rheumatol* 2000; **27**: 714–8.

12 Generini S, Giacomelli R, Fedi R, *et al.* Infliximab in spondyloarthropathy associated with Crohn's disease: an open study on the efficacy of inducing and maintaining remission of musculoskeletal and gut manifestations. *Ann Rheum Dis* 2004; **63**: 1664–9.

13 Ehrenpreis ED, Kane SV, Cohen LB, *et al.* Thalidomide therapy for patients with refractory Crohn's disease: an open-label trial. *Gastroenterology* 1999; **117**: 1271–7.

14 Huang F, Gu J, Zhao W, *et al.* One-year open-label trial of thalidomide in ankylosing spondylitis. *Arthritis Rheum* 2002; **47**: 249–54.

15 Maksymowych WP, Jhangri GS, Fitzgerald AA, *et al.* A six-month randomized, controlled, double-blind, dose-response comparison of intravenous pamidronate (60 mg versus 10 mg) in the treatment of non-steroidal anti-inflammatory drug-refractory ankylosing spondylitis. *Arthritis Rheum* 2002; **46**: 766–73.

Part 5 Managing IBD Outside the Gut

55 Prevention and treatment of osteoporosis

RICHARD MAKINS & JULIET COMPSTON

LEARNING POINTS

Osteoporosis

- Osteopenia and osteoporosis are common in IBD but not exclusively caused by steroids

- The risk of fracture is increased but in absolute terms is low

- Preventive measures include:
  - weight-bearing exercise
  - smoking cessation
  - control of the underlying IBD
  - minimizing the use of steroids
  - co-prescription of calcium and vitamin D supplements

- If treatment with bisphosphonates is unsuccessful, specialist advice should be sought

---

Introduction

Osteoporosis, as defined by the World Health Organization, is characterized by low bone mass and micro-architectural deterioration of bone tissue with a consequent increase in bone fragility and susceptibility to fracture [1]. Bone mineral density (BMD), measured by dual energy X-ray absorptiometry (DEXA), is expressed as the number of standard deviations (SD) above or below the mean BMD for young adults (T score) or the mean BMD for age-matched controls (Z score). Osteopenia is defined as a BMD T score between −1 and −2.5 SD and osteoporosis when the BMD

T score is lower than −2.5 SD [2]. With each SD decline in BMD, the subsequent risk of fracture increases between two- and threefold [3].

Skeletal mass accumulates during childhood, with peak bone mass being achieved in the third decade of life. Total bone mass is dependent on a combination of factors including genetics, physical activity, body weight, and diet. Ethnicity also has a role; people of African origin having a greater bone mass than those of European origin who, in turn, have a greater bone mass than Asians. After the menopause bone loss accelerates, with up to 15% being lost in the first 5 post-menopausal years, continuing at a rate of 0.5–1% per year thereafter.

Osteoporosis in IBD

The prevalence of osteopenia in patients with IBD is in the order of 40–50% with osteoporosis occurring in 2–30%. Several recent studies have documented a small increase in fracture risk in IBD.

A large case–control study from Denmark showed a 2.5-fold increased risk of fracture amongst women with Crohn's disease but failed to demonstrate any increased risk in men with Crohn's disease or in patients with UC. In addition, the observed fracture risk in female patients with Crohn's disease was seen to increase with increasing duration of steroid use [4].

In contrast, a large Canadian cohort study demonstrated similar fracture rates in patients with UC and Crohn's disease. This study, which looked at more than 6000 patients, found incidence rate ratios, compared with the healthy population, of 1.74 for spinal fractures, 1.59 for hip fractures, 1.33 for wrist and forearm fractures, and 1.25 for rib fractures. The incidence rate ratio for any fracture was 1.41 suggesting a 41% increased incidence of fractures occurring in all patients with IBD compared with the general population [5]. A further study, which utilized a large primary care database, confirmed an overall increase in fracture risk in IBD, particularly in patients with Crohn's disease and, in addition, highlighted that only 13% of patients who had already sustained a fracture were prescribed antifracture therapy [6]. Despite this, the absolute risk for the majority of patients remains low.

Risk factors

The pathogenesis of IBD-related osteoporosis may differ from that arising in the general population as a younger cohort is at risk and multiple contributory factors are involved. The prolonged use of oral glucocorticoids, ongoing systemic inflammation, malabsorption, vitamin D deficiency, malnutrition, and hypogonadism all potentially contribute to bone mineral loss [7].

Glucocorticoids lead to bone loss in a number of ways. A reduction in bone formation occurs by impairment of osteoblast activity, inhibition of insulin-like growth factor-1 (IGF-1) production, and reduction of circulating sex steroids. Increased bone destruction occurs via enhancement of osteoclast function and increased parathyroid hormone secretion. In addition, intestinal calcium absorption is reduced, an effect reversed by the administration of 1,25-dihydroxyvitamin D, while renal calcium excretion is increased.

Bone loss and associated increase in fracture risk occur rapidly following initiation of glucocorticoid therapy at *all* doses and increases in a dose-dependent fashion [8]. Fracture risk declines rapidly after cessation of therapy.

Disease activity is also likely to have a role as osteoclast function is promoted by circulating pro-inflammatory cytokines such as interleukins IL-1β and IL-6, and tumor necrosis factor α (TNF-α), thus reinforcing the need for the achievement of disease remission to inhibit bone loss.

Prevention

General measures
All patients should be encouraged to perform regular weight-bearing exercises, stop smoking, moderate their alcohol consumption, and ensure an adequate daily intake of calcium. This should be in the region of 1000–1500 mg (700 mg in 1 pint [568 mL] skimmed milk), which can be supplemented with 500–1000 mg of calcium if required.

Disease control
As the systemic inflammatory response maintains high levels of pro-inflammatory cytokines which promote inhibition of IGF-1, reduce appetite and enhance cachexia, and increase bone resorption, optimal disease control is vital to inhibit bone loss.

Timing of DEXA
Current recommendations are that postmenopausal women should have a BMD measurement at the menopause or when first diagnosed with IBD. For men aged over 50 years, BMD should be measured in all with Crohn's disease and those with UC who have received systemic steroids. Anyone experiencing a low trauma fracture or diagnosed with hypogonadism should also undergo BMD measurement [9].

When using oral glucocorticoids
The lowest dose of glucocorticoids should be used for the shortest possible duration and where possible non-systemic formulations utilized.

When receiving oral glucocorticoids all patients should also receive calcium and vitamin D concurrently. A recent Cochrane review update has confirmed the need for this co-prescription when a patient commences oral glucocorticoids [10]: the American College of Rheumatology recommends 800 units of vitamin D3 (cholecalciferol) daily. For glucocorticoid use for longer than 3 months, current recommendations suggest bone protection, with bisphosphonates, for all patients over 65 or those with a previous fragility fracture. In addition, patients younger than 65 years with a BMD T score of −1.5 or lower should receive treatment [11].

Vitamin D alone
Long-term oral supplementation with vitamin D alone has been shown to prevent bone loss in patients with Crohn's disease. In an Austrian study, 75 patients with Crohn's disease received either 1000 IU/day vitamin D for 1 year, or nothing. BMD increased significantly in those receiving supplements vs. controls, particularly if their baseline 25-hydroxyvitamin D levels were normal at enrollment [12].

TABLE 55.1 Prevention and treatment of osteoporosis in IBD.

General measures	Prevention	Treatment
Weight-bearing exercise	HRT or testosterone if hypogonadal	Bisphosphonates
Stop smoking		
Limited alcohol consumption	Prophylaxis of glucocorticoid-induced bone loss according to RCP guidelines [11]	Calcium and vitamin D
Ensure adequate calcium intake and vitamin D status		
Control underlying disease	Reduce dose of glucocorticoids to a minimum and use alternative formulations or alternative treatments if possible	Consider calcitonin, calcitriol, or raloxifene only as second-line option

RCP, Royal College of Physicians; HRT, hormone replacement therapy.

Hormone replacement therapy

The fracture risk in postmenopausal women is reduced with hormone replacement therapy (HRT) and this has also been demonstrated to reduce bone loss in women with IBD. In an open 2-year prospective study looking at 47 postmenopausal women with UC or Crohn's disease, HRT prevented bone loss regardless of IBD phenotype [13]. The risk–benefit ratio is discussed below.

Men with confirmed hypogonadism receiving glucocorticoids may benefit from testosterone replacement prior to initiation of other therapy although this has not been investigated in controlled studies.

Treatment

Once osteoporosis is diagnosed a range of stepwise treatment options exist. However, evidence for the treatment of IBD-associated osteoporosis is lacking and therefore current treatment recommendations can only be derived from data related to osteoporosis arising in the general population (Table 55.1).

Postmenopausal women

Bisphosphonates inhibit bone resorption. They can be administered orally (e.g. alendronate or risedronate) or as an intravenous infusion (e.g. pamidronate). The latter avoids potential poor mucosal absorption and the possibility of troublesome upper gastrointestinal side-effects. However, a recent, randomized, controlled trial has demonstrated oral alendronate to be well tolerated and safe in patients with Crohn's disease [14].

HRT is of proven benefit in reducing fracture risk in postmenopausal women in the general population. However, the return of menstruation and the increased risk of breast cancer and stroke make this an unattractive option for many women, and HRT is now regarded as a second-line option for the prevention and treatment of osteoporosis [15].

Raloxifene, a modulator of estrogen receptor function, does not promote breast cancer and may therefore be an alternative to traditional HRT, although there are no reports of its use in IBD.

Calcitonin acts by inhibiting bone resorption and can be administered by subcutaneous injection or nasal spray, but has not been used in IBD-related osteoporosis. Evidence for antifracture efficacy in postmenopausal osteoporosis is conflicting and the use of calcitonin is limited by its expense. Calcitriol, an active physiologic metabolite of vitamin D, increases intestinal absorption of calcium and can be used for the treatment of postmenopausal osteoporosis. There are no data relating its use in IBD-associated osteoporosis.

Premenopausal women and men

The absolute risk of fracture in premenopausal women and younger men remains low compared with older patients. As with postmenopausal women, bisphosphonates represent the mainstay of treatment in this group. However, bisphosphonates are contraindicated in pregnancy and should therefore be used with extreme caution in premenopausal women. As hypogonadism represents a risk factor for osteoporosis, hormone replacement should be considered in premenopausal women with prolonged amenorrhea and in men with biochemical evidence of hypogonadism.

Duration of therapy

BMD should be measured once every 2 years while on treatment. If there is no deterioration then treatment is usually continued for a minimum of 5 years but an alternative should be sought if the average annual bone loss exceeds 4%.

Conclusions

Patients with IBD, and in particular Crohn's disease, are at increased risk of osteoporosis and associated fractures compared with the general population, yet despite this the overall risk remains low. Uncontrolled disease activity and glucocorticoid use are key contributory factors. Preventative measures include lifestyle advice and cautious, limited use of glucocorticoids, with calcium and vitamin D supplementation. Following the diagnosis of osteoporosis treatment includes bisphosphonates and HRT.

References

1 Consensus development conference. Diagnosis, prophylaxis and treatment of osteoporosis. *Am J Med* 1993; **94**: 646–50.

2 WHO study group on assessment of fracture risk and its application to screening for post menopausal osteoporosis. *Assessment of fracture risk and its application to screening for post menopausal osteoporosis: report of a WHO study group* (WHO technical series 843). WHO, 1994.

3 Cummings SR, Black DM, Nevitt MC, *et al.* Bone density at various sites for prediction of hip fractures. *Lancet* 1993; **341**: 72–5.

4 Vestegaard P, Krogh K, Rejnmark L, *et al.* Fracture risk is increased in Crohn's disease but not in ulcerative colitis. *Gut* 2000; **15**: 993–1000.

5 Bernstein CN, Blanchard JF, Leslie W, *et al.* The incidence of fracture among patients with inflammatory bowel disease: a population-based cohort study. *Ann Intern Med* 2000; **133**: 795–9.

6 Van Staa TP, Cooper C, Brusse LS, *et al.* Inflammatory bowel disease and risk of fracture. *Gastroenterology* 2003; **125**: 1591–7.

7 Compston J. Osteoporosis in inflammatory bowel disease: therapy update. *Gut* 2003; **52**: 63–4.

8 Van Staa, TP, Leufkens HG, Abenheim L, *et al.* Use of oral corticosteroids and risk of fractures. *J Bone Miner Res* 2000; **15**: 993–1000.

9 AGA Technical Review on Osteoporosis in Gastrointestinal Diseases. *Gastroenterology* 2003; **124**: 795–841

10 Homik J, Suarez-Almazor ME, Shea B, *et al.* Calcium and vitamin D for corticosteroid-induced osteoporosis (Cochrane Review). *The Cochrane Library*, Issue 4, 2004. John Wiley & Sons, Ltd.

11 Working group collaboration of the Royal College of Physicians, the Bone and Tooth Society of Great Britain and the National Osteoporosis Society. *Glucocorticoid-induced osteoporosis. Guidelines for prevention and treatment.* The Lavenham Press, Suffcolk, 2002.

12 Vogelsang H, Ferenci P, Resch H, *et al.* Prevention of bone mineral loss in patients with Crohn's disease by long term oral vitamin D supplementation. *Eur J Gastroenterol Hepatol* 1995; **7**: 609–14.

13 Clements C, Compston JE, Evans WD, *et al.* Hormone replacement therapy prevents bone loss in patients with inflammatory bowel disease. *Gut* 1993; **34**: 1543–60.

14 Haderslev KV, Tjellesen L, Sorensen HA, *et al.* Alendronate increases lumbar spine bone mineral density in patients with Crohn's disease. *Gastroenterology* 2000; **119**: 639–46.

15 Chlebowski RT, Hendrix SL, Langer RD, *et al.* Influence of estrogen plus progestin on breast cancer and mammography in healthy postmenopausal women: the women's health initiative randomized trial. *JAMA* 2003; **289**: 3243–53.

56 Sclerosing cholangitis – what to do?

SUE CULLEN & ROGER CHAPMAN

LEARNING POINTS

Sclerosing cholangitis

- Magnetic resonance cholangiography is often sufficient to diagnose primary sclerosing cholangitis (PSC) and avoids the complications of endoscopic retrograde cholangiopancreatography (ERCP)

- Liver biopsy is not always necessary where typical features are present on cholangiography

- The evidence that ursodeoxycholic acid prevents progression of PSC is still poor but the suggestion that it may reduce the high risk of colonic cancer in these patients may become an indication for its use

---

Introduction

Primary sclerosing cholangitis (PSC) complicates approximately 2–5% of cases of UC. It is a progressive cholestatic liver disease characterized by concentric obliterative fibrosis and biliary strictures, eventually resulting in biliary cirrhosis and cholangiocarcinoma. Median survival from diagnosis to death or liver transplantation is around 18 years. In this chapter we discuss the controversies surrounding diagnosis of the disease, the use of ursodeoxycholic acid (UDCA), management of biliary strictures, and cholangiocarcinoma, the behavior of IBD in the context of PSC and optimum timing for liver transplantation.

Diagnosis

Most patients with PSC are diagnosed when asymptomatic with cholestatic liver function tests, performed routinely at IBD outpatient appointments. Symptoms, when they occur, usually consist of pruritus, fatigue, right upper quadrant pain, jaundice and, more unusually, cholangitis. Occasionally, PSC patients present with symptoms of advanced liver disease or cholangiocarcinoma. Endoscopic retrograde cholangiography (ECRP) is traditionally used to diagnose PSC and is still considered the gold standard; however, magnetic resonance cholangiography (MRCP) has been shown to be as sensitive where the best operator and equipment are available [1]. However, in view of the higher complication rate of ERCP, MRCP – if available – should be performed first. Liver biopsy is not undertaken routinely if typical biliary stricturing has been demonstrated by cholangiography, but is very useful in determining the stage of the disease and to assess for biliary dysplasia, which can be an early indication of the development of cholangiocarcinoma [2]. The typical histopathologic findings include "onion skin fibrosis," where concentric layers of fibrosis are laid down around bile ducts, portal inflammation, and periportal fibrosis. Diagnostic changes of PSC are only seen in approximately one-third of patients although some form of biliary disease can normally be identified.

Medical management of PSC

The medical management of PSC remains controversial, in part because of the lack of large trials with sufficiently long follow-up to account for the slowly progressive and fluctuating course of the disease. UDCA is widely used for a range of cholestatic liver disease and is the best studied therapeutic agent in PSC. Its mode of action is complex and still unclear. It may relate to the displacement of cytotoxic hydrophobic bile acids from the bile acid pool, stimulation

TABLE 56.1 Important trials of ursodeoxycholic acid (UDCA) in primary sclerosing cholangitis (PSC) (double-blind, placebo-controlled).

Author	Year	No of patients	Dose of UDCA/day	Trial period (months)	LFTs improved?	Symptoms improved?	Liver histology improved?
Beuers [3]	1992	6	13–15 mg/kg	12	Y	N	Y
Lo [5]	1992	23	10 mg/kg	24	Y	N	N
Stiehl [6]	1994	20	750 mg	12–48	Y	N	Y
Lindor [7]	1997	105	13–15 mg/kg	34	Y	N	N
Mitchell [4]	2001	26	20–25 mg/kg	24	Y	N	Y
Okolicsanyi [8]	2003	86	8–13 mg/kg		Y	Y	N
Olsson [9]	2005	110	17–23 mg/kg	60	Y	N	Not done

LFTs, liver function tests; N, no; Y, yes.

of hepatobiliary secretion thereby preventing the retention of toxic biliary constituents, an antiapoptotic effect on hepatocytes, or a range of other immunomodulatory and cytoprotective effects.

Several trials have investigated the use of UDCA in PSC (Table 56.1). Most demonstrated an improvement in liver function tests but only three showed improvement in liver histology, perhaps due to the use of inappropriately low doses of UDCA (13–15 mg/kg). Recent studies on the bile acid composition of PSC patients taking different doses of UDCA has demonstrated that biliary enrichment of UDCA increases with increasing dose reaching a plateau at 22–25 mg/kg. If this is the most important factor for its clinical effect, it seems likely that UDCA doses of up to 22–25 mg/kg may be more effective than lower doses [10]. Interestingly, the greatest effects of UDCA on biliary stricturing and fibrosis were found in the trial that used the highest dose [4]. UDCA is generally well tolerated although occasionally persistant diarrhea requires withdrawal.

UDCA may also prevent colonic neoplasia. Two studies of PSC patients undergoing colonoscopic surveillance demonstrated a reduction in the rates of dysplasia in UDCA-treated patients, while a non-significant reduction was seen in a third study [11–13]. However, to date, there is no firm evidence that the high rate of bile duct cancer seen in PSC is reduced by UDCA therapy, although a recent study found a significantly lower prevalence of cholangiocarcinoma in PSC patients coming to transplantation who had been treated with UDCA compared with those who had not [14].

Small studies using steroids in PSC have not shown benefit, and the combination of cholestasis and steroids is associated with accelerated bone loss. Other drugs, including a range of immunosuppressants, have shown slight benefits in small trials but, to date, no agent has proved to be unequivocally valuable. Combinations of UDCA, immunosuppressants, and antibiotics are being investigated, and there are hopes that this approach might be more successful; a pilot study using UDCA and metronidazole has shown encouraging results [15].

Management of strictures and cholangiocarcinoma

PSC is characterized by multiple annular strictures throughout the biliary tree. Tight strictures may precipitate deterioration in liver function and progression to cirrhosis. These "benign dominant" strictures can be treated endoscopically with stents or balloon dilatation although interpreting the results of studies using these techniques is difficult because of their small size and varying methodologies. Surgical bypass to drain the obstructed system into the gut is rarely used.

Cholangiocarcinoma develops in 6–20% of patients with long-standing PSC at a rate of 1.5% per year [16]. To date there are no clinical or laboratory parameters that accurately identify patients who go on to develop hepatobiliary malignancy. Risk factors, however, include recent diagnosis of PSC, no previous UDCA treatment, long duration of UC, previous colon cancer, high alcohol consumption, and smoking [14,17,18]. One study has suggested that an index combining two serum tumor markers, CA19-9 and CEA (carcinoembryonic antigen), might be helpful in identifying PSC patients with occult tumors but this has not been confirmed by other investigators [19]. Regular brushing of dominant strictures to detect early neoplastic transformation has a high specificity and positive predictive value for malignancy and high grade dysplasia, but its use is limited by a low sensitivity and negative predictive value. New cytologic techniques using molecular profiling to consider inactivation of tumor suppressor genes and mutations in oncogenes, for example, might prove useful in the future.

Management of PSC-IBD

IBD found in association with PSC has a specific phenotype, recently termed "PSC-IBD" [20,21], characterized by extensive, mild disease. There is a particularly high risk of colonic dysplasia and carcinoma in PSC-IBD patients (see Chapters 51, 52), with 31% in one series developing colonic neoplasia after 20 years of UC compared with 5% of patients with UC alone [22]. In view of this, PSC patients with UC should have colonoscopy annually. Recent reports have suggested that the course of UC worsens after liver transplantation despite immunosuppressive drug regimens [23,24]. PSC recurrence in the transplanted liver may also be more common in male patients with an intact colon [25]. It might therefore be appropriate to have a lower threshold for advocating colectomy in PSC-IBD patients. However, it should be noted that PSC patients have a higher rate of pouchitis following colectomy than other UC patients, and that PSC patients with ileal stomas who develop portal hypertension may bleed from peristomal varices.

Timing of transplantation

Liver transplantation is the only option for patients with advanced PSC, with 5-year survival figures of approximately 80%. In view of the variable course of PSC and the unpredicatable risk of developing cholangiocarcinoma, determining the optimal timing for transplantation is difficult. Transplantation earlier in the course of the disease reduces operative risk and the development of malignancy, however, PSC recurs in at least 30% of grafts, and colon cancer is a major cause of death in PSC patients after orthotopic liver transplantation [26,27]. Established cholangiocarcinoma is a contraindication to transplantation; however, results for patients transplanted with high grade dysplasia or cholangiocarcinoma *in situ* are not significantly different to all patients with PSC. Moreover, incidental discovery of cholangiocarcinoma in the explanted liver without lymph node involvement does not influence long-term survival [14,28].

Conclusions

Management of patients with PSC can be very challenging. Monitoring is difficult as liver function tests fluctuate during the course of the disease and do not necessarily reflect progression of the disease. Patients cannot yet be offered an established effective medical treatment although UDCA in high dose may slow progression of the disease and possibly prevent complications such as colorectal dysplasia. Patients and physicians must accept that hepatobiliary malignancy occurs commonly and cannot be reliably prevented or detected. Liver transplantation remains the mainstay of treatment for advanced disease but determining the optimum timing for transplantation can be difficult and early referral to a specialist unit is therefore appropriate.

References

1 Vitellas KM, Enns RA, Keogan MT, *et al.* Comparison of MR cholangiopancreatographic techniques with contrast-enhanced cholangiography in the evaluation of sclerosing cholangitis. *AJR Am J Roentgenol* 2002; **178**: 327–34.

2 Fleming KA, Boberg KM, Glaumann H, *et al.* Biliary dysplasia as a marker of cholangiocarcinoma in primary sclerosing cholangitis. *J Hepatol* 2001; **34**: 360–5.

3 Beuers U, Spengler U, Kruis W, *et al.* Ursodeoxycholic acid for treatment of primary sclerosing cholangitis: a placebo-controlled trial. *Hepatology* 1992; **16**: 707–14.

4 Mitchell SA, Bansi DS, Hunt N, *et al.* A preliminary trial of high-dose ursodeoxycholic acid in primary sclerosing cholangitis. *Gastroenterology* 2001; **121**: 900–7.

5 Lo SK, Hermann R, Chapman RW, *et al.* Ursodeoxycholic acid in primary sclerosing cholangitis: a double blind placebo controlled trial (abstract). *Hepatology* 1992; **16**: 92A.

6 Stiehl A, Walker S, Stiehl L, *et al.* Effect of ursodeoxycholic acid on liver and bile duct disease in primary sclerosing cholangitis. A 3-year pilot study with a placebo-controlled study period. *J Hepatol* 1994; **20**: 57–64

7 Lindor KD. Ursodiol for primary sclerosing cholangitis. Mayo Primary Sclerosing Cholangitis-Ursodeoxycholic Acid Study Group. *N Engl J Med* 1997; **336**: 691–5.

8 Okolicsanyi L, Groppo M, Floreani A, *et al.* Treatment of primary sclerosing cholangitis with low-dose ursodeoxycholic acid: results of a retrospective Italian multicentre survey. *Dig Liver Dis* 2003; **35**: 325–31.

9 Olsson R, Boberg KM, de Muckadell OS, *et al.* High-dose ursodeoxycholic acid in primary sclerosing cholangitis: a 5-year multicenter, randomized, controlled study. *Gastroenterology*. 2005 Nov; **129**: 1464–72

10 Rost D, Rudolph G, Kloeters-Plachky P, Stiehl A. Effect of high-dose ursodeoxycholic acid on its biliary enrichment in primary sclerosing cholangitis. *Hepatology* 2004; **40**: 693–8.

11 Tung BY, Emond MJ, Haggitt RC, *et al.* Ursodiol use is associated with lower prevalence of colonic neoplasia in patients with ulcerative colitis and primary sclerosing cholangitis. *Ann Intern Med* 2001; **134**: 89–95.

12 Pardi DS, Loftus EV Jr, Kremers WK, Keach J, Lindor KD. Ursodeoxycholic acid as a chemopreventive agent in patients with ulcerative colitis and primary sclerosing cholangitis. *Gastroenterology* 2003; **124**: 889–93.

13 Wolf JM, Rybicki L, Lashner BA. Ursodeoxycholic acid is not chemoprotective for colorectal cancer in ulcerative colitis patients with primary sclerosing cholangitis. *Gastroenterology* 2001; **121**: 2276 (Abstract).

14 Brandsaeter B, Isoniemi H, Broome U, *et al.* Liver transplantation for primary sclerosing cholangitis; predictors and consequences of hepatobiliary malignancy. *J Hepatol* 2004; **40**: 815–22.

15 Farkkila M, Karvonen AL, Nurmi H, *et al.* Metronidazole and ursodeoxycholic acid for primary sclerosing cholangitis: a randomized placebo-controlled trial. *Hepatology* 2004; **40**: 1379–86.

16 Boberg KM, Bergquist A, Mitchell S, *et al.* Cholangiocarcinoma in primary sclerosing cholangitis: risk factors and clinical presentation. *Scand J Gastroenterol* 2002; **37**: 1205–11.

17 Bergquist A, Glaumann H, Persson B, Broome U. Risk factors and clinical presentation of hepatobiliary carcinoma in patients with primary sclerosing cholangitis: a case–control study. *Hepatology* 1998; **27**: 311–6.

18 Chalasani N, Baluyut A, Ismail A, *et al.* Cholangiocarcinoma in patients with primary sclerosing cholangitis: a multicenter case–control study. *Hepatology* 2000; **31**: 7–11.

19 Ramage JK, Donaghy A, Farrant JM, Iorns R, Williams R. Serum tumor markers for the diagnosis of cholangiocarcinoma in primary sclerosing cholangitis. *Gastroenterology* 1995; **108**: 865–9.

20 Harewood GC, Loftus EV Jr, Tefferi A, *et al.* Concurrent inflammatory bowel disease and myelodysplastic syndromes. *Inflamm Bowel Dis* 1999; **5**: 98–103.

21 Loftus EV Jr, Harewood GC, Loftus CG, *et al.* PSC-IBD: a unique form of inflammatory bowel disease associated with primary sclerosing cholangitis. *Gut* 2005; **54**: 91–6.

22 Broome U, Lofberg R, Veress B, Eriksson LS. Primary sclerosing cholangitis and ulcerative colitis: evidence for increased neoplastic potential. *Hepatology* 1995; **22**: 1404–8.

23 Dvorchik I, Subotin M, Demetris AJ, *et al.* Effect of liver transplantation on inflammatory bowel disease in patients with primary sclerosing cholangitis. *Hepatology* 2002; **35**: 380–4.

24 Papatheodoridis GV, Hamilton M, Rolles K, Burroughs AK. Liver transplantation and inflammatory bowel disease. *J Hepatol* 1998; **28**: 1070–6.

25 Vera A, Moledina S, Gunson B, *et al.* Risk factors for recurrence of primary sclerosing cholangitis of liver allograft. *Lancet* 2002; **360**: 1943–4.

26 Gow PJ, Chapman RW. Liver transplantation for primary sclerosing cholangitis. *Liver* 2000; **20**: 97–103.

27 Graziadei IW, Wiesner RH, Batts KP, *et al.* Recurrence of primary sclerosing cholangitis following liver transplantation. *Hepatology* 1999; **29**: 1050–6.

28 Goss JA, Shackleton CR, Farmer DG, *et al.* Orthotopic liver transplantation for primary sclerosing cholangitis: a 12-year single center experience. *Ann Surg* 1997; **225**: 472–81; discussion 481–3.

Part 5 Managing IBD Outside the Gut

57 Thromboembolic disease: an under-recognized complication?

PETER IRVING & FERGUS SHANAHAN

LEARNING POINTS

Thromboembolic disease

- Patients with IBD are at increased risk of thromboembolic events

- Deep vein thromboses and pulmonary emboli are the most common, but not the only, thromboembolic events associated with IBD

- Thromboprophylactic measures should be considered for all inpatients with IBD

Introduction

Morbidity and mortality in patients with IBD are related not only to the direct effects of inflammation within the bowel but also to extraintestinal pathology. Thromboembolic (TE) phenomena are perhaps less frequently encountered than many other extraintestinal manifestations (e.g. arthritides; see Chapter 54) but, as they are potentially life-threatening, they must be considered important. Mortality associated with TE events in IBD has been described as being as high as 25% [1].

In this chapter we review whether there is an increased risk of TE disease in IBD, the predisposing factors and risk factors for developing TE complications in IBD, and what, if anything, can be done to prevent their occurrence.

Frequency of thromboembolic complications

Thromboembolism in association with IBD was first recognized in the 1930s, being described in a review of 1500 patients with IBD, 1.2% of whom were found to have had TE complications [2]. Subsequent attempts to describe the risk of developing a pulmonary embolism (PE) or deep venous thrombosis (DVT) were plagued by poor study design, particularly by the lack of control groups, leading to widely varying estimates of the frequency of TE events (for reviews see Quera and Shanahan [3] and Irving *et al.* [4]). Such were the difficulties in design, that it is perhaps unsurprising that clinical and postmortem studies described frequencies of TE events varying as widely as 1% and 41%. Indeed, while some studies suggested there was no increase in risk at all [5], many of the earlier studies may have overestimated the risk as they were performed in an era when surgical intervention for IBD was more common, and prophylactic measures to prevent DVT and PE were not used.

More recently, however, two well-designed studies have provided more robust data. Bernstein *et al.* [6] performed a population-based cohort study in which they examined hospital discharge data to identify patients admitted with either PE or DVT. Patients with IBD were compared with 10 age-matched controls from the general population, allowing the calculation of incidence rates of either DVT or PE of 40/10 000 person years for patients with Crohn's disease, and 50/10 000 person years for those with UC. In comparison with the general population, the increased risk was 4.7 (95% CI 3.5–6.3) for DVT and 2.9 (95% CI 1.8–4.7) for PE in Crohn's disease, and 2.8 (95% CI 2.1–3.7) for DVT and 3.6 (95% CI 2.5–5.2) for PE, in UC.

A similar, threefold increase in risk for patients with IBD compared with healthy controls was described by Miehsler *et al.* [7] in a study in which subjects answered questionnaires about their history of TE; radiologic confirmation of events was subsequently obtained by the investigators. Importantly, this increase in risk was found to be specific to IBD: neither an inflammatory group (patients with rheumatoid arthritis), nor a non-IBD bowel inflammation group (patients with celiac disease) had an increased risk of TE compared with their matched controls.

These two studies provide the strongest evidence to date of the level of risk of TE in IBD; however, the former also provided further information about the nature of the risk involved. In this study, older patients were, perhaps unsurprisingly, found to be at higher risk of DVT or PE than younger patients; however, the greatest *increase in risk* was found to be in those patients with IBD under the age of 40 years [6]. This finding echoed an earlier study suggesting that in IBD, TE events occur in younger patients than in those without IBD [5]. It appears that the risk of recurrence is also high, with 10–15% of patients with UC or Crohn's disease having recurrent events [8].

Although DVT and PE are by far the most common TE complications encountered in patients with IBD, they are not the only TE events to occur. Indeed, a search of the literature yields descriptions of thromboses of almost all peripheral, and even central vessels, including the aorta. However, why there is no increase in the incidence of ischemic heart disease in IBD is unclear, although the major confounding effect of tobacco smoking undoubtedly plays a part.

Thus, although there has been some debate over the years, it is now fairly well accepted that patients with IBD are at increased risk of TE disease compared with the general population, but why should this be the case?

Risk factors for thromboembolism in patients with IBD

Thrombocytosis associated with active IBD was first described over 30 years ago [9]. Indeed, the increase in platelet count was so marked in some of the patients described in this paper, that they were treated with busulfan. Increased platelet counts, probably related to interleukin-6-induced production of thrombopoetin by the liver [10], have subsequently been recognized as a sign of disease activity, an observation that can be of use in differentiating disease-associated from infective symptoms in Crohn's disease (Fig. 57.1).

Thrombocytosis, along with **increased platelet activation and aggregation** [11], is one of the better described

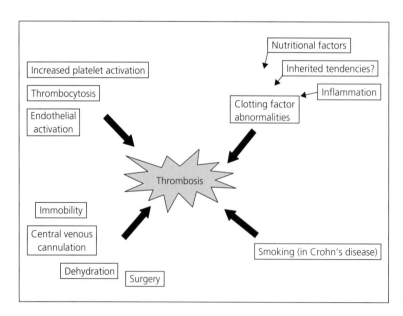

FIG 57.1 Prothrombotic risk factors in IBD.

prothrombotic tendencies in patients with IBD. Others, including inherited and acquired **procoagulant tendencies**, and **endothelial damage and activation**, are described in an ever increasing volume of literature, some of it contradictory. A recent review attempted to address some of these discrepancies by summarizing the results of papers published on the three most commonly inherited prothrombotic conditions (factor V Leiden mutation, G20210A mutation in the prothrombin gene, and homozygous C677T mutation in the methylenetetrahydrofolate reductase gene). No increase was found in their prevalence in patients with IBD compared with the general population [12]. It seems sensible therefore only to screen IBD patients who have had TE events for inherited thrombophilic tendencies if they have a family history of thrombophilia [3].

Abnormalities of the coagulation system found in patients with IBD are therefore more likely to be caused by other factors. **Nutritional deficiencies** of vitamins B_6 and B_{12} and of folic acid can cause hyperhomocysteinemia, which is itself a risk factor for thromboembolism. Drug-induced vitamin deficiencies (e.g. sulfasalazine- or methotrexate-induced folate deficiency) can have a similar effect. **Disease activity** (see below) may increase the risk of TE, for instance through the actions of inflammatory cytokines. Tumor necrosis factor-α, for example, decreases protein C activation and induces tissue factor (TF) expression on endothelial cells [13]. Moreover, treatment with infliximab appears to improve the prothrombotic state associated with IBD [14].

IBD predisposes towards thromboembolism in other ways: **immobility** (caused, for instance, by hospitalization); the need to undergo **surgery**; and diarrhea-induced **dehydration** all increase the risk of developing a DVT or PE. In addition, extremely unwell patients, or those needing parenteral nutrition, may require **central venous catheters**, thereby further increasing their risk of TE.

Are there any disease characteristics that predispose toward TE complications? A review of 98 IBD patients with TE complications revealed that most of those with Crohn's disease had colonic involvement while those with UC had extensive disease [8], suggesting that the increase in risk may correlate with the **extent of colonic involvement**, an observation previously suggested by others. However, although disease activity is probably an independent risk factor for TE, it is noteworthy that one-third of patients with TE complications have inactive disease [1] and that colectomy does not appear to protect against the risk of recurrence [8].

Prevention of thromboembolic complications

While no randomized controlled trials exist to confirm that the following interventions decrease the risk of developing TE complications, neither are these studies likely to be carried out. Recently published guidelines [15] advise using subcutaneous low molecular weight heparin for all inpatients with IBD. Likewise, the use of antithrombotic stockings, early post-surgical mobilization, and the avoidance of dehydration seem sensible. Screening patients at the highest risk of nutritional deficiencies (such as those with extensive small bowel disease or short bowel syndrome), using supplemental folic acid in those taking methotrexate or sulfasalazine, and avoiding central venous cannulation where at all possible may also be beneficial. Finally, while controlling disease activity is perhaps the primary aim of physicians treating patients with IBD, it may also decrease the risk of patients having TE events.

Conclusions

Thromboembolic events, although thankfully fairly rare, are an important cause of morbidity and mortality in patients with IBD. Simple interventions decrease the risk of developing DVTs and PEs and should be considered in all patients with IBD admitted to hospital, whether their disease is active or not.

References

1 Talbot RW, Heppell J, Dozois RR, Beart RW Jr. Vascular complications of inflammatory bowel disease. *Mayo Clin Proc* 1986; **61**: 140–5.

2 Bargen J, Barker N. Extensive arterial and venous thrombosis complicating chronic ulcerative colitis. *Arch Intern Med* 1936; **58**: 17–31.

3 Quera R, Shanahan F. Thromboembolism: an important manifestation of inflammatory bowel disease. *Am J Gastroenterol* 2004; **99**: 1971–3.

4 Irving PM, Pasi KJ, Rampton DS. Thrombosis and inflammatory bowel disease. *Clin Gastroenterol Hepatol* 2005; **3**: 617–28.

5 Grip O, Svensson PJ, Lindgren S. Inflammatory bowel disease promotes venous thrombosis earlier in life. *Scand J Gastroenterol* 2000; **35**: 619–23.

6 Bernstein CN, Blanchard JF, Houston DS, Wajda A. The incidence of deep venous thrombosis and pulmonary embolism

among patients with inflammatory bowel disease: a population-based cohort study. *Thromb Haemost* 2001; **85**: 430–4.

7 Miehsler W, Reinisch W, Valic E, *et al.* Is inflammatory bowel disease an independent and disease specific risk factor for thromboembolism? *Gut* 2004; **53**: 542–8.

8 Solem CA, Loftus EV, Tremaine WJ, Sandborn WJ. Venous thromboembolism in inflammatory bowel disease. *Am J Gastroenterol* 2004; **99**: 97–101.

9 Morowitz DA, Allen LW, Kirsner JB. Thrombocytosis in chronic inflammatory bowel disease. *Ann Intern Med* 1968; **68**: 1013–21.

10 Schafer AI. Thrombocytosis. *N Engl J Med* 2004; **350**: 1211–9.

11 Collins CE, Cahill MR, Newland AC, Rampton DS. Platelets circulate in an activated state in inflammatory bowel disease. *Gastroenterology* 1994; **106**: 840–5.

12 Papa A, Danese S, Grillo A, Gasbarrini G, Gasbarrini A. Review article: inherited thrombophilia in inflammatory bowel disease. *Am J Gastroenterol* 2003; **98**: 1247–51.

13 Nawroth PP, Stern DM. Modulation of endothelial cell hemostatic properties by tumor necrosis factor. *J Exp Med* 1986; **163**: 740–5.

14 Hommes DW, van Dullemen HM, Levi M, *et al.* Beneficial effect of treatment with a monoclonal anti-tumor necrosis factor-alpha antibody on markers of coagulation and fibrinolysis in patients with active Crohn's disease. *Haemostasis* 1997; **27**: 269–77.

15 Carter MJ, Lobo AJ, Travis SP. Guidelines for the management of inflammatory bowel disease in adults. *Gut* 2004; **53** (Suppl 5): 1–16.

58 Pulmonary manifestations: rare but real

PETER IRVING

LEARNING POINTS

Pulmonary manifestations

- IBD-related lung disease can affect any part of the respiratory tract and usually presents with cough and dyspnea

- It is more common in UC than Crohn's disease

- Drugs must be considered as a potential cause, particularly in patients with interstitial lung disease

- Pulmonary function testing, plain radiography, high resolution CT and biopsy may all be required for diagnosis

- Pulmonary manifestations of IBD are best managed with a respiratory physician

- Although heterogeneous, most IBD-associated lung disease is steroid-responsive

TABLE 58.1 Possible patterns of pulmonary involvement in IBD. For reviews see references [2,3,5].

Airways disease
Tracheitis
Chronic bronchitis
Chronic bronchiolitis
Bronchiectasis

Interstitial lung disease
Bronciolitis obliterans with organizing pneumonia
Pulmonary infiltration with eosinophilia
Necrobiotic nodules

Serositis
Pleural effusions

Vascular disease
Thromboembolic disease
Vasculitis

Drug-induced lung disease
Infection
Interstitial lung disease

Others
Granulomatous lung disease
Enteropulmonary fistulae

Introduction

When considering extraintestinal manifestations of IBD, involvement of the lungs does not immediately spring to mind. However, the pulmonary manifestations of IBD are, in fact, protean and may occur more frequently than is commonly realized. Here we describe these manifestations and discuss their relative importance (Table 58.1).

Airways disease

Airways disease is, of course, common amongst the general population, perhaps explaining why establishing a relationship between this and IBD has been difficult. Indeed, it is only in patients in whom no other cause of airway disease

can be identified that IBD-related lung disease is likely to be considered. However, since 1976, when a series of six patients was described with IBD and chronic bronchitis (five also had an obstructive pulmonary defect and four had bronchiectasis) [1], the association of otherwise unexplained bronchopulmonary disease and IBD has become increasingly recognized. Inflammatory disease of every part of the pulmonary tree, from the trachea to the bronchioles, is described in association with IBD and is probably more common in patients with UC than in those with Crohn's disease [2]. The inflammation is associated with airways narrowing and ultimately, if allowed to progress, bronchiectasis or bronchiolitis obliterans.

Airways diseases most commonly present with a chronic productive cough and are best diagnosed by pulmonary function testing and computerized tomography (CT) scanning (see below). Large airways disease frequently responds to inhaled steroids whereas small airways disease is more likely to require systemic steroids [3], while laser therapy may be required, in addition to steroids, to treat tracheal stenosis [2].

Interstitial lung disease

Interstitial lung disease is often associated with drug therapy in patients with IBD (see below) and therefore establishing a causal link with IBD itself is difficult. However, there are several descriptions of bronchiolitis obliterans with organizing pneumonia, pulmonary infiltrates and eosinophilia, and interstitial pneumonitis, as extraintestinal manifestations of IBD [2,3]. Necrobiotic nodules, which bear histologic resemblance to pyoderma gangrenosum, have also been described in association with UC [3] and Crohn's disease [4]. Fortunately, most such cases are responsive to systemic steroids, the use of which should therefore be considered [3].

Pleural disease

Pleural effusions, with or without other forms of serositis, are described in association with IBD. However, as with interstitial lung disease, establishing a link between pleural disease and IBD is difficult. Pleural effusions are certainly a rare complication in patients with IBD and may also be steroid-responsive [5].

Vascular disease

The risk of developing pulmonary emboli for patients with IBD is about three times that of the general population. This is discussed in Chapter 57 and is therefore not dealt with further here.

Vasculitis has been proposed as a pathogenic mechanism in Crohn's disease [6], and UC is associated with perinuclear–antineutrophil cytoplasmic antibodies (p-ANCA) (see Chapter 3), albeit in a different pattern to that normally seen in vasculitides. Pulmonary vasculitis is, however, only rarely reported in association with either UC or Crohn's disease, certainly far too infrequently to suggest a definite link. It must also be remembered that Wegener's granulomatosis can present with colitis.

Malignancy

It is well established that UC is a disease of non-smokers, while patients with Crohn's disease are more likely to be smokers (see Chapter 27). It is probably for this reason that in a study from Florence involving over 14 000 person-years of follow-up, lung cancer-related mortality was shown to be increased fourfold in Crohn's disease, but reduced by 70% in UC [7]. These findings are broadly consistent with other studies [8,9]. There is no convincing evidence of lung malignancy associated directly with IBD.

Others

Granulomatous involvement of the lungs in patients with Crohn's disease [10] raises the possibility of concomitant sarcoidosis or tuberculosis (see below). It has been suggested that sarcoidosis and Crohn's disease may even be different manifestations of the same disease [5]; it is likely that this question will be answered with the rapid increase in genetic data currently being produced. Again, the number of patients described with granulomatous lung disease is few. Still rarer is the description of enteropulmonary fistulae [11]; surgery appears to be the best treatment for such cases.

Drug-induced lung disease

Many of the drugs used to treat IBD can, albeit rarely, have pulmonary side-effects. 5-Aminosalicylate-containing drugs (5-ASA) have been reported to cause a variety of interstitial lung diseases, of which eosinophilic pneumonia is the most frequently encountered. Pulmonary fibrosis is less commonly reported. 5-ASA-related disease is idiosyncratic and normally occurs within the first few months of treatment. Although it is normally reversible with discontinuation of the drug, treatment with corticosteroids may be necessary if improvement does not occur quickly [12].

The use of methotrexate is associated with pneumonitis in patients with rheumatoid arthritis [13], although, to date, there are no reports of pulmonary toxicity when it is used to treat IBD. Nevertheless, methotrexate must be considered as a possible culprit in IBD patients who develop interstitial lung disease when taking the drug.

As the prescription of immunosuppressive drugs and biologic agents increases, so will the incidence of opportunistic pulmonary infections. Reactivation of tuberculosis is of particular concern in patients treated with infliximab (see Chapter 18), as is *Pneumocystis carinii* pneumonia in those on cyclosporine (see Chapter 16). In any event, vigilance and a high index of suspicion are recommended when using immunosuppressive therapies, particularly in combination with each other.

Pulmonary function tests and radiologic abnormalities

The majority of studies examining pulmonary function in patients with IBD demonstrate an increase in abnormal findings compared with controls. The most consistent abnormal finding is a decrease in the CO diffusion capacity. In one study of 82 mostly asymptomatic patients with IBD, a decrease in this measurement was found in slightly over 50% of patients with either UC or Crohn's disease [14].

Taking a different approach, of 17 IBD patients (three with Crohn's disease) presenting to a respiratory clinic with chronic pulmonary symptoms, 11 had abnormal pulmonary function tests, five had an obstructive pattern, four restrictive, and two mixed restrictive and obstructive tests [15].

In the same series, high resolution CT revealed bronchiectasis in three-quarters of patients. Others have noted that, particularly with airways disease, plain chest X-rays are frequently normal [2,16].

Etiology of lung disease associated with IBD

IBD-associated lung disease is more common in patients with UC than in those with Crohn's disease [3] and bronchopulmonary inflammation appears to be more common in females than in males [2]. Disease activity, however, does not clearly correlate with pulmonary involvement, with the exception of serositis, which is more common in active disease [2]. Pulmonary complications occur most commonly in patients with established IBD but are also found occasionally to predate or coincide with the onset of IBD [2]. It is also noteworthy that colectomy does not protect against the development of pulmonary complications; indeed, it has been suggested that this may even induce their development

[16]. This has led to the suggestion that there is an auto-immune basis to pulmonary problems in IBD; once the colon is removed, the inflammation "transfers" to the lung. The common embryologic origins of the gut and lungs add further weight to this interesting theory.

Conclusions

IBD-induced pulmonary dysfunction is probably not as uncommon as was originally thought to be the case. The limited literature to date suggests, however, that severe lung disease is, fortunately, rare. Nevertheless, larger studies are indicated to describe better this poorly understood extraintestinal manifestation of IBD.

References

1 Kraft SC, Earle RH, Roesler M, Esterly JR. Unexplained bronchopulmonary disease with inflammatory bowel disease. *Arch Intern Med* 1976; **136**: 454–9.

2 Camus P, Piard F, Ashcroft T, Gal AA, Colby TV. The lung in inflammatory bowel disease. *Medicine (Baltimore)* 1993; **72**: 151–83.

3 Camus P, Colby TV. The lung in inflammatory bowel disease. *Eur Respir J* 2000; **15**: 5–10.

4 Sanjeevi A, Roy HK. Necrobiotic nodules: a rare pulmonary manifestion of Crohn's disease. *Am J Gastroenterol* 2003; **98**: 941–3.

5 Storch I, Sachar D, Katz S. Pulmonary manifestations of inflammatory bowel disease. *Inflamm Bowel Dis* 2003; **9**: 104–15.

6 Wakefield AJ, Sawyerr AM, Dhillon AP, *et al*. Pathogenesis of Crohn's disease: multifocal gastrointestinal infarction. *Lancet* 1989; **2**: 1057–62.

7 Masala G, Bagnoli S, Ceroti M, *et al*. Divergent patterns of total and cancer mortality in ulcerative colitis and Crohn's disease patients: the Florence IBD study 1978–2001. *Gut* 2004; **53**: 1309–13.

8 Karlen P, Lofberg R, Brostrom O, *et al*. Increased risk of cancer in ulcerative colitis: a population-based cohort study. *Am J Gastroenterol* 1999; **94**: 1047–52.

9 Mellemkjaer L, Johansen C, Gridley G, *et al*. Crohn's disease and cancer risk (Denmark). *Cancer Causes Control* 2000; **11**: 145–50.

10 Omori H, Asahi H, Inoue Y, Irinoda T, Saito K. Pulmonary involvement in Crohn's disease report of a case and review of the literature. *Inflamm Bowel Dis* 2004; **10**: 129–34.

11 Singh D, Cole JC, Cali RL, Finical EJ, Proctor DD. Colobronchial fistula: an unusual complication of Crohn's disease. *Am J Gastroenterol* 1994; **89**: 2250–2.

12 Foster RA, Zander DS, Mergo PJ, Valentine JF. Mesalamine-related lung disease: clinical, radiographic, and pathologic manifestations. *Inflamm Bowel Dis* 2003; **9**: 308–15.

13 Alarcon GS, Kremer JM, Macaluso M, *et al.* Risk factors for methotrexate-induced lung injury in patients with rheumatoid arthritis: a multicenter, case–control study. Methotrexate-Lung Study Group. *Ann Intern Med* 1997; **127**: 356–64.

14 Kuzela L, Vavrecka A, Prikazska M, *et al.* Pulmonary complications in patients with inflammatory bowel disease. *Hepatogastroenterology* 1999; **46**: 1714–9.

15 Mahadeva R, Walsh G, Flower CD, Shneerson JM. Clinical and radiological characteristics of lung disease in inflammatory bowel disease. *Eur Respir J* 2000; **15**: 41–8.

16 Higenbottam T, Cochrane GM, Clark TJ, *et al.* Bronchial disease in ulcerative colitis. *Thorax* 1980; **35**: 581–5.

SUNIL SAMUEL & YASHWANT MAHIDA

59 Intestinal infections: mimics and precipitants of relapse

LEARNING POINTS

Intestinal infections

- Intestinal infections can mimic all forms of IBD and need to be excluded in new onset and established IBD

- Specific infections are particularly likely in some patient groups (after antibiotics, the elderly, recent travelers)

- Stool microbiology is mandatory, but negative results do not exclude infection

- Flexible sigmoidoscopy with biopsies can hasten diagnosis

Introduction

Clinical features of IBD, such as diarrhea, abdominal pain, and weight loss, also occur in gastrointestinal infections. These infections can sometimes cause diagnostic difficulty, especially in a patient presenting for the first time with symptoms of recent onset. It is well recognized that gastrointestinal infection may also provoke or even mimic a relapse of IBD. This chapter focuses on those gastrointestinal infections that should be considered in the differential diagnosis in patients presenting with their first attack of IBD, and those that may provoke or mimic a relapse. The role of Cytomegalovirus infection is considered in a separate chapter (see Chapter 44). A sound knowledge of the various clinical manifestations of infective etiologies will help the physician in making the appropriate diagnosis when confronted with difficult cases of diarrhea. This is particularly important in an era of increasing travel.

Infectious diseases of the intestine

Intestinal infectious diseases are common. In an English population-based cohort incidence study, intestinal infectious disease (defined as any person with loose stools or significant vomiting lasting less than 2 weeks, in the absence of a known non-infectious cause, and preceded by a symptom-free period of 3 weeks), occurred in 19.4 cases per 100 person years, of whom 1/6 presented to a general practitioner (GP) [1,2]. Of the cases seen by GPs, the most common viruses identified in stool samples were rotavirus group A and small round structured viruses. *Campylobacter* spp. were the most frequently isolated bacteria, *C. jejuni* being the predominant species identified (89%). Other common isolates in this study included *Salmonella* spp., enterovirulent *Escherichia coli* and *Clostridium perfringens* (enterotoxin-producing). Specific infections need to be considered in some patient groups. Such patients include those recently discharged from hospital and/or who have recently had antibiotics (*Clostridium difficile*), immunocompromised patients, and those with recent travel from a tropical or subtropical country (Table 59.1).

Infections to consider in differential diagnosis during first presentation of IBD

Clinical features

The duration of diarrhea is less than 14 days in most infections. Exceptions include protozoal infections (such as *Giardia*, *Cryptosporidium*, and *Entamoeba histolytica*) and infections in immunocompromised patients. Chronic or intermittent diarrhea (usually with occult blood) can also

TABLE 59.1 Infections to be considered in differential diagnosis of IBD.

Microorganisms	Other clinical features	Diagnosis	Special characteristics
Infections caused by invasive organisms presenting as bloody diarrhea			
Disease is due to invasion of intestinal epithelium and generally targets the distal ileum and colon			
Shigella species	Fever, fatigue	Stool mc&s	
Non-typhoidal *Salmonella* species	Vomiting, abdominal pain	Stool mc&s; rectal swab; culture biopsies	Ciprofloxacin can prolong fecal excretion of *Salmonella*
Campylobacter	Fever, abdominal pain	Stool mc&s	Chronic infection can simulate IBD
Escherichia coli • Enteroinvasive • Enterohemorrhagic	Fever, tenesmus, abdominal pain (*E. coli* O157:H7)	Stool mc&s	Antibiotics may increase risk of HUS in *E. coli* O157:H7 infection
Yersinia	Abdominal pain, fever, arthralgias	Stool mc&s; serology; barium and endoscopic studies	Ileal infection can mimic Crohn's
Infectious toxigenic organisms, usually presenting with watery, voluminous stools			
Disease is secondary to an enterotoxin effect on intestinal epithelium			
Vibrio cholerae *V. parahaemolyticus*	Rapid dehydration	Stool or rectal swab mc&s; phase contrast microscopy	
Enterotoxigenic *E. coli* (ETEC) Enteroaggregative *E. coli* (EAggEC)	Vomiting, abdominal cramps	Stool mc&s	Most common cause of traveler's diarrhea
Opportunistic infections causing diarrhea in immunocompromised people			
Cryptosporidium	Abdominal cramps, vomiting, wasting	Oocysts in fecal smears on acid-fast staining	Fecal–oral transmission
Cytomegalovirus	Fever, abdominal pain, hematochezia	Colonoscopy, biopsy	
Microsporidia (*Enterocytozoon bienusi*)	Cramps, malabsorption, weight loss	Spores in stool or intestinal biopsies	Fecal–oral transmission
Mycobacterium avium intracellulare	Abdominal pain, fever, weight loss	Acid-fast staining of stool and biopsies	Clarithromycin used prophylactically in AIDS patients
Mycobacterium tuberculosis	Fever, abdominal pain, weight loss	Intestinal biopsy and culture	
Cyclospora	Chronic intermittent diarrhea	Acid-fast staining of stool for oocysts	
Isospora belli	Chronic voluminous diarrhea and malabsorption	Acid-fast staining of stool for oocysts	Small bowel villous atrophy and eosinophilic infiltration
Organisms causing nosocomial diarrhea			
Clostridium difficile	Asymptomatic carriage to life-threatening pseudo-membranous colitis and toxic megacolon	Bioassay, enzyme immunoassay or PCR for toxin; Stool cultures	Flexible sigmoidoscopy may enable rapid diagnosis [7]
Viral causes of diarrhea			
Calicivirus (Norwalk-like), Rotavirus, enteric adenoviruses, astroviruses	Vomiting	Stool antigen by enzyme immunoassay	

TABLE 59.1 (*Continued*)

Microorganisms	Other clinical features	Diagnosis	Special characteristics
Parasitic causes of diarrhea			
Giardia lamblia	Flatulence, foul-smelling stools, anorexia, weight loss	Stool for microscopy; duodenal biopsy and aspirate; ELISA for stool antigen [13]	
Entamoeba (*E. histolytica*)	Bloody diarrhea, abdominal pain, fever, weight loss	Stool microscopy, antigen detection assay [5]	Serology has low specificity
Schistosomiasis (*S. mansoni, S. japonicum, S. haematobium*)	Abdominal pain, fever, bloody diarrhea	Stool and urine microscopy; colonic biopsy; serology (not diagnostic)	Polyposis in chronic schistosomiasis can mimic inflammatory polyps of UC
Specific diseases – Whipple's disease			
Tropheryma whippelii	Fever, arthralgias, abdominal pain, diarrhea, weight loss	PAS positive macrophages in small bowel biopsies; PCR	
Specific causes of diarrhea in men who have sex with men			
Chlamydia trachomatis	Bleeding, mucus per rectum, tenesmus, rectal pain	Antigen detection by direct fluorescent antibody or enzyme immunoassay; PCR; sigmoidoscopy and biopsies	Can mimic perianal Crohn's
Neisseria gonorrhoeae	Mucopurulent rectal discharge, bleeding, and anal itching/irritation	Gram stain of rectal discharge; Fluorescent labeled antigonococcal antibody; Culture of rectal swab	Patients should also receive a full treatment dose for *Chlamydia* as this frequently coexists
Treponema pallidum	Rectal pain, itching, bleeding, mucus discharge; anorectal masses and ulcers resembling chancre	Dark-field microscopy; Treponemal antibody tests	

ELISA, enzyme linked immunoabsorbent assay; HUS, hemolytic uremic syndrome; mc&s, microscopy culture and sensitivity; PAS, periodic acid–Schiff; PCR, polymerase chain reaction.

occur in intestinal schistosomiasis; diarrhea and hematuria in a patient who has recently been swimming in a lake in Africa may be due to acute schistosomiasis [3].

Bloody diarrhea is commonly caused by enteropathogenic bacteria. In patients presenting to 11 emergency departments in the USA, enteropathogens were identified in 30.6%, predominantly *Shigella*, *E. coli* O157:H7 (and other Shiga toxin-producing *E. coli*), *Campylobacter*, and *Salmonella* [4]. Bloody diarrhea can also occur in patients with amoebic colitis [5] and, in those less than 18 years of age, with *Yersinia enterocolitica* infection [6].

Fever is suggestive of an intestinal infection, although not specific for any microorganism. Sore throat has been reported to occur in nearly 20% of patients with *Yersinia enterocolitica* infection [6].

In patients with perianal Crohn's disease, leishmaniasis, histoplasmosis, *Chlamydia trachomatis* and herpes simplex virus infections should be considered.

Investigations

A very high erythrocyte sedimentation rate (ESR) may be due to *M. tuberculosis* infection, while eosinophilia can be caused by parasite infections, such as schistosomiasis. In addition to culture for enteropathogens, other stool tests can be helpful in those with appropriate clinical features. Such tests include microscopy for parasites, electron microscopy for viruses, detection of *C. difficile* toxins (by bioassay or enzyme linked immunoabsorbent assay [ELISA]) and antigen detection (e.g. rotavirus). In patients with suspected *E. histolytica* infection, an ELISA for its antigen in stool will help to distinguish it from the commensal *E. dispar* [5]. Detection of pathogenic microorganisms in stool samples by polymerase chain reaction (PCR) may become useful in the future.

Because bacteria (or their toxins) may not always be identified from stool samples [1,7], endoscopic examination can be particularly helpful. Colonoscopy in patients with acute severe bloody diarrhea has been reported to allow infectious colitis (from *Salmonella*, *Campylobacter*, and *Shigella* spp.) to be distinguished from UC [8]. As the main differences in the endoscopic appearances were seen in the left colon, flexible sigmoidoscopy should be equally effective in most patients. Pseudomembranous colitis resulting from *C. difficile* infection produces characteristic endoscopic appearances and flexible sigmoidoscopy has been shown to allow rapid diagnosis of this condition before the results of stool cytotoxin test are available. It is especially helpful in those with a (false) negative stool test [7].

Histologic examination of rectal and colonic biopsies can provide additional information. A number of studies (reviewed in Jenkins *et al.* [9]) have shown that specific histologic features (such as distortion of crypt architecture, crypt atrophy, increase in lamina propria cells, isolated giant cells, and epithelioid granulomas) enable IBD to be distinguished from acute infective colitis. Multiple large granulomas, especially with caseating necrosis, may result from tuberculosis, in which ulcers lined by epithelioid cells and microgranulomas along with disproportionate submucosal inflammation may allow distinction from Crohn's disease [10], particularly in the absence of acid-fast bacilli.

Where amoebiasis is suspected, examination of scrapings and biopsy samples for amoebic trophozoites should be undertaken [5].

Serologic tests can be useful but should be interpreted with caution because, first, circulating antibodies may persist after eradiction of infection (e.g. schistosomiasis), and second, subclinical infection may lead to high background seroprevalence for some microbial antigens.

In some patients with progressive intestinal disease resulting in severe inflammation, it may be difficult to distinguish IBD from intestinal infection, and treatment with antibiotics, to cover likely intestinal pathogen(s), in addition to corticosteroids may be required. In this setting, infections that can be exacerbated by corticosteroids should be excluded or treated. These include amoebic colitis and infection with *Strongyloides stercoralis*.

Infections that may mimic or provoke a relapse

It is generally believed that intestinal infection by pathogenic bacteria may provoke a relapse of IBD. Following the demonstration of the etiological role of *C. difficile* in pseudomembranous colitis in the late 1970s, there were conflicting reports of the finding and significance of *C. difficile* toxin in stool samples of patients with IBD suffering a relapse. Over the last 10 years, *C. difficile* infection has become a significant clinical problem, particularly among hospitalized elderly patients on antibiotics. Two recent retrospective analyses have reported the identification of pathogens in stool tests of 10.5% and 20% of patients with IBD in relapse [11,12]. *C. difficile* (via identification of toxin) was the most common pathogen identified and was associated with the use of antibiotics. Other pathogens included *Campylobacter* spp., *Salmonella* spp., and *Shigella* spp. Some of the patients responded to antibiotics only, implying that the infection was mimicking a relapse rather than provoking it. Because it is known that some healthy individuals are asymptomatic carriers of toxigenic *C. difficile*, further studies are required to determine the clinical significance of the presence of *C. difficile* toxin in stool samples of patients with IBD.

Conclusions

Clinical features usually allow intestinal infection to be distinguished from IBD. Diagnostic difficulty may arise in IBD patients presenting for the first time with severe symptoms. In addition to stool tests, flexible sigmoidoscopy can be particularly helpful. In those presenting with relapse of known IBD, the possibility of an infection either mimicking or provoking a relapse should be considered.

References

1 Wheeler JG, Sethi D, Cowden JM, *et al.* Study of infectious intestinal disease in England: rates in the community, presenting to general practice, and reported to national surveillance. The Infectious Intestinal Disease Study Executive. *BMJ* 1999; **318**: 1046–50.

2 *A report of the study of infectious intestinal disease in England.* Her Majesty's Stationery Office. 2000.

3 Ross AG, Bartley PB, Sleigh AC, *et al.* Schistosomiasis. *N Engl J Med* 2002; **346**: 1212–20.

4 Talan D, Moran GJ, Newdow M, *et al.* Etiology of bloody diarrhoea among patients presenting to United States emer-

gency departments: prevalence of *Escherichia coli* O157:H7 and other enteropathogens. *Clin Infect Dis* 2001; **32**: 573–80.

5 Stanley SL Jr. Amoebiasis. *Lancet* 2003; **361**: 1025–34.

6 Ostroff SM, Kapperud G, Lassen J, Aasen S, Tauxe RV. Clinical features of sporadic *Yersinia enterocolitica* infections in Norway. *J Infect Dis* 1992; **166**: 812–7.

7 Johal SS, Hammond J, Solomon K, James PD, Mahida YR. *Clostridium difficile* associated diarrhoea in hospitalised patients: onset in the community and hospital and role of flexible sigmoidoscopy. *Gut* 2004; **53**: 673–7.

8 Mantzaris GJ, Hatzis A, Archavlis E, *et al*. The role of colonoscopy in the differential diagnosis of acute, severe hemorrhagic colitis. *Endoscopy* 1995; **27**: 645–53.

9 Jenkins D, Balsitis M, Gallivan S, *et al*. Guidelines for the initial biopsy diagnosis of suspected chronic idiopathic inflammatory bowel disease. The British Society of Gastroenterology Initiative. *J Clin Pathol* 1997; **50**: 93–105.

10 Pulimood AB, Ramakrishna BS, Kurian G, *et al*. Endoscopic mucosal biopsies are useful in distinguishing granulomatous colitis due to Crohn's disease from tuberculosis. *Gut* 1999; **45**: 537–41.

11 Mylonaki M, Langmead L, Pantes A, Johnson F, Rampton DS. Enteric infection in relapse of inflammatory bowel disease: importance of microbiological examination of stool. *Eur J Gastroenterol Hepatol* 2004; **16**: 775–8.

12 Meyer AM, Ramzan NN, Loftus EV Jr, Heigh RI, Leighton JA. The diagnostic yield of stool pathogen studies during relapses of inflammatory bowel disease. *J Clin Gastroenterol* 2004; **38**: 772–5.

13 Addiss DG, Mathews HM, Stewart JM, *et al*. Evaluation of a commercially available enzyme-linked immunosorbent assay for *Giardia lamblia* antigen in stool. *J Clin Microbiol* 1991; **29**: 1137–42.

60 Microscopic colitis

DEBBIE NATHAN & PETER GIBSON

LEARNING POINTS

Microscopic colitis

- Microscopic colitis comprises lymphocytic and collagenous colitis

- Patients present with chronic watery diarrhea and macroscopically normal colonic mucosa

- It is most common in women in later life and has no relation to IBD

- Its cause is obscure, although drugs such as non-steroidal anti-inflammatory drugs and proton pump inhibitors have been implicated; some patients have associated celiac disease

- Treatment depends on severity, ranging from symptom relief with loperamide or colestyramine to budesonide and, exceptionally, more aggressive measures

- The prognosis is generally good

Introduction

Microscopic colitis (MC) is an idiopathic clinical syndrome consisting of the triad of chronic watery diarrhea, endoscopically normal colonic mucosa, and one of two characteristic histologic patterns: collagenous or lymphocytic colitis, differentiated by whether or not there is a thickened subepithelial collagen band. Whether the two conditions represent a spectrum of the same disease or separate entities is unresolved and currently of little relevance to clinical medicine.

MC was slow to be recognized – collagenous colitis (CC) was first described in 1976 and lymphocytic colitis (LC) in 1989 – because endoscopists believed that if mucosa appeared normal endoscopically, biopsies were unnecessary. MC is not generally included as a form of "IBD," but is seen as a distinct entity with different clinical presentation, his-

topathology, pathogenesis, and cause. While MC progressing to unequivocal IBD has been reported, this is unusual and when it occurs should be considered as two relatively common conditions occurring uncommonly together.

Epidemiology

High quality epidemiologic information on MC has been difficult to obtain because, first, most studies are case series, usually from referral centers, rather than population-based studies, and second, the condition is likely to be underdiagnosed in the community. Despite these limitations, clear patterns are emerging. MC has an incidence of 4–9 per 100 000/year [1,2] (LC being slightly more frequent than CC), which is not much lower than that of Crohn's disease. The prevalence of MC (10–15 per 100 000), however, is much lower than that of Crohn's disease because of its shorter natural history. Onset is mostly in the sixth decade [1,3] and, while female predominance has been generally reported for CC, sex distribution is less clear for LC. There is no evidence that MC is familial.

Clinical presentation

The symptoms and clinical course of these syndromes are highly variable. Patients typically describe watery, nonbloody diarrhea, often of sudden onset [4]. Stool frequency may fluctuate from 2 to 20 times per day. Other less frequent and non-specific symptoms include abdominal pain or discomfort, nausea, anorexia, weight loss, fatigue, fecal urgency, and incontinence. Electrolyte disturbances may occur if diarrhea is severe. There are no typical physical signs.

While the colonoscopic appearance of the colon is generally normal, patchy erythema or loss of normal vascular pattern may be found in up to 24% of patients [5]; in CC linear ulceration is occasionally seen. Imaging and laboratory investigations are usually unremarkable although inflammatory markers can be slightly raised. Fecal leukocytes may be present [6].

Natural history

The natural history of MC has been difficult to determine. A large Swedish study of LC reported spontaneous remission in a large proportion of patients, with a relapsing and remitting course in the remainder [7]. Data from populations with CC suggest that chronic continuous disease may be more frequent [6]. In general, MC is a benign condition, but can be debilitating and persistent. There is no evidence that MC is associated with an increased risk of colorectal cancer [8].

Pathology

As these syndromes are classified by their microscopic appearance, diagnosis is based on histopathology of colonic biopsies. The four key features are:
1 Increased density of intraepithelial lymphocytes in the surface compartment from a normal number of 4–10 lymphocytes per 100 epithelial cells, to a mean of 24 lymphocytes per 100 epithelial cells [9]
2 Evidence of epithelial injury in the surface compartment, most notably flattening of the cells and the presence of apoptotic cells, which are rare in the normal colon
3 A mononuclear cell infiltrate of lamina propria
4 Thickening of the subepithelial collagen table, usually exceeding 10 μm in CC

Because the histopathologic features are more prominent in the proximal than distal colon, the diagnosis cannot be excluded by distal colonic biopsies alone. Multiple biopsies are preferred for accurate classification, because the increased collagen table may be patchy. The accuracy of the histopathologic diagnosis is dependent upon the skill and experience of the pathologist. The diagnosis can be missed, or overcalled, especially with regard to the thickness of the collagen band and presence of mucosal inflammation in cross-cut sections [5].

Etiology and pathogenesis

While the causes of MC are generally not known, drug ingestion has been implicated in approximately 10% of patients, most commonly non-steroidal anti-inflammatory agents [2,4]. Other drugs, including ticlopidine, carbamazepine, serotonin reuptake inhibitors, proton pump inhibitors, amiodarone, and H_2 receptor antagonists, have been at least circumstantially associated with MC.

A minority of patients (up to 20%) presenting with MC prove to have celiac disease. In fact, 30% of patients with celiac disease may have colonic histologic appearances consistent with MC [2], which responds to a gluten-free diet. Furthermore, lymphocytic duodenitis is found in 5–10% of patients who present with MC. While some of these patients have celiac disease (and respond to a gluten-free diet), most have no response and have HLA-D phenotype inconsistent with celiac disease.

The remaining 70–85% of patients with MC have no obvious cause. The resolution of CC following ileostomy [10] and the similarity to findings found in celiac disease implicate an immune reaction to luminal antigen [6], but, other than gluten, none has been recognized. Infectious agents, such as *Clostridium difficile*, *Yersinia* sp., *Campylobacter jejuni* and the elusive Brainerd agent have been implicated. However, the possibility of an autoimmune pathogenesis is supported by concomitant autoimmune disease in up to 50% of patients with MC [3,7].

With injury to the surface epithelium, it is not difficult to understand the pathogenesis of the diarrhea seen in MC. Decreased colonic NaCl absorption has been documented [6], while bile salt malabsorption, present in less than 50% of cases [11], has provided more clues about potential therapy than cause.

Treatment

The evidence upon which the treatment of MC is based is poor. Many small observational studies have suggested efficacy with corticosteroids, 5-aminosalicylate (5-ASA), azathioprine, methotrexate, cyclosporine, antibiotics (particularly metronidazole), bismuth subsalicylate, colestyramine, octreotide, verapamil, pentoxifylline, antidiarrheals, bulking agents, and antispasmodics. Of five randomized controlled trials, only budesonide has sufficient data to yield meaningful conclusions [12]: three short-term studies involving 94 patients indicated that budesonide improves but does not heal CC, and is well tolerated.

Without a good evidence base, management has to be based upon common sense and extrapolation from experience in IBD. Any therapy must match the severity of the

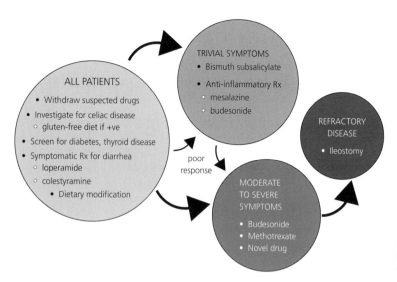

FIG 60.1 Suggested management approach to a patient with microscopic colitis.

illness and the clinical setting. It should take into account that patients with MC are generally elderly, that serious outcomes are very uncommon (and relate to the consequence of the diarrhea itself), and that MC often improves spontaneously. A suggested treatment plan is outlined in Fig. 60.1.

The initial approach must include cessation of any drugs that temporally might be incriminated, and investigation for celiac disease. If lymphocytic duodenitis is not associated with endomysial or tissue transglutaminase antibodies, HLA-D status can be helpful in the decision whether or not to pursue a gluten-free diet (a major undertaking for an elderly patient). Autoimmune conditions (especially thyroid disease and diabetes) should be considered.

Mild symptoms should be treated symptomatically, loperamide being the favored choice. Bile salt binders (such as colestyramine) can also be effective, leading to decreased diarrhea within 1 week in 3/4 patients in one open study [11]. Bismuth subsalicylate is another option with a good track record [13]. Dietary advice should be offered to all patients, but there are few data on which to base recommendations. Lactose intolerance is common in MC [3] and therefore avoidance of lactose and other dietary components that can induce diarrhea (especially sorbitol, free fructose, wheat, and onions) seems reasonable.

Anti-inflammatory therapy seems logical in those with more than trivial symptoms. Mesalazine-delivering drugs are often disappointing, only achieving a good response in

50% of patients [5]. Coated budesonide is well tolerated and efficacious, but does not induce healing, and, in more severe cases, might be needed for long periods. Prednisolone also seems to be of benefit in some patients, but relapse is almost invariable on withdrawal of the drug [14]. Because of its side-effect profile, it is best avoided.

In IBD, immunosuppressive agents are used in chronically active disease. This principle has also been applied to MC. Two groups from Australia have each found that oral methotrexate (10 mg/week) induces remission and often healing within 6 weeks with minimal toxicity [15].

Although evidence of efficacy for other drugs such as verapamil, antibiotics, and octreotide are lacking, they can be considered in resistant cases. Ileostomy is well documented to induce remission of CC, but should be reserved for very refractory patients.

Conclusions

Microscopic colitis is usually a benign condition and is more common than is generally appreciated. Determining its etiology and pathogenesis remains a challenge. Diagnosis is dependent upon the taking of multiple colonoscopic biopsies in patients with chronic diarrhea and requires an experienced pathologist. Therapy is largely empirical and "borrowed" from experience in IBD. More randomized controlled trials are needed to guide our therapeutic choices.

References

1 Fernandez-Banares F, Salas A, Forne M, *et al.* Incidence of collagenous and lymphocytic colitis: a 5 year population-based study. *Am J Gastroenterol* 1999; **94**: 418–23.

2 Pardi DS. Microscopic colitis an update. *Inflamm Bowel Dis* 2004; **10**: 860–70.

3 Koskela RM, Niemela SE, Karttunen TJ, Lehtola JK. Clinical characteristics of collagenous and lymphocytic colitis. *Scand J Gastroenterol* 2004; **39**: 837–45.

4 Bohr J, Tysk C, Eriksson S, Abrahamsson H, Järnerot G. Collagenous colitis: a retrospective study of clinical presentation and treatment in 163 patients. *Gut* 1996; **39**: 846–51.

5 Fraser AG, Warren BF, Chandrapala R, Jewell DP. Microscopic colitis: a clinical and pathological review. *Scand J Gastroenterol* 2002; **37**: 1241–5.

6 Tagkalidis P, Bhathal P, Gibson P. Microscopic colitis. *J Gastroenterol Hepatol* 2002; **17**: 236–48.

7 Olesen M, Eriksson S, Bohr J, Järnerot G, Tysk C. Lymphocytic colitis: a retrospective clinical study of 199 Swedish patients. *Gut* 2004; **53**: 536–41.

8 Chan JL, Tersmette AC, Offerhaus JA, *et al.* Cancer risk in collagenous colitis. *Inflamm Bowel Dis* 1999; **5**: 40–3.

9 Lazenby AJ, Yardley JH, Giardiello FM, *et al.* Lymphocytic colitis: a comparative histopathologic study with particular reference to collagenous colitis. *Hum Pathol* 1989; **20**: 18–28.

10 Järnerot G, Tysk C, Bohr J, Eriksson S. Collagenous colitis and fecal stream diversion. *Gastroenterology* 1995; **109**: 449–55.

11 Ung KA, Gillberg R, Kilander A, Abrahamsson H. Role of bile acids and bile acid binding agents in patients with collagenous colitis. *Gut* 2000; **46**: 170–5.

12 Chande N, McDonald JW, Macdonald JK. Interventions for treating collagenous colitis: a Cochrane Inflammatory Bowel Disease Group systematic review of randomized trials. *Am J Gastroenterol* 2004; **99**: 2459–65.

13 Fine KD, Lee EL. Efficacy of open-label bismuth subsalicylate for the treatment of microscopic colitis. *Gastroenterology* 1998; **114**: 29–36.

14 Munck LK, Kjeldsen J, Philipsen E, Fischer Hansen B. Incomplete remission with short-term prednisolone treatment in collagenous colitis: a randomized study. *Scand J Gastroenterol* 2003; **38**: 606–10.

15 Tagkalidis P, Gibson P, Bhathal P. Histological regression of severe and steroid-dependent microscopic colitis with oral methotrezate. *J Gastroenterol Hepatol* 2002; **17**(S): A104.

61 Diverticular colitis

LINMARIE LUDEMAN & NEIL A SHEPHERD

Introduction

Diverticular colitis (DC) is a condition poorly recognized by clinicians and pathologists alike and yet is one of the more important mimics of chronic IBD, clinically, endoscopically and histologically. The perplexities surrounding DC are multifactorial because of poor definition, its mimicry of other conditions and the use of multiple appellations to describe this condition. The terms segmental colitis, crescentic colitis, sigmoiditis and sigmoid colitis have all been used in the past but the term diverticular colitis is now preferred [1,2].

What is diverticular colitis?

DC describes the occurrence of luminal mucosal inflammation in the sigmoid colon affected by diverticular disease, irrespective of the presence or absence of diverticulitis (inflammation of the actual diverticula in diverticular disease). It is important to realize that diverticular disease itself is primarily characterized by the distinctive changes in the muscularis propria of the sigmoid colon, with or without mucosal outpouchings – DC may therefore be found in segments of bowel affected by diverticular disease, without, necessarily, evidence of diverticula themselves.

Although DC might be considered a rare condition because few cases are described in the literature, up to 25% of resected colons with diverticular disease may show some features of DC [2]. Bearing in mind the prevalence of diverticular disease in Western populations, one could therefore argue for a much higher prevalence of the disease than the literature would seem to attest. Possible reasons for the failure to diagnose DC, and the paucity of cases in the literature, may be that it is often a subclinical problem or that the symptoms have, erroneously, been attributed to chronic inflammatory bowel disease [3]. It is important to differentiate DC from UC and Crohn's disease as the treatment and prognosis may differ radically.

Clinical and pathologic features

Both diverticular disease and DC occur most frequently in the elderly population, as a lifetime of Western-style diet is usually a requirement for the development of sigmoid colonic diverticular disease. Patients with DC often present with rectal bleeding and/or a change of bowel habit with or without passage of mucus [4]. The endoscopic features may vary in severity and can include mucosal hyperemia, erosions, or edema. These changes are seen away from the orifices of the diverticula themselves, usually on crescentic folds of mucosa, hence the previously used term crescentic colitis [2].

The histologic features reflect the variability of the intensity of the inflammation and include a wide variety of findings ranging between mild inflammation with edema and telangiectasia, through the changes of mucosal prolapse to florid chronic active inflammatory changes closely mimicking C-IBD [2,4,5]. Clearly, the context in which the changes are found is of utmost importance when assessing the significance of the histopathologic findings.

Pathogenesis

DC may occur even before diverticular disease itself becomes manifest, in the condition of "pre-diverticular disease." This suggests that the catalytic event for the pathogenesis of DC is the intraluminal environment in the bowel [2,6]. However, it has been shown that DC is the final result of divergent pathologic factors. In the colon with diverticular disease, there is relative mucosal redundancy, leading to mucosal prolapse. These redundant mucosal folds are exposed to more mechanical stresses, especially when the stool is firm, leading to ischemia, ulceration, and inflammation [1,2]. Colonic ischemia itself may also be an important pathogenetic factor (Fig. 61.1). Other cases may represent a mass effect, where luminal inflammation is found directly overlying a peridiverticular abscess [7] or the result of increased exposure to intraluminal antigens and toxins because of relative stasis [8]. Rarely, there is an intriguing relationship between DC and UC (see below).

Differential diagnosis

DC is notorious for being a mimic of both Crohn's disease and UC. DC may also be mistaken for ischemic colitis. It is not always straightforward to differentiate all these conditions, clinically and pathologically and, indeed, they may coexist or be causally related to one another.

The distinction of DC from IBD can be problematic, especially the more severe forms of the disease, where there can be marked active chronic inflammation, ulceration, crypt abscess formation and crypt architectural distortion [2]. These microscopic features strongly mimic CIBD, specifically UC [1,2,4,5,9]. This form of DC may also respond to medications similar to that used in CIBD [1,4,8,10].

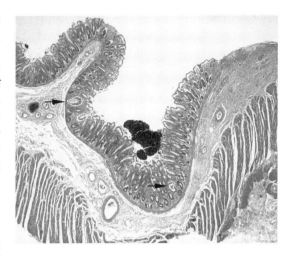

FIG 61.1 A low power histologic view of a sigmoid colonic resection with diverticular colitis (DC). The patient presented with rectal bleeding and blood is present in the lumen (center). The muscular wall of the sigmoid colon is thickened, typical of diverticular disease. The luminal mucosa is inflamed with two well-defined crypt abscesses (arrows). However, there is also ulceration with withering of the epithelium at the edge of the ulcer, typical of ischemia (at right). This case represents diverticular colitis due to relative mucosal ischemia in a known arteriopath. In this case the orifices of the diverticula were notably spared of the inflammatory changes and the ulceration, presumably because of the proximity of the diverticula to the arterial supply.

Ulcerative colitis

In endoscopic biopsy material it may be impossible to distinguish DC from UC as the histologic features may overlap. It is thus of critical importance that biopsies are taken from the rectum and from the colon proximal to the segment affected by diverticulosis and DC. In the latter, a rectal biopsy will be normal whereas it will show active disease in UC. Particular difficulties occur when there is relative rectal sparing in UC or when UC has been treated with enemas [11]. A good history together with the inclusion of rectal biopsies are therefore of the utmost importance in making the appropriate diagnosis.

There have been reports of cases, initially limited to the segment of colon affected by diverticular disease, that have subsequently evolved into classic distal chronic UC, involving rectal mucosa that had been entirely normal at the time of diagnosis of DC [1,4,5,10]. It has been postulated that the dynamic changes, fecal stasis and bacterial mucolysis that occur in diverticular disease provide the milieu that enables classic chronic UC to subsequently supervene [1,12]. Whatever the significance of this intriguing association, it is unusual and it remains possible that the association is merely fortuitous.

Crohn's disease

Here it should be emphasized that whilst granulomas, and indeed the other histologic hallmarks of Crohn's disease, are a characteristic feature of the disease, they are not specific to Crohn's disease and can be seen in many other situations, including diverticular disease/colitis [7,13,14]. It has been stated that there is a high rate of co-existence of Crohn's disease and diverticular disease, more so than the prevalence of either would suggest. This may be because granulomas and other features thought characteristic of Crohn's disease may be seen in isolated diverticular disease/colitis [13,14].

It may be difficult to differentiate DC and Crohn's disease on the basis of biopsies from the sigmoid colon alone and it is therefore important, as with the differential diagnosis of DC versus UC, to seek evidence of Crohn's disease elsewhere in the gastrointestinal tract, before making the diagnosis of Crohn's disease purely on the basis of biopsy material (or even a resection) from the sigmoid colon afflicted by diverticular disease. Even endoscopic features typical of Crohn's disease, such as aphthous ulcers, are well described in the sigmoid colon affected by DC [5].

It has been suggested that the co-existence of Crohn's disease and diverticulitis carries a worse prognosis with a more complicated clinical course than either disease in isolation [15]. To counter this, there is now increasing evidence that those cases with Crohn's-like features, isolated to the sigmoid colon affected by diverticulosis, have a remarkably good outcome following resection, with many patients showing no evidence of recurrence of "Crohn's disease" elsewhere [1,13]. This strongly suggests that many of the reported cases do not represent true co-existent Crohn's disease, but rather represent an idiosyncratic inflammatory response to the diverticular disease [1,2,13].

Conclusions

Diverticular colitis is a clinically rare, subclinically more common, form of inflammatory pathology of the luminal mucosa of the sigmoid colon in patients with diverticular disease. It usually presents with rectal bleeding and may show important clinical, endoscopic and pathologic mimicry of chronic idiopathic IBD. It may show fascinating, if uncommon, relationships with UC. Given the complete lack of controlled data, recommendations for treatment lack an evidence base. Nevertheless, the use of steroids and other immunomodulatory drugs, often used for IBD, for the treatment of DC may not be appropriate.

References

1 Shepherd NA. Diverticular disease and chronic idiopathic inflammatory bowel disease: associations and masquerades. *Gut* 1996; **38**: 801–2.

2 Ludeman L, Shepherd NA. What is diverticular colitis? *Pathology* 2002; **34**: 568–72.

3 Markham NI, Li AK. Diverticulitis of the right colon: experience from Hong Kong. *Gut* 1992; **33**: 547–9.

4 Gore S, Shepherd NA, Wilkinson SP. Endoscopic crescentic fold disease of the sigmoid colon: the clinical and histopathological spectrum of a distinctive endoscopic appearance. *Int J Colorectal Dis* 1992; 7: 76–81.

5 Makapugay LM, Dean PJ. Diverticular disease-associated chronic colitis. *Am J Surg Pathol* 1996; **20**: 94–102.

6 Mathus-Vliegen EM, Tytgat GN. Polyp-simulating mucosal prolapse syndrome in (pre-)diverticular disease. *Endoscopy* 1986; **18**: 84–6.

7 Gupta J, Shepherd NA. Colorectal mass lesions masquerading as chronic inflammatory bowel disease on mucosal biopsy. *Histopathology* 2003; **42**: 476–81.

8 van Rosendaal GM, Andersen MA. Segmental colitis complicating diverticular disease. *Can J Gastroenterol* 1996; **10**: 361–4.

9 Cawthorn SJ, Gibbs NM, Marks CG. Segmental colitis: a new complication of diverticular colitis. *Gut* 1983; **24**: A500.

10 Peppercorn MA. Drug-responsive chronic segmental colitis associated with diverticula: a clinical syndrome in the elderly. *Am J Gastroenterol* 1992; **87**: 609–12.

11 Spiliadis CA, Spiliadis CA, Lennard-Jones JE. Ulcerative colitis with relative sparing of the rectum: clinical features, histology and prognosis. *Dis Colon Rectum* 1987; **30**: 334–6.

12 Tsai HH, Dwarakanath AD, Hart CA, Milton JD, Rhodes JM. Increased faecal mucin sulphatase activity in ulcerative colitis: a potential target for treatment. *Gut* 1995; **36**: 570–6.

13 Goldstein NS, Leon-Armin C, Mani A. Crohn's colitis-like changes in sigmoid diverticulitis specimens is usually an idiosyncratic inflammatory response to the diverticulosis rather than Crohn's colitis. *Am J Surg Pathol* 2000; **24**: 668–75.

14 Shepherd NA. Pathological mimics of chronic inflammatory bowel disease. *J Clin Pathol* 1991; **44**: 726–33.

15 Berman IR, Corman ML, Coller JA, Veidenheimer MC. Late onset Crohn's disease in patients with colonic diverticulitis. *Dis Colon Rectum* 1979; **22**: 524–9.

Part 7 The IBD Service: Time for a Rethink?

62 Outpatient services – do doctors still have a role?

MARK KELLY & ANDREW ROBINSON

LEARNING POINTS

Outpatient services

- IBD has traditionally been managed by fixed hospital outpatient appointments

- However, patient-directed care with open access to hospital appointments is preferred by many patients and primary care physicians

- Such systems appear more cost-effective in the short-term, but long-term outcome is unclear

- Not all patients with IBD are suitable for, or prefer, patient-directed care

---

Introduction

A typical hospital serving a population of 250 000 people will treat approximately 50 new IBD patients/year and will provide services for up to 700 follow-up patients. Another 200 patients are likely to be managed by their primary care physician or receive no follow-up at all [1]. Some hospitals provide specialist IBD clinics with dedicated specialist nurses, pharmacists, and dietitians, while others have mixed gastroenterology clinics where IBD patients are seen alongside patients with other gastrointestinal conditions without specialist support services.

Patients with IBD require health services that are responsive to the changing requirements of their disease activity. Patients with complex, unresponsive, and frequently relapsing symptoms require greater specialist medical and psychosocial support than those with infrequent relapses or long-term quiescent disease.

The minority of IBD patients with frequently relapsing or chronic continuous disease require intense specialist monitoring and treatment, frequent fixed clinical review, medical and surgical input, and rapid access to medical advice; many of these patients will need surgery. For these patients, conventional secondary care-based management remains the most appropriate service.

Most patients with IBD run a relapsing/remitting course. Eighty-two percent of patients with UC have either intermittent relapses or remission 3–7 years after diagnosis and most patients' lives are relatively untroubled by their disease [2]. Three-quarters of Crohn's patients are fully capable for work at any given time following diagnosis [3].

Approaches to outpatient IBD management

The traditional service-centered model of health management based around fixed clinic visits, long-term hospital follow-up, and prescriptive treatment is poorly suited to the needs of IBD patients.

Most gastroenterologists follow up their IBD patients indefinitely [4]. Reported reasons for long-term hospital follow-up include: a perceived need for review of symptoms, medications and blood tests; unwillingness to discharge to primary care management; and a belief that patients expect hospital treatment [5]. Routine hospital follow-up for stable IBD patients represents a significant cost to health services and is inconvenient to many IBD patients who are often young and in employment. Prearranged clinic visits are unlikely to correspond with periods of disease activity; access to clinicians during exacerbations depends on clinic availability which may delay initiation of treatment; non-attendance rates are often high in this group of patients, and duplication of clinical activity in primary and secondary care is common [6].

Alternative approaches to chronic disease management where patients are supported to take an active role in monitoring and managing their disease have resulted in improved glycemic control in diabetic patients [7] and reduced morbidity in asthmatics [8].

A randomized trial of guided self-management and patient-directed follow-up in patients with UC resulted in a 70% reduction in outpatient attendances, earlier treatment of relapses and was preferred to traditional management [9]. In this trial, 203 patients with quiescent colitis were randomized to receive personalized self-management training and open access to hospital clinics instead of their usual management. Patients in the intervention group made an average of 0.73 hospital visits/year compared with 2.45 visits/year in the control group (Fig. 62.1). There was

a similar two-thirds reduction in primary care visits and a highly significant reduction in the delay between relapse and treatment.

Another IBD self-management study evaluated the effectiveness of a whole systems approach to treatment [10]. The intervention consisted of consultant training in patient-centered care, detailed written patient information, self-management training for patients with quiescent disease and patient-directed follow-up for those who did not require fixed appointments. Nineteen hospitals were randomized to intervention sites [9] or control sites [10] and 700 patients with Crohn's disease and UC were recruited for a 1-year trial. All patients were eligible for inclusion in the study although not all patients were stable enough to receive all elements of the intervention. For patients in the intervention group, consultation rates fell by 1.04/patient/year without any increase in primary care visits, quality of life and anxiety scores remained unchanged, enablement scores (a measure of patients' perceived control of illness) increased and there was an average cost reduction of £134/patient/year.

Williams *et al.* [11] compared open access clinics with fixed routine follow-up clinics and found that patients and primary care physicians prefer the flexibility provided by review on request. The study showed a slight reduction in hospital visits but there were no cost advantages. Some patients experienced difficulties making urgent appointments, highlighting the importance of adequate clinic capacity and structured access arrangements.

Multidisciplinary team

Over the last few years, IBD specialist nurses have become a key component of IBD service provision and are employed by one-quarter to one-third of British hospitals (see Chapter 63). They undertake a number of roles previously performed by medical staff including patient education, outpatient follow-up, medicine review, telephone advice, clinic triage, prescribing, GP education, and immuno-suppressant monitoring. They are seen as an invaluable resource by many gastroenterologists and their role is highly valued by patients. There is, however, little published evidence to support these widely held beliefs although there is uncontrolled evidence to suggest that IBD nurses may be a cost-effective addition to an established IBD department. Nightingale *et al.* [12] compared hospital visits, inpatient stays, and rates of disease remis-

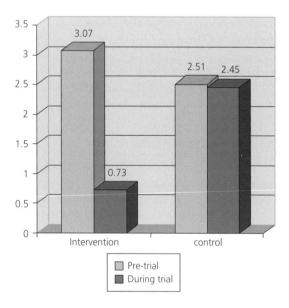

FIG 62.1 Annual hospital consultation rates before and during the self-management trial.

sion in the years before and after the appointment of an IBD specialist nurse. They reported a 38% reduction in hospital visits, a 19% reduction in inpatient bed stays, and an increase in remission rates from 63 to 69%. A nurse-led telephone helpline accounted for many of the reduced hospital visits.

Telephone consultations were the subject of a study by Miller *et al.* [13] in which routine clinic consultations were replaced by a nurse-led telephone support service. A total of 150 (of 155 patients invited) agreed to participate and received an evening telephone consultation based on a structured questionnaire. Most patients found this an acceptable and convenient service and only 23/150 patients required a clinic review for further assessment because of worsening symptoms.

What are the requirements for outpatient services for patients with IBD?

There are no minimum standards for the provision of IBD services but the British Society of Gastroenterology Guidelines for the Management of Inflammatory Bowel Disease propose the following as a basis for outpatient services [14].

• Rapid access to clinic appointments for patients with symptoms of IBD

• Rapid access to advice and clinic appointments for patients in the event of a relapse

• Adequate time and space in outpatients (and wards) to meet the unpredictable pattern of disease, allow discussion, explanation or counseling, and provide information or educational material

• Easy access to private, clean toilet facilities for patients

• Administrative and clinical support for different models of care (hospital-based, shared care systems with primary care, or patient-managed care)

• A multidisciplinary team that manages patients with IBD in hospitals that train specialists in the care of IBD patients.

Conclusions

Most patients with IBD have periods of remission punctuated by periods of disease activity. Traditional outpatient follow-up based on fixed appointments with doctors is being replaced by more flexible services incorporating guided self-management and open access follow-up. Many of the roles undertaken by doctors are now nurse-led and

face-to-face consultations can be replaced by telephone follow-up, which many patients find more convenient. Unlike most aspects of IBD management, there are few well-controlled studies evaluating the benefits of these changes and questions remain about the long-term outcomes of self-management, the cost-effectiveness of specialist nurses, the willingness of clinicians to transfer control to patients, and the flexibility of clinics to deal with unplanned demand. The basic principles of early diagnosis, rapid access for acute symptoms, and safe monitoring of therapy remain the key priorities of any IBD service.

References

1 Rubin GP, Hungin AP, Kelly PJ, Ling J. Inflammatory bowel disease: epidemiology and management in an English general practice population. *Aliment Pharmacol Ther* 2000; **14**: 1553–9.

2 Langholz E, Munkholm P, Davidsen M, *et al.* Course of ulcerative colitis: analysis of changes in disease activity over years. *Gastroenterology* 1994; **107**: 3–11.

3 Munkholm P, Langholz E, Davidsen M, *et al.* Disease activity courses in a regional cohort of Crohn's disease patients. *Scand J Gastroenterol* 1995; **30**: 699–706.

4 Probert CS, Jayanthi V, Mayberry JF. British gastroenterologists' care profile for patients with inflammatory bowel disease: the need for a patients' charter. *J R Soc Med* 1993; **86**: 271–2.

5 Burkey Y, Black M, Reeve H, Roland M. Long-term follow-up in outpatient clinics. 2: The view from the specialist clinic. *Fam Pract* 1997; **14**: 29–33.

6 Reeve H, Baxter K, Newton P, *et al.* Long-term follow-up in outpatient clinics. 1. The view from general practice. *Fam Pract* 1997; **14**: 24–8.

7 Anderson RM, Funnell MM, Butler PM, *et al.* Patient empowerment: results of a randomized controlled trial. *Diabetes Care* 1995; **18**: 943–9.

8 Kotses H, Bernstein IL, Bernstein DI, *et al.* A self-management program for adult asthma. Part I. Development and evaluation. *J Allergy Clin Immunol* 1995; **95**: 529–40.

9 Robinson A, Thompson DG, Wilkin D, Roberts C; Northwest Gastrointestinal Research Group. Guided self-management and patient-directed follow-up of ulcerative colitis: a randomised trial. *Lancet* 2001; **358**: 976–81.

10 Kennedy A, Nelson E, Reeves D, *et al.* A randomised controlled trial to assess the effectiveness and cost of a patient orientated self management approach to chronic inflammatory bowel disease. *Gut* 2004; **53**: 1639–45.

11 Williams JG, Cheung WY, Russell IT, *et al.* Open access follow up for inflammatory bowel disease: pragmatic

randomised trial and cost effectiveness study. *BMJ* 2000; **320**: 544–8.

12 Nightingale AJ, Middleton W, Middleton SJ, Hunter JO. Evaluation of the effectiveness of a specialist nurse in the management of inflammatory bowel disease (IBD). *Eur J Gastroenterol Hepatol* 2000; **12**: 967–73.

13 Miller L, Caton S, Lynch D. Telephone clinic improves quality of follow-up care for chronic bowel disease. *Nurs Times* 2002; **98**: 36–8.

14 Carter MJ, Lobo AJ, Travis SP; IBD Section, British Society of Gastroenterology. Guidelines for the management of inflammatory bowel disease in adults. *Gut* 2004; **53** (Suppl 5): 1–16.

The IBD Service: Time for a Rethink?

63 Shared care: tactical team selection

RESHMA C RAKSHIT & JOHN MAYBERRY

LEARNING POINTS

Shared care

A multidisciplinary approach to the management of IBD is important because:

- It empowers the patient
- It educates not only the patient but also the carers
- It engenders a spirit of partnership
- It is likely to improve quality of care

Introduction

The concept of multidisciplinary teams working for the benefit of patients has come to the fore during the last decade. Such teamwork should put particular emphasis on working together to deliver a coordinated, integrated service for consumers [1]. With the growing recognition of the social consequences of IBD and the complex nature of new treatments, the need for such teams is inevitable.

This form of teamwork is central to the postmodern organization of health care [2]. A multidisciplinary team gains from the cooperation between members. In other words, "the members of the team can produce more working co-operatively than separately" [3]. However, this is only true when team members are working with well-defined and common objectives.

The emphasis on teamwork has increased because of two factors. First, health care has become more specialized, complex, and technical. This has led to a range of specialists being involved in the care of patients with significantly increased interdependency [4]. Second, team-based organizations are more efficient, effective, adaptive, and cost-effective than unidisciplinary, bureaucratic ones [5].

In 1997, the Royal Commission on the National Health Service stated "We are in no doubt that it is in the patients' interests for multidisciplinary team working to be encouraged" [6]. In 1990, the NHS and Community Care Act advocated team care and collaboration between professionals. Such changes in approach will need to be reflected in the field of IBD.

The disease

The incidence of UC is 10–20 per 100 000 per year and of Crohn's disease is 5–10 per 100 000 per year for Crohn's disease [7]. Therefore, an average hospital, which serves a population of 300 000, has a new patient load of 45–90 cases per year with at least 500 people under regular follow-up. Because of the complex nature of diagnosis and management, a form of multidisciplinary approach has evolved over the years. However, as yet this has not been formalized which contrasts with the situation for other chronic diseases, where a shared care, multidisciplinary team approach is now commonplace.

Diagnosis, treatment, and management of complications involve several clinical specialities including gastroenterologists, gastrointestinal surgeons, radiologists, pathologists, nurse specialists, pharmacists, dietitians, and at times psychologists and social workers. However, the most important members of the team should be the patients and their family. For treatment to be successful, the patients needs to be well informed and agree to the plan of management decided in conjunction with their physicians [8]. They need to know how, where, and when to access treatment and so have greater control over their disease and its treatment [9]. Such an inclusive approach is seldom seen in practice and many patients still have to deal with paternalistic doctors.

In the next section we elaborate on the roles of different members of the team and provide evidence where available. However, evidence for these roles can be sparse and more research is needed.

Multidisciplinary team

Primary care
Traditionally, care of IBD patients has been shared between general practitioners (GPs) and hospital-based physicians. However, work from Middlesbrough [10] and Leicestershire [11] has shown that between 32% [11] and 70% [10] of patients are managed solely in the community. The introduction of computer-based registers will allow the care of such patients to be monitored to a common standard.

A study from Wales examined a shared care program (see Chapter 62) [12] in which patients had been randomized to routine hospital follow-up, or GP care with open-access hospital follow-up. Rapid access to secondary care was guaranteed for the latter group when considered necessary by either the patient or GP. Sixty-eight percent of GPs expressed a preference for this system. The advantages identified included stability of the patient's condition, access to specialists when needed, and the saving of time. However, the use of shared guidelines on treatment was less successful when implemented in Leicester, with a significant number of patients returning to hospital-based care [13]. This contrasted with a later study from Tunbridge Wells [14] which showed that guided primary care follow-up resulted in a net gain of 49 appointments in the secondary care sector over a 6-month period.

Interface and nurse-led care
One proposal from this study, [12] was of the need for specialist nurses in gastroenterology. Specialist nurses have been shown to be cost-effective in chronic disease management [15] and to reduce hospital admissions [16]; one IBD-related study showed a 38% reduction in hospital visits, a 19% reduction in inpatient stay, an increase in disease remission by 6%, and greater patient satisfaction. Ease of access to information on IBD, advice on avoidance of

illness, and maintenance of health were also noted [17]. Telephone helplines may also be effective in facilitating quick and appropriate access to secondary care; in a pilot study they reduced unnecessary follow-up and led to more rapid help during relapses [18].

The role of the specialist nurse in IBD is yet to be fully defined but includes:

1 Patient and family education and support
2 Nurse-led clinics with telephone helplines
3 Maintenance and monitoring of treatment, including immunosuppressive therapy
4 Inpatient support, including nutrition
5 Liaison with other members of the multidisciplinary team

For patients facing surgery, stoma nurses are considered mandatory. However, this view is not evidence-based. Indeed, a study examining psychological adjustment 10 weeks and 1 year after surgery found no benefit in patients seen by stoma nurses compared with those seen by representatives from an appliance company [19]. In another study, a failure of stoma nurses to provide appropriate advice to Asian patients was identified [20]; training of multidisciplinary teams about the needs of different ethnic and cultural groups would redress this problem.

Secondary care
The diagnosis and management of IBD can be complicated. A recent study reported the positive impact of a monthly multidisciplinary clinic involving a gastroenterologist, colorectal surgeon, and IBD specialist nurse. They were able to identify patients who needed surgery or infliximab therapy and reduce the time spent by specialists exchanging letters [21].

The core of such a team should include:
• a gastroenterologist
• a surgeon specializing in IBD
• a specialist IBD nurse
• a dietitian
• a pharmacist
• a social worker
• the patient

The team should also have close links with a radiologist, a pathologist and, when necessary, a psychologist and a clinical librarian; "PONDS" might be a suitable acronym (Table 63.1). The role of the physiotherapist and occupational therapist is well-established in multidisciplinary teams caring for patients with other chronic disabilities, but requires evaluation for those with IBD.

TABLE 63.1 To distinguish IBD-directed from traditional multidisciplinary teams, such teams could be known by the acronym PONDS.

P Patient, pharmacist, possibly psychologist and physiotherapist
O Others including occupational therapist
N Nurses
D Doctors, dietitian
S Social worker

The patient

The most important element of the multidisciplinary team is the patient. In one study, 50–80% of patients felt they were insufficiently informed about their condition and identified a lack of personal control over their lives as a significant problem [22]. Patient education, self-management, and a closer relationship with health care professionals can help address these problems.

The value of patient expertise in self-management of chronic diseases has been clearly demonstrated [23,24]. Empowerment of patients, which allows partnerships with the health care team, is cost-effective. In fact, the expert patient program was introduced recently in the UK as a centerpiece of the NHS approach to chronic disease management [25]. (The potentially beneficial effect of patient empowerment on provision of secondary outpatient care is discussed in Chapter 62.)

Conclusions

Multidisciplinary team involvement in IBD management offers significant advantages. The most important member of the team should be the patient. Patient education, partnership with the health care team, and a change in the attitude of both parties will enable more effective management. However, more research is needed in this field to identify the most efficient and cost-effective methods of IBD management.

References

1 Contested territory and community services: Interprofessional boundaries in health and social care. In: Soothill K, Mackay L, Webb C. (eds) *Interprofessional Relations in Health Care*. Edward Arnold.

2 Hartley P. *Group Communication*. Routledge, 1997.

3 Barney J, Hesterly W. Organisation economics: Understanding the relationship between organisations and economic analysis. In Clegg S, Hardy C, Nord W. (eds) *Handbook of Organisation Studies*. Sage, London, 1996: 114–47.

4 Northouse L, Northouse P. *Health Communication: Strategies for Health Professionals* (3rd edn). Appleton and Lange, Stamford, 1998.

5 Becker-Reams E, Garrett D. *Testing the Limits of Teams: How to Implement Self-Management in Health Care*. American Hospital Publishing, Chicago, 1998.

6 Bruce N. *Teamwork for Preventative Care*. Research Studies Press, Herts, 1980.

7 Loftus EV Jr. Clinical epidemiology of inflammatory bowel disease: incidence, prevalence and environmental influences. *Gastroenterology* 2004; **126**; 1504–17.

8 Clarke NM, Gong M. Management of chronic diseases by practitioners and patients: are we teaching the wrong things? *BMJ* 2000; **320**: 572–5.

9 Windsor R. Facing the challenges of long term care. *BMJ* 2000; **320**: 589.

10 Rubin GP, Hungin AP, Kelly PJ, *et al.* Inflammatory bowel disease: epidemiology and management in an English general practice population. *Aliment Pharmacol Ther* 2000; **14**: 1553–59.

11 Stone MA, Mayberry JF, Baker R. Prevalence and management of inflammatory bowel disease: a cross-sectional study from central England. *Eur J Gastroenterol Hepatol* 2003; **15**: 1275–80.

12 Cheung WY, Dove J, Lervy B, *et al.* Shared care in gastroenterology: GPs' views of open access to out-patient follow-up for patients with inflammatory bowel disease. *Fam Pract* 2002; **19**: 53–6.

13 Read AM, Stone MA, Rathbone BJ, *et al.* Production and evaluation of guidelines for the management of inflammatory bowel disease: the Leicester experience. *Postgrad Med J* 1999; **75**: 147–50.

14 Hayee BH, Basavarajaiah S, Harris AW. Guided primary care management of inflammatory bowel disease. *BSG* 2005; A405.

15 Blue L, Lang E, McMurray JJV, *et al.* Randomised controlled trial of specialist nurse intervention in heart failure. *BMJ* 2001; **323**: 715–8.

16 Mason JM, Freemantle N, Gibson JM, *et al.* Specialist nurse-led clinics to improve control of hypertension and hyperglycaemia in diabetes: economic analysis of the SPLINT trial. *Diabetes Care* 2005; **28**: 40–6.

17 Nightingale AJ, Middleton W, Middleton SJ, *et al.* Evaluation of the effectiveness of a specialist nurse in the management of inflammatory bowel disease (IBD). *Eur J Gastroenterol Hepatol* 2000; **12**: 967–73.

18 Miller L, Caton S, Lynch D. Telephone clinics improves quality of follow-up for chronic bowel disease. *Nurs Times* 2002; **98**: 36–8.

2 Can be structured to produce a patient-held record consisting of a disease summary and treatment – of particular value to patients when traveling or attending a hospital unfamiliar with their case

3 The database can be built to provide prompts and safety alerts. For example, interval since last colonoscopy, to facilitate appropriate timing of surveillance procedures; identification of patients on steroids who are not receiving treatment to minimize bone injury

For the specialist nurse

1 Facilitates protocol-guided care

2 Provides readily available information when responding to patients' enquiries without the need to locate the paper record

3 Supports postal, telephone, or open-access follow-up of patients

4 Facilitates monitoring of the nurse's own activity

For the general practitioner

1 Enables the automatic production of letters to general practitioners following consultations

2 Speeds up outpatient clinics, creating time for new referrals to be seen

3 Can be constructed to allow the general practitioner access to the database

For audit and research

1 Creates a disease register automatically as a by-product of patient care

2 Facilitates "look-back." For example: all patients on immunosuppressants for more than 4 years; any patient with dysplasia detected at colonoscopy

3 Identification of patients with specific disease characteristics suitable for inclusion in clinical studies

4 Allows studies to be performed using data collected within the database, avoiding the need for purpose-designed forms [5]

Creating an inflammatory bowel disease clinical database

Most databases have been created by enthusiasts and are used in individual departments, but there are one or two commercial offerings that have been developed in liaison with clinicians. An international database originating in Austria has growing exposure and is targeted particularly at recruitment to clinical trials and at accumulating aggre-

gate data (IBDIS) [6]. The very large number of data items collected on each patient make this database less suitable for day-to-day care of individual patients.

The wide availability of computer skills and database software mean that "home grown" databases are readily developed. This individual approach does not facilitate exchange of data between separate hospitals but is a quick and practical way of getting going. If the database uses common terminology derived from the nationally mandated coding system, SNOMED-CT, sharing of information between departments of gastroenterology becomes feasible. The British Society of Gastroenterology is assisting the UK national program in developing a complete list of the clinical terms in use in the care of patients with IBD. These terms should form the basis for the fields of a clinical database. By including clinical decision support in the database, further improvements in patient care and reduction of medical errors can be attained [7], at the expense of increasing the level of complexity in creating the database.

Populating the database

Once designed and built, the database only becomes useful when populated with patients' details. The ideal approach is to acquire patient data prospectively but usually there will be a large number of existing patients whose data must be added retrospectively. For the same reason that the database is so valuable, it can be very time-consuming to extract the relevant information from each patient's paper record. The skills of the IBD specialist nurse make him/her ideal for this task, which requires a depth of knowledge rarely found in administrative assistants, but the tedium of the task must be acknowledged and the time necessary made available. Entering details becomes quicker and easier with practice and updating information at the time of each patient contact should take only a minute or two. The benefits to the patient and the whole health care team make this effort ultimately rewarding.

Disadvantages of databases

There are some drawbacks to single disease clinical databases. Patients often have many medical problems and focusing only on the details held in the database can mean other diseases are overlooked. Countering this by creating specific databases for each possible disease becomes

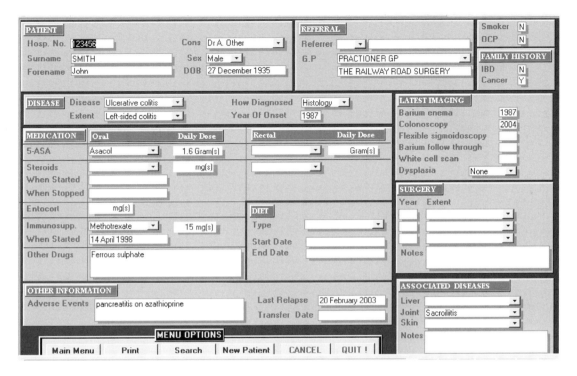

FIG 64.1 Screen shot of Inflammatory Bowel Disease database (IBD*base*).

logistically impossible to manage. In time, Connecting for Health [1], by providing access to each UK citizen's health record, will overcome these limitations and make IBD (and all other disease-specific) databases unnecessary.

Conclusions

The greatest benefit of an IBD database is the instant availability of all essential information when seeing a complex patient, facilitating a department's delivery of effective care [3], with the potential to reduce errors [7]. Beyond this, the adoption of agreed terminology in a standard database used by many institutions holds the potential to provide access to comparable data (made anonymous, if necessary) on very large numbers of patients for epidemiologic and intervention studies.

Health care is a complex task that requires accurate decision making based on interpretation of many pieces of information. Computer databases hold the key to easy access to this information, presented in an orderly manner (Fig. 64.1), and will become indispensable for high quality care.

Acknowledgments

I am grateful to Professors John Williams and Jonathan Brown for helpful discussions, and to Sister Juliet Rose for maintaining our own IBD database.

References

1 Connecting for Health. http://www.connectingforhealth.nhs.uk/
2 Rose J, Dunne I, Grainger SL. An electronic patient record for inflammatory bowel disease: helping patients and doctors. *Gut* 2001; **48** (Suppl 1): A87.
3 Williams JG, Cheung WY, Russell IT, *et al*. Open access follow up for inflammatory bowel disease: pragmatic randomised trial and cost effectiveness study. *BMJ* 2000; **320**: 544–8.
4 Black N, Barker M, Payne M. Cross sectional survey of multi-centre clinical databases in the United Kingdom. *BMJ* 2004; **328**: 1478–81.
5 Hutchings HA, Cheung WY, Williams JG, *et al*. Can electronic routine data act as a surrogate for patient-assessed outcome measures? *Int J Technol Assess Health Care* 2005; **21**: 133–8.
6 IBDIS. http://www.ibdis.net/project/index.asp
7 Kawamoto K, Houlihan CA, Balas EA, Lobach DF. Improving clinical practice using clinical decision support systems: a systematic review of trials to identify features critical to success. *BMJ* 2005; **330**: 765–8.

Index

DILEMMAS IN HEALTH CARE

Edited by Basiro Davey
Jennie Popay

PUBLISHED BY THE OPEN UNIVERSITY PRESS
IN ASSOCIATION WITH THE OPEN UNIVERSITY

OPEN UNIVERSITY PRESS

The Open
University   Health and Disease Series, Book 7

The U205 Health and Disease Course Team

The following members of the Open University teaching staff have collaborated with the authors in writing this book, or have commented extensively on it during its production. We accept collective responsibility for its overall academic and teaching content.

Basiro Davey (Course Team Chair, Lecturer in Health Studies, Biology)

David Boswell (Senior Lecturer in Sociology)

Richard Holmes (Senior Lecturer, Biology)

Kevin McConway (Senior Lecturer in Statistics)

Perry Morley (Senior Editor, Science)

Stephen Pattison (Lecturer in Health and Social Welfare, School of Health, Welfare and Community Education)

Clive Seale (Lecturer in Sociology, Goldsmiths' College, University of London, U205 Tutor)

Steven Swithenby (Senior Lecturer in Physics)

The following people have contributed to the development of particular parts or aspects of this book.

Sylvia Abbey (course secretary)

Steve Best (graphic artist)

Lucille Eveleigh (course co-ordinator)

John Greenwood (librarian)

Pam Higgins (designer)

Patti Langton (BBC producer)

Jean MacQueen (indexer)

Rissa de la Paz (BBC producer)

Liz Sugden (BBC production assistant)

Doreen Tucker (text processing compositor)

Authors

The following people have acted as principal authors for the chapters listed below.

Chapter 1

Basiro Davey, Lecturer in Health Studies, Department of Biology, The Open University.

Chapter 2

Stephen Harrison, Senior Lecturer in Policy Studies, and Gerald Wistow, Professor of Health and Social Care, both at the Nuffield Institute for Health, University of Leeds.

Chapter 3

Alastair Gray, Research Associate, Centre for Socio-legal Studies, Wolfson College, University of Oxford.

Chapters 4 and 5

Clive Seale, Lecturer in Medical Sociology, Department of Sociology, Goldsmiths' College, University of London.

Chapter 6

Gillian Pascall, Lecturer in Social Policy, School of Social Studies, University of Nottingham, and Kate Robinson, Professor and Dean of the Faculty of Health Care and Social Studies, Luton College of Higher Education.

Chapter 7

Nicholas Mays, Director of the Health and Health Care Research Unit, The Queen's University of Belfast.

Chapter 8

David J. Hunter, Professor of Health Policy and Management, Director of the Nuffield Institute for Health, University of Leeds.

Chapter 9

Helen Lambert, Lecturer in Medical Anthropology, Department of Public Health and Policy, and Klim McPherson, Professor of Public Health Epidemiology and Head of the Health Promotion Sciences Unit, both at the London School of Hygiene and Tropical Medicine.

Chapter 10

Richard Holmes, Senior Lecturer in Biology, Department of Biology, The Open University.

Chapter 11

Chris Pond, Director of the Low Pay Unit, London, and Jennie Popay, Director of the Public Health Research and Resource Centre, Bolton, Salford, Trafford and Wigan Health Authorities, North West England.

External assessors

Course assessor

Professor James McEwen, Henry Mechan Chair of Public Health and Head of Department of Public Health, University of Glasgow.

Book 7 assessors

Dr Mary Ann Elston, Lecturer, Department of Social Policy and Social Science, Royal Holloway University of London.

Nicholas Mays, Director of the Health and Health Care Research Unit, The Queen's University of Belfast.

Dr Bie Nio Ong, Senior Lecturer, Centre for Health Planning and Management, University of Keele.

Adrian Sinfield, Professor of Social Policy, Department of Social Policy and Social Work, University of Edinburgh.

Acknowledgements

The Course Team and the authors wish to thank the following people who, as contributors to the first edition of this book, made a lasting impact on the structure and philosophy of the present volume.

Nick Black, Alastair Gray, Steven Rose, Gerry Stimson, Phil Strong.

The editors and authors would like to thank the following for their advice in preparing the present volume:

Alastair Gray, George Davey Smith.